W9-BLF-917

American Sexual Character

*The publisher gratefully acknowledges
the generous contribution to this book
provided by the General Endowment Fund
of the University of California Press Associates.*

American Sexual Character

SEX, GENDER, AND NATIONAL IDENTITY
IN THE KINSEY REPORTS

Miriam G. Reumann

UNIVERSITY OF CALIFORNIA PRESS
BERKELEY   LOS ANGELES   LONDON

University of California Press
Berkeley and Los Angeles, California

University of California Press, Ltd.
London, England

© 2005 by the Regents of the University of California

Library of Congress Cataloging-in-Publication Data

Reumann, Miriam G., 1966–
    American sexual character: sex, gender, and national
identity in the Kinsey reports / Miriam G. Reumann.
        p.   cm.
    Includes bibliographical references and index.
    ISBN 0-520-23835-4 (cloth : alk. paper)
    1. Sex—United States.   2. Gender identity—United
States.   3. Institute for Sex Research. Sexual behavior in
the human female.   4. Kinsey, Alfred C. (Alfred
Charles), 1894–1956. Sexual behavior in the human
male.   I. Title.
HQ18.U5R48   2005
306.7'0973—dc22   2003022853

Manufactured in the United States of America
14   13   12   11   10   09   08   07   06   05
10   9   8   7   6   5   4   3   2   1

The paper used in this publication meets the minimum
requirements of ANSI/NISO Z39.48–1992 (R 1997)
(Permanence of Paper). ∞

ACC Library Services
Austin, Texas

CONTENTS

ILLUSTRATIONS

ACKNOWLEDGMENTS

For more than a decade, as this project grew from piles of disorganized notes into a slightly more organized dissertation and—slowly—into a book, I have accumulated intellectual debts along with endless drafts. At the Johns Hopkins University, Toby Ditz warned me that I seemed to be a historian, Neil Hertz taught me the pleasures of close reading, and Ruth Leys and Mary Poovey tutored me in the basics of both archival research and finely turned sentences. In the graduate program of Brown University's Department of American Civilization, dissertation director Mari Jo Buhle offered a model of rigorous and considerate criticism that I hope someday to emulate, while readers Richard Meckel and Anne Fausto-Sterling responded to odd questions and read chapter drafts with good cheer. Rich also educated me in the history of medicine, and Anne—whose offhand suggestion that I think about Kinsey helped to jump-start this project—endeavored to teach me the basics of science studies, both of which enriched this project a great deal. In addition to a hospitable and nurturing academic environment, Brown University provided financial assistance during my years of graduate study, including funds for travel to conferences.

Like most historians, I would be lost without librarians and archivists. The fine staffs of the Rockefeller and Science Libraries at Brown, especially Elizabeth Coogan and Beth Beretta of the Inter-Library Loan Department, cheerfully expedited my often obscure requests. Former and current staff members of the Rochambeau branch of the Providence Public Library also tracked down volumes for me, and I thank Jacquelyn Cooper, Tim McGinn, Susan Shoof, Michael Vallone, and Sarah Stanley Weed. The staff of the Kinsey Institute for Research in Sex, Gender, and Reproduction located images, letters, and pulp fiction on a 1999 visit and later expedited my requests for images from their collection. The cartoonist Charles Preston kindly granted permission for use of images from his *Cartoon Guide to the Kinsey Report,* and Robert Emlen and Terrence Abbott assisted me in photographing many of the images reprinted here.

The most important factor in the completion of this book has been my writing group, whose various incarnations have included Crista DeLuzio, Kathy Franz, Bill Hart, Joanne Melish, and Mari Yoshihara. Their presence kept me writing when nothing else could, and thanks to their eclectic research topics, I am prepared for trivia questions on adolescence, transportation, spirituality, Orientalism, and gradual emancipation. For the last seven years, during which it became the Not-Dissertation Group, Janice Okoomian, Kristen Petersen, and Eve Sterne have provided careful readings of draft after draft, along with warm friendship and emergency interventions into matters both syntactic and sartorial.

My family has shown endless patience with this project, and I thank Jack and Martha Reumann for encouraging their daughters' intellectual explorations, even when they range far from parental expectations. Amy Reumann and Rebecca and Andrew Reumann-Moore asked questions when I welcomed them and backed off when my response was a snarl, while Kyra and Maia Reumann-Moore provided welcome distraction. Charles Sadler offered invaluable support during a process that lasted even longer than he had feared, and also coined the best answer for those who expressed surprise at my subject: "This doesn't have nearly the impact on our lives that you're imagining right now." Judy, Ed, Beverly and James Flemer and Edie and Bill Evarts accepted my Kinsey preoccupation with good grace. Chrissy Cortina, Kathy Franz, Janice Okoomian, and Peter Cohen helped to make graduate school much more pleasant. I offer thanks to other friends and colleagues who supplied citations, humor, and commiseration, especially Jesse Berrett, Daniel Cavicchi, Peter Cohen, Lou Galambos, David Horowitz, Sarah Igo, Peter Laipson, and Pat Palmieri. Lundy Braun offered an invaluable line-by-line reading; I only wish I had half the smarts and tenacity needed to follow her suggestions.

Audiences at the Ninth and Tenth Berkshire Conferences, Social Science History Association, Third Carleton Conference on the History of the

Family, New England American Studies Association, and Pembroke Seminar for Teaching and Research on Women prodded me to ask new questions, broaden my sources, and refine my analyses, as did suggestions from panel commentators Regina Kunzel, George Chauncey, and Pat Palmieri. At the University of California Press, Monica McCormick and Randy Heyman guided me through the new and puzzling process of publication with patience. I owe great thanks to Regina Morantz-Sanchez and an anonymous reviewer for University of California Press who provided two painstaking readings of the entire manuscript, offering correctives and suggesting new approaches and insights. Project editor Laura Harger and copyeditor Bonita Hurd also offered invaluable help, catching errors and smoothing awkward prose. All mistakes and infelicities are, unfortunately, my own.

This book, and my life, was enriched by conversations with Jane Eliot Sewell about history, sexuality, and medicine, as well as by shared women's health activism, crab cakes, and laughter. She died before this book went to press, and her advice, her intellect, and her love will be sorely missed.

Introduction

IN 1948 AND 1953, the United States was rocked by events that observers compared to the explosion of the atomic bomb: the publication of *Sexual Behavior in the Human Male* and *Sexual Behavior in the Human Female*, respectively, popularly known as the Kinsey Reports.[1] These two massive sex surveys, compiled by the Indiana University zoologist Alfred Kinsey and a team of researchers, graphically presented the results of interviews with thousands of American men and women, including information on their age at first intercourse, number of partners, history of premarital and extramarital sex, incidence of homosexuality and lesbianism, and virtually every other imaginable sexual statistic. The studies' findings shocked experts and the public alike, as Kinsey demonstrated that much of Americans' sexual activity took place outside of marriage, and that the majority of the nation's citizens had violated accepted moral standards as well as state and federal laws in their pursuit of sexual pleasure.

Sexual Behavior in the Human Male and *Sexual Behavior in the Human Female* struck a nerve within the American public. Despite their complex graphs and charts and abstruse scientific language, the volumes became best-sellers and spurred unprecedented public discussion of national sexual practices and ideologies. Praised by some experts for their breadth, precision, and dispassionate approach to human sexuality, the books were also the targets of virulent criticism and were widely condemned as immoral, perverse, and damaging to the reputation of the United States. Upon the appearance of the first volume, Kinsey was simultaneously hailed as a liberator, denounced as a pornographer, compared to the scientific martyrs Darwin and Copernicus, and declared a Communist bent on destroying the American family, all themes that would persist in discussions of his work.[2] Public uproar over the volumes spread well beyond the world of science, as millions of Americans purchased and discussed them, rendering the reports' vocabulary and sensational findings a part of everyday knowledge. Kinsey's statistics on pre- and extramarital sex prompted a national forum on the state of the nation's morals and marriages, and his findings on the extent of same-sex sexual behaviors spearheaded debate about homosexuality in the United States. Omnipresent in postwar mass culture, the volumes featured centrally in discussions of virtually every topic imaginable, as references to the reports abounded in postwar political coverage, social science and medical writing, general-interest journalism, and even fiction.

This book examines the cultural dynamics and social dilemmas that informed the construction of *American sexual character*—a term I use to describe sexual patterns and attitudes that were understood as uniquely American—between the close of World War II and the early 1960s. It was initially spurred by my curiosity about why a sex survey repeatedly cropped up in discussions of topics that it ostensibly had nothing to do with. While scanning postwar books and articles, I was repeatedly struck by the pervasiveness of the two reports: articles on gender, marriage, and the family devoted extensive attention to the studies, but so did texts probing the effects of suburbanization, assessing the national zeitgeist, comparing Americans to their counterparts in other countries, and analyzing the state of contemporary theater. As I noted more such examples, I was struck by how often and how prominently the findings of the reports, along with public and media responses to them, featured in discussions of American society and national identity after World War II.

Postwar commentators saw Kinsey's research as expressing profound truths not only about Americans' sexual behavior but also about the nation itself, as charts and graphs from the two studies were brought to bear on analyses of America's class mobility and race relations, attitudes to work and leisure, and international political position. In brief, this book examines the processes by which Kinsey's statistical data became cultural narrative. It is not a history of the reports per se; rather, it maps the broader field of American sexual character by looking at themes and tensions in social scientists' and cultural critics' writings about sex in the United States.

It examines the ways in which normative categories such as heterosexuality, masculinity, femininity, and Americanness itself were constructed and questioned. In the process, it chronicles some of the microstruggles that constituted the meaning of sex, including popular responses to the two Kinsey Reports, discussions of the relation between sexual excess and popular literature, the changing legal meanings of obscenity, and homosexual activists' negotiation of scientific categories of normalcy and deviance.

DEFINING AMERICAN SEXUAL CHARACTER

My analysis of how the Kinsey Reports and other work on sexuality functioned to harness and rework notions of national identity is anchored by the concept of American sexual character. This phrase was not commonly used in the postwar United States, but its three terms, all widely used by authorities at the time, together capture some of the interwoven themes that characterized discussions of public and private life around the time of the Kinsey Reports. In juxtaposing them, I call attention to the mutual construction of postwar ideas about national identity, sexual life, and personal and community standards of behavior and ideology by exploring the relationship between these three terms. In this analysis of the discursive construction of sexuality in the modern United States, I examine contending definitions of sexuality and gender and explore how middle-class Americans during the postwar era negotiated a host of sexual possibilities. By reading various crises of American sexuality as responses to postwar worries about the stability and strength of the nation and its population, I map the ways in which new discursive practices emerged around American sexuality, examining why and how Americans thought that sexual behaviors were changing and how they related these changes to other developments in the United States during the cold war era.

The first key term, *American,* alludes to the centrality of nationalism, nation building, and national identity to postwar culture.[3] A recent resurgence of interest in nationalism has encouraged scholars to focus less on traditionally defined political processes than on the social and cultural processes that shaped changing conceptions of national identity. In the introduction to a 1996 collection of essays on nationalism, the historian Geoff Eley and the political scientist Ronald Suny note that, "if politics is the ground upon which the category of the nation was first proposed, culture was the terrain where it was elaborated," and they observe that recent literature has interrogated the "need to constitute nations discursively through processes of imaginative ideological labor—that is, the novelty of national culture, its manufactured or invented character, as opposed to its deep historical rootedness."[4] In Benedict Anderson's influential model, every nation is an "imagined community" in which citizens envision themselves as units in a collective, "because the members of even the smallest nation will never know their fellow members, meet them, or even hear of them, yet in the minds of each they carry the image of communion."[5] It is everyday beliefs and processes, not only spectacular events like wars, parades, or elections, that create and reproduce national identity. Identifying the 1950s as an era when interest in nationalism and nation building peaked, scholars argue that between the 1940s and 1960s the United States remade its economic, political, and social position, and that the period was thus marked by struggles to reestablish old models of nationhood and create new ones.[6]

During the 1950s, the United States—at perhaps the last moment in which many could still imagine a national public not riven by racial, class, gender, and other differences—defined itself in relation to a constellation of real and imaginary ideals, including both other nations and idealized Americas of the past. New themes also spurred and shaped postwar nation building. These included the postwar endorsement of middle-class status for many previously excluded groups like white ethnics and Jews; threats to the nation from the outside, such as the rise of international Communism; and dangers from within, such as Americans' alleged laziness, sensuality, consumerism, or any of a host of other characteristics.[7] The very factors through which the nation achieved and celebrated its postwar supremacy—possession of the atomic bomb; an enduring democratic government in the face of fascism, Communism, and revolutions abroad; economic prosperity; the mass production of consumer goods; and a cultural focus on family bonds and personal fulfillment—were double-edged swords. Nuclear knowledge made the United States internationally powerful but also promoted widespread fear and suspicion, and the specter of Communism prompted both celebrations of American democracy and crippling suspicions about internal subversion. Such paradoxes abounded in postwar culture: the economic prosperity that funded single-family homes and supported growing families also created new opportunities for single living, and the consumer economy lauded by boosters was accused of promoting a hedonism that subverted, rather than supported, national values.

The postwar era's teachings about sex fit perfectly into this contradictory pattern, as authorities simultaneously maintained that sexuality had the potential to ruin families and community standards and sought to harness its appeal for the maintenance of traditional lifestyles. The second word of my title phrase, *sexual,* thus alludes to the ways in which Americans brought sexuality into the public arena in the decade and a half after the end of World War II, making it a political and social topic as well as a personal one. The war changed the sexual landscape for many Americans, as wartime economic and social shifts promoted geographical and class mobility. War and its aftermath furthered dialogue about which of the domestic crises associated with war—desertion and failed marriages, promiscuity, same-sex sexual relations, and so on—were temporary eruptions and which were here to stay. When Kinsey's first study appeared a few years later, it provided vivid evidence of sexual change.

The reports, along with the host of other explorations of American sexuality that appeared in their wake, were received not only as collections of statistics but also as important statements about gender difference, social change, and American identity. Issues such as the increasingly direct depiction of sexual themes in the popular media, the future of the nuclear family, and the importance of sexual pleasure in marriage were also topics of heated discussion. Even more troubling to many was "unnatural" sex, and campaigns targeting "perverts," described as a threat to American security interests, drummed suspected homosexuals out of military and governmental service. As well as finding a far higher incidence of same-sex sexual practices than many had previously believed existed in the United States, the reports found that sexual behaviors long believed to be the province of homosexuals, including oral and anal sex, were in fact widely practiced by heterosexuals. Most Americans, according to Kinsey, believed fervently that "sexual behavior is either normal or abnormal, socially acceptable or unacceptable, heterosexual or homosexual, and many persons do not want to believe that there are gradations in these matters from one extreme to the other."[8] The report's statistics made these convictions increasingly untenable, as evidence suggested that the dividing line between heterosexual and homosexual was increasingly blurred.

Kinsey argued that many of the sexual categories Americans lived by were meaningless, claiming that "such designations as infantile, frigid, sexually over-developed, under-active, excessively active, over-developed, over-sexed, hypersexual, or sexually over-active . . . refer to nothing more than a position on a curve which is continuous. Normal and abnormal, one sometimes suspects, are terms which a particular author employs with reference to his own position on that curve."[9] In the postwar United States, as *normal* and *abnormal* threatened to lose all meaning, sex was both a pressing social issue and a rhetorical site for public discussions of American culture and identity. Literally, sexuality was surveyed, mapped, and theorized as never before. Metaphorically, sexual behavior was framed as a matter of politics, cultural change, and public policy.

In his analysis of "that quite recent and banal notion of 'sexuality,'" the philosopher and historian Michel Foucault points out the importance of examining how and why a culture's common wisdom about sex changes over time. The object of historical inquiry, he argues, is "not to determine whether one says yes or no to sex, but to account for the fact that it is spoken about, to discover who does the speaking, the positions and viewpoints from which they speak, the institutions which prompt people to speak about it and which store and distribute the things that are said."[10] As Foucault reminds us, discussions of sex are always about more than bodily behaviors. Postwar Americans made extensive use of sexuality as a category that expressed and explained other kinds of social concerns, demonstrating his assertion that modern identity included an injunction to catalogue and speak of sex.

A new language of sexuality—in which "sex" moved from a static, biologistic measure of the differences between male and female to a broad category that encompassed sexual practices, moral concerns, and social problems—reflected profound changes in the cultural meanings of sexuality. This transformation of sexual discourse was reflected not only in the proliferation and popularity of examinations of American sexuality but also in the ways in which sexual information was managed and categorized. Before World War II, articles about sex cited in the *Readers' Guide to Periodical Literature* were primarily medical in nature, with most sources falling under the category of "SEX (Biology)" and dealing with topics like venereal disease or sexual selection in the animal kingdom. After the war, the number of entries under "Sex" and its various subheadings expanded rapidly, demonstrating a quantitative increase in the production and dissemination of popular information about sex. The taxonomy of the *Readers' Guide* also changed, reflecting profound shifts in the ways sexual knowledge was organized and the expansion of terms for sexual acts. The number of categories nearly doubled, from eleven in 1939 to twenty in 1953, and new subheadings such as "Sexual Behavior" and "Sex Relations" accounted for an increasing share of works cited. After 1950, a new category, "Sexual," was added to accommodate the flow of articles that treated sex as an adjective rather than a noun, a cultural phenomenon instead of a biological condition or act. By 1957, new meanings had replaced old: the category of "SEX (Biology)" had vanished, reflecting an utterly altered sexual vocabulary.[11]

The third term I highlight, *character,* weaves throughout postwar literature on national identity and sexual and social change, uniting a cultural critique of the present with nostalgia for a simpler and idealized past. In their best-selling sociological treatise *The Lonely Crowd,* David Riesman and Nathan Glazer suggest that changes in personal relationships, work, and consumption were crafting a new—and to many, sadly diminished—type of American character.[12] Nineteen-fifties authorities often contrasted this contemporary brand of American character to that of earlier periods, alluding to the self-sufficiency of frontier settlers or the moral certainty of the Puritans. As the historian Karen Dubinsky observes, "Nation-building required more than the formation of political and economic infrastructures. In the 'human nation,' the proper sort of citizens, subjects with 'character,' was necessary."[13] Postwar nation building relied upon and incorporated notions about what kinds of sexuality were likely to aid or hamper national interests.[14] Character—usually understood as sobriety, commitment to labor, upward economic and social mobility, and dedication to both family and civic duty—was essential to the American democracy and civic life. It was also, according to social scientists, in decline.

The term resonated on other important levels as well, referencing a number of powerful forces that shaped postwar culture. *Character* sometimes connoted sexual chastity, a definition to which a Canadian journalist writing about Kinsey's second volume alluded when she noted that "Americans are sensitive about the sexual character of their women."[15] The concept of character also played on the tension between group identity and individualism, a theme examined by many social scientists of the era. Individualism was one of the most crucial differences between American democracy and Communism, and warnings about the dangers of conformity often reminded the public of the need to understand themselves and encourage their personalities to flourish. At the same time that individuality was lauded, however, Americans were also appealed to as members of a group and praised for their civic-mindedness and "togetherness," whether measured on the level of family, community, or nation.

The term *American sexual character* thus suggests the ways in which a range of postwar discourses—having to do with the family, national security, popular culture, consumption, work, racial difference, and political affiliation, among others—borrowed from a common vocabulary.

Wilhelm Reich, a former disciple of Freud whose writings attracted the attention of both American admirers and the state, urged disciples to strive for "genital character," a state of physical, mental, and sexual health free from the repressions and neuroses that plagued most modernists. Social and cultural advance or decline, he believed, largely depended upon the genital character of a people, since "the character structure is the congealed sociological process of a given epoch."[16] Few went so far as Reich in drawing these links, but numerous mainstream mental health and social science professionals associated sexual beliefs and behaviors with the psychological health and character of the nation. As sex became viewed as a key to civic as well as personal identity, social scientists and mental health professionals argued that specific forms of sexual behavior either contributed to or endangered the health of the individual, one's familial and social relationships, and the body politic and were thus constitutive of the national character. As a result, the trope of character was crucial to postwar debates about sexuality and national identity, often serving as a bridge connecting the two.[17] The emerging "American sex revolution," one well-known sociologist warned, not only threatened individual happiness but also posed grave dangers to nothing less than "the well-being of the nation itself."[18]

SEXUAL AND SOCIAL CHANGE

The nation's changing sexual patterns were discussed by people across the political spectrum, including self-defined sexual liberals, libertarians, and conservatives. In postwar debates over sexuality, however, traditional political labels were not always reliable or helpful. The midcentury political consensus known as cold war liberalism was a flexible and extensive category, and in battles where the cultural and the political merged, seemingly similar concerns could emerge from vastly different places.[19] Conservatives and liberals alike, for example, at some moments worried that Americans lacked basic sexual knowledge, and at others lamented the omnipresence of sexual information in the mass media. Both those who identified as sexual freethinkers and those who embraced traditionalism critiqued Americans' alleged materialism and consumerism and complained that the modern focus on sex threatened to rob it of emotional meaning.

Along with a host of conservative social scientists who argued that national and international stability depended upon an immediate desexualization of American mores and morals, liberals like the sociologist David Riesman deemed the national focus on sex to be a new and particularly dangerous form of consumerism that distracted modern Americans from their civic duties.[20] In an assessment of the assumptions and motives of postwar authorities who produced information on American sexuality, an important distinction emerges between sexual pessimists, who foresaw the decline and collapse of the nation in changes in the sexual status quo, and idealists, who envisioned a new sexual order as liberating and empowering. Those who believed that sexual behaviors outside marriage were potentially dangerous generally agreed that public attention to matters of sex was pathological, while believers in sexual liberalism cast the same behaviors as a welcome reversal of puritan repression. The definition of sex as a liberatory force, along with the belief that truths about sex can be unearthed and examined, was an important concept in the twentieth-century United States.

In the years after World War II, political and sexual respectability were closely linked and the social and political order that many saw as crucial to national stability was based upon deeply polarized gender roles and a conservative deployment of sexual energy.[21] When the liberal sexologist Albert Ellis charged that "most Americans are sexual fascists," his choice of terms underlined the connections made between private behavior and the nation's moral and political character during the cold war.[22] So too did charges that sexual investigators, or certain sexual acts, were un-American or Communist. Sexual deviance, whether understood as homosexual activity, promiscuity, interracial sex, or any other arrangement that violated the prescribed path of monogamous sexual expression within marriage, was coupled rhetorically with political subversion. At the same time, the marital bond and the sexual satisfaction identified with it were viewed as cornerstones of family happiness and national stability. The tension between these two themes—American sexuality as a sign of cultural disintegration and political weakness or as the locus for familial and social cohesion—shaped postwar discourse on sexuality. Whether commentators on American sexual character championed new forms of sexual dissent or called for a return to traditional practices and beliefs, they shared a firm belief that Americans' sexual behavior could and did shape their moral character, civic roles, and political future.

Americans had worried and written about sex before, of course, and observers had long drawn connections between the national interest and sexual behavior by punishing sexual expression that took place outside marriage or between "inappropriate" partners. The social purity movements of the nineteenth and early twentieth centuries, agitation for marriage reform in the 1920s, and intermittent campaigns against prostitution all defined various forms of sexual misconduct as pressing social problems and sought to correct them through education, moral suasion, and punishment.[23] In her work on racial and sexual violence, the historian Lisa Duggan argues that legal and medical discourses work to mobilize "a specifically American version of normative national sexuality" based on proper gender roles, whiteness, and respectability.[24]

The specifics of what counts as "normative national sexuality" have varied: in the early nineteenth century, class- and race-based notions of respectability were crucial to individual reputations and community maintenance, while more recently the AIDS crisis has rendered concepts of health and disease central to normative sexuality. Americans after World War II, however, outstripped earlier generations in the fervor with which they made sexuality a legitimate topic and the extent to which they insisted on its relevance to postwar social problems. Experts disagreed, often vehemently, about exactly what was wrong with modern sexuality, but virtually all commentators who addressed the subject diagnosed grave problems with American behavior and mores. Sex surveys since the turn of the century had focused most often on bohemian urbanites or on marginalized groups such as prisoners, the poor, and the "feeble-minded," reflecting investigators' conflicts over whether sexual behavior could best be understood by viewing the normative or the abnormal. Kinsey's postwar studies, and the public debates about sex that they fostered, instead addressed the private behavior of "average" Americans. Nonmarital and nonreproductive sexuality had often been the subject of moral panic, but in the postwar United States even marital heterosexual behaviors were studied and interrogated, believed to reveal vital information about the state of the nation.[25]

A crucial development shaping postwar culture was the rise of a national mass media and a public receptive to its claims. As the number and variety of media outlets expanded after the war, so too did the parameters of allowable news. Popular magazines openly discussed homosexuality and sexual techniques, and experts complained that Americans were obsessed with sex. The psychiatrist Albert Ellis lamented the "average" citizen's ignorance in his book *The American Sexual Tragedy,* while the conservative *Reader's Digest* issued the plaintive query "Must we change our sex standards?"[26] Articles in women's magazines counseled, "We must face the facts about sex," asked "Do Americans commercialize sex?," and encouraged readers to "check your sex I.Q."[27] As the historian Joanne Meyerowitz argues, the media's discussions of Americans' sexual behavior sometimes "expanded the process by which some readers identified new options for themselves in the popular culture."[28]

Debates about American sexuality also reflected competing claims to knowledge and authority. As older definitions of normalcy and deviance came under attack in the wake of new research, the qualifications required to be an authority on sex changed. Physicians, psychiatrists, pulp novelists, sexologists, social scientists, homophile activists, and self-styled typical Americans, among others, presented competing narratives and claims about sexuality. The vast majority of published authors writing about sex were white male professionals, but as the parameters of "sexual expert" became more fluid, especially by the late 1950s and early 1960s, traditionally disenfranchised voices were increasingly vocal in debates about sex. In one collection of articles on the Kinsey Reports, for example, authorities included not only representatives from medicine and psychiatry but also a theologian, a literary critic, and the anonymous "Mrs. W.," who spoke as a wife and mother.[29] The public and private figures who spoke of sex had various motives, which included criticizing specific groups or behaviors, diagnosing social ills and prescribing correctives, titillating, and making money. In this torrent of analysis, sexual definitions and meanings intertwined with other topics that concerned Americans during the postwar years, ranging from the possibilities posed by the new affluence and leisure to the problems presented by changing gender roles, race relations, and definitions of the family.

This book chronicles the ways in which national identity, sexuality, and "character" intersected in postwar culture, interrogating the spaces where these terms construct, complicate, and contradict one another. *Sex* was an important term in postwar civic discourse, as existing and ideal relationships between people and nations borrowed from, and were configured as, domestic and social relationships. Nationalism, a recent theorist argues, "is inseparable from gender and sexuality," since "sexuality plays a key role in nation-building and in sustaining national identity" even as the powerful rhetoric of national identity "becomes the language through which sexual control and repression (specifically, but not exclusively, of women and homosexuals) is justified, and masculine prowess is expressed and exercised."[30] Just as much of the burgeoning postwar literature of sex drew on and articulated concerns about the nation, so too did narratives of nationalism rely upon ideas about sex.[31] Gendered and sexualized descriptions of the United States and other nations abounded in postwar culture: journalists and social scientists worried that the nation was "weak" and "soft," while State Department policy makers drew upon a rhetorical system in which the nation was depicted as stalwartly male. European countries were viewed as feminized sexual conquests or potential marriage partners, and the USSR was represented as an aggressive sexual competitor.[32] More literally, experts compared American sexual behavior to patterns found in other countries and grimly concluded that the nation's mores were unique and often destructive.[33]

The postwar United States thus offers a particularly dramatic case study in what Foucault terms "the way in which sex is 'put into discourse[,]' . . . the forms of power [it takes], the channels it takes, and the discourses it permeates."[34] Rather than a private behavior that could escape surveillance, sex—even when carried out in private—was increasingly understood to be a public act fraught with social consequences. Authorities argued repeatedly that sexual disarray did not merely harm individuals but was a national danger. The American Social Hygiene Association cautioned worried citizens that through "the right use of sex" they could build solid families and a united nation. But what was the right use of sex, and who decided?[35]

Historians of gender and sexuality have usually focused on the experiences of specific groups, asking, for example, how lesbian and gay communities changed after the war, or whether sexual liberalism empowered or harmed women. This book takes a different approach, examining how postwar Americans debated the topic of American sexuality and what role it played in their discussions of other national problems. Many of reformers' suspicions about modern sexuality—for example, the belief that changing sexual norms would lead to mass marital failure, the disappearance of heterosexuality, or a decline in American character—were vague threats, impossible to measure. The concerns and anxieties that these reformers articulated, however, were very real, and battles over such topics were fought bitterly by all concerned. Americans' hopes and fears about sex mattered, regardless of how realistic or fantastical, how prescient or paranoid they were. "Culture," as the anthropologist Marilyn Strathern has phrased it, "consists in the way analogies are drawn between things, in the ways certain thoughts are used to think others."[36] For postwar Americans, national identity was configured in sexual terms. By looking both at what activities or ideas constitute *sex* and at the cultural status of *sexuality* at a given moment, one can trace the ways in which ideological battles about sexuality mirror and mask other social changes. In the postwar United States,

American sexual character was a legitimate topic in its own right, as well as a trope for other social and cultural problems. Contesting definitions of how sex should be regulated and managed and who was qualified to speak about it aired in the popular and scientific presses. Responses to the Kinsey Reports brought together debates about national identity, consumption and consumerism, family and gender roles, and racial and political liberalism.[37]

In examining postwar concerns about sexuality and national identity, the most important documents that I draw on are of course Alfred Kinsey's *Sexual Behavior in the Human Male* (1948) and *Sexual Behavior in the Human Female* (1953). I see these two reports as a Rorschach test for postwar Americans: Kinsey's statistics were and are capable of many interpretations, and my focus here is how these dry numbers were given meaning. Commentators on the reports were variously struck by the project's sheer volume, the novelty of hearing how thousands of ordinary Americans actually conducted their sex lives, and the tension between titillation and objective science that the studies created. Beyond these factors, though, the reports' immense popularity and controversy stemmed from something else: the studies offered a set of data through which critics, experts, and casual readers could address the sexual and social changes surrounding them. For American readers, the Kinsey Reports *were* sex, stripped of emotional nuance and physical momentum and distilled into numbers and tables.

The Kinsey team's findings served as the basis for many different kinds of claims about American sexuality and national character, and their repeated use by authorities who wished to comment on social problems makes them an ideal point from which to explore gender and sexual roles during the 1950s. The reports were important not only for the new data they presented but also because they reaffirmed and provided evidence for ideas already found elsewhere in popular culture. In fact, it was the ways in which the reports wove together the familiar with the startlingly new that made them such compelling cultural touchstones, capable of supporting dramatically different agendas. At once scientific documents, signs of the changing limits of public discourse, metaphors for changing patterns of sexual behavior, and sites for projecting cultural hopes and concerns, the reports confronted Americans with a complex and often unflattering self-portrait.

Kinsey's work spurred a host of popularizers, detractors, and imitators, and their work makes up the next tier of my primary sources. Responses to and appropriations of the studies were many, from scholarly symposia to joke books and novels, from articles in women's magazines and confessionals to news coverage in scientific journals and newspapers.[38] The reports were a leitmotif in postwar culture, and I engage a wide range of sources throughout this book, including work on postwar national character; advice literature regarding dating, marriage, and sexuality; mass-market literature popularizing Kinsey's findings; reviews of and commentaries on the reports; social science literature; articles from psychiatric journals; and fictional and film sources.

Ideas about American sexual character in the postwar United States were part of a powerful discourse that imagined the nation as middle class, white, and well assimilated to the dominant culture. As postwar industry and increased access to higher education expanded, many Americans whose ethnic or religious identities had kept them on the margins of the American mainstream in previous generations took on or secured middle-class status, culturally and economically. Americans who were working class or nonwhite, along with those who transgressed gender boundaries or violated moral codes, served as the outsiders against whom the expanding middle class defined themselves. With these demographic and cultural changes in mind, I attempt throughout the book to consider the blind spots and silences of available sources. Some of these spring from the ways in which the postwar authorities I read compartmentalized their discussions of American sexuality. Although these authorities addressed a wide range of issues in their analyses of social and sexual change, some sexual issues and experiences received relatively little attention: incest, intergenerational sex, and rape and other forms of sexual violence, for example, were most often framed as criminal matters rather than incorporated into discussions of everyday adult sexuality.[39] Other silences in my sources stem less from postwar experts' organization of knowledge than from their assumptions about what narratives, categories, and people mattered. Sexual literature facilitated some viewpoints more than others, and authors were predominantly male, overwhelmingly white, and drawn primarily from elite groups like scientists, cultural critics, educators, and journalists. Virtually all of them also had to negotiate issues of respectability and prurience, positioning their work as sober fact, lurid sensationalism, and every combination in between. In interrogating their work, I have tried to consider the multiple roles of and silences about class, racial, and other differences in postwar literature on national character and sexuality, along with the ways in which these authors' analyses were shaped by the subjects they chose and audiences they anticipated.

Beginning with a brief portrait of the reports and the cultural moment into which they emerged, the book moves from a general overview of the place of sexuality in postwar social thought to more focused readings of sources that target and analyze specific problems and populations. Each chapter examines a different facet of the overarching discourse of American sexuality and national character. The topics on which I focus—which include the two Kinsey Reports on women and men, the politics of marriage, and the changing meanings of heterosexuality and homosexuality for Americans—played a distinctive role in the burgeoning postwar discourse on sexuality. Each chapter provides a case study of what the political historian Kyle Cuordileone calls "the way erotic imagery and gendered dualisms can structure a historical narrative," and in each I draw on a different set of sources to paint an interlocking portrait of postwar anxieties about American sexual character.[40]

Chapter 1 sets the stage by examining postwar social scientists' concerns about the state of American character and offers an overview of how they united concepts of national identity, character, and sexuality. Experts declared various crises in American sexuality, compared the sexual mores of the United States to those of other nations, and outlined theories accounting for what many referred to as the "sexualization" of national culture. Assessing the ways in which many of their worries about leisure, affluence, and other major social problems with little apparent connection to sexual behavior in fact drew on and spoke to anxieties about the changing meanings of sex and gender, I argue that the cultural project of rethinking and centering sex offered postwar Americans an avenue through which they could debate the meaning of being American.

Chapters 2 and 3 examine how the married pair served as the central figures in discussions of sex during the 1950s. What was the relationship among the statistical male and female of the reports, actual American men and women, and the ideological formations of "man" and "woman," most often represented as a white-collar husband and suburban housewife? Through an analysis of the differing ways the Kinsey Reports on American men and women were received, these chapters examine postwar authorities' psychological and cultural explanations of masculinity and femininity, especially the ways in which they related sexual behavior to normative gender roles.

The final two chapters consider in turn the two most widely discussed types of sexual relationships, marital heterosexuality and homosexuality.

Chapter 4 illuminates the ways in which Americans saw marriage as changing and analyzes the place of marital sex in debates about healthy and unhealthy marriages. Experts offered a model for modern marriage that stressed egalitarianism, sexual knowledge, and reliance upon professional advice. In examining the ways in which advice books described and valorized heterosexual intercourse as the cornerstone of modern marriage, I illuminate the connections that experts during the 1950s made between sexual and gender roles. Chapter 5 turns to the changing cultural meanings of same-sex sexual activity during and after World War II. I argue that homosexuality, which received unprecedented national attention after the appearance of Kinsey's statistics, was depicted in the mainstream press as simultaneously alluring and dangerous. As experts debated the apparent increase of homosexuality, many articulated a deep concern that Americans were particularly susceptible to it, linking same-sex sexuality to broader concerns about American character.

In the epilogue, I consider how different sexual subjects, such as the average American, the married couple, the modal man or woman, and the homosexual, were constructed by and participated in the overall discourse of American sexual character during the 1950s. I also discuss important sex surveys after Kinsey's and offer some suggestions about how conceptions of American sexual character have operated in more recent discussions of national identity and sexual behavior.

The cultural project of collecting data about sexual behavior and discussing its significance offers experts and their audience—both in the postwar United States and today—the opportunity to discuss the meaning of being a modern American. As researchers dissected American sexuality, they expanded the role of sexual topics in civic discourse and extended the meanings of sex. The often-paradoxical stock characters they created—the impotent or philandering husband, the frigid or adulterous wife, the latent homosexual, and the modern American dangerously susceptible to the manipulations of the media or in search of therapeutic understanding— enacted narratives of sexual change and possibility in the postwar era, and continue to do so today.

ONE

"Sexual Order in Our Nation"

American Sexuality and National Character
in the Postwar United States

Our present-day sexual literature is a
literature not of sex, but of society.

DIANA TRILLING
"Men, Women, and Sex"

AS WORLD WAR II DREW to a close and the United States adjusted to peace, journalists, politicians, and authorities hailed a spirit of national optimism. Before Pearl Harbor, the publishing magnate Henry Luce had urged citizens to "create the first great American Century," and the country could now heed his call to be "the powerhouse from which the ideals spread throughout the world."[1] Americans had emerged victorious from the international conflict, surviving the war with less loss of life and more of its services and infrastructure intact than other combatant nations. In contrast to defeated Axis powers and to European allies, shortages and rationing were short-lived. Wartime industries had rescued the nation from the lingering depression, postwar assistance programs such as the GI Bill promised class and economic mobility, and Americans' savings and pent-up consumer demand would fuel an era of economic growth and prosperity. The production of consumer goods boomed, real wages rose steadily, and home ownership became attainable by many Americans who had never before been able to afford it. Military, governmental, and civic authorities all lauded a return to "normal" life, urging citizens to put the upheavals and dislocations of war behind them and devote themselves to work, leisure, and family life.

Beneath this apparent national confidence, however, lay an undercurrent of worry as the postwar United States faced new international and domestic conflicts.[2] A host of anxieties fed a national mood of self-examination as well as a celebration of American exceptionalism. Rebuilding a normative society after World War II was complicated by a number of factors: Americans dreaded a recurrence of war, a fear soon realized in the Korean conflict; the specter of national annihilation was made painfully concrete by cold war maneuverings and the spread of nuclear weaponry; minor economic slumps continued to evoke fears of renewed national depression; and racial segregation and postwar red scares raised unsettling questions about the true extent of democracy and the state of civil liberties. Amid this tumult of postwar social change, however, what most disturbed many observers were changes in the nation's sexual patterns.

Between the late 1940s and early 1960s, authorities articulated their concern about the nation's condition and future by linking them to the state of American sexuality, situating Americans' sexual behavior as both cause and consequence of a host of ills. Experts rang a series of alarms: traditional morality was being ignored as a new sexual license swept the land; gender differences seemed to be blurring, as men were becoming increasingly passive and sexually troubled while women grew more sexually demanding; the institution of marriage was troubled; and same-sex sexual behavior was increasing. The United States had led the way to triumph in a world war, but as the nation struggled to adjust to peace, observers asked, What kind of a country was it going to be? Were traditional moral codes vanishing, and if so, what would replace them? As social scientists, historians, journalists, and others examined the nation's mores, worries about Americans' sexuality, character, and future intensified and intertwined.

THE "SEXUAL CONSEQUENCES OF WARFARE": AMERICAN MORALITY IN WORLD WAR II

Many of the authorities who saw American sexuality as an important social issue during the 1950s believed that the nation's sexual license and moral decay were rooted in the war years. The management of soldiers' and civilians' sexuality, maintenance of long-distance marriages, and arrival of war brides all focused state and public attention on Americans' sexual behavior. A number of social scientists believed that the war years offered new opportunities and justifications for illicit sex. GIs, the sociologist Francis Merrill argued in 1948, had been emboldened by the "greater sexual laxity traditionally allowed the soldier as a partial recompense for the risk of his life." The war had thus "accelerated the sexual emancipation of unmarried boys and girls that was already well under way."[3] Venereal disease and illicit sex—both hetero- and homosexual—flourished in the unsettled conditions of military barracks.[4] Social changes on the home front also loomed, because, for many American women, sex with a soldier took on patriotic appeal. During wars, a psychologist noted, "a new and strange philosophy grips the country . . . [as] war creates a pathological interest in sex."[5] A 1945 *Time* report on the United States at war found that although no "great moral collapse" had yet come to pass, American women's sphere and sexual behavior alike were changing. Despite the privations of war, the magazine noted pointedly, "fun is there, even now, if a woman wants to take it. Some have."[6] Military personnel abroad were being exposed to all manner of temptations, American girls from all social levels were indulging in sexual experimentation, and many soldiers wives' showed no sign of settling down to wait faithfully by the fire. Experts worried: Would these trends end with the war, or did they pose a long-term threat to the nation?

After D day and victory in the Pacific, the immediacy of war receded for most Americans, but fears about moral chaos did not. Many experts believed that the experience of war had permanently unsettled Americans' behavior and that peace would not bring with it a return to prewar morality. "Morals, we understand, are a little out of date," the philosopher G. W. T. Patrick commented caustically in the *Ladies' Home Journal* as the war drew near to a close.[7] Concerned that war had dramatically altered traditional social and economic relations, and that fears of a recurrence of warfare would further unsettle Americans' morale, he predicted that the near future would bring "more and more people flocking to taverns and nightclubs[,] . . . more and more gambling and drinking and license of sex among both young and old." He also warned that "the present confusion about morals and moral sanctions in the minds of our young people is a matter more serious than any of our troubles in the field of economics and finance." Given such grave problems, Patrick saw no solution but to turn to experts, and proposed a sort of New Deal to revitalize American morals. If a brain trust of professionals from every discipline were formed to tackle these problems, he believed, their recommendations—backed by "the authority of science"—would pave the way for a resurgence of traditional American morality, ensuring a brave new postwar world.[8] In his analysis of the war's toll on the United States, the sociologist Ernest Groves argued that one of the "major hazards of war" was the "abnormal sex situation" it fostered. The "sexual consequences of warfare," he added, were "not dealt with frankly, which makes them all the more dangerous to marriage happiness and social welfare."[9] Groves's diagnosis of sex as a pressing national problem and his plea for candid discussion of the "sexual consequences" of social change were common themes in the late 1940s, but the increasingly open discussions of American sexuality often served to fan fears rather than allay them. Patrick's vision of a mass of national experts turning their attention to Americans' sexual behavior would come true during the next decade and a half, as would his hope that "the authority of science" would feature prominently in sexual discourse. However, the evidence that sexual commentators studied and the conclusions they drew differed drastically from what he had optimistically hoped for.

Experts insisted that sex was a serious topic. It had "entered the realm of discussion," one sociologist wrote in 1949; authorities increasingly recognized that "changes in sex behavior are taking place . . . [and] they need to be subjected to further study."[10] During the war years, military and civilian authorities had seen sexuality as one of several problem areas, identified by popular and official wisdom alike as threatening to the war effort.[11] Anarchic female sexuality was identified as a prime threat to the war effort, and military and public health campaigns warned patriotic Americans about the dangers of loose "victory girls" who might deliberately or inadvertently carry secrets to the enemy and venereal disease to the troops.[12] Hasty war marriages promised to pose additional social problems in the years after the war, and experts braced themselves for trouble from the American women and girls whose war experiences encouraged them to view themselves as sexual actors. Simultaneously, concerns about homosexuality featured prominently in experts' counsel about how to manage both soldiers abroad and civilians on the home front.[13] At war's conclusion, the topic of sex was not wholly incorporated into the privatized realm of the family but remained high on the national agenda, as scrutiny of the sexual behavior of any and all Americans—even "normal" and "average" men and women—intensified.[14]

In the decade and a half after the war, sex assumed a central and unprecedented place in discussions of America's troubles and future. According to the popular media, older moral norms were breaking down. So rapidly were American mores changing that, in the 1955 introduction to a paperback reprint of her 1949 study, *Male and Female,* the anthropologist Margaret Mead observed that many of her observations about dating and courtship were passé, since after only a few years "a new pattern of sex relationships is emerging."[15] Wartime experts had tended to focus on threats by and to specific sexual populations, localized problems that could be blamed on the exigencies of war or solved by bureaucratic and legal intervention. After the war, however, in a time of peace and prosperity, sexual anxieties ran deeper and more broadly. Troubling statistics could no longer be blamed on temporary dislocations but instead bespoke deep-rooted national problems. When they wrote and spoke of sexual crises in the years after the war, experts increasingly attributed them to sweeping changes in the nation's social and cultural life rather than to temporary causes. As they studied sex, scientific and cultural authorities made it central to postwar thought, a symbol of accelerating social change and of the possibilities and problems of American identity.

POSTWAR SEXUALITY AND THE POLITICS OF EVIDENCE

In 1948, anxieties about American morality intensified when a team of researchers headed by the Indiana University zoologist Alfred Kinsey published *Sexual Behavior in the Human Male*. The volume, which reported the sexual experiences of over five thousand American men, was the largest and most detailed work of sexual science ever conducted. In the past, the authors (pictured in figure 1) explained, such a "thoroughly objective, fact-finding investigation of sex" would have been impossible to conduct, but modern Americans showed "an abundant and widespread interest in the possibilities of such a study" (4).

Instantly dubbed the Kinsey Report, *Sexual Behavior in the Human Male* offered the perfect site around which Americans' inchoate fears about sex could crystallize. It revealed that virtually all American men violated the dominant culture's code of respectability, along with the law, by engaging in sexual activities outside of marriage. Of the cross section of "average" American men whom he had interviewed, Kinsey informed readers, nearly all masturbated, most engaged in petting or intercourse before marriage, approximately half confessed to extramarital affairs, and a similar number had engaged in homosexual sex (see figure 2). Less than half of all male orgasms, Kinsey's figures revealed, resulted from the socially validated outlet of marital intercourse.[16] The volume's authors stressed the extent and range of American men's sexual activity, noting that their data "represent[ed] an accumulation of scientific data completely divorced from questions of moral value and social custom" (3).

Figure 1. *Left to right:* Kinsey with Martin, Gebhard, and Pomeroy. (Photo by William Dellenback; reprinted by permission of The Kinsey Institute for Research in Sex, Gender, and Reproduction, Inc.)

Five years later, fears about the extent of sexual and social change were again confirmed when Kinsey and his associates published *Sexual Behavior in the Human Female,* which covered the sexual lives of nearly eight thousand American women. This second volume was greeted with even greater fanfare than the first, as newspapers and journals clamored for tours of Kinsey's Institute for Sex Research (later renamed the Kinsey Institute for Research in Sex, Gender, and Reproduction) and advance copies of his data. It was also condemned more vitriolically than its predecessor, because the American women Kinsey described were likely to have engaged in premarital coitus, and, after marriage, nearly half had flouted their vows to engage in petting or intercourse with partners other than their husbands.[17]

Kinsey had little control over the volumes' reception. The Indiana team had begun taking sex histories during the late 1930s and had completed

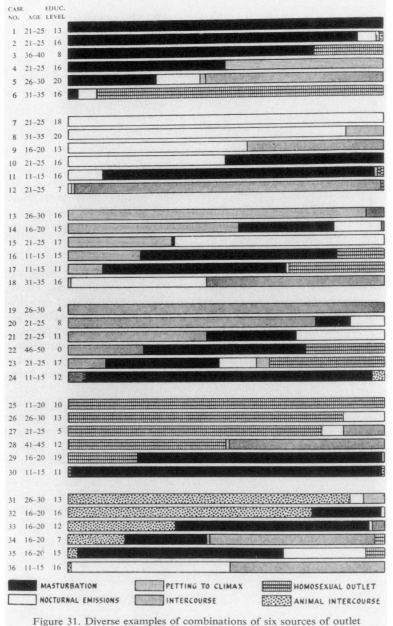

Figure 31. Diverse examples of combinations of six sources of outlet
Each bar shows a combination of outlets used by one individual.

Figure 2. As this figure suggests, Kinsey's data was complex and voluminous, requiring careful interpretation. From Kinsey, Pomeroy, and Martin, *Sexual Behavior in the Human Male,* 196. (Reproduced by permission of The Kinsey Institute for Research in Sex, Gender, and Reproduction, Inc.)

the bulk of its interviews for the first volume during the mid-1940s; but despite the authors' reminders that the cohort most heavily represented in the reports was born around the turn of the century, readers repeatedly interpreted the volumes as snapshots of the present. One of Kinsey's most important findings—that sexual behavior changed gradually, and that the social and behavioral transformations evident in his informants' histories had long roots—was buried under this popular impression that the study referred primarily to contemporary postwar Americans. Similarly, Kinsey's subject pool and data-gathering methodology shaped his work in significant ways that received little attention in the press.

Race is a prime example. The first volume broke informants down into eleven "race-cultural groups" and, opting for a cultural rather than bio-medical model, explained these as cultural and social divisions based on such factors as region of upbringing and adult residence "rather than racial background in the exclusively biologic sense." Kinsey further undercut the idea that race is biological by adding that any individual "may be placed in two or more of these groups," and incorporated a final confusing twist with the terse note that the current volume "is confined to a record on American and Canadian whites" (76). This statement is clarified by a notation that "we do not yet have enough histories of Negroes to warrant their inclusion in the analyses that have been made in the present volume" (393). But throughout the volume, there are scattered references to case histories of African American informants, including "a 39-year-old Negro who had averaged more than three [ejaculations] per day from 13 to 39 years of age" (217) and two "Negro males [who] were still potent at age 90" (237). *Sexual Behavior in the Human Female* addressed the issue of race earlier and more clearly, declaring in the second paragraph of the first chapter that it was based on the "case histories of 5940 white females," and referencing the descriptive category of "white females" throughout the remainder of the study (3). In both cases, the authors' chosen categories and explanations were confusing: the Kinsey team collected sex histories from different racial groups but decided to integrate sex histories together rather than break results down by race. This move, which I address in later chapters, reflected the team's stated belief that their samples were insufficiently large for separate analysis but also testified to their conviction that racial differences in sexual behavior were minor, if even measurable at all. Their arrangement of data effectively presented the volumes as histories of white American sexual behavior, accentuating their shock value.

Another of Kinsey's most cherished theories—that class background and regional difference were fundamental in shaping adult sexual behavior, especially among men—was largely ignored by readers and reviewers, who read the reports' American subjects as middle class. Their stance reflected the postwar investment in a myth of universal middle-class status. One of the defining characteristics of the suburban developments that proliferated during the period and came to dominate the national imagination was their reflection of an upwardly mobile vision in which class was irrelevant and individuals were free to remake themselves. Second- and third-generation Jews, white ethnics, and working-class Americans were encouraged to imagine themselves as members of the white middle class, embracing normative culture and aspiring to middle-class opportunities. Within this conception of a classless and homogenous United States, shared national identity drew people together far better than any economic, religious, or ethnic differences could keep them apart. In a 1957 speech, the Senate Majority Leader, Lyndon Johnson, argued that labels such as *manager* and *worker* were outmoded, since modern Americans envisioned themselves as equal citizens. Both "the carpenter who built this rostrum" and "the man who paid his wages . . . think of themselves first as American men and their wives think of themselves as American women. And they are perfectly right in doing so."[18] Members of the expanding middle class, especially the white ethnics and religious minorities previously unable to afford the material and cultural costs of membership, took complementary gender roles, an intense personal life, and sexual pleasure within marriage—all hallmarks of the new American sexuality so hotly debated by experts—as important markers of their new status.

Kinsey's books offered a disquieting representation of average Americans, and reaction was immediate, passionate, and divided.[19] Half of *Good Housekeeping*'s readers, representing "fairly typical American families and institutions," objected to the reports' publication.[20] *Life* magazine castigated the first volume as "an assault on the family as the basic unit of society, a negation of moral law, and a celebration of licentiousness," and a Catholic periodical denounced both studies as being "at war against purity, against morality, against the family."[21] A national convention of physicians condemned the books for furthering a "wave of sex hysteria."[22] The reports, such sources claimed, would encourage premarital sex, adultery, and homosexuality, corrupt children, and plunge the nation into moral and sexual anarchy. Other authorities, however, hailed the studies as a welcome corrective to decades of repression, declaring that they would encourage open discussion of sex and hasten the end of American puritanism. According to the psychoanalyst Albert Deutsch, one of Kinsey's most enthusiastic advocates, the studies were "a powerful battering-ram" against "the accumulated sex taboos of centuries."[23] The sex researcher Harry Benjamin took liberatory rhetoric even further, declaiming that "Lincoln freed the slaves from their shackles. The work of Kinsey and his collaborators should be a powerful factor in freeing human society, from fantastic tribal taboos, from ecclesiastic prejudices, and from the savagery of medieval laws. This may indeed," Benjamin concluded grandly, "be known as the 'Alfred C. Kinsey age.'"[24]

Benjamin's proposed nickname for the postwar era never quite took, but Kinsey's work was discussed by journalists, politicians, and cultural critics as well as scientists, and the studies' effect was dramatic. Whether embraced or denounced, Kinsey's results quickly assumed indispensable status, as no discussion of American social change was complete without reference to them. Both volumes rapidly became best-sellers despite their sober packaging, relatively high cost, and often-impenetrable language, and both were popularized for even broader audiences through exhaustive media coverage.

Criticisms of Kinsey's work and of its putative effects generally fell into four camps: religious, moral, nationalistic, or psychoanalytic, each with its own distinctive objections. Some of the most vehement protests came from clergy who condemned the reports for downplaying noble emotions like love and altruism to focus on the physiological aspects of sex. Their complaints ranged from heated denunciations of Kinsey's work as "glaringly anti-Biblical" and "sewerage for the stream of life" to more measured evaluations of the implications of his "extreme form of naturalism" for modern Americans.[25] Not all religious respondents to the reports repudiated them—pastoral psychologists, for example, often questioned Kinsey's quantitative approach but also lauded the reports' usefulness and saw themselves as participating in, rather than opposing, postwar conversations about American sexual character.[26]

Another set of critics drew on a more traditional moral vocabulary to combat Kinsey's work. Such detractors, who lamented changes in gender roles and family life, saw Kinsey's work as injurious to the moral codes of readers (especially women) and thus likely to foster confusion about appropriate moral behaviors and beliefs. Some objected to Kinsey's effrontery in conducting the studies at all, others merely to the volumes' wide dissemination and the publicity they received.

Still others based their criticism of Kinsey's work and its possible effects on civic interests, arguing that his findings would serve to undercut the nation's prestige or weaken family ties. No less an enforcer of right than J. Edgar Hoover, director of the Federal Bureau of Investigation, cast Kinsey and his colleagues as anti-American, warning, "Whenever the American people, young or old, come to believe there is no such thing as right or wrong, normal or abnormal, those who would destroy our civilization will applaud a major victory over our way of life."[27]

A fourth major source of anti-Kinsey sentiment was psychiatry. Although only a minority of the nation's mental health practitioners were psychoanalysts, their cultural authority reached unprecedented heights after World War II, as the discipline's insights were lauded in popular books, magazine articles, and Hollywood dramas.[28] Practitioners held strong opinions on the reports and the new sexual cultures they described. They criticized the reports for their quantitative nature, which ignored the psychoanalytic truism that only continued and intense individual treatment could elicit valuable clinical material, as well as for Kinsey's calm acceptance of behaviors that most psychiatrists classed as neurotic or worse. Orthodox Freudians who dominated the profession's elite ranks were especially incensed by the widespread publicity given the reports' findings, with many questioning Kinsey's belief that informants would or could tell the truth about their sexual behaviors.[29] Other social science and mental health professionals showed greater divergence in their opinions about the reports, with marriage counselors, in particular, often enthusiastic about the potential that new sexual information held for improving marriage and increasing personal happiness.

Different strands of opposition to Kinsey's work often combined, sometimes in unexpected ways. The jeremiad *I Accuse Kinsey!,* for example, printed protests from the conservative Southern Baptist pastor E. J. Daniels, the mainstream Christian evangelist Billy Graham, and the gynecologist William S. Kroeger, among others. Authors differed dramatically in their critiques but agreed that the reports were "dangerous to the mental, moral, and physical health of our country."[30]

Kinsey's adherents also diverged, admiring his work for reasons ranging from its contribution to scientific knowledge to its potential to liberate Americans from hidebound sexual norms. Supporters are in some ways more difficult to characterize than opponents, since few professional groups approved unanimously of the volumes; instead, positive reactions reflected a diverse constituency of supporters and a wide range of reasons for admiring the studies.

What united opponents and admirers was the fervor with which they greeted Kinsey's work. Rather than regarding the reports as merely collections of data, they saw them as revealing something crucial about contemporary American social and cultural mores and about the nation's future. According to Sylvanus Duvall, a professor of social science and religion who commented on the dramatic response to the studies, the reports were significant because their figures shattered readers' worldview. The average American, he explained to readers of *Pastoral Psychology* magazine, was "agitated" about the reports "for the same reason that our spiritual ancestors were agitated about Galileo."[31] Duvall's suggestion, that sexual behavior and identity were as important to contemporary Americans as belief in a divine order had once been, implied that Kinsey's charts and graphs rendered previous knowledge false.

The reports catalyzed a massive national project to examine and explain sex. Although Kinsey's exact figures were hotly contested, other medical professionals and scientists also documented rates of sexual activity that shocked and alarmed readers. Sexologists believed that premarital and extramarital heterosexual intercourse were on the rise, and that many Americans' accustomed range of sexual practices was also expanding. A mid-decade survey found that college students increasingly engaged in such previously taboo—and still illegal—practices as oral sex and manual genital stimulation.[32] Statistics on same-sex sexuality offered further evidence of upheavals in Americans' sexual behavior. Shock and outrage greeted Kinsey's finding that nearly half of American men had participated in homosexual activities to the point of orgasm, but others agreed that the incidence of homosexuality was on the rise.[33] Estimates of the percentage of covertly homosexual men in the nation ranged from a shocking one in six to a more reassuring, although still unsettling, one in twenty.[34]

These statistics, and the alarm that greeted them, raise a question: Did sexual patterns themselves really change during and after the war, or only Americans' perceptions? It is difficult to disentangle evidence of changes from public attention to sexual problems and the rise of an increasingly sexualized popular culture. Rates of venereal disease and premarital pregnancy did rise during the war years and may have reflected increased sexual contacts and changes in patterns of dating and mating. Explorations of homosexual lives during the war, for example, suggest that geographical and job mobility offered many gay men and lesbians increased opportunities to meet potential partners and to learn about homosexuality. Overall, Kinsey's work points to slow and gradual shifts in sexual behavior during the first half of the twentieth century rather than any sudden and dramatic leaps; but whatever the extent of actual change, Americans believed that sexual behaviors had accelerated and taken on new forms in recent years, and they searched for explanations and solutions. The reports offered a focus for the national preoccupation with sexuality, but they did not cause the trend.

Everywhere observers looked, they saw mounting evidence that American sexual behaviors were changing, and observers noted again and again that American culture was becoming sexualized. In an address to the American College on Obstetrics and Gynecology, a prominent physician diagnosed the entire nation as being caught in the grip of "sex hysteria."[35] The "cult of super-sex," a journalist concurred, was "infesting" American culture and had already "invaded every aspect of our lives."[36] A sociologist noted sorrowfully that, since the end of the war, the United States had entered "one of those recurring periods in which there is considerable confusion of family values and in which interest in and concern with sex is a sort of major pastime."[37]

As one sociology textbook put it, Americans were embracing a new philosophy of "the naturalism of sex."[38] In the process, many worried, they were becoming a nation of sexual outlaws. When a marriage therapist coolly informed her audience of fellow professionals that "the chances are nine out of ten that you are a sex criminal," she was expressing a sentiment that was to be frequently reiterated.[39] The reports fed a growing critique of the nation's sex laws, which many legal authorities saw as archaic and out of touch with actual practices. The postwar period did see a panic over the category of offenders who would come to be called sexual predators, but postwar concerns about sex were directed primarily at mainstream behaviors or at those that threatened to become so.[40] Prostitution was largely dismissed as a minor social problem, while private, consensual, sexual contacts, and even marital behaviors came under increasing scrutiny.

As they evaluated new sexual data, authorities were particularly worried by their observation that it reflected the behaviors of respectable, average women and men rather than marginalized subgroups or deviant minorities. Many noted that it was the decent middle-class boy and girl next door, rather than the lower classes, foreign born, or criminals, who were responsible for the changing demographics of sexual behavior. Kinsey had commented in the first report on "a definite increase in the amount of intercourse with girls who are not prostitutes," and others agreed that middle-class youth were increasingly likely to engage in sexual activities ranging from kissing to heavy petting to intercourse.[41] The psychiatrist Lawrence Frank singled out as the most important aspect of Kinsey's research the finding that "young men today are apparently seeking and finding a variety of sexual relationships—and with girls who are not prostitutes."[42] The pediatric gynecologist Goodrich Schauffler backed up Frank's observations when he described the "young girls in serious trouble" he encountered in practice as "sweet, nice, 'normal' girls like your daughter and mine."[43]

To many, the breakdown of traditional sexual morality went hand in hand with the growing instability of traditional gender arrangements. Despite a return to the domestic sphere by many working women after the war, the number and percentage of women—even mothers of young children—who worked outside the home increased steadily throughout the 1950s and early 1960s. Evidence that gender roles were neither eternal nor assured emerged on a mass scale during the 1950s. When the sexologist George Henry republished data from his 1930s study *Sex Variants* in a more accessible format designed for the "helpful enlightenment" of mid-1950s readers, its new title, *All the Sexes,* spoke to a bewildering proliferation of sexual possibilities.[44] One alarmed social scientist entitled his cautionary screed *The Disappearing Sexes* and warned that factors including the recent "revolution in sexual morality" were "working to eliminate differences between the sexes."[45] Even biological sex differences seemed less certain. The 1952 sex change operation of Christine Jorgensen, which was widely reported in the American news media and which received a great deal of alarmed attention in discussions of changing gender roles, provided a troubling physical dimension to discussions of the mutability of sex and gender.

Everywhere they looked, postwar commentators saw evidence of the new "concern with sex" reflected in the popular culture. Nonfiction works like the Kinsey Reports reached best-seller lists, and the popular press featured information and advice that would have been deemed too explicit only a few years before: *Newsweek* magazine noted in 1949 that newspapers had recently begun to feature "frank questions about sexual relations—and equally frank answers."[46] Fictional works that dealt with previously taboo topics, such as Henry Miller's *Tropic of Cancer* and Grace Metalious's *Peyton Place,* extended the limits of respectable reading. The poet and novelist George Viereck surveyed the state of contemporary fiction in 1954 and noted approvingly that, after decades of "sentimental mush" and "bloodless character portraits," in recent years "American writers [have] discovered sex."[47]

Not all observers were as sanguine as Viereck about this development. "The heavily advertised novel," one columnist complained, "features three illicit affairs to the chapter. The newsstand at the neighborhood drugstore is ablaze with 'Illegal Lover,' 'Cash-and-Carry Love,' 'Thrills from a Stranger.'"[48] "American fiction," a reviewer noted with equal disapproval, "has become the most licentious literature that ever enjoyed popular distribution."[49] Popular taste, these critics feared, was becoming irremediably cheapened. As authors were forced to meet the public's demand for sexual explicitness, titillation would drive out artistic integrity. One critic painted a grim view of American belles lettres when he predicted that "prose, already verging on the emotionally lush, will become tropical, over-ripe, with exotica of all types flitting through it. Sexually starved heroines will turn positively carnivorous. Sadism will be substituted for love. The unconscious homosexual overtones will be more consciously focused."[50] The extent of sexual themes in popular fiction also interested the federal government, and in 1952, congressional investigators charged publishers with "the dissemination of artful appeals to sensuality, immorality, filth, perversion, and degeneracy."[51]

American literature was not the only medium affected by increasing sexualization. A writer for *Life* magazine argued that advertising had so capitalized upon Americans' sexual interests that "Americans not only think of sex as the ultimate goal of all their social and economic activity" but also "actually buy automobiles and refrigerators for reasons that are, at least in part, sexual."[52] A landmark 1949 advertising campaign for Maidenform brassieres, in which women dreamed of going about everyday activities clad only in lingerie, evoked criticism for its scantily clad models and explicit voyeurism but proved wildly successful.[53] In *The Hidden Persuaders,* his 1957 attack on the manipulations and growing influence of the advertising industry, the social critic Vance Packard charged that a barrage of sexual images had rendered people "jaded and permissive." Echoing the literary critic Alfred Towne's worry that Americans were becoming inured to increasing sexual display and required more explicit images, Packard noted that images of attractively clothed bodies were no longer adequate to sell merchandise; now it took "overtones of masochism, body exhibitionism, etc." to appeal to consumers.[54]

Similar controversies arose over the depiction of sexual themes in American theater and film, leading reviewers and cultural critics to complain that postwar Americans' taste for sexual themes was leading to the debasement of artistic standards there as well. The Production Code of the motion picture industry, which had long ruled Hollywood with an iron fist and dealt in moral absolutes—no rapes, no seductions, no double beds for couples, and no adulteries unless the participants were punished—was gradually giving way to a system of greater moral relativism, permitting language and images previously deemed unacceptable.[55] The classic noir tale of adultery and murder *The Postman Always Rings Twice* (1946) was described by *Newsweek* as "as explicit as it can be," but was overtaken by the 1956 film *Baby Doll*, which *Time* characterized as "just possibly the dirtiest American-made motion picture that has ever been legally exhibited."[56] *Postman* and *Baby Doll* had a good deal of competition—to many, it seemed that all American films were being negatively affected by the new mandate of sexual explicitness. By the early 1960s, even many liberals, like the radio and television commentator John Crosby, found that sexual themes had permeated popular culture to a disconcerting extent. In his article "Movies Are Too Dirty," Crosby conceded that the trend toward sexual directness had some positive effects, as a few directors were producing magnificent films unconstrained by former taboos; but he added that far too many were simply cashing in on the new openness about sex. The palate of the American filmgoer, Crosby believed, had become jaded. Illicit sex, adultery, and rape were commonly depicted in recent films, not to mention "lesbianism in *The Children's Hour*, male homosexuality in *Victim*, child molesters in *The Mark*, nymphomania in *The Chapman Report*, cannibalism in *Suddenly Last Summer*."[57] Significantly, Crosby's analysis of popular culture and sexuality equated the United States' cultural sensibility with the sensational and the cheap. The sexually themed films Crosby singled out for praise, such as *La Dolce Vita* and *Virgin Spring*, were European.

The "sexualization" of the mass media was made possible by an accompanying revolution in the court system. During the 1950s and early 1960s, the nation's legal system recognized and furthered an expanding sexual discourse through decisions that widened the range of protected speech. In the series of cases that culminated in the landmark 1957 *Roth v. United*

States decision, a California publisher indicted for sending obscene literature through the mail pleaded that the definition of *obscenity* and *pornography* was too subjective to pass constitutional muster, and that prevailing judicial norms were out of step with most Americans' tastes and tolerances. Although the publisher's conviction was upheld by the Supreme Court, his argument, and the brief filed by the new Supreme Court justice William Brennan, signaled the liberalization of allowable speech. Brennan's Court, in the words of one legal scholar, "acted to legitimize and constitutionalize the public discussion of sex."[58] In a landmark 1959 case that involved the right of a motion picture company to exhibit a film deemed—and widely agreed to be—"immoral," the nation's leading legal authority declared that the First Amendment right to free expression outweighed any potential threat posed by sexual speech. Speaking for the Court, Justice Potter Stewart not only held that sexual ideas were protected in their capacity as artistic or socially relevant productions but also said that they were overtly political and protected as such: "What New York has done," he wrote, "is to prevent the exhibition of a motion picture because the picture advocates an idea— that adultery under certain circumstances may be proper behavior." The First Amendment, he continued, "protects advocacy of the opinion that adultery may sometimes be proper, no less than advocacy of socialism or the single tax."[59]

By declaring that unpopular sexual ideologies were as protected as political ones, and indeed *were* political, the Court not only allowed for the production and exhibition of sexual material but also insisted that sexuality was central to civic identity.[60] Court decisions upheld authors' right to publish—and the public's right to read—explicit texts like Vladimir Nabokov's *Lolita* (1955) and Allen Ginsberg's *Howl* (1956). As narratives aimed at promoting sexual arousal became a protected form of speech, the "public discussion of sex" grew increasingly frank and voluminous.

SEXUALITY, POLITICS, AND THE PROBLEM OF NATIONAL CHARACTER

As these debates about the status of sexual free speech suggest, a central theme of postwar discourse on American sexuality was the relation between private sexual behaviors and the public interest. In 1956, when the Harvard sociologist Pitirim Sorokin described the "greatest threat to American democracy since the rise of Fascism in Europe," the enemy he saw was not China, the Soviet Union, or even internal political subversion;

rather, it was the national preoccupation with and abandonment to sex. Sorokin warned:

> A peculiar revolution has been taking place in the lives of American men and women. Quite different from the better-known political and economic revolutions, it goes almost unnoticed. Devoid of noisy explosions, its stormy scenes are confined to the privacy of the bedroom and involve only individuals. . . . It has no revolutionary army to fight its enemies . . . no politbureau directs it. Without plan or organization, it is carried on by millions of individuals, each acting on his own. . . . Its name is the sex revolution.

If left unchecked, Sorokin continued, the emerging phenomenon he labeled "the American sex revolution" promised to result in the "disintegration . . . [of] marriage and the family" and ultimately threatened nothing less than "the well-being of the nation itself."[61]

This linking of sexual and political threats demonstrates how American sexual behavior offered critics both a specific issue around which to rally and a trope through which to identify and critique other social changes affecting the nation. Like members of the Court, Sorokin argued that sexual acts had to be understood as political, and that Americans' changing moral standards were equivalent to shifts in their political ideologies. Paradoxically, this revolution posed a greater threat to American culture than would an invading army—rather than attacking from without, it played on Americans' innermost weaknesses and desires. The central flaw in American character, many experts feared, was that postwar citizens would prove incapable of reconciling their personal desires—for ease, affluence, and pleasure—with the interests of the state.

Sorokin was not alone in seeing Americans' sexual character as a Trojan horse carrying the potential for national destruction. A wide range of contemporary thinkers drew similar associations between private sexual behaviors and the condition and fate of the nation, seeing sexual chaos as the cause or symptom of other problems. Sylvanus Duvall argued that all sexual activity, especially any taking place outside of marriage, was a public matter. Rather than a private affair concerning only consenting individuals, he argued, illicit sexuality affected a wide cross section of the nation. Irregular sexual liaisons had an effect upon apparatuses of the state, such as the health departments that tracked venereal disease. They also affected the "general public," who bore the social and economic costs of raising illegitimate children and caring for families broken up by adultery and divorce; acquaintances and families, who drew lessons from the conduct they observed; and future generations, who would grow up surrounded by sexual chaos.[62] Since the social costs enacted by immorality were high, the state could legitimately step in to survey and control sexual behavior.

Sexuality and the state were linked by representatives of both the right and the left. It was common for journalists and experts to describe sex outside of marriage as a Communist idea that would foster political chaos in the United States, but the progressive commentator Lewis Mumford added an anti-McCarthy twist to the equation, warning in 1954 that the nation's continuing climate of political suspicion would lead to "regressive reactions" that included "purposeless sexual promiscuity."[63] Calls for state intervention into Americans' sexual lives came most often from social and religious conservatives, but self-described liberals and libertarians also championed the state's interest in regulating or liberating Americans' sexual behaviors, a development that points up the difficulty of applying labels of left and right to many of the period's sexual commentators.

Sexual Practices of American Women, a 1953 work by Christopher Gerould that combined data on female sexual physiology and behavior with an appeal for a "true sexual morality" based on openness, offers an example of the multiple uses to which sexual rhetoric could be put. Arguing that "Americans are faced with a serious failure" and that "if our sexual patterns are flawed and imperfect, our whole lives and personalities must suffer," Gerould drew familiar associations between the nation's sexual patterns and its political character.[64] His proposed remedy, however, went a step further than many. Modern Americans, he noted sorrowfully, were "the most immoral people on earth in terms of sexual morality, precisely because our sex behavior is governed almost entirely by rules and conventions instead of by free choice between the good and the bad." To solve this dilemma, the United States should adopt what he called the "Four Sexual Freedoms" to assure freedom of information, education, law, and choice. Alluding to Franklin D. Roosevelt's 1941 "Four Freedoms" speech, a list of ideals that had become enshrined as sacred obligations of the modern state and entitlements of the nation's citizenry, Gerould boldly identified sexual liberalism as a central concern of the nation and underlined the relationship between a private sexual life and a public civic one.

The exact connections authors drew between sexual irregularities and their social consequences varied. Narratives of sexual danger could and did attach to specific kinds of acts or bodies: homosexuality was often rhetorically linked to political subversion and the betrayal of male institutions, women's extramarital sexuality associated with the decline of female nurturance and motherhood, and male heterosexuality viewed as potentially becoming either passive or excessive, either of which would threaten family life and gender roles. Most often, though, a generalized sexual chaos—heterosexual promiscuity, premarital sex, petting, mate swapping, homosexuality, and any other sexual behaviors deemed perverse—was depicted as the route to a similarly broad-based social and cultural anarchy. As a pastor and social worker noted in 1950, sexual problems were often "symptomatic" of national dilemmas and despairs, including cold war political fears, apprehensions of economic decline, and worries about familial strength, so much that "for man or woman, sexual life has become an anxiety and an anguish."[65]

A vivid example of both postwar alarm at the sexual state of the nation and the ways in which the language of sex was used to talk about other kinds of social problems is *The Split-Level Trap,* a 1960 exposé of suburbia by the psychiatrist Richard Gordon and the psychologist Katharine Gordon. The book opens with a description of life in Bergen County, New Jersey, stressing inhabitants' material success and quest for serenity and security. Instead of a new Eden, however, settlers find a modern hell where they fall victim to ulcers, depression, schizophrenia, and suicide. Their individual and collective problems are driven by and expressed through misplaced sexual desires or acts, and many of the Gordons' vignettes of the dark side of suburban life attest to a pervasive violence and anomie expressed through sexual chaos:

> As night falls, three teen-age boys visit the home of a girl in one of the town's more expensive sections. The girl's parents are out for the evening. She lets the boys in. The boys take turns with her on the living room couch.
>
> In the darkness between two houses, a young man creeps up to a window and looks in. He is disappointed, for the housewife he sees is fully clothed. He disappears into the darkness to look for another window.
>
> Down at the police station . . . a wild-eyed young mother comes in. She begs to be locked up. She talks incoherently of performing sexual perversions with her husband and stabbing her new baby.[66]

In this narrative, as in a host of similar analyses of postwar American life, inappropriate sexual urges and behaviors represent the flip side of the American Dream. *The Split-Level Trap*—promoted as "a Kinsey Report on suburbia"—suggests that affluence could not protect Americans from danger. The kind of sexuality that concerned the Gordons and other social scientists was not one that affected individual bodies so much as it targeted something broader. Experts feared that sexuality was taking on a preeminent role in the national consciousness, shaping not only the ways in which Americans thought but also what they did and with whom. As they constructed American sexuality as a privileged signifier of national identity, postwar experts were relying upon a central trope in postwar thought, that of American character.

The historians Beth Bailey and David Farber argue that postwar Americans, in reaction to international turmoil and the perceived need for a strong and united nation, "seemed obsessed with questions of self-definition."[67] This process of self-definition often relied upon what the historian Eric Sandeen calls the "overt American exceptionalism that pervaded 1950s popular culture."[68] Americans had a long tradition of theorizing an exceptional national character—a collection of common traits, beliefs, and behaviors that united an otherwise diverse group—but this trope loomed increasingly large in the national cosmology during the postwar years. In a 1950 text designed for a popular readership, the historian Henry Steele Commager described the American past as one that had produced an identifiable set of shared values and attributes, and called the result of this "blending of inheritance, environment, and experience" a "distinctive American character."[69] "The important questions about any nation," Commager declared elsewhere, "as about any individual, come back to character."[70]

Many midcentury intellectuals posited a specific and identifiable kind of American character as having directed the nation's past and as continuing to dictate its shape in the present. Theories of national character aimed at understanding the *mentalité* of the Axis nations proliferated during World War II, as authorities sought to aid U.S. intelligence by understanding combatant peoples.[71] Psychologists and anthropologists gauged enemy nations' motivations, often rendering international conflict in the language of psychology. Germans flocked to National Socialism, a popular theory suggested, because Teutonic swaddling practices produced citizens eager to adopt demagogues like Hitler as protective father figures. Japan, by contrast, produced a "highly distinctive national character" that emphasized group loyalty and rendered its people fierce and effective warriors.[72] After the war, national character studies, spearheaded by T. W. Adorno and colleagues' influential study *The Authoritarian Personality* (1950), focused more on the relationship between a nation's political and economic structure and its people. The delineation of national character assumed paramount importance not only within the social sciences but also as a tool for negotiating America's place in the emerging world order.

Significantly, the language used by many theorists implied that this order, and nations themselves, was gendered. In the postwar United States, the diplomatic historian Michelle Mart argues, "traditional gender roles were applied to individuals as well as nations; in these representations, the United States was a masculine country that took responsibility for other, 'weaker' nations."[73] Trouble on the home front thus threatened not only individuals but also the nation's interests abroad. If American men's aggressiveness and strength of character were in decline, then how could their nation save other countries from Communism?[74]

Scholars insisted that studies of national character offered valuable information that could be drawn upon for political and military use in national crises.[75] The British anthropologist Geoffrey Gorer, whose 1948 book *The American People: A Study in National Character* provoked a firestorm of controversy with its critical portrait of American culture, stated forcefully that nothing less than "the future peace and prosperity of the world" depended on identifying and understanding the differences between national characters. Accurate portraits of national character, Gorer argued, "are our only safeguard against the inconceivable horrors of another war, or the horrors, only slightly less grim, of totalitarian domination."[76]

The extension of this analysis to the United States, where the search for a collective and uniquely "American" personality type would preoccupy theorists of varying disciplines and convictions for more than a decade, provides the richest example of the range offered by national personality studies. *And Keep Your Powder Dry,* by the anthropologist Margaret Mead, written early in the war under government sponsorship in order to stir up home-front patriotism, opened up new possibilities for American scholars. Their own culture, Mead's work argued, offered a rich lode for study. Theorists of American identity uncovered in the nation's culture a unity and coherence of belief systems that made "American character" a blanket of interlocking and mutually supportive traits from cradle to grave. "The way in which people behave," Mead asserted about American culture, "is all of a piece, their virtues and their sins, the way they slap the baby, handle their court cases, and bury their dead."[77]

Over the next decade, social scientists turned new eyes upon American society, concentrating on excavating and assessing what seemed to be distinctively American traditions.[78] Gene Wise argues that American studies scholarship of this period was characterized by the assumption of a homogeneous and historically enduring "American mind" and the mission of "prob[ing] for the fundamental meaning of America."[79] Historians, psychologists, journalists, anthropologists, and all manner of other cultural critics wrote about "our culture" and "the American mind," presuming that some unified and synchronous set of values bound together a population of over 150 million.[80] The Harvard philosopher Ralph Barton Perry noted that what he termed the "pervasive and identical character of the American mind" stemmed from the triumph of shared culture over geographical, racial, and ethnic differences. "Common Americanism," Perry argued, was "something discernible and recognizable" that knit Americans together into a common unit.[81]

Warren Susman has argued that the early twentieth century saw a shift from character to personality as the dominant trope for self-consciousness. Character, he argues, is a nineteenth-century concept concerned with steadiness, reliability, and the dedication of oneself to some greater good. Personality, on the contrary, evokes glamour, persuasiveness, and charm, all quintessential twentieth-century traits needed to prosper in a competitive consumer society. The rise of personality, though, did not bring an end to character, and here I am concerned with its use to define a specific set of traits.[82] Character was a useful trope for postwar commentators because it stressed the shared nature of group beliefs rather than individual differences. The term's very old-fashionedness hearkened back to an idealized American past and downplayed racial and class differences.

The cultural critic James Donald reminds us that "a nation does not express itself through its culture; it is cultural apparatuses that produce 'the nation.'"[83] The concept of American character was vital to the production of the postwar nation. The notions of America and the typical American whose character these academicians worked with were powerful ideological constructs, distinct from—though supposedly recognizable as—actual inhabitants of the contemporary United States. Character served as a kind of cultural capital, its amount and quality constantly measured and assessed by journalists and other worried observers.[84] Soon after the war, a *Life* editorial noted that the precipitous decline in character spelled disaster for the nation's economic recovery and its morals alike. Arguing that "the wealth of nations does not consist in natural resources but in the character of the people," *Life* stressed that "the family is the basic cell responsible for the production of those people and that character."[85]

Theorizing the national character, and dissecting its flaws and uses, served as a form of ideological nation building in which national identity was consolidated or disputed through narratives that described Americans to themselves.[86] The trope of American character thus served several functions for postwar Americans. It allowed authorities concerned about the nation's status to rework long-standing ideas of American exceptionalism by trying to capture what made Americans different from citizens of other nations. The popular notion of an inheritance of uniquely American character, based in Puritan roots and hardened by the travails of the frontier, bore a great deal of ideological weight. In its most positive form, this narrative offered hope that Americans formed a united citizenry possessed of what it took to win a cold war. In the hands of postwar experts, American character was an almost infinitely malleable and useful construct. According to the logic of national character, if all Americans ostensibly shared a common heritage and set of attributes, then differences in achievement must be caused by individual failure rather than social or structural forces. Little wonder, then, that when the U.S. government published *Amerika,* a magazine of articles in Russian distributed in the USSR as part of a program of cultural exchange, one of its first articles mapped out the concept of American character for Soviet readers.[87]

The discourse of character, however, also could and did serve as a site for national self-examination and critique. A worried undercurrent to the celebration of American character during the late 1940s and 1950s was the widespread fear that this character was changing in ways that threatened the United States' economic, technological, and ideological dominance. The nation's position of superiority appeared increasingly precarious as other countries attained nuclear capacity throughout the 1950s. The launching of *Sputnik* by the USSR in 1957 confirmed for many the worry that Americans had become lulled into complacency by too much leisure and affluence, and prompted renewed national critique of American habits. A new kind of character was emerging, one described by the sociologist David Riesman as "other-directed" and by William Whyte as an "organization man" shaped by the demands of corporate culture and stifled by "conformity."[88] In mid-decade, when *Time* magazine devoted a cover to the pressing question "What is the American character?," it worried that "the American self-picture has gone out of focus."[89] As authorities searched for and interrogated the alleged "weakness" and "decadence" of contemporary American culture, they returned again and again to American sexual behavior, which served at once as a cause and a symptom of national decline.

CREATING AMERICAN SEXUAL CHARACTER

Observers had drawn connections between Americans' sexual behavior and the nation's stability and strength before, of course. Sexual nonconformity had often been associated with political radicalism, and law and custom had rewarded premarital chastity, especially for women, while defining adultery, bastardy, and sodomy as threats to public order. During the postwar years, however, concerns about American sexuality took on new urgency. Again and again, prominent cultural critics and social scientists took American sexuality as the starting point and central focus for critiques of postwar national culture. Many maintained that American sexual mores were hypocritical, harmful, and badly in need of reform. "In almost no department . . . is there so much false direction, misinformation, and invalid expectation as in sex, love, and marriage," counseled a neurologist and psychiatrist in 1950.[90] In his 1954 study of "the attitudes, myths, and feelings of the average American," the liberal psychotherapist Albert Ellis documented Americans' simultaneous preoccupation with sexual topics and pervasive unhappiness and dubbed it the "American sexual tragedy."[91] Commentators of all stripes were struck by the glaring gap between Americans' professed moral code and their actual behavior. Before the release of *Sexual Behavior in the Human Male, Science Illustrated* reported with distress that it would "show a great schizophrenic split between what Americans do and what they believe they do, what they practice and what they preach. These facts show Americans as furtive, self-righteous, unobjective and intolerant in their sexual beliefs and practices."[92] "Our sex morals," the psychologist Lawrence Frank affirmed, promoted "all manner of evasion, subterfuges, fraud, hypocrisy, deceitful practices, and an immense amount of human misery and conflict."[93]

Overwhelmingly, commentators expressed concern about the effects this "revolution in contemporary morals" was having upon the nation. The sociologist Sorokin, of course, held that the "sex revolution" resulted from national laziness, and he located promiscuity and "sex-mindedness" as the primary dangers to democracy. Riesman, too, stressed the growing importance of sexuality to the average American, arguing in *The Lonely Crowd* that, as middle-class citizens became more other-directed, they transferred sex from the realm of private and personal experience to a competitive arena, becoming what he called "consumers of sex."[94] Americans, usually defined unquestioningly as white and affluent, hungered for new varieties of experience in their sex lives just as they did in their leisure activities.

As this reference to Americans as sexual consumers suggests, postwar concerns about sex resonated with a contemporaneous ambivalence about consumer capitalism. Numerous observers equated the nation's preoccupation with sex and its love affair with newly available shiny cars, homes, and appliances, likening postwar consumers' spending sprees to orgies of another kind. Both kinds of pleasurable consumption were good in their place, logic dictated, but too much unbridled acquisition—whether of sexual partners or Buicks—was bad for the national interest, as well as the individual soul.

The social critics who viewed Americans' allegedly increasing sensuality as part of a larger shift in national priorities were indeed witnessing an important historical transition in the nature of capitalist consumption. The celebration of character, as we have seen, coexisted with fears that traditional citizenship was eroding, replaced by a competing understanding of citizenship organized around materialist and cultural entitlements rather than political rights.[95] After all, as David Potter's *People of Plenty* and other explorations of American character argued, postwar abundance was profoundly reshaping the nation's patterns of work and play.[96] During the cold war, American citizens increasingly affirmed their national and class identity through acts of consumption. Jennifer Scanlon argues that consumption, whether imaginary or literal, took on new valence as "consumer goods functioned as one of the most important means to distinguish the pampered U.S. citizen from his or her apparently deprived Soviet counterpart."[97] What Lizabeth Cohen calls the "landscape of mass consumer culture"—the types of items available for purchase, the social spaces in which such purchases took place, and the gendered cultural meanings assigned to consumption—expanded dramatically during the years after World War II. The 1950s, Cohen argues, were central to an "important shift from one kind of social order to another," and authorities lauded the American consumer's role in stimulating the economy and creating a culture of widespread homeownership, higher education, and expanding—and apparently universal—membership in the middle class.[98] Even religion seemed to participate in this process, as the much lauded postwar rise in Americans' religious adherence was described as a theologically indistinct "civic religion" that celebrated family and national unity as much as it did any specific theological tradition. In *Protestant-Catholic-Jew,* the sociologist Will Herberg argued that intermarriage among white ethnics from different national and religious traditions hastened assimilation into a universal middle class at the cost of authentic ethnoreligious practices and beliefs.[99]

The Columbia University sociologist Daniel Bell, who had hailed the "end of ideology" at the close of the 1950s, placed the rise of this assimilated and consuming middle class at the center of his dramatic reassessment of the period a decade later. Rather than critiquing the bankruptcy of the left and right, he located the major fault of the United States in what many saw as its greatest postwar triumph: the spread of consumer capitalism. The national culture, he argued, had become "prodigal, promiscuous," and ever more voracious in its appetite for pleasurable experiences and goods. Significantly, Bell believed that the traditional American "character structure inherited from the nineteenth century—with its emphasis on self-discipline, delayed gratification, restraint—is still relevant to the demands of the social structure; but it clashes sharply with the culture, where such bourgeois values have been completely rejected—in part, as we shall see, and paradoxically, because of the workings of the capitalist system itself."[100] It was this increasingly individualist ethos of pleasure, rather than economic and political forces, that threatened Americans' character and national stability. The increasing centrality of consumption wrought profound changes in Americans' definitions of citizenship, the state, and collective national identity. Many of the critics who first identified and warned against changing sexual patterns such as the impermanence of marriage, rise of temporary sexual liaisons, and lure of sensuality, were in part using sexuality as a proxy for these larger transformations.[101]

Theorists of American sexual character relied upon a series of basic truisms, with sexual behavior resonating with concepts of health or illness, normalcy or deviance. "Poets and psychologists," a physician explained, "agree that an adult's sexual activity represents the epitome of his personality: if all goes well in this area, a state of health is reflected; and if there is not a state of health, then in some fashion sooner or later, the sexual life reflects the illness."[102] Since a nation's sexual patterns similarly mirrored its health or decay, signifying its adequacy to function in a changing international milieu, the nation as a whole was often seen as sharing a distinctive sexual character. Experts stressed the need to look at sex as a national system, one in which Americans' collective failures and beliefs were writ large. The journalist Howard Whitman argued that "the sexual character disorders which stem from faulty sex education may greatly influence our adult society, not necessarily through the warpings of one man or a small group of men but through the warpings of all of us."[103] According to a physician, the nation's attitude toward sexuality was pathological and unbalanced: "As a nation, we are preoccupied—almost obsessed!—with the superficial aspects of sex; you might say, with sex as a form of amusement."[104]

Authors often contextualized their criticisms of American sexual ideology with references to other peoples and nations, arguing that the laxity of American morals and the heightened value placed on sexual pleasure in the United States weakened the nation's interests abroad as well as at home. Statistics on sex and marriage were compared to those from other countries, underlining the belief that social change was not merely a natural consequence of modernization but instead expressed something endemic to American culture.[105] Americans' sexual character, in short, made the country look bad in an increasingly competitive and crucial international marketplace, subverting the nation's battle for international political influence. "In the years following World War II," as the historian Mary Dudziak puts it, "the United States had an image problem." The international media drew repeated attention to failures of democracy, such as racial segregation, panics over internal dissent, and rampant consumerism. Internationally this image problem was deemed so significant that diplomats and the Federal Bureau of Investigation joined to censure and censor public figures whose criticism of the country might reach foreign ears.[106] Postwar liberals and conservatives alike noted time and again that negative international opinion regarding the United States harmed the nation, and many saw American sexual behavior as a particularly sensitive topic. The author John McPartland observed in 1947, even before the revelations of the first Kinsey Report, that "our sexual habits have become something of a worldwide scandal."[107] Similarly, the émigré author Andre Visson commented disapprovingly in a 1948 guide to American ways that "a favorite target for European criticism is the American approach to sex." Internationally, Visson believed, anti-American sentiment was often based on "the most fantastic ideas about sex life in the United States."[108] "By 1955," one sexologist believed, "the American people have become sex-minded to such a degree that it has attracted attention at home and abroad."[109] Experts worried about the effects such beliefs could have on international opinion, with one Sovietologist reporting apprehensively that, within the USSR, "the Kinsey Report is a revelation of the dirt and depravity into which American civilization has fallen."[110] This concern only grew over the next decade. A 1958 article in *Cosmopolitan* magazine observed that "our new preoccupation with sex and sexuality have been noted time and again by visitors from abroad," and a 1960 guide to censorship in the United States remarked that Americans' sex-consciousness was so pronounced that "visitors from other civilizations sometimes think us sex mad."[111]

The anthropologist Gorer, whose *The American People* had offered a particularly unflattering depiction of the national character, agreed. Foreign readers, he observed in a 1950 article, often cherished an "erotic myth of America," a fantasy in which "all the women are in heat" and male heroes "respond with equal fervor and superhuman potency, each fornication described in minute detail." To Europeans still feeling the pinch of postwar reparations and grimly engaged in rebuilding their shattered economies, America was coming to stand as a symbol of excess. In the place of prewar cultural cartography, which had assigned France the role of sexiest nation, Gorer posited that a "new myth" was "growing up in Western Europe . . . the myth of the United States as a [place] in which there are endless opportunities to indulge . . . all one's erotic . . . daydreams." This perception, the anthropologist warned U.S. readers, was "one of the more important components in the fear which many Europeans feel concerning the spread of American culture and influence."[112]

These concerns were widely shared, as American boosters displayed deep concern with international opinion. Government agencies and private initiatives alike disseminated positive images of the United States abroad as part of the cold war effort, and many examples of what Richard Pells calls "cultural diplomacy" were designed to manage images of the United States as a site of moral decay.[113] This was especially true in western Europe, where in West Germany, for example, the "American consumer goods and cultural exports [that] posed a threat to German culture and traditions" were viewed simultaneously as dangerous and possessed of an "extraordinary allure."[114] In the charged context of the cold war, as the United States sought ideological alliances abroad, its image as a "sex-mad" nation could harm key diplomatic and military relationships. When the National Council of Catholic Women declared the first Kinsey Report to be "a disservice to the nation," they recognized and affirmed the intimate links between sexual behavior and national character, as did cartoons in which suave Europeans exploited American sexuality for profit or amusement (see figures 3 and 4).[115]

"FEELTHY KINSEY CHARTS, M'SIEUR?"

Figures 3 and 4. Opinions from abroad: cartoons from Charles Preston, ed., *A Cartoon Guide to the Kinsey Report,* 46, 12. (From the *Wall Street Journal*—permission, Cartoon Features Syndicate and Charles Preston.)

If American sexuality held the potential to damage U.S.–European relations, its effect on cold-war tensions elsewhere was even more dramatic. Edmund Bergler, one of many psychiatrists to denounce Kinsey's findings, objected to the first report partly because its conclusions "will be politically and propagandistically used against the United States abroad, stigmatizing the nation as a whole in a whisper campaign."[116] Others shared Bergler's concern: "In Soviet eyes," an American expert on the Soviet Union reported in 1951, Americans were perceived as having "sunk so low that we are interested only in sexual pathology. Our family has decayed, our morals have disintegrated. We are hardly human anymore."[117] Idealized national images of family life played an important symbolic role in

"——MAKES ONE FEEL SO VEREEEE LUCKY, JUST TO
BE FRENCH!"

the ongoing battle for ideological supremacy waged by the Soviet Union
and the United States, and indications of American moral decline led
inevitably to political embarrassment.

The specifics of European analyses—for example, the very different
charges that Americans were puritans obsessed with policing others' sexuality or that they were licentious and immoral—mattered less than did the
ways in which such commentary lent credence to broader national fears
about retaining political and cultural capital abroad. Sexual excess, moral
relativism, and gender chaos weakened America's stature in the eyes of allies
and enemies alike, and the statistics of the Kinsey Report threatened the
international balance of power. Drawing on a rhetoric that resonated with
contemporary worries about political subversion, Sorokin argued in *The
American Sex Revolution* that, by their increasing promiscuity, Americans
"undermine their own position, influence, prestige, and authority much

more than do all the Communists and other subversive revolutionaries taken together."[118]

At the same time that sex stood as a major social problem, however, it simultaneously figured in some analyses as part of the possible solution to national dilemmas. Authorities agreed that properly channeled sexuality could revitalize marriages and cement family and community ties. Rather than reflecting depraved "sex-mindedness," such theorists believed, the public's preoccupation with sexuality could be turned to a calm public discussion of sexual issues, marking Americans as rational, mature citizens interested in improving their nation. Abraham Stone, a respected sex advice author who served at Columbia's Institute for Psychological Research and later as director of the Sanger Institute, countered criticism of Kinsey's data with the claim that new and accurate information on sexual behavior would instead ultimately assist in nation building, since "the sounder the family, the stronger the social body."[119]

Liberal commentators thus viewed the new openness about sex as a tool for promoting civic order. Employing a rhetoric of enlightenment, they insisted that, once armed with new knowledge about sexual behaviors and functions, Americans could manage their sexual relationships with a new maturity. The Vassar sociologist Joseph Folsom even suggested in a review of the reports that better understanding of the nation's sexual life could lead to dramatic improvements in international understanding. Connecting Americans' erotic preoccupations to their political and military undertakings, he asked, "Would a population which spends much more of its time in a state of mild erotic feeling be as prone to competitive tensions, to hatreds, and to aggressions, as one which is intent either upon the quick relief of erotic feeling or upon preventing its arousal?"[120] Few social scientists proposed such a crudely libidinal model of the relationship between sexual behavior and national or international tensions, but virtually all saw sex as having implications for the national interest.

Such concerns led inevitably to a wide range of recommendations about the nation's future sexual policies. Whether they welcomed Americans' preoccupation with sexuality or viewed it as dangerous, virtually all experts who addressed the topic of American sexual mores agreed that they needed reform. Not surprisingly, the experts who criticized American repression and hypocrisy generally applauded the spread of sexual information and increased sexual freedom, while conservatives who decried the increase in sexual liberalism called for a return to traditional restraint and decorum. Sorokin, for one, based his plan for "a sane and joyous sexual order in our nation" on a return to traditional morality: his plan both emphasized the repression of homosexuality and called for social support for monogamous marriage.[121] Despite their differences, though, both optimistic advocates of sexual freedom and pessimistic experts who decried recent developments believed that the disjuncture between Americans' moral codes and their sexual behavior called for attention.

From the process of reading a nation's strengths and failures from its sexual conduct, it was a short step to recommending policies that would produce solid values and citizenship. The fallout from the inconsistencies between Americans' beliefs and their behavior went well beyond the individual to affect the body politic, experts argued. One author of sexual advice stressed the connections between a well-ordered sex life and national political identity when he advised readers that they "cannot afford to sit back and do nothing about the tragedies resulting from sex ignorance. It is our combined responsibility to persuade others in need of enlightenment that a more intelligent adjustment to our sexual needs results in better parenthood, fewer divorces and sex crimes, and better citizenship for the country as a whole."[122] A reviewer for the *New York Times Review of Books* drew an even more direct connection between the cultural project of understanding sexual behavior and the political one of improving social relations when he described the first Kinsey Report as offering not only "invaluable aid in the study of our complex social problems" but also "data that would promote tolerance and understanding and make us better 'world citizens.'"[123]

Social conservatives also drew a direct relationship between sex and the social body, but they saw the role of such information as wholly destructive. A 1956 congressional report found that the increasingly "loose portrayal of sex . . . serves to weaken the moral fiber of the future leaders of our country."[124] The entire nation, another commentator disapprovingly remarked, was suffering from a "sex addiction" that distracted it from more important matters.[125] The Harvard sociologist Carle Zimmerman, in a widely reprinted response to the first Kinsey Report, warned that the postwar focus on sexuality threatened both familial happiness and national political stability. In times of social unrest such as the present uneasy moment, he explained, "society goes on a sex happiness jag." Zimmerman, like other family experts, responded to this unredeemed pursuit of pleasure by encouraging a resurgence of "traditional family" models and morals, which could act as a bulwark against the linked evils of sexual radicalism and political upheaval. If left unchecked, sexual disorder would lead directly to national and international political chaos and even annihilation. "If you cannot control the values about the womb," Zimmerman reasoned, "you also cannot control the values about the atomic bomb."[126] To adherents of both the left and the right, the political fate of the nation was inextricably allied with the private sexual behavior of its citizens.

The diverse group of experts who examined American sexuality concurred that the sexual behavior and ethos of a nation's population were both important clues to and determinants of that nation's strength. One commentator recognized the cyclic nature of declarations of sexual crisis but singled out the nation's current state of sexual crisis as unique. He argued that contemporary Americans were "by no means the only generation which has found itself bewildered by that mysterious human potency we call sex," but that "there is something peculiarly ironic about the situation our own generation faces. We are, by all odds, the best-educated victims of sexual crisis in history. There has probably never been such open, unabashed discussion of sexual matters as there is today—not a flagrant, defiant openness which delights to flaunt the problem, but a serious, dogged openness which seeks a cure for the problem in education and discussion."[127]

In this statement, as in many others that experts made about the postwar United States, two contrasting ideas about sex collided. Some authorities, in a classic example of Foucault's repressive hypothesis, lauded what they saw as a new sexual openness and predicted an end to sexual ignorance, hypocrisy, and disease. In the modern United States, according to this optimistic viewpoint, Americans were ideally positioned to investigate sex and discover solutions to individual and societal sexual problems. If Americans could understand and perfect their sexual behavior, then all of society would benefit. Modern information, whether it came from Kinsey's investigators, psychoanalysts, or other sex experts, could make it possible for enlightened sexual policies to emerge from the current confusion, policies that would strengthen marriages, heighten individual happiness, and create a useful sexuality that served the national interest.

This progressive view of American sexual character, however, coexisted with a darker, more pessimistic one in which, rather than offering a solution, the new information on and frankness about sex exacerbated existing social problems and even created new ones. Authorities like Sorokin and Zimmerman saw only dire consequences resulting from the new spirit of sexual freedom and believed that political and social chaos would result from Americans' tolerance of premarital sex and homosexuality. American sexuality, they warned, was characterized by selfishness and the decline of traditional values and, if left unchecked, would lead to chaos, with sexual categories and gender roles collapsing.

By locating transformations in the meaning of sexuality as both the cause of and cure for recent changes in American life, experts embedded sex within a matrix of other social changes and related American identity to the expression and articulation of a changing, modern sexuality. Cultural critics who turned their attention to American sexual character thus agreed that sex in America was changing, but they were far from unanimous about the value and consequences of such changes. Sex, to postwar Americans, stood as synecdoche for many of the most exhilarating and frightening possibilities of affluence and social change.

CONCLUSION

In the introduction to her 1997 study of sexuality and citizenship in the United States, the cultural theorist Lauren Berlant observes, "Something strange has happened to citizenship. Now everywhere in the United States intimate things flash in people's faces: pornography, abortion, sexuality, and reproduction; marriage, personal morality, and family values. These issues do not arise as private concerns: they are key to debates about what 'America' stands for, and are deemed vital to defining how citizens should act."[128] Berlant sees the ideological association of citizenship and sexuality as a recent occurrence, fostered by the competing demands of various identity-based movements that came to prominence in the 1960s. I argue instead that "intimate things" have long been prominent in "debates about what 'America' stands for," and that the 1950s were a crucial moment in this genealogy. Sexual behavior is often framed as a matter of national interest: in welfare policy, presidential elections, military recruitment, and court decisions, among other areas, certain kinds of sexuality have been lauded and others condemned for their putative effects on the nation. During the postwar era, however, the relationship between sex and civic interests was mapped with exceptional fervor.

Americans' sexual character was thus positioned as the site for a wide range of national hopes and anxieties during the postwar years. The Canadian historian Karen Dubinsky reminds us that "changes such as economic upheaval or shifting patterns of race or gender relations" are often "cloaked and reinterpreted socially as crises of sexuality."[129] The postwar discourse of American sexual character provides voluminous evidence that

Americans understood a wide range of concerns about changing gender relations, family patterns, demographics, politics, and international relations in sexual terms. The reports, and the broader discourse on American sexual behavior in which they took on meaning, received intense public scrutiny precisely because they embodied so many tensions within postwar culture. A collection of distinctive national types emerged from the discourse of American sexual character: the young single man or woman negotiating sexual pleasure and marriageability, the reproductive nuclear family made up of a housewife-mother and businessman-father, and the increasingly feared, yet often unrecognizable, sexual deviant, among others, were familiar characters in postwar narratives of sexual and social change. In creating and deploying these characters, politicians, social scientists, filmmakers, and theorists of "the American character" all negotiated a richly symbolic minefield of sexual, gendered, and racial meanings in constructing their definitions of American identity and their prescriptions for the postwar era.

Authorities' disquiet at the centrality of sexuality, and their fears of American decline, bespoke a deep concern with the instability of sexual and gender categories and a prevailing fear about the nation's future. Kinsey maintained that accurate information about American sexual behavior would aid professionals in engineering a better society; Margaret Mead testified to the effect of social change on Americans' sexual behavior and decried the new focus on sexual information in the media; Sorokin worried that sexual excess would lure Americans away from their civic duties; and Riesman lamented the passing of inner-directed Americans who kept their private lives private. A host of other social critics expressed concern for the citizen seduced by brazen depictions of sex in the mass media, or lauded the opportunities that sexual liberalism offered for personal happiness. Each of these scenarios addressed a deep anxiety about the effects of sex on Americans' present and future.

Ultimately, much of the mass of postwar writing on sex, social change, and American character was designed to elicit a socially useful sexuality. Proper American sexual character—both a set of practices and an implicit national policy—would unite modernity and tradition. This ideal sexuality, commonly described as "healthy" or "normal" and contrasted to a varying list of "unhealthy" behaviors and types, was characterized as civic minded. Normalcy was an elusive concept, though, and it sometimes seemed that, as new sexual information was uncovered and disseminated to the general public, consensus on what constituted average or ideal behavior became impossible. Americans never quite agreed upon what an ideal or appropriate sexuality might look like, but their debates offered a host of competing visions. Sexuality offered postwar Americans a language that could be used to describe behaviors and ideologies alongside other kinds of social change.

Successive chapters look more closely at the ideological work performed by the postwar discourse of American sexual character by examining the types it most often depicted: the average man and woman, the married couple, and the homosexual. These categories were constituted in 1950s sexual literature both as sites that required identification and interrogation and as populations who received advice and information specifically tailored to their needs. Each was a site of ideological battles over proper sexual behavior. The postwar literature of American sexuality—even at its most graphic, pedantic, or alarmed—was never just about sex. Rather, it told and retold stories about gender, the social realities of postwar life, and sexual and national identity, stories through which Americans aired and tried to make sense of the changes that surrounded them.

TWO

"A Missing Sense of Maleness"

Male Heterosexuality, Sexual Behavior in the Human Male, *and the Crisis of American Masculinity*

WHEN *SEXUAL BEHAVIOR IN THE HUMAN MALE* appeared in 1948, reaction to the volume was instantaneous and impassioned. Kinsey's study spurred a national referendum on sexual behavior, prompted new research on related topics, and provided ammunition for social reformers of all stripes. The report also, however, affected Americans' understanding of gender norms and relations, focusing popular attention on the relation between ideal codes of masculinity and actual male sexual behavior, and promoting discussion of what it meant to be a man in the atomic age. Kinsey and his team, as one social scientist put it, might be "mainly concerned with a descriptive account of sex habits," but their data and the public's reception of it "reveal more of the cultural dynamics in such behavior than they perhaps realize."[1] In the process of providing a blueprint of American men's sexual behavior, *Sexual Behavior in the Human Male* illuminated what the lawyer Morris Ernst called Americans' "cultural fantasies" of masculinity and male sexuality.[2]

Kinsey's book took on meaning for readers and reviewers at a time of widespread concern about the state of American masculinity. A decade after the report's appearance, the historian and critic Arthur Schlesinger Jr. declared that the contemporary United States was suffering from "a missing sense of maleness."[3] The nation, the critic warned darkly in an article titled "The Crisis of American Masculinity," was increasingly "more and more conscious of maleness not as a fact but as a problem. The ways by which American men affirm their masculinity are uncertain and obscure. There are multiplying signs, indeed, that something has gone badly wrong with the American male's conception of himself."[4] Schlesinger's sense that masculinity was imperiled was shared by many other commentators on postwar society, and it is within the context of this discourse that I analyze postwar debates about male sexuality and national character.

To many observers, it seemed that the social and cultural shifts transforming the nation posed a profound threat to American men. In their discussions of topics as varied as American politics, labor, leisure, and family life, authorities questioned whether masculinity was in decline. In contrast to the volatile and often problematic terrain of femininity, the existence and lineaments of a specifically male identity had often been assumed to be self-evident and obvious to the observer. Certain kinds of men—heterosexual, white, able-bodied, and financially comfortable— held unquestioned title to masculinity, with more problematic modes of masculinity represented by those whose sexuality, race, body, or class placed them outside of the normative ideal. The postwar years, however, saw attention paid to maleness that was unprecedented in its scope. Theories of marriage and family, patterns of class formation and consumption, and mass culture all focused popular and expert attention on the shifting boundaries and meanings of masculinity.

During the nineteenth and early twentieth centuries, authorities had periodically decried the "feminization" of civic culture, bemoaning the loss of traditional masculine vigor and aggression. As the historian Nancy Bristow suggests, declarations that middle-class white masculinity was in crisis "continued a lengthy and often anxious public conversation about maleness that has been an almost constant feature of American culture since its inception."[5] As this conversation ebbed and flowed, each anxious rediscovery of the nation's imperiled masculinity addressed new themes, and its specific trajectory could differ dramatically over time. Depression-era discussions of masculinity had focused on the effects of unemployment, while World War II discourses addressed war's emotional and physical effects on soldiers. Postwar discourse on masculinity, by contrast, was notable for its intensity, its expansiveness, and its focus on the plight of average heterosexual white men.

Although expert and popular opinions over what exactly had "gone badly wrong with the American" male differed, commentators agreed that American men's public and private lives were undergoing fundamental change. They described the postwar male as a subject whose definitions of masculinity, sense of self, and sexual behavior all differed dramatically from his father's. Beginning well before the war's end, social scientists questioned how American GIs would adjust to peacetime, and their interrogations continued over the next decade and a half. Despite the apparent reassurance offered by a marriage and baby boom, masculine roles and norms seemed forever altered. As family experts preached egalitarianism, and white-collar workplaces stressed flexibility, questions persisted about how modern American men were to demonstrate traditional manly virtues.

Many of Americans' deepest anxieties about masculinity were articulated in relation to male sexuality. Sexual performance has long been crucial to American definitions of manliness, but the exact nature of the relationship between sexuality and normative masculinity has shifted over time. Modern discourses that insisted on the centrality of sex to personal identity, the nation's interests, and the character of its citizenry targeted Americans regardless of their gender, constituting both men and women as modern sexual subjects. A range of sexual possibilities—from exclusive homosexuality to exclusive heterosexuality—as well as every gradation in between, offered different models of sexual subjectivity to mid–twentieth century Americans. Panics about homosexuality and sex crimes presented men as ridden by hidden passions that threatened the community. At the same time, the average male, a middle-class white husband and father, was revealed to have his own problems. The experts whose advice filtered into mass consciousness by way of popular literature announced and interrogated a series of paradoxical crises in male identity and masculinity. Suburban living and a family-centered ethos were accused of dulling men's competitive edge at the same time that changing corporate policies and demands of the workplace forced them to compete more aggressively than before. New definitions of masculinity coexisted uneasily with calls for a return to traditional standards of virility and manliness. Declarations of masculine decline and crisis drew on the findings of the first Kinsey Report and other information on male sexuality, spurring a series of ideological struggles over the meaning of male sexual behavior and character. Were transformations in men's roles affecting their sexual performance? What kind of premarital sexual patterns produced the best husbands and fathers? Were men inherently more sexually aggressive than women, or might the male sexual drive or capacity be lower than the female?

The recurrence and urgency of such questions attested to a pervasive sense of crisis around masculinity and male sexuality, as postwar Americans stressed connections between sexual performance and imperiled masculinity. Links between the two were signaled by increases in diagnoses of homosexuality, impotence, and sexual inadequacy, as well as by the related concern that women were assuming control over heterosexual sex and by media speculations about the effects of changing male sexual behavior on the culture at large. Through their proclamations of what constituted appropriate masculinity and sexual behavior, experts redrew the parameters of masculinity, negotiated old and new models of sex and gender, and articulated contemporary social problems in sexual terms.

SEXUAL PRISONERS OF WAR: MASCULINITY IN WAR AND PEACE

Many of the themes that would feature prominently in postwar debates over American masculinity emerged during the war years. Returning soldiers were lauded in advertising, government propaganda, and the popular press as virile defenders of the nation, entitled to the gratitude and devotion of civilians. One typical journalistic treatment of their return, penned by a recently demobilized sergeant, paid homage to "the magnificent American male."[6] However, beneath the master narrative of victory ran an undercurrent of distress. The GI was a contradictory figure, and postwar fears about men's emotional, physical, and psychological stability struck at national definitions of maleness and encouraged Americans to examine modes of masculinity.

Two seemingly opposed possibilities dominated debates about the effect of war on American men. Some experts theorized that the experience of war had rendered the GI excessively violent, while others propounded the equally disturbing possibility that war had instead made him weak.[7] Men, the first theory ran, had been debased and rendered brutish by their participation in warfare, and it would be difficult for them to resume peaceful civilian lives.[8] One manual for the wives of returning veterans cautioned that "it is impossible to tell men to go and kill an enemy and risk their lives doing it, and expect them at the same time all to be honest, chaste, kind and unselfish."[9] As the reference to chastity suggests, male sexual urges were a particular source of concern. A military spokesman warned that combat training, along with soldiers' exposure to the horrors of war, "may liberate further expression of the male sexual urge in the postwar period."[10] Soon after, a journalist argued that the war had unleashed inherent male sexual aggressiveness, and therefore, according to police, "many men in our society are tottering on the edge of sexual maladjust-ment and sex crime."[11] Male hypersexuality and sexual aggression threat-ened to disrupt postwar family and civic life, and "normalcy" called for reeducation of men in civility and gentility.

Other experts took a very different tack, fearing that instead of toughen-ing men war had made them passive, fearful, and effeminate. The massive unemployment of the depression had raised fears about male decline that the war years did nor quell. Military and civilian experts launched blister-ing critiques of inductees' performance on physical and psychological tests, raising concern about the caliber of the average American male. Indeed, the inadequacy of potential draftees was a national scandal, and conster-nation spread beyond professional therapeutic circles into the broader culture. The tension between these two views of men's inherent qualities—aggression and predatory sexuality, on the one hand, and passivity and sexual failure, on the other—characterized postwar discussions of mas-culinity, as male sexual behavior was often envisioned as a zero-sum game in which contradictory traits had to be carefully balanced. These two modes of describing American men alternated in almost schizophrenic fashion throughout the postwar years. The suggestion that men were inherently aggressive brutes could be oddly soothing if the alternative was widespread weakness and emotional and physical collapse—and the reverse was also true. No matter which characterization of men domi-nated, in the years after the war one thing was clear: despite the successful reconversion of the nation to civilian production, a celebratory reaffirma-tion of the family, and a much lauded return to predepression normalcy, fears about the caliber of American men and the effects of their wartime experiences lingered.

Anxieties about the reintegration of veterans into their families and society attested to the potential legacies of the war for male bodies and psyches. One military psychiatrist translated his professional fears into laymen's terms when he explained that the "soldier who did so much to make America secure returned to situations that made him and his family feel insecure."[12] Diagnoses of impaired masculinity proliferated: when a team of Boston physicians who examined male veterans found that many were experiencing nervousness, anxiety, marital difficulties and alco-holism, their diagnosis was "male hysteria," a masculine variant of the quintessentially female disorder.[13] Others found that war caused a conta-gious unwillingness to fight again, and American men were accused by no less a judge than FBI director J. Edgar Hoover of shirking their duty to serve in the military. Only a few years after the conclusion of World War II, Hoover reported that men drafted for the Korean conflict were attempting to escape conscription in record numbers, and he branded contemporary Americans as "example[s] of mankind at its worst."[14] In *Generation of Vipers,* his 1945 polemic on modern gender relations, Philip Wylie described the average American male as cowed by female domination. Along with other experts, he asserted that, under the pernicious influence of greedy and parasitic women, American men had become too subservient to assert themselves in battle during war or develop into healthy maturity in peacetime.[15]

Ultimately, the varied pictures of postwar American manhood that authorities painted shared one central theme. Whether the experience of war had rendered American men brutes or proven their incapacity to measure up to earlier ideals of manhood, it had altered them profoundly; when former soldiers returned home to reenter existing families and create new ones, they brought wartime pathologies with them. As the nation geared up for a return to peacetime "normalcy," questions persisted. How would men who had lived under the regimentation of military life and experienced combat adjust successfully to family life after V-day? And conversely, how should the nation receive those who had been rejected by the military as physically or emotionally unfit?

"WHAT HAS UNMANNED THE AMERICAN MAN?": THE POSTWAR MASCULINITY CRISIS

Given the prevalence of wartime fears, it is not surprising that, in the years after the war, changes in and threats to American masculinity remained popular topics in the media. Underneath the presumption that all healthy men would demonstrate their maturity by creating flourishing careers and stable families lay widespread worries about their actual ability to do so.[16] As the historian Rickie Solinger has noted, postwar culture betrayed "a deep concern about the postwar capabilities of adult males to sustain their traditional role of domination within the family and in the culture at large."[17] Experts of all stripes drew upon the increasingly powerful language of science and psychology to pen unflattering descriptions of contemporary men, sympathetic considerations of their plight, analyses of changing gender roles, and predictions for the future.

The years after World War II, which saw a focus on the home and family and heightened attention to developments in the social and psychological sciences, offered fertile ground for discussions of shifting definitions of masculinity. In 1948, the social welfare activist Edith Stern commented in the popular magazine *American Mercury* that men were due for the public scrutiny to which American women had been subjected in recent tracts. In an essay titled "The Miserable Male," Stern observed:

> I feel it is high time that some sympathy also be extended to the other half of humanity. After all, modern man in his own way is just as biological as modern woman and yet, poor devil, what an unnatural, psychologically ruinous life he has to lead. . . . For the way his problems have been overlooked; for the psychically devastating repressions of his masculine drives and instincts imposed by our civilization; for his frustrations and anxieties, my womanly heart goes out to miserable modern man.[18]

Despite her sardonic tone, Stern did believe that the time was ripe for a new examination of American men's behavior and status. Modern life, she suggested, was frustrating men's "natural" bent toward aggression and sexual promiscuity. The increasing autonomy of women, the dull routines of marriage, and the drabness of workaday life after the excitement of wartime, combined with what she termed the "widely deplored feminization of our culture," were creating a nation of men who were "maladjusted, miserable," and "bordering on panic."[19]

During the next decade and a half, physicians, psychologists, journalists, and other experts would join Stern in examining changes in American masculinity, revealing a wide range of opinions about contemporary American men and their problems. Many postwar theorists of such abstract concepts as American character or "the national mood" of course focused implicitly on changes in politics, work, and culture that affected men and women alike. But a growing chorus of voices addressed the problems of American men as a distinct group, making evident the gendered dimensions of postwar social change. "The first detailed discussions of the 'male sex role,'" the sociologist R. W. Connell notes, "appeared in American social science journals in the 1950s."[20] Critics focused on the cultural and social production of masculinity, on what Stern termed its "frustrations and anxieties," as never before.

As critics like Stern and the popular and prolific anthropologist Margaret Mead noted after the war, it was perhaps inevitable that, as authorities debated women's changing place in society, men's positions should also receive increased attention. Mead, whose best-selling works rendered her a respected authority on gender, sexuality, and cultural differences, observed that American men had always defined their identities in contrast to those of women. Shifts in women's activities, such as the slow but steady increase in the number of married women in the workforce after the war, resulted in a complementary questioning of male roles. To Mead, gender identity was always conditional and contingent, and masculinity was especially precarious in the modern world. "Maleness in America," she argued, "is not absolutely defined, it has to be kept and re-earned every day, and one essential element in the definition is beating women in every game that both sexes play, in every activity in which both sexes engage."[21] If men no longer won at "every game," then masculinity could indeed appear precarious.

Postwar research in the physical and social sciences underlined the contingency of masculine identity by suggesting that there was no such thing as an essential masculinity. Women had successfully performed many traditionally male jobs during the war, and even after male workers returned to take their places, concern lingered that "manly" jobs could be performed by women. The appearance of virility offered no guarantee: a "frail, feminine stenographer in the outer office is often more ruthlessly masculine in her outlook than her helpless boss," one business magazine advised readers, adding that outmoded ideals of masculinity and femininity hampered the productivity of all workers. "In a flexible society such as ours," the author reassured worried male readers, "having attributes of the opposite sex is an asset."[22] A number of other authorities appealed to men to rethink their roles. After the usual mapping of the nation's declining stock of masculinity, a journalist concluded hopefully that American men were "developing in [a] new direction" as they "relinquished old notions" of patriarchal authority.[23] The anthropologist Ashley Montagu's *The Natural Superiority of Women,* a much discussed best-seller, similarly asserted that, as sex roles evolved, "men will have to give up their belief in masculine superiority."[24]

Other commentators were less sanguine about postwar transformations in gender roles, and they located shifts in the composition and meaning of the family, changes in the workplace, altered gender roles, and the increasing femininity of mass culture as problematic for male identity. When he described a crisis of American masculinity in 1958, Schlesinger was only articulating what many others had already defined as a widespread problem. The American man, one psychiatrist wrote in 1951 in a professional journal on marriage and the family, was at once "expected to live up to the ideal of the good provider and strong masculine figure" and beset by "contradictions in our culture which make the achievement of this ideal an increasingly difficult one for the male."[25] The psychologist Lawrence Frank agreed that male roles were less clear than they had even been. "Boys and men growing up today," he advised readers of *Look* magazine in 1955, "are much more confused about what they should and should not do to fulfill their masculine roles."[26] Margaret Mead agreed, noting that "something has happened to the position of men," and "all the thrashing about over the position of women, over 'conformity' and 'security,' is a sign that we are beginning to realize it."[27]

Americans' worries about the apparent crisis in masculinity were articulated in a wide range of venues. The *Reader's Digest* featured articles on men's changing domestic roles; a professional journal on the family outlined "the new burdens of masculinity"; the urbane men's monthly *Esquire* asked plaintively, "What has become of the old-fashioned man?"; and the popular magazine *Collier's* punningly inquired, "The U.S. male: is he first-class?"[28] The fronts on which masculinity seemed threatened also proliferated, as *Cosmopolitan* expressed concern about "the decline and fall of the American father," and the *New York Times* vented irritation at women's takeover of public spaces, lamenting that "the male sanctuary is all but done."[29] *Playboy* magazine, which offered a model of masculinity emphasizing leisure and consumption, both mocked and took up the refrain, decrying "the womanization of America," on which it blamed "the increasingly blurred distinctions between the sexes in this country."[30] Significantly, the crisis in masculinity was one of only a few postwar social problems believed to cross racial lines. Analyses of masculine crisis among blacks drew on the same explanatory categories used to assess white men, and according to the sociologist St. Clair Drake, who analyzed the prevalence of male desertion among African American families, "Negro men leave home not because they are Negroes but because they are men."[31] Whether married or single, black or white, professional or blue collar, American men stood together as a group when it came to the gender problems they faced: by 1962, the author Morton Hunt could refer in passing to "social critics who do a brisk business in condemning American men *en masse* as unmasculine."[32] Confusion, disintegration, decline—the language used by commentators on masculinity was striking and their drift unmistakable. The "magnificent American male" had apparently declined to a browbeaten and morose specimen, proof of the nation's debased masculinity.

At its most dramatic, this rhetoric of crisis expressed a fear that men not only were becoming culturally feminized—through their participation in traditionally female activities, their roles in egalitarian families, or their consumption of popular culture—but also might literally become female in body. One psychiatrist opened a 1949 article with the provocative observation that, "biologically speaking, the sexes seem to be less differentiated than formerly," and speculated that hormonal makeups were changing to mirror men's and women's new roles.[33] A pair of experts who wrote widely on gender issues argued that "the characteristics that men possess because of the biological fact of their sex may be changed in many ways by the social set-up or the culture in which they live."[34] The widespread publicity given to the 1953 sex change of Christine Jorgensen, widely described as a "normal" man—an honorably discharged veteran, even—who nevertheless insisted that he was essentially a woman, also threatened the stability of masculinity as a category.[35] As other cases received news coverage as well, the *American Mercury* summed up many Americans' concerns in a breathless series of questions: "How secure is anybody's sex? What is it to be a man or to be a woman? How much sex change is possible for a human being? Can a man and a wife walk into a hospital and come out roles reversed, Joe turned into Jane, Jane into Joe?"[36] Although "roles" are specified here, not anatomies, the choice of the hospital as the site where such a transgression might take place is revealing, as is the example of "a man and a wife." A more literal rendering of sexual chaos, in which penises, vulvas, and economic and familial authority were exchanged over operating tables, would be hard to find. The dramatic image of men and women trading genitalia, sexual scripts, and cultural space spoke to the depths of postwar Americans' fears.

Why—during peacetime and at a moment characterized by a generally healthy economy, a burgeoning birthrate, and an embrace of familial values—did so many authorities see American masculinity as declining and endangered? As Schlesinger asked rhetorically, "How to account for this rising tide of anxiety? What has unmanned the American man?"[37] Social scientists and journalists who addressed these questions identified a plethora of reasons for the masculinity crisis. Much of their attention focused on the crucial areas of the workplace, the nuclear family, and the gendered national character. In the process of describing and analyzing the behavior of men in these problem areas, they not only probed men's changing experience but also suggested new definitions of masculinity.

The American workplace featured centrally in experts' analyses of male malaise. According to Talcott Parsons, perhaps the preeminent sociologist of the era, the masculine role was based on one crucial activity. "Virtually the only way to be a real man in our society," he wrote, "is to have an adequate job and earn a living" for a family.[38] This vision became increasingly possible for many workers after the war, thanks to the reforms of the New Deal, the rise of the Congress of Industrial Organizations, and employers' increasing endorsement of the family wage. Workers of the 1950s, however, were more likely than previous generations to work all of their lives for someone else, whether in blue- or white-collar jobs, and the vaunted American ideal of independent entrepreneurship increasingly gave way to a pattern of laboring for growing conglomerates. As workplace autonomy dwindled, massive shifts in the organization of labor forced postwar Americans to reexamine the equation of masculinity with independent labor.

Theorists who related the postwar "masculinity crisis" to changes in men's public roles as workers argued that the requirements of professional and wage work had altered along with the nation's economy. Middle-class white men composed both David Riesman's "other-directed" lonely crowd and William Whyte's army of drones who labored for the "organization" at the cost of an authentic self. Both of these models assumed that contemporary Americans were less self-reliant and entrepreneurial—in short, less masculine—than their fathers and grandfathers had been. Riesman and Whyte described the new workplace as one that demanded flexibility rather than brute strength and rewarded the traditionally feminine skills of negotiation, compromise, and sociability rather than aggressive individualism.[39] The sociologist Herbert Marcuse also contrasted a mythic past to the contemporary American workplace run by faceless bureaucracies. Drawing equally from a Marxist perspective and the language of pop psychology, he argued that, "with the rationalization of the productive apparatus," personal relationships with peers and mentors had vanished. "At its peak," he maintained, "the concentration of economic power seems to turn into anonymity: everyone, even at the very top, appears to be powerless before the movements and laws of the apparatus itself."[40]

The new workplace was a feminized and feminizing space. The salesman or advertising executive, the model worker within this new order, was valued for the very other-directedness that signaled a troubling loss of traditional masculinity and independence. One sociologist studying male roles noted that male white-collar workers were now encouraged to develop "traditionally feminine forms of behavior for ingratiating superiors [and] customers," a shift that went far toward explaining the increasingly common male "feeling of being threatened by women in industry."[41] A workplace in which men were depersonalized, anonymous, feminized and "powerless" stood as a potent threat to masculine autonomy.

By the mid-1950s, critiques of the white-collar workplace as hierarchical and dehumanizing had become commonplace. Social scientists and novelists alike viewed white-collar men as alienated workers, and both saw middle-class males as dreaming of escaping a life of commuting, corporate subservience, and suburban domesticity in order to fulfill dimly imagined wishes for bohemian freedom. When Tom Rath, the hero in Sloan Wilson's popular novel and film *The Man in the Gray Flannel Suit,* chose to reject career advancement in exchange for personally satisfying labor, audiences applauded.[42] So pervasive was the belief that the American workplace was a degrading place for men that, in *The Split-Level Trap,* Richard Gordon and Katharine Gordon strung together a series of familiar images to describe the average suburban male as "a man running up a down escalator . . . rushing for the morning train with breakfast half-eaten and undigested, fighting to hold his place in a jungle-like world of business, working and studying and worrying far into the night, relaxing too little, hounded by ulcers, and finally struck down by heart disease."[43]

As both fictional and ethnographic treatments suggest, transformations in the American workplace had repercussions that extended beyond men's nine-to-five lives. Employers, experts often noted, controlled more of their employees' lives, dictating not only the manner in which they performed their work but also where they could live and the opinions they might express. Such control fostered a sense of powerlessness among workers and could decimate their self-confidence: "When The Company does your husband's choosing for him," one article warned American wives, "he can lose pride in himself as an individual."[44] Thus the dictates of the postwar workplace could affect a man's sense of self, familial and social relations, and, according to the author Norman Mailer, even his sexuality, since "when a man can't find any dignity in his work, he loses virility."[45] Instead of providing American men with a site in which to prove their strength and exercise entrepreneurial skills, the modern workplace now often seemed to offer only humiliation and emasculation.

Another major arena to which experts turned in their examination of postwar masculinity was the American family, placing a spotlight upon men's roles as husbands, fathers, and family heads. It was commonly noted by social scientists and delineators of American character that men had lost much of their former authority within the family. Indeed, the typical American male, as described by the anthropologist Geoffrey Gorer, was seen as having "so completely given up any claim to authority that the family would constantly risk disintegration and disaster" if not for the efforts of his wife.[46] Other experts concurred, with many of the sociologists surveyed for a 1955 conference on the American family observing a disturbing and widespread "decline in [the] authority of husbands and fathers."[47] A 1956 article in a women's magazine described the new American domestic ideal in unsettling terms: in "any suburb on a Sunday afternoon," women "look like keepers of a prosperous zoo and the men like so many domesticated animals inside it."[48] Metaphors of male servility abounded, with a science writer describing the average man as "a lowly automaton that changes diapers and gets mama's breakfast," and one sociologist asking bluntly, "Are husbands slaves to women?"[49]

Experts often juxtaposed these ambivalent descriptions with a lament for lost patriarchal authority. One 1955 article, "The Decline and Fall of the American Father," which appeared in the middlebrow mass-circulation journal *Cosmopolitan,* was typical in its comparison of past and present. Opening with a photograph of a Victorian family with a stern paterfamilias surrounded by his docile wife and brood, the article warned that the tranquil domesticity captured in that image had vanished: "Fifty years ago father was a god around the house[;] . . . today he's a bumbling stranger." Citing evidence from sources in popular culture and the social sciences, the author, Morton Hunt, argued that "we live in the era of Father's fall from power and prestige." From his former lofty position as "the lord of the household, fount of wisdom and dispenser of justice, he has shriveled to a mere financial accessory of the home—a profitable boarded guest."[50] Hunt nostalgically described an earlier era in which male clout was unassailable, sharply contrasting with the matriarchal present. "In those days," he reminisced, "Father was faintly Godlike. His wife called him 'Mr. Smith' (or whatever his last name was), even in bed. She asked no questions about money or about his companions outside of the home; she used dulcet tones and sweet blandishments to win favors. The children were silent and respectful in his presence, and aunts, uncles, and other contingent members of the family bowed to his opinions and quailed before his wrath."[51] Due to men's extended daily absence from the suburban home and the increasing expectation that they participate in child care, Hunt warned, male presence and authority in the household had eroded. Simultaneously, women had usurped many previously male prerogatives, from political involvement to disciplining children and earning part of the family income.

As Hunt's rhetoric suggests, discussions of the problems faced by men returned again and again to one target: women. Whether authors blamed women's laziness and love of leisure for men's soul-killing drudgery or targeted their aggressive pursuit of careers as the cause of men's literal or figurative impotence, they continuously saw women themselves, along with the feminine values they embodied, as a primary cause of a range of social problems. At the same time, though, their discussions of women's role in the demasculinization of the nation were tempered by ambivalence, as postwar ideals of masculinity also stressed the importance of men's involvement in maintaining the tenor of the home, borrowing from a model that Margaret Marsh calls "masculine domesticity."[52] Rebellion against women, often expressed as a yearning for the return of male dominance in families and society, coexisted uneasily with coverage of American men's expanding role within the home as passionate husbands and loving parents, intimately engaged in family life.

Individual families and the nation as a whole were depicted as paying the price for changing gender roles, as the crisis in masculinity threatened the well-being of the next generation. The lack of a proper "model of maleness" for every child, a mental-health expert cautioned, would ultimately produce a generation of troubled men, as sons would "develop into men who are sissies, poor husbands, or latent or overt homosexuals."[53] According to the psychoanalyst Bruno Bettelheim, the juvenile delinquency widely cast as a new and dangerous social problem in the 1950s was "often no more than a desperate attempt" by mother-ridden boys "to assert their maleness."[54] Although daughters received less attention, they too could be damaged by the American male's lack of vigor. "The young woman who has been deprived of an adequate image of maleness," the same observer who had warned of male "sissies" wrote, "may simply withdraw from male society, in which case she may become incapable of sexual response."[55] The masculinity crisis also hampered the formation of new families, as pervasive "feelings of emotional immaturity and insecurity" fed the "widespread fears of men to accept the responsibilities of marriage and fatherhood."[56]

Whether they assigned primary responsibility to changes in work, family, or gender roles, authorities joined the nation's manliness problem to the fate of the country itself. It was always "the *U.S.* male" or "the

American Father" whose masculinity was imperiled, not modern manhood in general. Experts repeatedly stressed that the social and cultural patterns that produced the postwar crisis were specifically American in nature, and the national culture was commonly described as both feminine and feminizing. In a 1950 symposium on mass culture convened by the American Academy of Arts and Letters, the poet Randall Jarrell argued that in contemporary society "we are all women together, and can hear complacently the reminder of how feminine this consumer-world of ours is."[57] New stars like James Dean and Montgomery Clift projected an image of vulnerability and sensitivity, and postwar Western films such as *High Noon* (1952), *Shane* (1953), and *Broken Arrow* (1956) featured flawed and troubled heroes. Further underlining the connection between American national character and male dysfunction, popular experts often invoked men from other countries as icons of a naturalized and unproblematic masculinity. American men, a female journalist stated in 1949, should "study the European male" in order to avoid "losing their manhood."[58] William Barrett, editor of the *Partisan Review,* drew a sharp contrast between European men and their American counterparts when he described the latter as "furtive and giggling, more like boys out of school than grown men."[59]

American politics was another realm endangered by feminine values.[60] Schlesinger's equation of manliness with a healthy national character, first expressed in his 1949 call in *The Vital Center* for "a new virility in public life," became a common trope.[61] Cold war commentators repeatedly linked sexual abnormality and gender inversion to political radicalism, suggesting that each sprung from darker aspects of modern American culture. The phenomenon that Kyle Cuordileone describes as "an excessive preoccupation with—and anxiety about—masculinity in early Cold War American politics" framed political subversion as one symbol of the masculinity crisis.[62]

Gendered assumptions about American character came into play in the realm of international politics as well, as intellectualism and liberalism were coded as feminine and the traditionally "masculine" traits of independence, pioneer spirit, and competitiveness were feared to be vanishing. When liberals were denigrated as "pink," the term alluded to their insufficient masculinity as much as it did their alleged Communist sympathies. Schlesinger's attention to masculinity and his rhetoric of decline and failure reflected a growing swell of concern. National debates over the alleged weakness of liberal intellectuals, suspected treachery on Capitol Hill, and

Communist dangers such as Ethel Rosenberg (who, the press reported, bullied her husband) and the "Red spy queen" Elizabeth Bentley all represented threats to American political interests in terms of femininity and effeminacy.[63]

Commentators diagnosed an assault on middle-class manliness and warned of its effects on the nation and its culture. Obsessively rehearsing a narrative of nationwide decline, social disarray, and familial and gender collapse, they pictured a country in which masculinity had become a besieged and precious resource. Authorities differed on the primary reasons for and sites of this process—for some, it was the independence of American women that led to a decline in male confidence, whereas for others it was war, family life, politics, or popular culture. What they shared was a belief that central institutions of modern American life were inimical to the development and maintenance of male authority, and that postwar national culture promoted a process of psychic if not actual emasculation.

The language these experts used made clear that the polity was threatened by a lack of manly virtue, whether it was identified as femininity, effeminacy, or degenerate sexuality. Modern manhood, it appeared, was dangerously like womanhood. In *Look* magazine's evocation of "the American male," the everyman Gary Gray, whose name evokes the garb of the prototypical suburban businessman, begins to reclaim his lost masculinity only when he realizes how utterly he has been feminized by modern demands for conformity and security and questions how he had "allowed this rape of his privacy and integrity?"[64] Gray's feminized position as the subject of sexual violence marked loss of self as a natural position for women but a new and dangerous development for the middle-class man.

This destructive process was envisioned as being historically as well as nationally specific. When experts contrasted the contemporary American man with earlier generations, they generally found him to be seriously lacking. The author of *Look*'s 1958 series on "the American male" confided to readers that "scientists worry that in the years since the end of World War II, he has changed radically and dangerously; that he is no longer the masculine, strong-minded man who pioneered the continent and built America's greatness."[65] The liberal columnist Dorothy Thompson described her countrymen as exemplars of that "American prototype, the timid soul who will accept anything rather than make trouble." Looking back nostalgically to a past of aggressive individualism, Thompson commented bitterly that for contemporary American men "the organization is always right and the free individual always wrong."[66] Although Thompson's more liberal critique of postwar conformity was politically far removed from Morton Hunt's nostalgia for Victorian male supremacy, their writings drew a similar contrast between craven postwar men and their independent forefathers, highlighting a narrative of masculine decline.

Postwar writers linked very different phenomena—a decline in men's power within the family, changes in the organization of white-collar labor, and the demands of life in a consumer society—to form the discourse of imperiled masculinity. The connections they drew between declining masculinity, male discontent, and social collapse suggested that the postwar "crisis" in masculinity was seen as far-reaching, threatening devastation not only for individual men but also for their family members, communities, and the nation as a whole. Whether expressed as familial disarray, unhappiness, or the decline of national stability, the projected social cost of the failure of American manhood was high.

THE MASCULINITY CRISIS AND MALE HETEROSEXUALITY

Men's sexual behavior lay at the center of postwar analyses of American masculinity. Not only did virtually all authors who addressed changes in male roles allude to the centrality of sexuality to masculinity, but the dominant rhetoric of the postwar discourse of failed manhood was itself sexual, as American men were repeatedly depicted as "shriveled," "emasculated," "feminized," and as having lost their "virility." When the sexologist Edward Podolsky examined American soldiers after World War II, he argued that they suffered from "desexualisation" and a list of ailments that included sterility, venereal disease, "sexual anaesthesia" and "sexual negation." Proclaiming that the paramount duty of the Allied nations was *to reclaim their prisoners of war sexually,"* he outlined a grand vision of masculine rejuvenation that included the mass administration of sex hormones to those unmanned by the pressures of war.[67] Despite its science fiction flavor, Podolsky's plan mirrored the agenda of other American experts, who located sexuality at the heart of masculinity and looked to it as both symptom of and cure for the masculinity crisis.

The 1948 publication of Alfred Kinsey's *Sexual Behavior in the Human Male* served to intensify discussions of the topic. The first Kinsey Report was regarded by public health officials and physicians as offering scientific facts against which generalizations about American male sexuality could be measured and upon which policies for appropriate sexual character and behavior could be based, even as it was condemned for its subject matter and conclusions. The study was repeatedly described as larger, broader, more ambitious and—to many—more accurate than any previous sex surveys. Queries regarding the men who had participated were rare, however, perhaps due to popular acceptance of the phenomenon of men talking publicly or privately about sex. In contrast to the scrutiny that Kinsey's female subjects would receive a few years later, surprisingly little attention was devoted to the actual men who contributed their histories to *Sexual Behavior in the Human Male.* The report, however, signaled a new level of public attention to male sexuality, with many reviewers commenting that the volume removed sexual information from the realm of the stag party or locker room to the more respectable arena of science.

From the moment the study appeared, commentators on a wide range of social issues drew on the graphs and charts contained in its 788 densely packed pages to define normalcy and deviance (see figure 5). The public also flocked to the weighty tome: "Nearly everyone who can read," the *Yale Review* noted, "apparently wishes to have a look at it."[68] Its status as a much discussed best-seller, greeted with reactions ranging from acclaim to disgust, confirmed the emergence and public recognition of male sexuality as a legitimate social problem. The responses that it elicited provide historians with voluminous information about what it meant to be a man in the postwar United States.

Sexual Behavior in the Human Male offered a complex and confusing picture of its subjects. Kinsey explained that Americans' "code of morals, our social organization, our marriage customs, our sex laws, and our educational and religious systems are based upon an assumption that individuals are much alike sexually, and that it is an equally simple matter for all of them to confine their behavior to the simple pattern which the mores dictate."[69] In sharp contrast to these assumptions, Kinsey argued that American males were notable for their diversity, and that their sexual behavior varied dramatically with men's age, class, region, and religion, as well as across each individual's life span.

According to the report, sexual behavior was profoundly shaped by men's class background. "Upper level" men reported having more diverse sexual practices than their working-class counterparts, a pattern valued by Kinsey for being closer to the "biologically natural." Although they had fewer partners, upper-level men were considered by Kinsey to be more attentive to their partners' needs and more willing to experiment in the

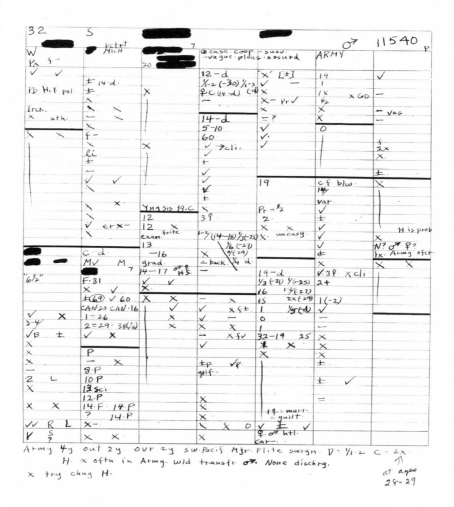

Figure 5. Code sheet recording a sexual history interview. (Photo by IU Photographic Services; reprinted by permission of The Kinsey Institute for Research in Sex, Gender, and Reproduction, Inc.)

pursuit of sexual satisfaction. The average, educated professional man, the report asserted, "considers nudity almost an essential concomitant of intercourse" (366), and his sexual encounters typically featured "considerable manual petting between partners, particularly on the part of the male" (367). Working-class males, in contrast, had a higher incidence of sexual activity but a more limited erotic repertoire, and thus copulated more frequently but with less finesse. "Many persons at this level," Kinsey noted, "strictly avoid nudity," with "some of the older men and women in this group tak[ing] pride in the fact that they have never seen their own spouses nude" (367).

These class differences in sexual attitudes and behavior were neatly summed up in Kinsey's discussion of oral eroticism. "Many a college male," he observed, "will have kissed dozens of girls, although he has had intercourse with none of them. On the other hand, the lower level male is likely to have had intercourse with hundreds of girls, though he may have kissed few of them" (369). Kinsey's hyperbolic descriptions in the report of two different modes of male sexuality effectively split masculinity into two camps: working-class men were virile and enthusiastic sexual subjects, while upper-class men were connoisseurs. Working-class male sexual patterns exemplified some aspects of "traditional" masculinity, while upper-class men, whose behavior was described as the direction in which most American males were evolving, more closely resembled the modern ideal found in the pages of sex advice literature. As experts reported, the sexual values of the upper class were replacing long-standing working-class mores, as an emphasis on female sexual pleasure and orgasm replaced male potency as the determinant of male sexual prowess.[70] The kind of sexuality valued by the authors of sex manuals and advice literature combined working-class vigor with upper-class sophistication, striking an uneasy balance between competing, and often contradictory, ideals.

The emphasis on class background as the primary determinant of male sexual behavior worked to obscure the seemingly absent but crucial variable of race and, especially, the perception of sexual differences between whites and African Americans. As noted earlier, Kinsey did not segregate data by race in *Sexual Behavior in the Human Male,* a choice that would be repeated in *Sexual Behavior in the Human Female;* instead, he opted to divide data by eleven different "race-cultural groups." Although he viewed human sexual behavior as biologically based, a repertoire of acts common to all mammals, Kinsey drew on a decidedly environmental model of human behavior in formulating his model of these groups. He saw race as an almost arbitrary signifier, arguing that "the subject's place of birth, his place of residence during childhood and adolescent years, and the ancestral home of his parents"—only one of which bore much relationship to contemporary biologic notions of "race"—were the factors that "decide the race-cultural group to which he belongs."

Kinsey further emphasized the cultural and environmental definition he gave to race when he added that membership in any of these groups was conditional and could shift over time, since any individual "may be placed in two or more of these groups" (76) depending on his familial, economic, and regional affiliations. In this model, the histories of poor Southern whites and blacks were likely to share similarities and to differ dramatically from those of college-educated easterners of any race or background. As Kinsey remarked, "educated, upper level Negroes may have as little comprehension of a lower level Negro community as upper level white persons would have" (388).

Once he had prepared the ground by carefully defining race in terms of culture and habit rather than biology, Kinsey turned to the role that it played in his investigations. The study, he explained, "is confined to a record on American and Canadian whites," although "we have begun accumulating material which will make it possible to include the American and Canadian Negro groups in later publications" (76). Race was thus a ghostly presence in the report, evident in Kinsey's methodological and theoretical models of human diversity but absent from the statistical portions of the published reports. As befitted his authorial stance as a dispassionate scientist and his personal beliefs in a cultural etiology for sexual behavior, Kinsey downplayed the existence of racial differences in sexual behavior, arguing that "Negro and white patterns for comparable social levels are close if not identical," and stressing that it was "impossible to generalize concerning the behavior of a whole race" (393). Rather than analyzing this approach to race, and taking seriously Kinsey's dismissal of biologistic definitions of race, reviewers generally ignored the absence of an African American presence in the Kinsey Report, framing normal and deviant sexuality alike as white.

The finding that drew by far the most comment from reviewers was the extent to which American men's sexual behavior was both illegal and immoral. Less than half of all male orgasms stemmed from marital intercourse (568), with most stemming from premarital, extramarital, oral, same-sex, masturbatory, or bestial sexual activities. Most of these activities were classified as sex offenses, and each violated the dominant code of morals. Sexual lawbreakers, Kinsey noted in a widely publicized aside, "constitute more than 95 per cent of the total male population. Only a relatively small proportion of the males who are sent to penal institutions for sex offenses have been involved in behavior which is materially different from the behavior of most of the males of the population" (392–93). The volume, as one legal expert commented, proved that "almost everything which the human male does in his sex life is against the law."[71] The unavoidable conclusion that American men did not live up to the code that supposedly governed their behavior was trumpeted in the media and discussed across the nation.

Despite the reference in the Kinsey book's title to a biological entity, the "human male," the report was immediately recognized as evidence of unique national behavior patterns. "Kinsey's study," one expert pointed out, was not a description of universal male behavior, but instead reflected "the way the *American* male behaves under a given type of social restraint."[72] Over the next decade, as commentators weighed in on the study and incorporated its findings into discussions of the masculinity crisis, they argued that American men suffered from a wide range of sexual disorders, that they had become "oversexualized," and that many lacked erotic knowledge and expertise. Although *Sexual Behavior in the Human Male* was greeted with shock and outrage in many quarters, this criticism was complicated by new cultural anxieties about masculinity, anxieties that Kinsey's figures both furthered and assuaged. At a moment when social scientists and the mass media openly declared their worries that American men were less masculine than previous generations, that they were literally as well as figuratively impotent and emasculated, then a portrait of American manhood that emphasized sexual voraciousness and variety offered hope. The first Kinsey Report depicted American men as far more sexually unbounded than did popular mythology, which often painted them as drudges whose sexual desires were subordinate to those of their wives. At the same time, many of the study's findings—especially those on the extent of homosexuality—ran directly counter to American ideas of the ideal male sexual subject. As observers of the "masculinity crisis" drew on Kinsey's work, they aired competing notions of male sexuality and visions of masculinity.

"THE AMERICAN MALE IS A SEXUAL DISASTER": CHANGING STANDARDS AND SEXUAL PROBLEMS

Virtually all postwar experts agreed that modern masculinity was founded upon an imperative to be actively sexual, equating normative male sexuality with a strong biological and psychological drive. The sex educator Lester Kirkendall, in a 1958 review of literature on male sexuality, found that "the implication in the literature is that this physical drive is imperious in its demands. Such words as 'torment,' 'torture,' 'misery,' 'insistent,' and 'compelling' are used to describe it."[73] The anthropologist Ashley

Montagu noted sardonically that, in America, masculinity was synonymous with sexual performance, as men "seem to be in a chronic state of sex irritation, and are ready to indulge in intercourse with any presentable female at almost any time."[74] And Margaret Mead underlined the gendered nature of such beliefs when she observed that, for men, "the demon to be avoided at all costs is lack of potency, defined in a number of quantitative ways—frequency, time, interval before rearousal, accuracy in judging the strength of his own impulse. There is an implicit assumption for males that if one copulates one is happy."[75] Genital sexual activity had long been so central to any definition of masculinity, a psychiatrist agreed, that its lack was enough to stamp a man as unmanly. "The chaste man in our society," he observed, was "incorporated into the feminine world" and likely to be "ostracized from his group."[76]

Given the direct equation between masculinity and sexual function, as measured by erection, heterosexual copulation, and orgasm, evidence of male heterosexual dysfunction could be acutely distressing. Problems ranging from inadequate performance to impotence to homosexuality were believed to be on the rise, and they elicited anxious attention, analysis, and recommendations. In the process, popular coverage undermined many traditional assumptions about the "naturalness" of male sexual prowess.

A recurring theme of experts who documented the various "crises" afflicting the American male was that impotence was affecting more and more men every year. One journalist called it "one of the commonest and most distressing disorders that the doctor is called upon to treat," and *Newsweek* asserted that, as a result of an epidemic of impotence, "the American Male is a sexual disaster" who would "rather work than make love."[77] Kinsey discussed it only briefly, arguing that impotence was rare in men under sixty (209) and suggesting that those rare cases with no physical basis could often be traced to the effects of sexual inhibition (297, 545). To many, though, the disorder served as more evidence of men's physical and sexual decline. Other male sexual problems were less clearly defined than impotence but even more troubling. A number of experts proclaimed that American men lacked sexual savvy. Abraham Stone, author of a marriage manual, estimated that at least 25 percent of American men suffered from some sort of sexual dysfunction, and he believed that impotence was often merely the end result of the far more common male affliction of sexual ignorance or clumsiness.[78]

As in the broader discourse of failed American masculinity, comparisons to men of other nations were frequent and invidious. The Italian film actress Silvana Pampanini, writing in *Esquire* magazine, offered her own expert testimony on national sexual differences when she complained of American men that "as lovers, they always fail. They are all sweaty boys." Compared with men of other nations, Americans were chronically short on seductive techniques, and "it would take an American regiment," the actress observed regretfully, "to produce the adult passion of one Italian man."[79] According to another sex expert, the psychiatrist and prolific author Frank Caprio, it was distressingly apparent that many American men were "SEXUALLY INADEQUATE," "anything but God's gift to women," since their "ignorance of the average woman's emotional make-up and of the proper sex technique is colossal."[80] Caprio went on to indict American men not only of clumsiness based on misinformation, which could be corrected by seeking proper counsel, but also of a willful sexual selfishness. "Few men really understand how to perform the act of intercourse adequately," he claimed, adding that "there is no excuse for a husband who has done nothing to prepare himself for the responsibilities which he is expected to assume as the more active partner in marital relations."[81]

As Caprio's comments suggest, the standards by which masculine sexuality was evaluated were changing. American men's sexual prowess increasingly came under fire as they were accused of lacking both sexual capacity and erotic knowledge: a 1946 survey of men's sexual knowledge concluded that "a large cross-section of American manhood" exhibited "broad areas of ignorance concerning sex in all its manifestations."[82] A few years later, the marriage advisor and minister Margaret Blair Johnstone concurred. Based on the requests for advice that she received, Johnstone advised readers, *"If you are an average man, the chances are you have slightly less correct information and considerably more misinformation about sex than the average woman of your acquaintance."*[83] Even the optimistic Kinsey, who usually approved of American males' expansive and often illicit sexual behaviors, offered some damning comments on their sexual prowess. "The male's difficulties in his sexual relations," he noted in *Sexual Behavior in the Human Male,* "include a lack of facility, of ease, or of suavity in establishing rapport in a sexual situation. . . . Few males achieve any real freedom in their sexual relations even with wives. Few males realize how badly inhibited they are on these matters" (545). In modern scientific parlance, both "lack of facility" and "inhibition" were coded as extremely negative qualities.

Not surprisingly, a literature offering diagnosis and treatment proliferated alongside analyses of male sexual ignorance and inadequacy. As

Caprio's reference to every man's responsibility to "prepare himself" suggests, the genre of sexual advice literature expanded dramatically during the postwar years. The authors who urged men to revitalize their sex lives drew on Kinsey and others to preface their advice with a critique of men's sexual knowledge and performance. "I must admit," Caprio confessed with apparent regret, "the average husband could well stand instruction in the art of love. His approach is crude and often brutal; he is more concerned with satisfying his own desires than those of his wife."[84] Such rhetoric underlined the widely shared belief that sex was increasingly significant and called for the dissemination of new knowledge, but authors also offered cautionary tales about how that knowledge should be exercised.

The link between healthy masculinity and assertive heterosexuality, experts suggested, had become both more important and more tenuous in recent years. As divisions between the genders blurred or collapsed, sexual behavior took on greater importance in defining manhood. David Riesman pointed out in a 1958 lecture that the "greater 'femininity' [that] is being increasingly permitted to educated men in this country" had a "curious consequence"—that "they cannot clearly and unequivocally define themselves as men by their roles." The solution that many middle-class men had found to this dilemma, according to Riesman, was to define themselves as sexual agents, asserting their masculinity in "the one physiological way which appears irrefutable."[85] Other evidence supported Riesman's theory: *Playboy* magazine, published by the entrepreneur Hugh Hefner from 1953 onward, defined sexual consumption, rather than sportsmanship, family, or workplace success, as central to modern masculinity.[86] Tellingly, Hefner proudly described himself as a "pamphleteer" for Kinsey's findings, underlining the report's foundational role in making male sexuality a topic of public interest.[87]

Although popular and medical opinion often identified healthy adult masculinity with aggressive and goal-directed sexual urges, evidence suggested that actual practices did not always reflect these cultural ideals. Postwar publicity about male sexual problems belied easy assumptions about the "imperious" male sex drive, and the idea that there existed only "one physiological way" to assert male sexuality was countered by Kinsey's findings on sexual range. The new focus on men's sexual variability and vulnerability, and on the changing sexual demands of women, positioned male sexuality as being increasingly threatened and in flux. Was male sexuality truly an inexorable force with only one "natural" and positive goal, experts asked, or was it instead flexible, variable? Although the imperative to be actively (hetero)sexual remained a cornerstone of postwar theories of male sexuality, popular opinion on the ways in which that imperative was to be exercised changed. In the emerging economy of sexual adequacy, the simple "ability to perform" was no longer enough to reassure men of their virility. Instead, they were encouraged to expand their sexual repertoire, to focus as much or more on their female partner's pleasure as on their own, and to achieve a new level of sophistication in their sex lives.

Men, some authorities suggested, were devastated by this heightened climate of sexual expectation, which demanded that males be simultaneously sexually assertive, sensitive, and knowledgeable. The historian Elizabeth Lunbeck argues that, as modern psychology attributed increasing importance to sex, inadequacy exacted a "far more disabling toll" upon men than upon women. "For men," Lunbeck explains, "sexual deficit was at once singularly specific—denoting failure of the sexual apparatus, impotence most commonly—and overwhelmingly inclusive, undermining the whole of a man's masculine identity."[88] The identification of sexuality as a privileged component of individuality and expression of gender identity grew even stronger by the 1950s, meaning that male sexual dysfunction was experienced as a sign of inadequate sex role adjustment and a troubled self. According to some experts, men who appeared uninterested in sex did not merely have a naturally lower sexual drive or capacity than their "normally sexed" counterparts; instead, their lack of interest in intercourse bespoke a host of psychological and physical problems and, indeed, removed them from membership in the class of normal men. "Undersexed males," as described by one endocrinologist, were "notoriously petty, selfish and old-womanish," a set of attributes far removed from any masculine ideal.[89] In a cultural climate where the continuing demand that men be sexually assertive and successful combined uneasily with critiques of male sexual knowledge and performance, it is not surprising that male sexual vulnerability was central to postwar discourses of sexual and social change.

In the years after the war, entrepreneurs drew on such charges of male ignorance in creating an audience for their wares. Continuing decades of appeals to middle-class male audiences, sex authors built an industry out of educating male desire, joining with advertisers to sell a popular vision of manliness that combined physical strength and competence with a modern appreciation for sexual pleasure. In addition to stressing the respectability and scientific accuracy of their works, many authors pointed out that sexual selfishness or lack of knowledge branded a husband as immature and irresponsible. The negative effects attributed to American men's alleged sexual ignorance and insensitivity were legion. Caprio blamed the vast majority of cases of female frigidity and subsequent divorce and marital unhappiness on awkward and selfish husbands, commenting that "the sexual blunders which these 'clumsy lovers' commit tax the imagination."[90] Responding to such fears, the designer of a course on "responsible husbandhood" counseled that "good husbands should read what leading physicians recommend about sex techniques, study the needs and potentialities of their wives and work out with their wives sex intercourse programs that are mutually satisfying, not just husband satisfying."[91]

Experts laid out a wide range of possible sexual problems to be avoided. Any man might fall short of the standard of masculine prowess by being too timid or too aggressive, by ejaculating prematurely or not at all, by desiring sex too often or too rarely, or by such qualitative blunders as approaching sex with a lack of imagination, which one expert scornfully referred to as "handl[ing] their sex as they would a business transaction."[92] The zone of appropriate male sexuality was a narrow one and demanded constant self-scrutiny on the part of its subjects. Such enumeration of potential sexual problems and heightened attention to men's sexual responsibilities helped to transform dominant ideas about masculinity. By challenging traditional notions about male sexual knowledge and prowess, pointing out that women were often both more informed about sex and more sexually explorative than men, and highlighting men's alleged difficulty with women's increasing demands, the postwar discourse on sex challenged many traditional views of male sexuality.

Some of the contradictions inherent in this discourse emerged in experts' ambitious projects to educate men. The sexual education of husbands was an important aspect of advice literature, and many physicians and other sex experts prescribed it as the treatment for male sexual ignorance and inadequacy. The effects of sexual education on masses of males, reformers believed, would be dramatic. Caprio, whose alarm at sexual ignorance was so profound that he published nine books on the topic, enumerated a long list of "major benefits that would result if the members of our male fraternity availed themselves of the sex education they need and each one made a sincere endeavor to bring about a better sexual adjustment in his life." Effects included a reduction in sex crimes, the halving of the divorce rate, less marital unhappiness and a diminished need for psychiatry, sharp declines in the rates of abortion and venereal disease, an "appreciable decrease in female homosexuality" as men became better lovers, and a nationwide trend toward "greater maturity and stability of character . . . and inevitably better citizenship."[93] Once American men received what the marriage and sex counselor Paul Popenoe somewhat ominously termed "re-education," they would be able to satisfy wives who expected modern and skilled sexual partners, thereby cementing marital stability. Men, however, needed to learn to value these goals and to seek out information on their own. The modern and "sexually adequate" man was urged to engage in a modern ritual of confessing his ignorance about sex and seeking the assistance of scientific experts, defining himself simultaneously as a Foucauldian subject, a modern citizen, and, in Riesman's term, an "acquisitive consumer of sex."

The most common explanation for men's alleged sexual faults was simple ignorance. But some observers saw a different reason for men's bedroom problems: women's increasing demands were harming American men and causing sexual chaos. The idea that traditional, male-centered sexual pleasure was being altered by new female demands was widespread. Since "the modern male is being directed toward a new goal in sex relations," *Look* magazine warned, his own needs were being downplayed in favor of female satisfaction, resulting in widespread sexual disinterest. "Today's American male," the magazine concluded, "has even lost much of his sexual initiative and control; some authorities believe that his capacity is being lowered."[94] Authorities expressed a great deal of concern over the power women held to sexually shame men. One woman physician noted pointedly that "the bride has her husband's self-esteem at her mercy," and that a careless or vindictive woman could "build an edifice of humiliation" by cruelly mocking her husband's attempts at lovemaking.[95]

New heterosexual expectations placed heavy demands on men. As the marriage experts Judson and Mary Landis noted in a 1952 article, "American men of today have some problems with which their grandfathers were probably not bothered. In those days, no one questioned that sex was for men." In the present climate of heightened attention to sex, however, many were "unprepared psychologically for wives who are fairly uninhibited sexually."[96] *Cosmopolitan* magazine likewise informed readers that "marriage does not solve the sex problems of the American male," since he "can no longer take his wife for granted sexually, nor regard her sexual responses as a right due him." According to Abraham Stone, roles had become so reversed that the average American man "may now find himself faced with *her* sexual demands, hearing that *he* isn't active enough."[97] The psychiatrist Edmund Bergler took these fears to their logical culmination when he worried that American men's sexual needs were being subordinated to women's demands *"that men perform preparatory acts on them before insertion."*[98] Others concurred that women's excessive demands on their husbands fostered male sexual dysfunction, since male anxiety was largely "due to the modern wife, who realizes she is entitled to enjoy sex."[99]

Postwar authorities contended that healthy men were naturally sexually knowledgeable and desirous, even as they documented widespread male sexual failure. How could fears that men were becoming feminized and desexualized coexist with the much touted evidence of their sexual voracity? Adding to the confusion, some authorities maintained that men's sexual debilities or incapacities were caused by the same factors that promoted their hypersexuality. These analysts of American masculinity believed that American patterns of dating and courtship produced men who were simultaneously sexually overstimulated and inadequate as sexual partners. After an adolescence spent surrounded by sexual stimuli, and after years of negotiating for access to girls and women whose objective was to avoid intercourse, the married or engaged man could not make the transition to a mature and healthy adult sexuality. The "modern man in the United States," Popenoe sorrowfully conceded, was often arrested at an early stage of sexual development, as more and more adult men replaced "normal aggressiveness" with "the infant's desire merely to enjoy his sensations on what is almost an auto-erotic basis."[100] Middle-class Americans' courtship norms, which featured extended dating and premarital petting, were partly to blame for this problem. According to the sexologist Albert Ellis, American men, "literally by the millions, become so sexually excited and trigger-finger tuned by continual non-concluded sex arousal that they acquire varying degrees of impotence; they frequently garner tremendous feelings of anxiety, guilt, and sexual inadequacy; and they become so generally supersexualized or debilitated that the eventual achievement of the average kind of marital sex relations is hardly likely to satisfy their unrealistic desires."[101]

For the anthropologist Geoffrey Gorer, it was not difficult to reconcile these seemingly opposed findings. A vocal critic of American mores, Gorer drew on broader stereotypes of the national character to describe American men as simultaneously weak and aggressive. Kinsey's male subjects, he commented, like most American men, "do not easily tolerate physiological discomfort, and will get rid of it some way or other. Just as there is in the United States very low tolerance of even mild hunger or thirst or cold[,] . . . so relatively mild gonadal pressure will be relieved somehow, almost as a health measure."[102]

The tension between male hypersexuality or aggression and passivity continually reappeared in the work of sex experts. According to the sociologist Ernest Burgess, American men were torn between "two conflicting conceptions" of sex. While women were socialized to integrate their impulses into familial relationships, literally domesticating their sexuality, men faced a more difficult developmental task, as "sex is likely to become detached and to be defined and discussed apart from and even as if antagonistic to these other roles." The "ideal of masculinity," he elaborated, became "associated with toughness, with physical exploits, with profane and obscene language, and with unrestrained sex behavior," leading to sexual problems.[103] Within this discourse, male sexuality could only be imagined as a game in which contradictory traits—passivity and aggression, sensitivity and dominance—had to be carefully balanced. Normative masculinity was a difficult balancing act, and much postwar commentary on male sexuality attempted to negotiate between a sexual voraciousness that risked clumsiness and a modern definition of sexual skill that for many seemed suspiciously effete and female-centered. The kind of mature sexuality valorized by commentators on American sexual character called for balancing traditionally "male" aggression with the modern, "female" goals of education, finesse, and heterosexual mutuality. Men were encouraged to seek sexual knowledge in order to maintain their marriages, communities, and ultimately the social order; yet behavior that was excessive or misdirected also prompted fears of national decline.

Male homosexuality, which I examine in greater detail in chapter 5, served as a vital—though often unarticulated—term in postwar discussions of male sexuality. Diagnoses of male passivity and weakness, along with sexual problems such as lack of interest or facility, often rested on a set of assumptions that linked gender inversion to same-sex desires and acts. Postwar purges of suspected homosexuals in government, along with increased concerns about the visibility of homosexuality in popular culture and everyday life, spoke to the connections many Americans saw between changing male behaviors and sexual deviance. When contrasted to homosexuality and effeminacy, male heterosexual aggression and hypersexuality may have seemed preferable to many.

Discussions of the nature and proper deployment of male sexuality mirrored the welter of often conflicting theories about American masculinity. The normative male was instructed to be sexually forceful, yet gentle; he was assumed to possess instinctive knowledge about sex yet also encouraged to admit his ignorance and seek information from experts. Such conflicting recommendations revealed a longing for a seemingly simpler past, when men were men, women were women, and sex was effortless and pleasurable. Modern life, many experts seemed to agree, had complicated notions of gender and sexual performance, altering drives, behaviors, and psyches.

CONCLUSION

In the postwar United States, sexuality served as a fulcrum for debates about how to measure and define masculinity. Virility and virtuosity, united, became the hallmark of the modern male sexual subject, but the attainment of this ideal was always fraught with conflict. American men may have been encouraged to assert themselves as powerful and knowledgeable heterosexual subjects as a corrective to wartime and postwar concerns about effeminacy, weakness, and loss of traditional masculinity, but the strategy of positioning male sexual behavior as a site from which to refute the discourse of masculine crisis was not entirely successful. Throughout the decade, fears that male sexuality was imperiled were aired side by side with criticism of men's aggressive and illicit sexual behaviors.

Theories of masculinity often position male heterosexuality as an easily assumed and unproblematic identity. Analyses of male roles in the sexual revolutions of the modern United States, whether in the 1920s, 1950s, or later, have often focused on men's access to women as sexual objects, positioning sex as a paradigmatic form of modern male consumption. As the postwar "masculinity crisis" and anxious responses to the first Kinsey Report suggest, however, American ideologies of manhood—even for many heterosexual, white, middle-class men—were far more ambivalent and riddled with contradiction than such views would indicate. The effects of heightened postwar attention to masculinity and male sexuality were complex. Within the overarching discourse of American sexual character, connections between masculinity and male heterosexual activity took on enhanced importance as a balanced and fulfilling sex life became associated not only with physical health but also with emotional well-being, domestic harmony, civic balance, and personal liberation. At the same time, however, the figure of the average American male, whether painted as feminized and impotent or as overly aggressive and lacking in sexual finesse, served as a troubling symbol of postwar social crisis. The man who appeared in the pages of sex literature ready and willing to confess his sexual faults and learn new sexual attitudes and skills performed important cultural work. His remaking into a faithful yet sexually knowledgeable and potent husband assuaged anxieties about female dominance and cultural concerns about the status of American men. The new kind of masculinity lauded by authorities had dangerous implications, however. By encouraging open discussion of sexuality, critics feared, the nation could indirectly encourage heterosexual promiscuity and homosexuality and ultimately further a sensualist ethic that would lead to familial and national decline.

In 1962, *Esquire* magazine, which had carried numerous articles during the preceding decade examining the plight of the American male, complained, "Crises of masculinity be damned, the problem is the crisis of femininity."[104] Many of the social developments that were shaping male sexuality, including the spread of sexual information, the embrace of domesticity and the nuclear family, and the intense focus on Americans' sexual character and its effects, affected women as profoundly as they did men. Some postwar problems, such as the apparent epidemic of male sexual dysfunction and general decline of traditional masculinity, were indeed seen largely as caused by women. As *Esquire* suggested, any sustained focus on male sexuality seemed to lead inexorably to the demands and failings of heterosexual men's female partners, especially the stock character often referred to as "the American wife." *Sexual Behavior in the Human Male* had laid out questions about women that Kinsey and his team promised to address in their next volume. The two volumes, however, elicited very different public reactions.

THREE

"Much the Same Desires as Men"
Sexual Behavior in the Human Female
and the "American Woman"

SEXUAL BEHAVIOR IN THE HUMAN MALE had prompted a public uproar and made American sexual behavior a popular subject of discussion among scientists, politicians, and commentators on popular culture. Five years later, anticipating the publication of *Sexual Behavior in the Human Female*, the public braced itself for even more shocking revelations. While the first volume had spawned unprecedented coverage of Americans' sexual behavior and focused attention on the gap between moral ideals and actual practices, the second volume entered into an already heated discourse on sex in the United States. In addition, its focus on a specific group—white women who were predominantly middle-class and married—automatically rendered its results, in the words of one magazine, "stronger stuff" than those of the first volume.[1]

Sexual Behavior in the Human Female confirmed some long-standing ideas about women's sexuality, but it also allowed for the development and articulation of new, often conflicting theories of female desire and behavior. In their responses to the report, which received even more popular attention than had its predecessor, experts addressed the question of what kinds of female sexual behavior fostered or threatened public interests. Theories of female heterosexuality had often relied on an opposition between "good" and "bad" women, defined as sexually chaste versus sexually active. Although this dichotomy was still powerful, its influence was on the wane and, ultimately, it could not serve to satisfactorily explain the findings of the Kinsey Report and what women's changing sexual behavior meant culturally to postwar Americans. In fact, experts' reliance upon the figure of the average American woman helped to call into question the very existence of a uniform female heterosexuality or a normal femininity.

Popular readings of and responses to *Sexual Behavior in the Human Female* revealed a growing anxiety about the stability and naturalness of traditional female roles and the sexual double standard. As Americans discussed the volume, their popular ideal of the average American woman—white, middle-class, usually married, and presumably heterosexual—was increasingly contested. The reception of the Kinsey Report on female sexuality shows widening rifts in this image: the gulf between women's prescribed social and sexual roles and their actual desires and behaviors could no longer be ignored.

THE CULTURAL CONTEXT OF FEMALE SEXUALITY

Much of the commentary that anticipated and greeted *Sexual Behavior in the Human Female* insisted that female sexuality had hitherto been an unexamined topic, but neither Kinsey's study nor the ideas about female sexuality that countered it emerged from a void. Insistence on the topic's novelty allowed critics to position themselves as daring moderns and to link contemporary sexual behavior to recent shifts in American culture rather than take a longer view. Earlier popular and scholarly works on women's social roles and on female sexuality had familiarized readers with major theories. Within this literature, two different paradigms of female sexuality struggled for dominance. In the first, women were portrayed as passive and sexually quiescent; in the second, their sexual desires were seen as rapacious and socially destructive.

Both visions were shaped by the increasing popular interest in and acceptance of psychological thinking. Although the number of Americans actually in analysis was never large, psychoanalysis reached a peak in popularity after World War II, as therapeutic culture and expert advice were popularly celebrated. The period's emphasis on personal fulfillment and happiness emphasized sexual pleasure, as did the postwar celebration of marriage. High expectations for personal life had been an important feature of upper-middle-class intellectual life for some time, but during the postwar years the audience for these ideas expanded. As the children and grandchildren of immigrants formed families—or, as noted in later chapters, explored same-sex attractions—unprecedented numbers embraced an ethos of exploration and personal entitlement in their personal lives, including their sexual lives. Whether they sought the familial happiness promised by women's magazines by participating in quizzes and reading columns designed to evaluate their degree of happiness and adjustment or by exploring their psyches with representatives of the burgeoning mental health professions, Americans' intense scrutiny of the self became a leitmotif of the era. Indeed, for many upwardly mobile young Americans, the process of defining themselves as belonging to the middle class entailed adhering to secular values of self-knowledge and personal improvement as much as it did abandoning urban ethnic neighborhoods for suburban subdivisions.

Freudian theory and its variations contributed to the ideal of female sexual passivity. In their often oversimplified American incarnation, such analyses stressed profound differences between male and female character and desires, with women's sexuality inextricable from their maternal yearnings and sense of lack. Influential texts like Marynia Farnham and Ferdinand Lundberg's *Modern Woman: The Lost Sex* portrayed female sexuality as essentially receptive. According to these authors' famous description of women's sexual responsibilities, a woman's "role is passive. It is not as easy as rolling off a log for her. It is easier. It is as easy as being the log itself. She cannot fail to deliver a masterly performance, by doing nothing whatever except being duly appreciative and allowing nature to take its course."[2] A decade later Dr. Marie Robinson, another psychiatrist-turned-advice-author of the period, described the "grown-up, truly feminine woman" in similar terms, urging the reader to recall that

> a great part of her personality is organized around her maternal instinct[,] and that the chief characteristic of that instinct is a pleasure in giving, an unappeasable altruism that always puts her husband and children before self, even to the point of risking her own life and welfare. Her central activities revolve around her nest building and child rearing. Her personality is characterized by a deep intuitiveness about others. She is inward and passive, her energies devoted to that deepest of all needs, the procreation of the race of man through her own body. Her husband, by contrast, is aggressive, occupied basically with his struggles in the outside world. Her stage, the focus of her central interest, is the home and its preservation and happiness.[3]

For Farnham and Lundberg, Robinson, and a host of other popular experts, female sexuality mirrored women's psychological and biological natures—women were receptive, passive, and sought pleasure through service to others.

This belief that female sexuality was based upon passivity and maternal instinct had long lived in tension with another set of ideas, one that insisted instead that women were at least as sexually desirous as men. This viewpoint, which emphasized the centrality of desire to female sexuality, was bolstered during the war years when the news media featured alarming evidence that American women were engaging in premarital and extramarital sex. At the close of the war, news of "victory girls" may have slipped from the front pages, but anxieties about uncontrolled female sexuality did not abate. According to the historian Leisa Meyer, the war years "catalyzed popular fears about women's sexual and economic independence," and these fears continued to resonate in peacetime.[4] After being confronted with wartime evidence of women's sexual transgressions, experts from the social and biological sciences focused new attention on women's sexual behavior and its effects.

Observers insisted that women were in the vanguard of the sexual and social changes that were altering the country. In 1947, the philosopher John McPartland argued that changes in the nation's moral code "were determined by our women. Not that our women became bad—the term is meaningless—but that they reflected the changes in our culture, while men tended to lag."[5] According to this influential argument, it was the behavior and ethos of average heterosexual women that most directly influenced national shifts in mainstream sexual behavior and character. Fritz Wittels, one of a number of authors who attempted to scoop Kinsey's second report by publishing his own study of female sexuality in the early 1950s, similarly depicted women as the standard-setters of modern American culture. The current "sexual revolution," Wittels maintained, is "more or less a woman's revolution."[6] The anthropologist and psychoanalyst Abram Kardiner agreed that "the whole question of sex morality pivots about the behavior of the female, not the male."[7] Kinsey's discovery that the decade of birth was a significant factor in women's sexual behavior also suggested that women were more responsive to social changes than men.

According to the postwar biological and social scientists who turned their attention to "the behavior of the female," contemporary American women faced a host of potential problems in their efforts to enjoy a mature sexuality. At one end of the spectrum of possible fates for women lay frigidity. Robinson maintained that "the problem of sexual frigidity in women is one of the gravest problems of our times. . . . No other public health or social problem of our time even approaches this magnitude." Since "over 40 per cent of women suffer from it in one or another of its degrees or forms," its effects spiraled beyond individual women to affect their husbands and children, making frigidity "a major danger to the stability of marriage and to the health and happiness of every member of the individual family."[8] Estimates of the extent of frigidity among American women varied but were significant even among those who did not share Robinson's orthodox Freudianism. Some experts believed it could affect as much as "70 to 90 per cent" of American women.[9] The noted marriage counselor and advice columnist Paul Popenoe warned readers of the *Ladies' Home Journal* in 1953 that "few serious handicaps to marriage are as common as frigidity." Repeating the common association of frigidity with upper-class status, a correlation that he and other eugenicists found troubling, Popenoe noted that, among wives with a high school or college education, "at least one-third have some difficulty of this kind."[10]

Although frigidity loomed as a major issue in much of the literature on women's sexuality, it coexisted in the work of physicians and advice authors with the seemingly very different problem of women's excessive sexual activity, especially outside of marriage. Anecdotal and survey evidence of this trend abounded even before Kinsey's figures appeared. In one 1947 poll, a majority of American women agreed that they had become "less strict" in their morals in recent years, and *Good Housekeeping* reported in 1950 that "a substantial proportion of today's young girls have sexual relations before marriage."[11] This decline of traditional morality was particularly pronounced among "respectable" girls. As one expert summed up the trend, any "male in search of sexual excitement can now find it with girls of his own class and often his immediate group."[12] Science even raised the alarming possibility that women's sexual capacity was greater than that of men: a biologist from the University of California warned the readers of *Nation's Business* magazine in 1952 that "women can achieve the sex climax up to 100 times as often as a man."[13]

Virtually all authorities who commented on female sexuality believed that women's behavior indicated the state of the nation's morality and culture and offered valuable clues to its future. Thus, the postwar years witnessed intense disputes over the evolving roles of American women. Academics, women's magazine writers, and federal commissions surveyed, interrogated, and assessed working wives, the mothers of young children, and other average women.[14] Changing evaluations of women's sexual behavior and ideas about proper female sexuality were intimately connected to these issues, since theories about women's psychology and their roles within the family, workplace, and polity were consistently intertwined with assessments of their sexuality. The psychologist Amram Scheinfeld underlined both the urgency of these links and the vital position of women when he noted that "the sexual behavior of our women is even more crucial to our society than that of our men," and that therefore "any misunderstanding about it can be even more harmful."[15]

As in the complementary discourse of masculinity and male sexuality, transformations in sexual behavior were juxtaposed with shifting patterns of labor and family relationships, as the apparent dualism regarding female sexuality mirrored larger debates about women's roles outside the bedroom. Women were central to the logic of postwar American nationalism, not only as wives and mothers but also as independent actors. Their presence in the political arena signaled modern gender relations rather than the subservience of Third World women or the constant labor associated with women in the Soviet Union. As Joanne Meyerowitz points out, U.S. women played a vital role in cold war discourse by proving that women in democracies were free both to devote themselves to domesticity and nurturance of their families and to vote and engage in other civic activities. In her investigation of postwar popular magazines, Meyerowitz found a "bifocal vision of women both as feminine and domestic and as public achievers" as mass culture celebrated their public roles and promoted a gendered strategy for fighting the cold war.[16] When the editor of *McCall's* magazine famously coined the term *togetherness* to characterize postwar life, it not only celebrated increased family unity but also gestured toward women's "wider range of living." In the past, according to *McCall's*, women had dwelt in "a rosy realm of fashion and folderol" and had been dismissed as "mysterious and unpredictable creatures given to vagaries and vaporings." Modern American women had "carve[d] out large areas of living formerly forbidden to your sex." The magazine saluted the fact that *"today women are not a sheltered sex."*[17]

Whether expected to refute or confirm new sexual patterns—whether to be sexually knowledgeable and experienced or essentially passive and enmeshed in the world of the home—women played a central role as both subject and audience in the discussion of female sexuality. Feminine virtue was one bulwark upon which cold-war thought rested. Tamar Mayer suggests that the place of women in the cultural logic of nationalism is often based on their roles as agents of "biological and ideological reproduction" and predicated on their sexual purity. "Only pure and modest women can re-produce the pure nation," Mayer notes, as "without purity in biological reproduction the nation clearly cannot survive."[18] Although this formulation provides a starting point from which to analyze the relationship of women, sexuality, and nationalism, postwar ideologies of American womanhood were far more complex than a focus solely on purity would suggest. As others have noted, American women were framed as being different from their counterparts in other countries. It was important to national legitimacy for them to be seen as unhampered by political oppression, domestic responsibility, and male domination and as free to enjoy leisure, consumer resources, and egalitarian family lives, as well as free to play public roles as civic housekeepers.[19]

While postwar authorities debated how their roles were changing, battles over the nature, proper expression, and limits of female sexuality were part of a broader debate over private and public female roles. Mayer's analysis suggests the importance of women's sexual character to national identity, as postwar democracy depended on women's activities for reproduction and socialization. An upright citizenry was based upon nurturing and moral mothers, and the suburban home, which served as an inducement to labor, consumption and national pride, was predicated upon a vision of a nuclear family with clearly segregated roles and duties. A certain kind of American woman emerged as a powerful political trope, perhaps most directly in the 1959 "kitchen debate," in which Vice President Richard Nixon lauded the glories of American labor-saving devices—and the leisure they provided to American women, which kept them younger looking and more attractive than their Soviet counterparts—for the benefit of an unimpressed Khrushchev.[20] Average women's lives, moral standards, and sexual behavior thus held crucial implications for the legitimacy of American culture and politics.

"THE COMPOSITE AMERICAN WIFE" AND THE AVERAGE AMERICAN WOMAN: RESPONSES TO THE SECOND REPORT

Within this context of intense concern with female sexuality and its implications for American character, readers looked to the second Kinsey Report for quantitative data on American women. The first report had raised tantalizing questions about women's sexual behavior, and speculation about the second volume took on increasing urgency as its proposed publication date drew near.[21] Given the numbers of men who had reported premarital and extramarital sex, what results would similar

Figure 6. Kinsey interviewing a female subject. (Photo by William Dellenback; reprinted by permission of The Kinsey Institute for Research in Sex, Gender, and Reproduction, Inc.)

queries of women elicit? Were women keeping pace with men's sexual behavior? Commentators took it as self-evident that the new volume would be more controversial than *Sexual Behavior in the Human Male*. Speculation ran rife on what it would contain, with interested readers and commentators braced for shocking revelations.[22] "If the first Kinsey report created a sensation," one magazine editorialized, "the second is likely to outdo it, since it will deal with the sexual behavior of American women."[23] The furor caused by the report on men, another magazine concurred, "was a mere puffball explosion, compared to the forthcoming report" on the "touchier subject . . . [of] women's sexual behavior."[24] Rumors flew and copycat texts surfaced as the book racked up massive advance sales. Writers vied for invitations to the project's offices, and magazine editors reserved space on their covers for Kinsey's statistics. A few intrepid women even described the details of their actual or fantasized interviews with Kinsey to magazines, which guessed how these isolated narratives might compare to the conclusions of the completed study (see figure 6).[25] A poll of

Newsweek readers revealed that coverage of *Sexual Behavior in the Human Female* was ranked as equaled in public interest only by the possible advent of a third world war.[26]

The belief that women's sexuality held the potential to endorse, indict, or transform modern American society emerged clearly in the hopes that experts expressed for the report before its actual findings became known. A few reviewers who had been dismayed by the findings of *Sexual Behavior in the Human Male* prayed that the second volume would present a more reassuring picture of American morality. The psychiatrist Edward Strecker spoke for many when he expressed his desires regarding the second report. Since Kinsey's first offering had presented such a grim view of American sexual mores, he explained, he devoutly hoped that the second would vindicate them, and that "the record of the composite American wife will redeem her erring spouse, statistically."[27]

Other authorities were less sanguine about Kinsey's likely conclusions and predicted that the book would wreak havoc on the morality of American girls and women. One journal editorialized against the publication of the second report with the warning that society "may already be seeing the unintentional fruits of the first Kinsey Report" in public records of crime and maladjustment, and cautioned that "the liberty of a free press which permits Dr. Kinsey to publish his findings is in serious danger of being abused."[28] The forthcoming volume, another author grimly concurred, "looks like a definite troublemaker" threatening to "damage sex relations and sex dignity for millions of decent and honorable women."[29] *Your Life* magazine perhaps summed up prevailing opinion best when it predicted the volume's likely effects: "Not a few folk assume that woman is a fragile vessel, made of finer clay than man; that she doesn't, or shouldn't, enjoy sex, certainly she shouldn't talk about it, and if she does talk about it the truth is not in her. The forthcoming Kinsey Report is bound to prove that whatever the truth of such beliefs, it's far from the whole truth."[30]

When this eagerly anticipated and much discussed document finally arrived in bookstores around the nation in September 1953, its findings did not disappoint those who expected controversy. The study, based on interviews with 5,940 women from all over the United States, revealed that approximately half had experienced premarital coitus and more than four in ten had engaged in either coitus or petting to orgasm outside of marriage. The "biggest shockers in the new Kinsey Report," according to a typical profile of the volume, all disputed long-held myths about women that depicted them as less interested in sex than men. On the contrary, one of the first reviews claimed, American women were often aggressively sexual, as measured by their quickness to arousal, pleasure in orgasm, and long-term sexual drive.[31] The marriage counselor Emily Mudd, who penned several approving articles on the report, noted that "American women emerge from all those pages of careful analysis with far more sexual drive than they have ever been given credit for."[32]

The explosion of banner headlines and cover stories that greeted the book's release offered a wealth of popular opinions on the report's relevance and proper place. Mainstream sources asked, What had American women told the Kinsey team about their sexual behavior? Were the study's findings accurate? Should it have been published, or even undertaken at all? And, most pressing, what effects would its conclusions have on its female readers and on the nation's moral standards? Not unlike the broader culture's ambivalence about female roles, evaluations of and responses to the report were contradictory. While many experts accepted the report as generally trustworthy, more than a few attacked the character of Kinsey's informants or accused the researchers of inventing or manipulating their data. Reviewers' opinions varied dramatically, depending both on their assumptions about female sexuality and on which aspects of Kinsey's massive study they chose to focus. Some news sources read the report as a shocking indictment of American women, while others interpreted the same statistics as proof that the nation's female population was safely chaste.

Life magazine's coverage caught this tension graphically when it featured three separate pieces on *Sexual Behavior in the Human Female* in a single issue. The centerpiece of the coverage, an article by the magazine's editor, Ernest Havemann, trumpeted, "The Kinsey Report on Women: Long-Awaited Study Shows They Are Not Very Interested in Sex," and went on to sympathize with the "average woman" who "often comes to regard herself as the frigid exception to the passionate female world" displayed in popular fiction. In the second of the magazine's three reviews, the novelist Kathleen Norris deemed the book literally "incredible!" and argued that its evidence of petting and extramarital activity by some women "could be harmful" to female readers. Easily differentiating between "human females" and American women, she sniffed that respondents had clearly been "of an easily recognized sort," since "genuine women" could only regard sex as a sacred marital trust, part of the "proud estate of being wife, homemaker, mother." The magazine's third assessment of *Sexual Behavior in the Human Female* was penned by the novelist Fannie Hurst, whose credentials as author of the 1930s novel and film *Back Street* apparently qualified her as an expert on illicit sexuality. Hurst took a cautiously approving stance toward the report, maintaining that the study had been approached "with decency and dignity" and would "lead to better understanding between sexes" during "the social revolution through which we are now muddling."[33]

As the divergence of opinion within this single source suggests, Kinsey's 1953 volume elicited a dizzying range of responses. To some extent, this resulted from the complexity of Kinsey's figures. In its 842 pages of cramped print, the book contains 334 detailed tables, presenting statistics on topics ranging from the percentage of high school dropouts born in the 1930s who ever engaged in oral sex to the active incidence of dreaming to orgasm among moderately devout Protestant women. Exactly what this wealth of data had to offer the public, how readers were to extrapolate from this information, and how the tables and charts of the report related to actual, living women were questions for which all readers had to formulate answers. Even experts could not easily agree on what the data proved: in the words of a panel from the American Statistical Association, charged with evaluating the data, "It would have been possible to write two factually correct reports, one of which would leave the reader with the impression that KPM's work was of the highest quality, the other that the work was of poor quality."[34] To lay readers, the complex statistics were often meaningless: the *New Yorker* argued that "much of the volume consists of tables and charts" so confusing that the "ordinary reader can no more appraise its contents justly than he can appraise those of a manual on prestressed concrete."[35]

Readers' and reviewers' confusion as to what the report "really" said was not merely indicative of their misunderstanding of complicated statistics, though: more profoundly, it spoke to a representational crisis regarding American female sexuality. The widely varying interpretations of the report offered by American reviewers bespoke a serious and widespread cultural confusion. Could the sexual behavior of about six thousand women scattered around the United States, or that of the millions across the nation to whom they allegedly corresponded, be accurately represented? How faithful were women to their marriage vows? Were they exemplars of restraint or excess?

Sexual Behavior in the Human Female offered a host of conflicting answers. It could be read, two sociologists grumbled, both as "a disappointing documentation to dampen the fantasies of younger males" and "as confirmation of the grumpy suspicions of veteran husbands."[36] Faced with such voluminous data, American opinion consolidated the mass of information in the Kinsey Report by judging which categories and figures mattered and which did not. Kinsey's finding that more than 20 percent of America's married women had had illegal abortions received virtually no comment in the mainstream press, for example, and his statistics regarding lesbianism received less attention than those on male homosexuality had five years earlier. Instead, the majority of popular attention focused on the sexual behaviors of heterosexual women, with the most often-cited figures being the percentages of women who had experienced premarital coitus (50 percent), extramarital coitus (26 percent), or extramarital petting to orgasm (16 percent). Given a dense and interminable tome crammed with charts and graphs, how did readers turn them into comprehensible and assimilable information? What could the report be used to prove, and what did it mean to postwar readers?

In addressing these and related questions, scientists, journalists, and other reviewers of the report turned again and again to one figure, the average, or "typical," American woman. From Kinsey's statistical tables, garnered from a study of 5,940 women diversified by age, geographical location, sexual orientation, marital status, class, and education, reviewers conjured up a single modal woman who could embody the most controversial findings of *Sexual Behavior in the Human Female*. This iconic woman allowed commentators to both air and elide profound cultural contradictions governing American female sexuality. The normal or average— the two terms were often used interchangeably—American woman, a category assumed and interrogated in hundreds of books and articles, allowed commentators to address the social dilemmas presented by American women's unruly and often indecipherable sexuality. As this mythic average woman emerged from the Kinsey Report, her presence effectively displaced many of the complexities of the original lengthy document. Simultaneously representing subject and audience, individual woman and collective women, she embodied Kinsey's data and rendered statistical abstractions comprehensible.

The averageness of the women Kinsey interviewed was a constant refrain in reviews of the second report. Although the project's researchers cautioned readers against generalizing too rapidly from the sample represented, they did claim that the book's findings were "typical of . . . not an inconsiderable portion, of the white females living within the boundaries of the United States."[37] The nearly six thousand women whose sexual histories formed the basis for the volume came from a variety of regions, class backgrounds, and occupations. Kinsey's sample, one author reported, ranged from "housewives, Y.W.C.A. secretaries, women's club leaders, [and] professional women" to "Salvation Army lasses and . . . clergymen's wives."[38] Another noted that "Dr. Kinsey's interest must be in the typical individual," adding that although his interviewees might not match the nation's female population in every particular, they "are not, at any rate, remarkably abnormal or subnormal."[39] Kinsey and his team, as another journalist phrased it for women readers, had spent years "tracking down the truth about *you,* the elusive, reticent female."[40]

Even before the report appeared, commentators drew connections between its numbers and the behaviors and beliefs of actual women. Whether they spoke in condemnation of the report or in its defense, they consistently represented these women in familial terms. Philip Wylie had earlier referred to the report's subject as "the composite American wife," and according to a New York State politician who sought to bar the report from the U.S. mail, Kinsey's work "hurls the insult of the century against our mothers, wives, daughters, and sisters," tarring all American women by implying that any could assert their sexuality outside the containment of marriage.[41] One troubled commentator presented the report's findings in extremely intimate terms when he commented that "Dr. Kinsey and his colleagues tell us that a goodly proportion of our wives are unfaithful."[42] Reviewers' tendency to read the report in personal terms also led them to pit Kinsey's "females" against real ones: one described the study in adversarial terms as a case of "American women vs. the Kinsey Report."[43] Similarly, when the *Indianapolis Star* reported that Kinsey and his staff left their headquarters in Bloomington for a research trip before *Sexual Behavior in the Human Female* appeared, the paper editorialized, "You can either smile and nervously change the subject after calling a woman unfaithful, or you can get out of town."[44] And in the *Reader's Digest,* another journalist closed a scathing indictment of Kinsey's study and its likely effects with the reassuring tableau of a real-life young GI and his wife and baby, whom the journalist had recently encountered: "The young woman was dreamily awake, her head snuggled against her husband's shoulder, and I watched her eyes look up at him adoringly, then move down to the baby, then back to her husband again." This writer, through his illustration of one flesh-and-blood woman and her family, brought the discussion of women's sexuality away from charts and statistics and back to where, in his opinion, it belonged: to "motherhood—and love."[45]

The ways in which these reviewers interpreted the report reflected their view of middle-class, white, married American women who were both the principal subjects of and major audience for the report. Confronted by endless ranks of numbers that defied understanding but needed to be translated into accessible terms for a mass readership, observers went to the perceived heart of the matter, defining women in relation to their social roles as wives. When narratives about Kinsey's male interviewees appeared in the press, they were invariably testimonials by prominent medical and scientific authorities to Kinsey's interviewing skills and scientific acumen. When women were the interviewees or the potential readers, very different relationships were evoked. Whether portrayed as a sister, a daughter, a young wife, or a mother, the average American woman invoked by the media in relation to the report was a character tailor-made to question rather than endorse the accuracy of Kinsey's numbers.

By interpreting Kinsey's findings through the medium of a fictive average woman, commentators could use her to dismiss the evidence of the report. Indeed, many posited that the women Kinsey interviewed, with their rich histories of petting, premarital intercourse, and noncoital sex techniques, simply did not and could not exist. The novelist Kathleen Norris, in one of the three reviews commissioned by *Life*, questioned the motives of any woman so depraved as to submit herself to the interview process. "Dr. Kinsey and his associates," she wrote acerbically,

> claim that they reached their conclusions after getting statistics upon the most delicate, the most secret affairs of the hearts of 5,940 women. . . . How does the questioning start? Some women must answer with a stinging blow to the left eye of the interlocutor. But some women answered. . . . Believe me, Dr. Kinsey, the women who told you of such girlhood and postmarital sex experiences were of an easily recognized sort: the sort who wrote themselves letters from imaginary lovers in high school days and have gone right along into womanhood fabricating sensational affairs.

"Genuine women," Norris concluded, "don't talk about it."[46]

Such charges of female duplicity often featured in discussions of Kinsey's data. "Figures may not lie," one commentator wrote, "but many of the women probably did."[47] Claims that women are likely to be liars or, more benignly, unreliable narrators worked to diminish the report's threats. In many cases, women's alleged propensity towards falsehood could even be a source of humor. One cartoon collected in *A Cartoon Guide to the Kinsey*

Figures 7 and 8. Cartoons from Charles Preston, ed., *A Cartoon Guide to the Kinsey Report,* 7, 42–43. (From the *Wall Street Journal*—permission, Cartoon Features Syndicate and Charles Preston.)

"OF COURSE, I EXAGGERATED A TEENSY BIT."

Report, for example, depicted an American everyman reading *Sexual Behavior in the Human Female* and then sallying forth in search of female companionship. At day's end, after being ignored by a succession of women, he returns home in disgust to thrust the report into the trash. A related suspicion found expression in another cartoon from the same collection, in which a woman fresh from her Kinsey interview confides to a friend, "Of course, I exaggerated a teensy bit" (see figures 7 and 8).

The issue of veracity had rarely if ever surfaced in popular discussions of the first Kinsey Report. Although a few commentators speculated about the men who had provided its statistics, discussion was usually limited to noting the class background or prison experience of different subgroups represented in the study. For Kinsey's male subjects, there was no parallel debate about whether they had exaggerated, minimized, or fantasized their sexual histories. When women talked about sex, the cultural stakes were different. Whether because of preexisting assumptions about women's inability to tell the truth, concern about the propriety of women talking to male interviewers, or the wish to deny the accuracy of the report's findings, a sizeable number of reviews alluded to women's well-known tendency to embroider, exaggerate, or outright lie.

Another group of authors followed a different strategy: they granted that the women whose experiences went into *Sexual Behavior in the Human Female* actually existed but categorized them as an aberrant minority unlike truly average or typical women with more conventional sexual histories. The sociologists A. H. Hobbs and W. M. Kephart argued that "the 5,940 white, non-prison females who were willing to describe their sexual activities in minute detail for Professor Kinsey's second volume" were a "distorted sample," more educated and less conventional than "women in general."[48] Any women willing to discuss their sexual histories with a male interviewer, a journalist speculated in advance of the report, were inevitably "ill-balanced, frustrated, confused exhibitionists" who were "victims of maladjusted sexual lives," rather than representatives of "those millions of other women whose religion, modesty, and reticence would keep them from a heart-to-heart talk with a Kinsey investigator."[49] The marriage counselor Judson Landis went a step further, writing that "the women Kinsey studied" displayed "types of behavior that seem to approach the behavior of prostitutes."[50] The orthodox Freudian psychiatrist Edmund Bergler, perhaps fuming at Kinsey's dismissal of the vaginal orgasm, posited that "either these woman were perverted masochists, and therefore not 'typical' of American women, or they were pulling Kinsey's leg," and declared them "automatically suspect" as neurotics or prostitutes.[51]

If the danger of unrestrained sexuality could be so easily diminished by locating it in a handful of deviant women, it remained safely contained. Such women, critics suggested, were anomalous: the American public might be distressed at the revelation that so many prostitutes existed, and perhaps puzzled at how Kinsey had unerringly located them, but it could reject his data, assured that the woman who mattered, the typical middle-class American mother, wife, daughter, or sister, was not reflected in its pages. As one reviewer soothingly phrased it, the report's assertions "may be referring not to people you know, but to a couple of other females somewhere else."[52] These debates about the report offered a graphic version of the deep cultural dualism about women's sexuality that allowed

"THERE GOES ROCKLAND COUNTY'S KINSEY REPORT."

Figure 9. Cartoon from Charles Preston, ed., *A Cartoon Guide to the Kinsey Report,* 13. (From the *Wall Street Journal*—permission, Cartoon Features Syndicate and Charles Preston.)

them to be displayed as two groups, one pure and maternal and the other abandoned and actively sexual. What lay at the heart of this division was a deep anxiety that these two drastically different women could not be separated, that they were in fact the same figure.

For readers and reviewers unwilling to accept that Kinsey's subjects were either liars or an aberrant minority, only one option remained: to accept Kinsey's numbers as an accurate reflection of the behavior of average American women. One cartoon that played off of this assumption depicted a female figure described as a wealthy suburb's local version of the report (see figure 9). Another, published in several newspapers, featured Kinsey as a bohemian artist painting a portrait of a female model. His canvas is not visible to the reader but can be seen by the model, who reacts with shock and anger.[53] Some of the reviewers who believed that the report accurately captured American women's sexual behavior found glee in shattering illusions. One magazine warned bachelors contemplating marriage, "We'll give you four-to-one odds she's not a virgin. The ladies of the nation may howl at that one, but they provided the statistics. And a party named Kinsey will give you only three-to-one that she stays faithful to you after you've married her."[54] Plotting the odds against female sexual fidelity became a national pastime: the *Saturday Evening Post* used gambling jargon to comment on the volume, joking, "This Kinsey Report says that Womanhood is about as reliable as a 20-to-1 shot in a race for maiden two year old fillies. . . . Can you imagine how a guy could work while spending the morning muttering to himself, 'It's 8 to 5 the wife is out with the grocer's boy right this minute. And if the grocer's boy ain't seventeen yet[,] the odds jump to 8 to 1!'"[55]

Whether they accepted or disputed the findings of *Sexual Behavior in the Human Female,* both consumers and critics of the report saw its figures as significant because they indicated broader social changes. Many believed that Americans' sexual character was actually being changed—either liberated or perverted, depending on the viewpoint of the observer—by the recent outpouring of information on sex and incitement to a new standard of sexual activity. The expectation that middle-class wives and mothers be sexually knowledgeable and fulfilled—an ideology that had emerged during the 1920s in the writings of sexual reformers influenced by both feminism and Freud—had trickled down to a mass audience. The postwar imperative for Americans to embrace the freedoms of individualism and democracy, along with a related emphasis on egalitarian marriage, lent a cold-war twist to the idea that modern women were entitled to—even expected to—enjoy sexual pleasure. Along with their freedom to "vote, attend college, become doctors, lawyers, [or] engineers," a commentator on modern women's roles mused, American women now "have a right, even a duty, to have a full, rich sex life."[56]

Sexual responsiveness and pleasure had become as much a part of women's cultural role as were domesticity and self-fulfillment. "In the last years," the analyst Theodor Reik wrote approvingly, "under the influence of psychological knowledge acquired through reading books and articles or listening to lectures, modern woman sometimes feels that her cooperation in sex is necessary and that she does not fulfill her part by acting the 'victim' of the sexually excited man." Noting the popularity of works on sex directed at a female audience, Reik concluded that, despite a long-standing tradition of female sexual passivity, a "slow change in women's attitude toward the question" was under way, producing "women who feel that they too are responsible for success or failure in sexual relations."[57] Margaret Mead tartly noted that "in the United States positive sex response has come to be defined as something women ought to have, like the ability to read."[58] Authorities often linked this development to Kinsey's work: according to one attorney, "The new Kinsey report demonstrates that women are awakening on all levels of sexual expression—which is all to the good."[59] And the sexologist Albert Ellis lauded the trend, predicting after the report was published that "the American women of tomorrow will probably equal or surpass American men in their sexual responsiveness."[60]

Some of the commentators who shared this belief that the modern woman was becoming more sexually aware were less sanguine. They believed that, instead of freeing women to enjoy sex, the increasing cultural emphasis on female sexual entitlement destroyed female happiness, threatened marriages, and posed a grave threat to the nation. Rather than being a "natural" development or the flowering of a long-denied potential, women's increasing interest in and expectations about sex were imposed on them by sensationalist and misguided media "experts." The author John McPartland wrote disapprovingly that the average American wife was becoming "increasingly conscious of sex, due in no small part to the consistent emphasis on sexual values in practically everything she sees, reads, or hears."[61] The biologist Robert Odenwald similarly held that modern women were being subjected to sinister propaganda, arguing that, "if it is true that wives in the past were kept ignorant of the pleasures of sex, it may be equally true that today's brides are overly aware of them." Due to glowing media depictions of sexual pleasure, Odenwald grumbled, young women believed they had a "right to petting and other forms of sex stimulation," and "the modern girl has as many orgasms behind her when she marries as her grandmother had at the menopause."[62] In this analysis, *Sexual Behavior in the Human Female* came in for sharp criticism because it was seen as persuading vulnerable women to engage in behaviors they would not have contemplated without the report as a model. According to *Life Today* magazine, the dangers of Kinsey's second study lay in the possibility that American women would be "inspired or assuaged by Mrs. Jones' confessions of sex variations."[63]

The sociologist and marriage expert Paul Landis generally approved of the increasing emphasis on sexuality in modern marriage but warned that it could harm women by suggesting that their marriages were unsatisfactory or abnormal. In the past, Landis explained, women had accepted the belief that "sex pleasure was a sin . . . a necessity, a duty performed in exchange for the security of her home and children." Recently, as a result of "the flood of information now available on sex problems," American women were suddenly encouraged to express desire and to demand orgasm. Landis believed that such expectations raised women's hopes unrealistically, and that this "new attitude, which has brought so much joy, has also brought with it a great deal of unhappiness."[64] Other authorities concurred, warning against the dangers that sex and marriage manuals posed for unwary women.[65]

The effects of women's increasing sexual expectations could be devastating. In *The Split-Level Trap,* their exposé of the dark side of suburban living, the sociological team Richard and Katharine Gordon offered a vivid case study of "Gina," a young housewife whose aberrant desires drove her to a breakdown. Like many other modern women, the Gordons argued, Gina had become unstable because "she lived in a modern mobile society which has made women more knowledgeable about sex." "In the old-time American communities" of the past, the Gordons noted,

> people didn't talk about sex much, nor did they have mass-communication media in which sex was continually thrown at them. Indeed, there were many wives in those towns who went through life without ever knowing that it was possible for them to enjoy the sexual experience— they saw intercourse simply as a duty to their husbands. Women today are more informed. And this has created problems. Knowing that it is possible for her to achieve sexual enjoyment, hearing other women talk about it, seeing it portrayed in realistic (and often surrealistic) detail on the movie and TV screen, the modern wife may fret more when deprived of it than did the wife of fifty years ago.

Under the influence of such mass media sources, Gina "made wild demands on [her husband] John. . . . [She] wanted to experiment with new techniques and positions she had heard and read of, some of which were unusual and most of which she had been taught to think of as perversions." Her husband was "horrified and frightened," and Gina ultimately suffered an emotional and physical breakdown.[66]

As the Gordons' concern attests, Americans' changing sexual behaviors and ideologies were linked again and again to visions of gendered, as well as sexual, disorder. The sociologists A. H. Hobbs and W. M. Kephart, writing in the *American Journal of Psychiatry* soon after the release of the second report, maintained that chroniclers of the sexual scene shared a secret agenda to destroy American mores and wreak havoc upon the nation. If the current trend toward sexual freedom and experimentation continued, they argued, the institution of marriage would become meaningless. Wives would desert their families to pursue affairs, and the "brave new sexual society of Dr. Kinsey" would decimate the traditional family. Yearning for a social geography in which women were wives and mothers within the home, rather than sexual subjects outside it, Hobbs and Kephart described the present as a nightmarish vision of sexual and gender chaos. "Who, but a short time ago," they asked, "would have dreamed that cigarette-smoking, bar-hopping, pants-wielding females would operate streetcars and taxis, weld steel, and serve in the armed forces?" Further associating anarchic female sexuality with the breakdown of the family, the authors proposed satirically that Kinsey's ideas would lead to young girls' being "'conditioned' toward erotic responsiveness and sexual dalliance instead of home-making, child-bearing and rearing, premarital chastity, and marital fidelity."[67] If current trends continued, such watchdogs warned, the influence of modern sex experts—a group into which they lumped scientific surveyors and mass media popularizers alike—would foment gender ambiguity and social chaos.

In such scenarios, women's emerging and potentially destructive sexual expectations and capacity stood partly as a proxy for their real and imagined demands in other areas of American life. The flip side of the kind of obeisance shown to "our wives, mothers and daughters" was the virulent misogyny often directed at middle-class women in sources like Philip Wylie's infamous *Generation of Vipers,* which portrayed "Mom" as a selfish, grasping automaton who survived by preying on hardworking males. As Wylie says scathingly of the American woman, it is "her man who worries about where to acquire the money while she worries only about how to spend it, so he has the ulcers and colitis and she has the guts of a bear."[68] At the same time, the discourse on modern American women's sense of sexual entitlement also mirrored social and cultural demands made *of* many postwar women—that they disaffiliate from their origins to create new nuclear families, leave behind ethnic and religious ties to the past, and trade old attitudes and behaviors for middle-class norms.[69] Unlike the first report, *Sexual Behavior in the Human Female* did not present its subjects' class as an important category. This reflected widespread assumptions that women's class position was less fixed than men's, since they took their class status from their fathers and husbands rather than from their work and expressed it more through cultural than economic markers.

One way in which experts bridged the distance between hypersexuality and frigidity and wedded the new emphasis on women's "natural" sexual needs with cultural norms was to couple satisfying sexuality with heterosexual pair bonding and monogamous marriage. According to the Barnard professor Charlotte Muret, the "permanence" of marriage was "very favorable, not to say necessary, to women in their sex relations." Women's "passions," Muret expounded, "are often slow in developing, but tenacious. Their emotional and affective life depends on stability for complete flowering, and temporary love relationships seldom bring happiness to women of the highest type, even if they are driven to accept them."[70] Marie Robinson also endorsed marriage as the sole site of real sexual pleasure for women, approvingly describing the normal woman as one whose sexuality depended upon that of her husband. Couples could experience sexual abandon together, but the normal wife, "despite her very pronounced wantonness with her husband[,] . . . has no promiscuous urges whatsoever."[71] These authors domesticated female desire and orgasm by embedding them within a long-term and socially sanctioned relationship, drawing a sharp distinction between healthy female desire legitimized by marriage and unhealthy desire, characterized by promiscuous and temporary social relations.

A few experts even added an evolutionary twist to this view. The psychotherapist Abraham Franzblau, whose 1954 book *The Road to Sexual Maturity* blended psychoanalytic wisdom with religious and philosophical advice, argued that modern women's ability to be sexual at all times was a recent development to which they were as yet unaccustomed. Unlike men, who were genetically programmed to seek sex, the "female being is historically a novice to pleasure" and therefore "cannot as yet succeed easily each time in striking the right note or achieving the perfect harmony."[72] Under these circumstances, women could only learn to enjoy sex within a secure and stable marriage. "The human female," Franzblau elaborated,

> is slow to arouse to the pitch of orgasm. It is as though the broad plateau of ecstasy can be reached only after climbing over the top of a high hill. In a happy marriage, the female lives up near the top and can reach the peak with ease. The constant renewal of love and devotion and the mutuality of the relationship keep her in a state of high sexual potential. The unhappy female has to make her way each time from the very bottom of the hill. It is too much of a climb, in most cases, and except with a rare partner, she does not make it.

The moral to be drawn from this evolutionary law could not be clearer: given the physical and psychic limits of women's sexual character, mon-

ogamous marriage was the best, if not only, site for female sexual fulfillment. For couples in long-term marriages, sex "is enjoyed more and
more as the years roll by, while those who are unhappily married or who
take sex as they find it under other forms of relationships are apt to grow
more and more uninterested and anesthetic with time."[73]

Female orgasm, these commentators warned, was difficult to attain and
available only to married women. Femininity was by no means divorced
from sexual pleasure—indeed, it depended upon it, as persistently frigid
women were labeled unwomanly—but sexual pleasure was firmly connected to marriage and, for many, to motherhood. As Marie Robinson put
it, orgasm served as "a reward equal to none," making "the constant giving
done by the woman seem not only worth while but highly desirable."[74] In
this view, sexual pleasure, even more than children or financial support,
provided women's reward for completing the developmental steps that led
to mature womanhood. Circumventing this process by engaging in sex
outside of marriage was thus not only immoral but flew in the face of
psychological, biological, and evolutionary laws.

Popular culture also reflected the fear that average American women
were enjoying a covert and illicit sex life. At the same time that *Sexual
Behavior in the Human Female* and the morals of the American woman
were being discussed in the popular press, the best-selling book *The Three
Faces of Eve* offered a parallel narrative of conflict between sexual respectability and excess.

Eve, a narrative version of a psychiatric case study penned by two psychiatrists, reenacted the increasingly familiar cultural struggle between an
active, sexual, single woman and a passive, faithful married one. The plot
twist in this case was that the two personalities, plus a third, were housed
within one body. This "fantastic true story of a young housewife who was
three women in one body" presented a demure American wife and an
inappropriately sexual single woman united together.[75] Eve White, the
presenting personality, is a quiet married woman, described as "demure"
and rather "colorless." Her husband characterizes her as "a patient[,] indus-
trious wife [and] a devoted mother" (15), and according to her psychiatrist
she is "almost unaware of passionately erotic impulses" (11). Her alternate
personality, Eve Black, in contrast is "reckless" and "provocative" (23). She
describes herself as single and childless, enjoys trysts with other men, and
castigates Eve White's husband for his sexual selfishness (31). The narrative deals with attempts to integrate the docile Eve White and the seductive Eve Black, types whose surnames echoed racialized assumptions about

sexual restraint and abandon. The text's contrast between opposing types of American womanhood parallels popular response to Kinsey's work. After all, one of the many cartoons to locate humor in the idea that all American women were alike—and sexually suspect—made its point merely by juxtaposing a thick volume labeled "Kinsey Report" with the caption "Judy O'Grady and the Colonel's Lady . . . !"[76] In its similarly graphic representation of the "innocent housewife" as being allied to her "unrecognized twin" (29–30), the popular book and film *The Three Faces of Eve* captured many of the same themes featured in the public's reception of *Sexual Behavior in the Human Female.* The figure of Eve, like commentary on the report, warns that a demure appearance may mask sexual excess and that no one can know the truth about women's sexual behavior.

Women's potential sexual behavior evoked a disquiet that emerged clearly in humor. Cartoons that referenced the reports often featured the scenario of a husband reading *Sexual Behavior in the Human Female* and then applying its conclusions to an actual woman, usually his wife (see figures 10, 11, and 12). In one, a woman implores her husband, who is reading the report, to "stop staring at me!" In another, a Kinsey-reading husband remarks to his wife, "Wouldn't you say[,] dear, his figures on infidelity are much too high?" The husband, his back to the door of their home, cannot see his curvaceous, negligee-clad wife engaged in a passionate embrace with the milkman. In perhaps the most dramatic rendition of this theme, another cartoon depicts a man who brings home a copy of the second report and reads it while darting uneasy glances at his wife, who knits placidly in an adjoining chair. Outraged by his reading, he crosses the room with the report in hand and strikes her across the face, leaving her with a black eye.[77] This scene, which finds comedy in the juxtaposition of statistical generalities with a particular domestic ménage, underlines the ways in which the statistical findings of the report were applied to average women and suggests the fears that underlay humorous takes on the report.

In fiction and fact alike, the exact relationship between "nice" women and other kinds was a source of deep anxiety. The sociologist Joseph Folsom raised alarm by suggesting that the boundary between wives and sex workers was blurring, since, as "the line between the prostitute and other sexually active women becomes less clear," observers noted "an increasing diffusion of non-marital intercourse through the female sex as a whole."[78] A 1953 manual for married couples initially struck a more soothing note when it counseled men that women who had been sexually active before marriage could still become faithful wives. The reverse, however, also held true. "There is no fixed law for determining the future morality of one's wife," the authors warned male readers, since the fact "that she is intact on her wedding night is no guarantee that she will not slip from her pedestal five years hence."[79] The price women paid for premarital "slips" could be high: in one postwar survey of marriage and family life, several wives complained that their sexual activity with the men they later married caused their husbands to denigrate their morals and to assume that they were likely to have affairs in later life.[80] This recurring fear of the adulterous woman was supported by the popular belief that women's sexuality was more secretive and hidden than men's, impenetrable even to experts—indeed, one of the hundreds of novelty items that referenced the reports was a notepad with each blank page headed "What Kinsey Knows about Women."[81] As the author of another sexual guide for men phrased it, "Every woman possesses a *dual* personality made up of her conscious or outer self, which is misleading, and her unconscious or inner self, which represents more than likely her *true* self."[82] Like "Eve," American women could appear to be sedate housewives while hiding lives of sexual excess. The split between what Kinsey referred to as Americans' "overt" beliefs and their "covert" acts was thus especially fraught in the case of married women.

A number of tensions—between different kinds of women, traditionalism and modernity, and sexual innocence and knowledge—were caught in a short story featured in *Good Housekeeping* in 1951. "Susan McViddy Finds Out What She's Missing," one of the realistic dramas that were a staple of women's magazine fiction, proclaimed its topical theme with the announcement, "We think we know one woman who isn't going to be bowled over when Dr. Kinsey's new report is issued."[83] The story opens when Susan McViddy, a young wife and mother, is "selected [as] a sexual guinea pig" and visited by an interviewer for a "cross-examination concerning the sex habits of the American woman." Shocked by the questions she is asked, and disturbed by her ignorance of the sexual techniques and behaviors detailed by her interviewer, Susan realizes that "sexually she was a babe in the woods" (40). Worried by her perceived sexual shortcomings, she turns to popular literature for advice, filling out a magazine questionnaire on marriage (modeled, perhaps, on those devised by Clifford Adams in *Good Housekeeping*'s chief competitor, the *Ladies' Home Journal*). Based on her score, the column advises her, "Your marriage is on the rocks sexually. Consult a psychiatrist, doctor, or marriage counselor immediately" (40). Panic-stricken,

"STOP STARING AT ME!"

Figures 10, 11, and 12. Male readers and the second report: cartoons from Charles Preston, ed., *A Cartoon Guide to the Kinsey Report,* 33, 112–13, 125. (From the *Wall Street Journal*—permission, Cartoon Features Syndicate and Charles Preston.)

"WOULDN'T YOU SAY DEAR, HIS FIGURES ON IN-FIDELITY ARE MUCH TOO HIGH?"

Susan reproaches herself for failing her husband and immediately makes the suggested appointment with a proper authority. When she informs her husband of her intention to "correct my inadequacy as a physical partner" and apologizes for his years of frustration, he is angry at her foolishness. Imploring his wife to "please stop falling for everything you read," he declares, "Your husband says if there's any physical inadequacy around here, he likes it fine!" (186). Scales falling from her eyes, Susan realizes that her marriage was always solid and that the new sexual norms she has encountered are foolish ones that threaten solid marriages. The story ends

1.

2.

3.

4.

5.

CAVALLI

6.

as, brimming with contentment, she returns to her interrupted task of vacuuming the chandelier.

"Susan McViddy Finds Out What She's Missing" offers an incisive critique of Kinsey's study and of the new sexual standards. Expert sexual advice is portrayed as irrelevant to average women like Susan (and the readers of *Good Housekeeping*), and surveys like Kinsey's, along with the industry of sexual and marital advice that was built upon them, are dismissed as incapable of capturing what truly matters about sex. Rather than contributing to personal happiness and adjustment, the gospel of female sexual fulfillment preached by experts threatens to tear a family apart. Cultural productions like "Susan McViddy" spoke to some women's discomfort with modern sexual advice and information, offering a critique of the postwar emphasis on female sexuality that blended conservative and liberal elements. Traditional values are reflected in the story's message that women's sexuality is rooted in the domestic and familial realm, as well as in its view of Susan as easily led by male authorities and in need of correction by her husband. Other elements of the story, however—especially its rejection of expert advice and critique of female sexual fulfillment as another burden placed on women—echo a more liberal, even potentially radical, view of female sexuality. Although readers of "Susan McViddy Finds Out What She's Missing" may have cheered the heroine's rejection of the cultural demand that women be sexually knowledgeable and responsive, ultimately the Kinsey Report and the sexual experts who offered interpretations of it had the final word, as *Good Housekeeping* followed other women's magazines in featuring the volume when it appeared three years later.

"THIS DOESN'T APPLY TO ME!": RACE AND THE AMERICAN WOMAN

The ways in which mainstream commentators who addressed a middle-class and predominantly white readership responded to *Sexual Behavior in the Human Female* are thrown into relief by comparison to the volume's reception among the African American press and, in particular, by black women. As with the first report, Kinsey's team had conducted interviews in African American and other minority communities, and his overall statistics included nonwhites, but the data was not broken down by race. This lack of racial categorization made it impossible for readers to segregate or assign Kinsey's findings by race. In fact, in their volume on women the Bloomington team went even further in their efforts to remove any suggestion of racial difference from their study. Unlike its predecessor, *Sexual Behavior in the Human Female* announced its subject as "*white* American women" and lacked index entries under "Negro" or "race." The few white reporters who addressed this issue usually repeated Kinsey's explanation that he did not yet have enough Negro or other nonwhite respondents to constitute adequate samples, but most simply ignored the question in their hurry to discuss the report's implications for average— that is, white—American women. Although a significant number of reviewers quibbled over the report's accuracy by arguing that Kinsey's study was too heavily biased toward urban women or midwestern ones or, as we have seen, those "of an easily recognized sort," none addressed in any depth one of the most obvious facts about the American woman depicted in its pages. The average American woman, in the Kinsey Report as in the popular media, was white.

Kinsey ostensibly merged white and nonwhite data in *Sexual Behavior in the Human Female* simply because his sample of African American women was not broad enough to be statistically valid.[84] Kinsey was sometimes disingenuous about his motives, however, and by the time the second volume was being readied for publication he was experienced in avoiding and shaping controversy in order to promote serious discussion, rather than permit dismissal, of his work. This suggests an alternate reading of why African Americans are absent from the reports.

African Americans and other racialized groups, as Toni Morrison points out, have often been viewed in the United States, and in Western thought in general, as a "surrogate and enabler" of the discussion of sex, the "marker . . . of illicit sexuality."[85] This was especially historically true for African American women. While black men were often seen in American racial mythology as either sexual predators or examples of impaired masculinity, African American women often represented lax morality and sexual availability, in relation to which respectable white femininity was constructed.[86] So strong were midcentury associations between black women and sexual license that, when the African American actress and singer Dorothy Dandridge headlined at the Los Angeles nightclub the Mocambo in 1953, publicity agents arranged for cigarette vendors to display copies of the second report. This marketing ploy counted on the public to overlook the fact that African American women were not included in its figures and instead to view Dandridge, and African American women in general, as sexually available to the consumer.[87]

I believe that Kinsey's choice to blend nonwhites into the general statistics of his report rather than list them as a separate category was spurred by a refusal of racial categorization that paralleled his denial of biological differences between hetero- and homosexuals. Downplaying race as a factor in shaping sexual behavior also fit his agenda of foregrounding class and other environmental differences as instrumental in shaping sexual behavior. Whatever his intentions, Kinsey's strategy regarding race and its representation interrupted or bypassed the prevalent white association of African Americans with sexual deviance and excess. It also made it impossible for commentators to dismiss his figures on the grounds that nonwhites inflated overall averages. Despite the researchers' repeated insistence that race had not proven to be a significant category, such assumptions about nonwhite women still surfaced: one journalist claimed erroneously but tellingly that "Negroes and women with prison histories are missing from the study since their sexual patterns vary so radically."[88] In general, though, the removal of nonwhite women made it difficult for such charges to be made. Statistics could not be simply ascribed to blacks and dismissed, and the report's findings had to be understood as based on the behavior of white women. Although the structure of *Sexual Behavior in the Human Female* made it difficult for hostile or suspicious reviewers to dwell on the lack of attention to African American women, one group of commentators, from the African American press, did speculate on the roles played by race in Kinsey's statistics.

Both the power of the "American woman" ideal and the strength of cultural associations between black women and sexual licentiousness were evident in the response of African American newspapers and journals to the volume's release. Although one analyst of Kinsey's work has dwelt critically on the implications of African Americans' exclusion from the report, at the time the African American press responded approvingly to both Kinsey's volume and his decisions regarding the representation of black women.[89] Five years before Kinsey's second report appeared, an African American interviewee who reported on her experience in *Ebony* framed her participation as a form of racial uplift, condemning the widespread phenomenon of "whites who take it for granted that Negroes are far more active sexually than their white brothers and sisters" and anticipating that the study would interrupt misguided assumptions about race-based differences in sexual behavior.[90]

When it was eventually published, experts who usually deplored the omission of minorities from social and scientific studies maintained that in this particular case, the exclusion of African American women was a blessing. The columnist Marjorie McKensie of the *Pittsburgh Courier* struck a typical note in her coverage of the volume. Although McKensie declared it to be "a shame that Negro women have been left out of the Kinsey report on women," her headline declared proudly that "the Negro woman still has her privacy and her mystery," and she gleefully noted of whites who were curious about African American sexuality that "the poor dears will have to go on looking."[91] When *Ebony* published four separate articles on the report in one issue, its coverage opened with the approving observation that, when the report appeared, "Negro women can swagger confidently past and say 'This doesn't apply to me!'"[92] Although *Ebony* questioned Kinsey's decision to use only white interviewers, the general tone that the magazine took toward the project's exclusion of African Americans was positive. The issue included a report on the wishes of "some Negro women" who hoped that "they would be left out of the new book," since "the average Negro woman does not want anyone probing into her personal sex habits."[93] *Ebony* also featured a sociologist's explanation that African American women were "afraid of being misquoted or misunderstood, afraid that erroneous judgments would be made about them," an eventuality that the report's ultimate organization prevented.[94] When the issue at hand was female sexuality, middle-class blacks' postwar call for inclusion was trumped by gendered respectability. Both the *Courier* and *Ebony* were relieved to be able to assign sexual transgression to white women, confirming that the report's focus on subjects who were all white and largely middle class interrupted the widespread cultural association of African Americans with sexual deviance and excess. This focus also pre-empted any dismissal of the report's averages on the grounds that non-whites might have inflated the figures for all. Ironically, the Kinsey team's exclusion of African American women reinforced the gravity of its conclusions: if white, largely middle-class wives and mothers were reporting greater sexual experimentation, then factors in the national culture, rather than poverty or female biology, had to be implicated.

The division of women into two classes, one pure and the other sexually available, had long been a central feature of American sexual cosmology. Whether it was structured by race or by respectability, though, such a split became increasingly untenable as American women's changing sexual desires and behaviors became headline news. As statistics on women's sexual behavior flooded the market, alongside advice literature and scientific and popular accounts of sex, it became increasingly difficult to avoid the suspicion that the average woman—white, middle-class, heterosexual, and married—was indeed engaging in the behaviors Kinsey had described.

AMERICAN WOMEN IN FACT AND FICTION:
REPRESENTING *THE AMERICAN MARRIED FEMALE*

A number of fiction writers found the plot device of the sex survey irresistible. In the standard narrative, the survey's subjects are female and investigators male, sex studies promote sexual and marital disarray, and the story inevitably ends with the creation or renewal of a central family unit. In Victor Menzies and Jean Bernard-Luc's *The Fig Leaf,* a British novel published the year after the second report was released, an American female professor visiting a French country house wreaks havoc by distributing copies of the reports and conducting her own survey. As she interrogates members of her host family, she continually compares their experiences to Kinsey's statistics and counsels them to change their sexual patterns in order to be more up-to-date. In the end, American sociology and modern sexual mores are trumped by the linkage of sex and love, as couples flee to haylofts to escape the scrutiny of science, and as the American sexologist herself is unfaithful, crushing her French husband.[95]

American novelist Joseph Hilton Smythe's *The Sex Probers* (1961) offered an even more disquieting portrait of the havoc wrought by sex surveys (see figure 13). When a mild-mannered sociologist agrees to analyze data from his small university town, his family is torn apart by the experience. His academic tenure is threatened when his participation becomes known; tearful women call him late at night to beg him to discard their interview data; he uncovers evidence of his teenage daughter's lesbian affair; and he conducts affairs with two neighboring women after reading their histories. Despite these dramatic events, Smythe insists on the importance of the sex survey as a social phenomenon and on its transformative potential. By the book's conclusion, which features a paean to the importance of sex education, the researcher's frigid wife agrees to revitalize their marriage and his teenage daughter, recovering from her doomed lesbian affair, shows a new interest in boys. Several other marriages are reborn due to the sexual complications that ensue when the researcher is given access to intimate details regarding women in his community: in one case, the sexologist teaches a timid local wife how to properly seduce her husband, ensuring marital bliss; in another, he converts a lesbian student to heterosexuality by introducing her to a strapping football player.

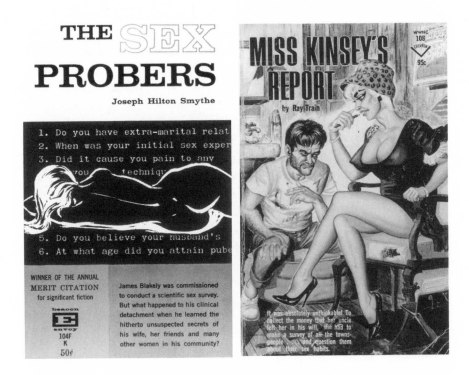

Figures 13 and 14. Fictionalizing the report. *Left:* Cover, Joseph Hilton Smythe, *The Sex Probers. Right:* Cover, Ray Train, *Miss Kinsey's Report.*

Somewhat farther down the scale, the pulp novel *Miss Kinsey's Report* features a buxom but sexually unawakened sociologist heroine who must conduct a sex survey in a small town in order to receive a legacy from a wealthy relative (see figure 14). "Miss Kinsey" experiences near-seduction by an older woman, experiments with aphrodisiacs in the company of swingers, and is raped not once but twice in the course of her interviewing duties. After detailing these and other sexual encounters, the novel closes with a proposal of marriage and the heroine's reflection that "there is only one, true sexual responsiveness in the world . . . the responsiveness that is inspired by true love alone."[96]

As these plot summaries suggest, the sex-survey theme allowed writers, publishers, and readers alike to enjoy sexually themed plots garbed in social significance. *The Sex Probers* claimed sociological significance by relating the themes of the text to larger social realities, promising that the book was "certain to be read and discussed by all who have wondered whether studies of sex cannot go too far."[97] As in most melodramatic genres, the sex survey allowed authors to depict a wide range of sexual behaviors, then repudiate them at the end. The sex survey also provided an excellent vehicle through which authors could meditate on gender relations, marriage, the public role of the expert, and changing American sexual character.

Seven years after the publication of *Sexual Behavior in the Human Female,* a number of issues that had dominated popular responses to the volume resurfaced in the novel *The Chapman Report,* by far the most popular of the fictional appropriations of Kinsey's work. In this 1960 best-seller by Irving Wallace, which was subsequently made into a popular film, a team of researchers working on a report titled *A Sex History of the American Married Female* visit an upper-class California suburb in search of interview subjects.[98] The novel and film follow a group of women (six in the novel, four in the film) as they reveal their sexual histories to researchers, a process that leads each woman to reminisce about her past, assess her present, and make decisions about her future. In classic trashy-novel style, the inquiries of the outside investigators provide the impetus for characters to interact sexually and otherwise, and for readers to observe and judge their actions. The central love story of Paul (one of Chapman's assistants) and Kathleen (a widow whom he interviews) takes place against a more sober plot in which the apparently benevolent sex researcher Dr. Chapman is exposed as venal, untrustworthy, and a bad scientist.

It is immediately evident that *The Chapman Report* is modeled upon Kinsey's project. The fictional Chapman and his team produce studies of American males, then females. Following the publication of his first survey, Wallace writes, the title character "became a household name, a bedroom name, a springboard for jokes and leers and learned commentaries." The "Chapman Report," as the press referred to *A Sex Study of the American Bachelor,* became an integral part of the American scene.[99]

Although Wallace asserted that his characters were fictional, reviewers could not help but note the similarities between Chapman and another famous sexologist, with one commenting that "the author's attempt to dis-associate his character from Kinsey offers the only genuine humor in the whole book."[100] *The Chapman Report* speaks in a language of sexual exper-tise familiar to readers from newspapers and magazines: Dr. Chapman and his assistants compare their own fictional statistical findings to Kinsey's and other studies, commenting on similarities and divergences. An oppos-ing scientist, Dr. Jonas, whose more spiritual approach to sex makes him a foil to Chapman's statistical focus, also quotes contemporary sexual authorities, and Wallace devotes a lengthy paragraph to listing the contents of Jonas's library on American sexuality (143–44).

Throughout the novel, Wallace identifies the genre of the sex survey and the topic of American sexual behavior in general as issues of immediacy and importance. The novel begins with an epigraph from Nelson Foote, a family expert who had criticized Kinsey's work, lamenting the modern separation of sex from love and marriage (i). In an introduction titled "To Many Women and a Few Men," Wallace further links his novel to the zeitgeist of the 1950s. Describing the sex researcher as "a phenomenon of our time," he identifies his work as being set in the present, "an age preoccupied with sex, with surveys, with confessions, with statistics" (viii). Early on, a central character predicts that some day in the future, Chapman's survey "would be a freak symbol of his decade and its obsessive concern with sex" (17), a stance that presumes a rational move away from the "obsessive" discussion of human sexuality in a more enlightened future.

Between romantic interludes, characters engage in extended debate about the nation's changing sexual norms, the state of contemporary gender relations and marriage, and the possible effects of sex surveys on American morality, debates that mirrored those of contemporary social commentators. Dr. Jonas, whose fears about the institution of the sex survey will ultimately be vindicated in the novel's finale, tells a representative of the Chapman team that he is concerned about "the permissive effect your data has, the sudden undermining of long-taught ideas about right and wrong." Jonas also questions the effects of the interview process on female volunteers. "You set off the chain reaction and then let the women go," he tells the hero, Paul, an assistant sex researcher, "and I sometimes wonder, Go where, to what? What are they like afterwards, what becomes of them?" (163).

The characters Chapman interviews fit into the broader social category of troubled and bored middle-class white women. Describing his idyllic suburban setting and the women who inhabit it in terms that evoke Betty Friedan's *The Feminine Mystique*, Wallace writes:

> The secret climate of The Briars, held as private as any Masonic rite, was, for most of its women, one of empty monotony, boredom, confusion. More often than not, the natives—as the parlor joke went—were restless. The malady was American and married female, but the women of The Briars chose to believe that it was exclusively their own. . . .
>
> Inarticulate for the most, they wanted more—but exactly what they wanted they could not explain, even to themselves. (12)

Collectively described as average upper-class American women, the women whose stories are told in *The Chapman Report* are presented as easily recognizable social types, each of whom featured in media responses to the second Kinsey Report. As identified by the back cover copy, they include "a nymphomaniac, an inhibited intellectual, a frigid wife, a father-dominated bride, an adulteress, and an aggressive career woman," a virtual rogue's gallery of popular types of middle-class white womanhood. Although reviewers criticized the woodenness of the characters and melo-drama of the plot, the majority read the array of women as reflections of existing types of "real" women. One critic paid the author a dubious compliment when he noted that "each of the women emerges as if in silhouette from the pages of any good true confessions magazine," casting the female characters as sleazy and simplistic but also as mirroring both reality and the problems posed by mass culture.[101] As occurred in the media coverage of *Sexual Behavior in the Human Female* seven years earlier, the women represented in Chapman's sex survey are depicted as ordinary women whom the reader might unknowingly encounter. "I don't think we're any different from women anywhere," the central female figure argues, a view supported by their statistical profile (18).

Dr. Jonas's fear that the interview process will set off a "chain reaction" of harmful effects is substantiated, as each female character faces a crisis after her participation in the sex survey. The "nymphomaniac" is gang raped, the "inhibited intellectual" has an unsatisfying affair, the "aggressive career woman" decides to trade sex for a promotion, and Kathleen, the "frigid wife" and heroine, learns to enjoy sex under the tutelage of Chapman's principled assistant, Paul. The women's participation in the sex survey fosters a growing consciousness of themselves as sexual beings, entitled to pleasure, and this consciousness brings about their fates. As in other Wallace novels, events progress rapidly and dramatically. One of Chapman's assistants, obsessed with a survey participant, stalks, rapes, and murders her; the shrewd Dr. Chapman manages to cover up the scandal; and the researcher Paul—the putative hero, along with the skeptical scien-tist Dr. Jonas—resigns in disillusionment. At the novel's close, Paul and Dr. Jonas set up a practice as marriage counselors, engaging in the business of piecing together relationships rather than destroying them through misguided sex research. Sexual knowledge, this ending proclaims, is dangerous when popularized. It belongs in the private setting of the coun-selor's office or clinic, not spread before the public in best-selling books, just as sex should be relegated to marriage, where most critics of Kinsey and Chapman alike believed that it belonged.

The novel concludes with its sexually troublesome female characters either banished, like the murdered adulteress, or reintegrated into happier, monogamous marriages. A new and therapeutic social order has triumphed in which both sexuality and science are kept in their place: proper sex is marital, emotionally fulfilling, and springs from love, while proper science is rigorous and avoids sensationalism. Both, used carelessly, promote selfishness, misery, and social decay.

Ultimately *The Chapman Report* criticizes both the sex survey and the centrality of sex to American culture, an ironic position for a novel marketed with the tag line "Would have been banned in Boston." The characters' drive to seek out sexual activity and disseminate sexual information is depicted as dangerous, and the novel warns against the public study of sex. As Kathleen, the central female protagonist, prepares for her interview with Dr. Chapman, she reflects that she "was not prepared to disclose her private secrets to a band of strangers, to disrobe figuratively before a group of leering male voyeurs." Contemplating refusal, however, Kathleen "instinctively realized any objection would not be understood and would make her sexually suspect" (16). Sex in the post-Kinsey United States has become overburdened with significance, Wallace argues. Representative women like Kathleen—and *Good Housekeeping*'s Susan McViddy—are powerless to refuse participation in sex surveys and to reject the corollary belief that such surveys offer models of sexual conduct. It is only after each has her eyes opened by a wise and authoritative male who blends the functions of expert and love object that she can criticize the commercialism and sensationalism that modern culture attaches to sexuality.

The fictional narrative of *The Chapman Report* gives free run to the darkest fantasies inspired by Kinsey's work and, more generally, by the postwar discourse on sex as a social problem. In a nation filled with adulterous and sexually voracious women, the novel suggests, social order will collapse, precipitating betrayal, violence, and even death, until sex can be restored to its proper place as the cement for monogamous marriages. Ironically, however, the conclusion of Wallace's novel could not completely endorse traditional morality, much as critiques of the Kinsey Report's ethos could not get around the nagging presence of its figures. In the novel's final vignette, which takes place nearly a year after its main events, several of the women characters gather together again. The previously frigid woman is now happily married and pregnant, and the former nymphomaniac has benefited from psychiatric treatment and reconciled with her husband. As the women mingle, conversation turns to Chapman's "recently published book, *A Sex History of the American Married Female*." The women whose varied sexual histories it contains are outraged by the book's conclusions about the extent of infidelity. In the novel's final paragraph, as the surviving female characters discuss the study, the most indignant is Teresa Harnish, the married "inhibited intellectual" whose affair with a football player many years her junior formed one of the book's subplots. Ursula Palmer, the text's "aggressive career woman" who narrowly avoided an affair after coming under Chapman's influence, reads from the study:

> "You'll find it in the appendix," Ursula was saying. "He states baldly that in communities like this, and he means ours, too, over twenty-nine per cent of married women up to thirty-two years old are having, or have had, extramarital relationships, and thirty-eight percent—mind you, thirty-eight per cent—have committed infidelity by the age of forty-five. Now, what do you think of that?"
>
> "I'll tell you what I think," said Teresa Harnish. "That dreadful book should be classified as fiction, not nonfiction, that's what I think."
>
> And almost everyone in the group solemnly agreed. (383)

In this grand finale, the community whose bed hopping has electrified readers for nearly four hundred pages unites to agree that the statistics of the Chapman Report are incorrect and dangerous. By giving the last word to the adulterous and hypocritical Teresa, however, Wallace suggests that women's denials of sexual misbehavior are hypocritical and false. Despite the novel's resolute condemnation of Chapman, the sex researcher's work remains popular, influential, and—damningly—true. In closing, Wallace offers a disquieting suggestion that the findings of the Chapman Report, like those of the Kinsey study upon which it was based, cannot be so easily dismissed.

CONCLUSION

If the average American women interviewed by Kinsey could break their marriage vows, then how secure could familial and national stability be? A few of the contemporary authors who commented on the battles over the report's reception noted the ideological bonds that joined women's sexual behavior to ideals of national character and predicted the possible effects of their rupture. The Canadian journalist Eleanor Rumming reflected on the furor caused by the report by linking it explicitly to the rigidity of American sexual and gender mores. "The North American attitude towards sex," she wrote, "is not a mature one."

> In particular, Americans are sensitive about the sexual character of their women. Motherhood and virginity, in many sections of the U.S.A., enjoy a prestige far beyond anything which may be reasonably attributed to their importance in society. In the ideal woman of the nation, as shown in popular magazine pictures, and in the idols of Hollywood, these two admired states of being are united; the breasts, symbols of motherhood, are heaved and padded into an extreme development; the loins, the seat of love, are so small as to suggest virginity and perhaps under-development. A nation which sees women in this image will not like to learn that women have much the same desires as men do.[102]

Advertising copywriter Elizabeth Kidd struck a similar note when she argued in the advertising trade publication *Printer's Ink* that the report challenged the myth of the "ideal" female. In showing the sexual range and variation of real women, she suggested, *Sexual Behavior in the Human Female* threatened to explode a cherished and widespread fantasy. According to Kidd, the American man "has made up an 'ideal woman'—a sort of Marilyn Monroeish phantom endowed with instant, utter response to him—and introduced her liberally into his literary works, his books and plays, where his wife can see her and make comparisons." This false "ideal woman of the nation," like Rumming's, embodied faithfulness and full sexual response, while real women, by contrast, displayed a wide range of sexual behaviors. The report, Kidd believed, would go far to convince men of the falsity of their cherished image, since "the 2 or 3% of women Dr. Kinsey found who live up to those ideal specifications" were few and far between.[103]

The cultural historian Mary Poovey has argued that mid-Victorian-era society reserved its most vehement opposition for what she terms "border cases," issues or individuals that "threatened to relocate difference" by finding it lurking in unexpected places. Especially fraught, according to Poovey, are revelations of difference that "uncover it *in woman,* the very subject upon whose self-consistency the ideology rested." Such troubling discoveries "had the potential to challenge the social arrangement of separate spheres and everything that went with it."[104] In the postwar

United States, the discovery of women's sexual subjectivity outside the bounds of marriage was such a case. The average woman, whether represented directly as one of the 5,940 subjects of the Kinsey Report or more broadly as an actual or potential consumer of the volume, was at once the standard by which American womanhood was measured and the border case that threatened to expose the impossibility of that standard. Cultural and sexual expectations of women had altered since the nineteenth century, as postwar authors' mingled disdain and nostalgia for the vanished Victorian family suggests, but popular ideologies of gender and sexuality still maintained that women were essentially different from men. Following the conceptual split between "bad" and "good" women, American women were expected to exercise their sexuality only within carefully demarcated boundaries. The report stated that the average American woman was far more complex than the ideal.

For those who accepted its findings, the report shattered the public fiction of middle-class white women's sexual fidelity within marriage and chastity outside it. The publication and ensuing national discussion of *Sexual Behavior in the Human Female* was a moment in which the gap between what Kinsey called the "covert" and the "overt" of female sexuality— and, beyond that, of American women's prescribed roles—was presented so graphically that women could neither be universalized or separated into two opposing groups.[105] The adulterous wife of fiction and cartoons, like her counterpart in the pages of social science and medical journals, blurred cherished distinctions. Rigid separation between good and bad women could no longer be sustained in the face of changing sexual mores. And although some commentators used the idealized figure of the American woman to oppose the findings of the report, their attempts to attribute aberrant sexuality to only a minority of women were never completely successful.

The long-term effects of *Sexual Behavior in the Human Female* and related literature were as complex and paradoxical as their reception. The report not only offered a site in which conflicting beliefs about female sexuality were articulated, but also shaped cultural expectations of women, as did the torrent of sexual advice directed at women during the postwar era. New norms made it difficult for women to define sexual pleasure in ways that ran counter to the new discourse or to avoid sex by claiming frigidity or disinterest.[106] Despite claims that they would expand sexual possibilities for women, these norms instead often replaced one narrow range of appropriate responses with another. Women's magazines like

Good Housekeeping and the *Ladies' Home Journal* exemplified this complex stance. Such sources often rejected works like Kinsey's and critiqued the new cult of expert sexual advice, condemning the widespread popular discussion of sex and emphasizing a more traditional model of female heterosexuality that connected women's fulfillment to traditional marriage. They also, however, featured articles that promoted Kinsey's work as relevant to the average woman, encouraged readers to "rate" themselves against norms determined by sex experts and to seek advice from them, and, within limits, urged sexual knowledge and experimentation. In the process of promoting sexuality as the core and site of expression for the authentic self, they raised expectations for marriage.

FOUR

"I'm a Much Better Citizen Than If I Were Single"

Remaking Postwar Marriage and Reconfiguring Marital Sexuality

Society is interested in the nature of marital intercourse because it is interested in the maintenance of the family.

KINSEY, POMEROY, AND MARTIN
Sexual Behavior in the Human Male

POSTWAR AMERICANS SIMULTANEOUSLY EMBRACED MARRIAGE as the cornerstone of personal fulfillment and believed it to be in crisis. They endorsed the institution in unprecedented numbers, as the vast majority of the population chose wedlock over single life and marriage became increasingly central to national ideology. Simultaneously, however, experts also critiqued marriage, diagnosing a host of contemporary problems and speculating about its future. Kinsey's studies reported that less than half of Americans' sexual activity took place between spouses, and observers lamented the prevalence and devastating effects of premarital sex, infidelity, divorce, and other ills. In 1953, a philosopher tracing the past and contemporary states of marriage noted that "the divorce rate in the United States is three out of every five marriages—and still going up. It is obvious that there must be something seriously wrong with the institution of marriage—or with our interpretation of it—to cause so many divorces."[1] The same year, the historian Sidney Ditzion captured the opinion of many other social scientists when he observed that the "good old family, called 'domestic' by those who prefer it to its newer forms, is certainly disappearing; and there are few who look forward to its return."[2]

These authors' observations that patterns of marriage and family organization had changed drastically were not unusual, and their hopes and fears for the future of American marriage were shared by many other contemporary experts. Scientists, psychologists, sociologists, and demographers declared that marriage was imperiled, as did the proliferating class of experts who taught high school and college courses in marriage, published in professional journals, and offered advice through the mass media.[3] Their offerings were eagerly studied by a generation of Americans newly attuned to both psychological theories and sexological evidence, who applied them to their own marriages.[4] The American marriage, experts stated, was threatened as never before, and the proliferation of theories about and findings on the nation's marriages bespoke great concern for the institution's changing form and uncertain future. At its best, Americans' sexual character was expressed through solid and happy marriages. At its worst, it produced unstable unions or, worse, threatened the very institution of marriage.

To postwar observers, the marital relationship meant many things. At a moment of intense pronatalism, it was the necessary setting for the birth and rearing of legitimate children.[5] Universally understood as an intensely private realm based on an emotional bond between unique individuals, it promised personal happiness and fulfillment. At the same time, it united individuals in something larger than themselves, cementing their ties to community and nation. It was, in addition, the central, and to some the only proper, setting for sexual expression. Caught "between promiscuity and repression," as one author described them, single men and women faced a terrible dilemma: should they restrain their impulses or engage in illicit sex outside of marriage?[6] Either choice might well doom them to "crippled personalities." Calculating the right time to marry and the right choice of partner, along with navigating decisions about premarital sex, was crucial to mental health. "Psychiatrists' offices," one representative of the profession warned, "teem with men and women suffering from guilt complexes because they indulged in premarital sex relations, and with equal numbers who are frigid or impotent because they were too long repressed and frustrated."[7]

Only marriage could safeguard American couples against these dire fates by offering a safe and sanctioned site for their sexual urges. The marital contract allowed partners exclusive sexual access to one another and barred sexual contacts with any outside their original bond. Since heterosexual expression lay at the heart of most Americans' notions of marriage, the dramatic transformations in sexual behavior and morals outlined by social scientists and cultural critics after World War II held important implications for marriage. Such trends as the increased sexual autonomy of women, the expansion of marital sex beyond coitus, and the rising reliance upon information provided by experts were all factors in the changing landscape of marriage. "The family," a 1947 sociology textbook noted, "is becoming more an erotic relationship." Elaine Tyler May describes the model postwar family as one in which "ideas of happiness, patriotism and reproduction" combined with "an unprecedented focus on sexuality" to produce the cultural ideals of the "eroticized marriage and the sexualized home."[8] Even as it promised unprecedented sexual pleasure and personal happiness within marriage, though, this eroticization raised troubling implications. Could the "oversexualization" some critics saw afflicting American culture be properly integrated into existing models of marriage, or should marriage provide a bulwark against improper sexuality? Did the new focus on and public discussion of alternative sexual behaviors threaten marriage or offer new ways to revitalize it? What role, exactly, should sex play in marital adjustment?

In addition to its reproductive, emotional, and sexual aspects, marriage was also widely understood as a civic relationship that could either undermine or shore up the nation's stability in times of anxiety. A former GI interviewed by *Better Homes and Gardens* magazine in 1947 expressed a popular belief in simple terms: "Being a married man—with one child already and another on the way—I'm sure I'm a much better citizen than if I were single."[9] Virtually all experts agreed with his equation of marriage and civic responsibility. The state of American unions, they believed, offered an index to the nation's success in living up to its ideals. As members of a miniature democracy within a much larger one, married couples in the United States were understood simultaneously as insistently private units outside of state control and as legal entities whose health and morals were the proper topic of social debate.[10] As postwar opinion makers both celebrated and scrutinized the American family, its role as a unit in the fabric of nationalism was inextricable from the intimate bonds that held it together.

It is the relationship between these two understandings of marriage—as a personal sexual relationship and as a public civic one—that this chapter addresses. In the years after the war, as authorities drew the public's attention to Americans' ignorance about sex, to often-unruly sexual behavior, and to the dangers that these posed for the nation, marriage emerged both as the site of new problems for the nation and as their solution. Modern

Americans' sexual character threatened nothing less than "the social fabric of our civilization . . . [and our] national welfare," the physician and sexual advice author Frank Caprio declared, since "it was the quality of the relationship between husband and wife that determines the security of the family, the group, the country." If Americans were properly educated about sex, Caprio believed, they would naturally create healthy and productive marriages, produce children, and assist in reproducing the modern state.[11]

Sex played a critical role in assessments of and remedies for American marriage. As postwar experts struggled over the role of sex in marriage, they created new ideals that would dramatically alter the meaning of marriage, often in ways they had not intended.

THE "MARRIAGE CRISIS": MARITAL STABILITY IN WAR AND PEACE

Not least among the disruptions caused by World War II was its effect on American marriages. Experts painted an alarming picture of the war's influence: some singles contracted hasty, ill-advised marriages, whereas others indulged in premarital sexual contacts while in the military or at war jobs. Enforced separations resulted in extramarital affairs as husbands and wives encountered new social situations and cultural norms. Geographical dislocation, separation, and economic forces also encouraged many to delay childbearing, further straining traditional marital bonds. Married and single people alike, one commentator noted with disapproval, often reacted to the upheaval of war by displaying "hedonistic life adjustments in sex relationships."[12] Not surprisingly, concerns around marriage, nonmarital sex, and their social consequences would continue to resonate throughout the postwar years.

In the immediate wake of the war, marital and familial relationships took center stage as a topic of national concern. The American GI who had married a foreign national while abroad, the war worker parted from her fiancé, and the teenage "victory girl" spurred by patriotism or profit to consort with soldiers were all commonly invoked in postwar discussions. Several of these scenarios were featured in the popular 1946 film *The Best Years of Our Lives,* in which three demobilized soldiers returning to their midwestern homes are faced with problems in adjusting to interrupted relationships with girlfriends and wives.[13] Rejuvenating established marriages and creating new ones took on paramount importance in the nationwide effort to return to peacetime routine, and the fate of individual marriages was seen as inextricable from the nation's social and economic future.[14] "In a world of chaos," one sex manual proclaimed, "there remains only the solid structure of the home."[15]

Gloomy predictions of postwar familial chaos proliferated. The psychiatrist William Menninger believed that peace would challenge Americans' mental health and family stability. "What did the war do to the home?" he asked rhetorically. It created "a crisis," in which "one out of three American marriages ends in divorce": "we must all admit that family life as we have known it is being changed."[16] "Marriage," a psychologist concurred in 1945, "is headed for some of the bumpiest weather in its age-old existence."[17] The "wholesome family" anchored by "a permanent pair of parents" was widely believed to be "seriously threatened," a 1947 *Life* editorial warned readers.[18] The same year, a college sociology textbook not only affirmed that wartime marriages were troubled but also gloomily predicted that "many marriages entered into *after* the war will also be unstable."[19]

Experts from all fields urged marriage: single women were warned of a "male shortage" and deluged with advice on how to find and hold a man, recent brides were advised to cater to their returning husbands, and pundits worried about the strength of hasty wartime unions.[20] One professor of education lectured, "If the family fails, it might well be impossible for industry and the government to succeed."[21] The links drawn between individual marriages and the condition of the nation were far from subtle: "You married him," one magazine writer exhorted her female audience, "now stick with him" for the sake of "this wonderful country of ours."[22] A number of authorities encouraged early marriage and urged the state to fund matrimony for those who could not afford to marry without aid.[23] Such a program, one argued, would contribute to the "serious business of saving young people from frustration, of preserving the American home, [and] of stemming the tidal waves of promiscuity, delinquency and divorce." Early marriage was also supported because it was seen as reflecting traditional American practices. "In the America which conquered a wilderness," the same author observed pointedly, "it was unthinkable that a young couple should marry without being given a few acres of land . . . or the old house by the meadow." Modern parents could do no less, and many recommended that they finance their married children's education and housing.[24]

Although their intent was to promote traditional morality, those experts who enthusiastically promoted early marriage inadvertently fueled the very sexual liberalism they opposed. By insisting on the right of teenagers and young adults to marry and enjoy a sexual life, they endorsed the idea that sex was a personal right, necessary to a full life. Healthy American men and women, as a New York senator who urged early marriage explained in 1948, were "biologically mature" by their teens but, due to taboos against teen marriage and against premarital sex, were "still leading the lives of children at twenty."[25] Urging parents and the state to accept this sexual maturation and aid young Americans in legitimately gratifying their sexual needs ultimately authorized youthful sex.

The nation's marriage rate and birthrate did not support the gloom of immediate postwar predictions for long. Despite fears of a postwar decline in the marriage rate, Americans married in record numbers at an early age. Trends over the preceding century had included an increase in the age of both sexes at marriage; fewer children, which were born later in life due to deliberate spacing; and growing public acceptance of legal separation or dissolution as possible ends to an unhappy union.[26] During the 1950s, these trends reversed themselves for the first and only time since industrialization. By late in the decade, the median age of marriage had dropped to a twentieth-century low of 20.1 for women and 22.3 for men, with nearly half of all brides married before their nineteenth birthdays. Retreating rapidly from its postwar peak of nearly eighteen per thousand, the divorce rate hovered at around ten per thousand until the mid-1960s.[27]

Statistical trends told only part of the story, because they reflected a marital imperative evident at all levels of the popular culture. The historian Wendy Kline has argued that positive eugenics—encouragement of marriage, childbearing, and dedication to family by middle-class white Americans, especially women—helped to shape postwar demographic shifts.[28] A leading marriage and family expert held that, with the possible exception of "the sick, the badly crippled, the deformed, the emotionally warped and the mentally defective, almost everyone has an opportunity to marry," and opportunity was routinely translated into expectation.[29] American psychoanalysis promoted marriage as the key to mental health, directing a campaign to "resanctify the heterosexual family, investing domesticity with deep personal, ethical, and sexual meanings previously attached to extrafamilial forms of personal life."[30] This celebration of marriage trickled down to the less elite opinion-makers—a popular science monthly noted sternly that the reasons single Americans offered for their state were groundless rationalizations, indicative of deep-rooted psychoneuroses and phobias.[31] The equation between singleness and emotional imbalance was a common one, and an individual's unmarried status was often cited as both cause and reflection of larger personal problems.

"Studies show," an article announced portentously, that "bachelors and spinsters [are] more likely to be neurotic than married people."[32] One influential study recommended compulsory state-funded psychotherapy for any Americans who reached the age of thirty without having exchanged wedding vows.[33]

As such programs suggest, rhetorical constructions of the state played an integral role in postwar debates over marriage. In the past, authorities believed, community standards had regulated the selection of partners and the conduct and endurance of marriages. In the present, however, such safeguards had collapsed. As Americans moved from rural areas to cities and the burgeoning suburbs, family and community surveillance of their marriages lessened. Direct state control over marriage had likewise diminished as divorce became easier to obtain and the state's role in punishing violations of marital vows was declining.[34] Authorities who correlated the nation's strength with that of its families strove to instill in their audience the determination to create solid marriages by blending older notions of duty with the emergent ethos of individual pleasure, all presented in the language of the social-scientific expert. They also moved to psychologize forms of deviance that might interfere with long-term national interests.

Postwar opinion on interracial and intercultural marriage offers a case in point: authorities who addressed so-called mixed marriages carefully endorsed racial, religious, and ethnic tolerance but advised that such unions were generally not prudent. Authorities approved of marriages between second-generation white ethnics from different backgrounds, and they advised that cross-class marriages could be successful, but they claimed that the desire to flout racial and religious taboos was evidence of neurosis in one or both potential spouses. According to one authority, "Willingness to suffer severe penalties in order to marry a particular person raises serious questions about the emotional normality of the individuals involved," and it was "highly doubtful that a person willing to go to such extremes is emotionally sound enough to marry anyone."[35] Another authority held that interracial marriage was usually an example of "blemish mating," in which one partner, usually a white female, has "a serious blemish which would ordinarily rule her out as a marital partner for most people."[36]

A number of commentators noted the strength of the cultural imperative to marry. David Riesman observed in 1949 that young women "today feel under almost as great a pressure to get married as did their pre-emancipation ancestors. In a certain way, they are under greater pressure, since all sorts of psychological aspersions are cast at them if they stay single too long." Men, too, felt an obligation to marry—in order to avoid being thought homosexual, among other reasons.[37] As a physician and a psychologist observed in their 1956 book of advice on common problems for the lay reader, the unmarried were commonly seen as "derelict in their duties to society." In the current social climate, the authors elaborated, "marriage is regarded popularly as a cure-all for neurotic symptoms, for intellectuality in women, for excessive preoccupation with work or a career in men, and even for some physical ailments," a view they found troubling.[38] Such reservations were rare, however, and the vast majority of observers enthusiastically endorsed the marriage boom. By the early 1950s, critics who had warned of a postwar marriage dearth were praising American couples for their marriage mindedness, their fecundity, and the economic prosperity they fueled through their rising consumption of housing and goods.

However, even in the face of the marriage and baby boom and a divorce rate that stabilized at half its earlier height, the concerned tone of earlier writings on the state of marriage and the family lingered, reflecting an "unparalleled ambiguity and anxiety about family life."[39] In the words of one concerned journalist, the nation was in fact witnessing nothing less than "the crack-up of the twentieth century marriage."[40] "As far as our national welfare goes," one physician admonished married couples, "merely increasing our population by bringing babies into the world is not enough. It is the quality of the relationship between husband and wife that determines the security of the family, the group, the country."[41] If marriage fostered a solid citizenry, then threats to it spelled disaster for the nation's economy, personal happiness, and social stability. Experts worried that modern Americans were becoming weak and selfish, too focused on the pursuit of individual pleasure to make a success of marriage. In the face of a sexual revolution, was marriage becoming obsolete? Or were Americans merely experiencing a shift in its meaning and functions? One writer summed up the stakes in a 1946 essay in *Harper's:* "If the failure of marriage is an indication of an unhealthy and degenerating culture, then that's us. If it isn't, we are causing ourselves and our children a great deal of frustration, bewilderment, and personal tragedy by outlining one set of rules, and then encouraging them to play the game some other way."[42]

As experts' rhetoric suggests, many believed that the failure of American marriages mirrored a more general national decline. Implicit in their warnings about the prevalence and effects of divorce were fears that the

United States compared poorly to other nations. Marital collapse, observers noted again and again, was "a peculiarly American problem," far more common than in other countries.[43] Shortly after the end of the war, Margaret Mead argued that "the most serious thing that is happening in the United States, the most significantly important, is that people enter marriage now with the idea that it is terminable."[44] "Divorce," another article began forthrightly, "has become an American bad habit."[45]

Why was American marriage alone seen as so threatened and likely to fail? Immediate postwar concerns about marriage made a certain amount of sense—no one could know that a baby boom was soon to occur, and worries about recession and declining population were widespread after World War II. What calls for more explanation is why worried commentary on marriage persisted, and even grew, during what was in many ways marriage's heyday in the modern United States. As authorities offered diagnoses of and correctives to the "marriage crisis," they connected the blame for marital failure to perceived flaws in the national character. Americans were heeding the call to marry, to be sure, but observers diagnosed their motives as immature and selfish and decreed that many marriages were unlikely to be either harmonious or lasting. Postwar citizens, many suggested, lacked the commitment of earlier generations and instead viewed the institution as temporary. The nation, one *Reader's Digest* contributor worried in 1952, was exhibiting an "increasing disregard for the dignity of marriage, especially notable in the casual attitude of the oncoming generation."[46] The authors of a sex manual published the following year noted sorrowfully that the "decline" of marriage in the United States "is an acknowledged fact, a constant reproach to our society and way of living."[47]

As Americans' sexual character was denigrated, and as increasing selfishness and individualism were blamed for contributing to the failure of marriage and of community life, more and more commentators called on the state to oversee and support damaged unions. Marriage educators routinely incorporated existing or proposed governmental agencies into their plans for the revitalization of the nation's marriages, underlining the natural link they saw between private and civic life. Some observers urged changes in the legal system or in federal welfare policies as a way of safeguarding marriage. John Sbarbaro, a Chicago judge, was so alarmed by marital failure that he proposed that the federal government fund and administrate compulsory courses in marriage, as well as adopt laws that forbade hasty marriage and made separations far more difficult to obtain. "The state," the jurist argued, "has a deep interest in each marriage from its beginning, for in successful marriage is to be found the very basis of the welfare of the nation. Actually, the affairs of two people who plan to wed—or divorce—cannot be solely their own concern. The manner in which they manage their marriage must also be the concern of the state."[48]

Social and behavioral scientists from liberal Ashley Montagu to conservative Marynia Farnham and Ferdinand Lundberg were sufficiently concerned about the fate of the American family unit that they proposed federal programs designed to assist family life. The aims and mechanics of such programs varied drastically: Montagu's called for both parents to work a four-hour day so they could share child care, while Farnham's promoted new federal laws curtailing female employment and imposing punitive taxes on bachelors.[49] Another commentator, writing in *Christian Century*, instead proposed legislation limiting the number of marriages that any one individual could contract.[50] What is significant about this trend is that so many authors, writing from very different political and cultural perspectives, saw the promotion of family life as a legitimate use of government resources. Although these suggestions were never taken up seriously, many experts shared the concern they exhibit for the potential effects of marital unhappiness on the nation's interests.

Journalists and social scientists offered comparative statistics proving that divorce and its ills were a uniquely American phenomena, not simply a reflection of international chaos or modernization. One guide that drew typically unsettling comparisons between America and other nations reported that "the United States, with 381,000 reported divorces, exceeded by 231,000 the total number granted in Canada, England, Wales, France, West Germany, Yugoslavia, Switzerland, and Japan."[51] Another authority lamented that the nation's divorce rate was seven times that of neighboring Canada and more than twice that of Sweden, reputedly the home of modernity and sexual laxity.[52] Such comparisons inevitably worked to the detriment of the United States. "As a nation," one magazine writer commented sardonically, "we are a blue-ribbon winner: the United States leads all Europe and the Americas in divorce rate."[53]

The authorities who predicted mass marital collapse were incorrect: although the divorce rate spiked in the years immediately after World War II, it did not spiral out of control during the 1950s but returned to a figure close to prewar rates and remained there.[54] Authorities' vast overestimation of the incidence of divorce was not merely a case of incorrect forecasting, however; their continuing concern about the rate of divorce, along with their alarmed insistence that marital failure was a pressing national problem, points to the strength of the anxieties about social change and American character that lay underneath the surface celebration of marriage and domesticity. To distressed observers, the frequency of divorce stood as an indicator of comprehensive changes affecting American marriages and expressed something crucial about the American character. Divorce was no longer limited to the wealthy or the dissolute but had reached the middle class. Respectable citizens, observers worried, were accepting legal dissolution "not as a symbol of defeat and the death of a marriage, but as a way to solve problems and win a new life."[55] When the virginal ingenue of *The Best Years of Our Lives* fell in love with an unhappily married man and proclaimed to her shocked parents, "I'm going to break up that marriage!" audiences cheered.[56] Like other postwar developments, the apparent acceptance of divorce was a national fault that mirrored broader problems in the American character. The admission that unhappy marriages could be dissolved instead of fixed was another example of the pervasive national "softness" and self-indulgence that worried a host of cultural critics.

Increasingly often, the specter of unhappy and unfulfilling marriage provoked as much concern as did divorce. One of the authorities who noted the high American divorce rate did not let matters rest there but fretted that, when these already appalling numbers were swelled by the 25 to 40 percent of Americans whose marriages were intact but unhappy, "the proportion of family discord is amazing."[57] "Unhappiness in marriage is a great national problem," a college administrator and theologian similarly observed in the *Christian Century,* since "studies show that as many as one-third of marriages may be unhappy though still intact."[58] The psychiatrist Kenneth Appel wrote about his appalled "discovery of the extent to which marital maladjustment appeared in patients, masquerading or expressing itself unconsciously in unhappiness, vocational ineffectiveness, alcoholism, psychosomatic symptoms, nervous illness, mental disease, and even suicide."[59] Divorce was only the tip of an iceberg of unhappy, though technically intact, marriages. Faced with widespread projections of such an epidemic of marital disarray, experts searched for explanations and solutions. In the process, they documented profound shifts in the contemporary meaning of marriage and the requirements and demands of those who entered into it.

Postwar domestic prosperity both enabled and threatened marriage, as the same rising incomes that allowed for early marriage, an increasing birthrate, and all the accoutrements of middle-class family life could also support divorce, single life, and sexual hedonism. Leisure and affluence brought many benefits, but prosperity could also enable more to dodge family responsibilities, whether through engaging in leisure outside the family unit or leaving unsatisfactory marriages rather than remaining for economic reasons. The day-to-day stresses of modern-day affluence threatened to utterly alter marriage and perhaps even make it obsolete. "Our wealthy, mobile society" one study suggested, "is as rough on marriage as it is on individuals," and the marriage and family educator Paul Landis noted the emergence of the "individualistic marriage [that] clearly places pleasure above responsibility and duty."[60] Distressed by their findings, experts repeatedly emphasized that marriage was not solely a private relationship but involved broader civic issues. The Christian educator Sylvanus Duvall, for example, stressed to readers, "Your family does not exist in a social vacuum. It is part of a community, of a social and economic system."[61] Postwar Americans' dedication to individual pleasure over collective stability suggested that their commitment to marriage was dwindling, with dire social consequences in store.

Commentators on marriage elaborated a number of theories about the nation's apparent epidemic of collapsing and threatened marriages. Updating earlier suggestions that marital dissolution was caused by the temporary upheavals of the war, some observers attributed the continuing failure of American marriages to a general sense of social crisis during the 1950s. The prominent sexologist Frank Caprio echoed prevalent concerns when he suggested that cold-war fears could lead to a decline in marital fidelity, especially among husbands. "During every cataclysmic period in history," he observed, "there is a new excuse to toss out the rules. . . . The times are reckless, the future dim. Perhaps there won't even be any, in this atomic age, so why waste energy preparing for it? Why deny yourself anything in the present?" Such nihilism about the nation's future might seem attractive, but it promised disaster. "Many a husband acting on this philosophy," Caprio concluded soberly, "has spoiled his own marriage, dissipated his children's chance for a normal life, and damaged the lives of the women he seduces."[62]

Others suggested that young couples were simply ignorant of the demands of marriage. Formerly embedded in a matrix of extended family and community from a similar ethnic and class background, the typical young married couple was now likely to be geographically and socially mobile.[63] As nuclear families grew more isolated, psychological experts and the mass media moved to take over the roles once presumably filled by extended families and community norms, and commercial advice about marriage proliferated. Indeed, representatives from the burgeoning world of popular psychological advice constantly asserted Americans' alleged need for information and assistance in their personal lives.

Marriage education manuals had been popular in the United States at least since the turn of the twentieth century, and public interest in psychological information grew after Americanized versions of Freudian psychoanalysis became fashionable in the 1920s. During the postwar years, however, psychologically oriented advice reached a mass audience as affordable texts on the topic appeared and popular magazines featured advice columns. Coverage of marriage and sex was crucial to this growing cultural industry, with narratives of relationships gone wrong often focusing on couples' sexual problems and incompatibilities. In 1948 the popular women's magazine the *Ladies' Home Journal* began to feature a regular column called "Making Marriage Work." Penned by the psychology professor Clifford Adams, who also authored several volumes on sex, columns included quizzes designed to reveal incipient marital problems. Adams's quizzes, which included "Are You Enhancing Your Appeal?" "What Factors Favor Good Sexual Adjustment and a Happy Marriage?" and "Ask Yourself: Am I a Successful Working Wife?" worked to popularize the ideas of academic marriage experts.[64]

The *Journal* expanded its pedagogic function a few years later to include another regular feature on improving marriage. Based on case studies, the popular column "Can This Marriage Be Saved?" featured a husband's and wife's separate accounts of their marital problems and offered advice designed to resolve them, "saving" their marriage from collapse. Such productions presumed that American men and women lacked the knowledge needed to make their marriages successful but could learn—with exposure to psychological expertise—how to attain marital success. Abraham Stone noted approvingly in 1954 that marriage counseling "is today emerging as a new social science and social art" as "young people come to the counselor for information and guidance before marriage; and they come after marriage when difficulties arise in their marital adjustment."[65] Rooted in marriage-education literature, this new material was distinguished by its close attention to the role of sex and by its omnipresence—as the fictional Susan McViddy's experience suggests, women were inundated with advice literature on sex.

Some observers thought that too much expert advice could be worse than none at all and argued that the new marital imperative, with its insistence on the centrality of personal fulfillment and happiness, had a detrimental effect on marital stability. Rather than lauding marriage experts for improving the institution, they blamed them for raising unrealistic expectations. The American wife, one marriage counselor declared, "today is told so many things that she often doesn't know what to believe." The advice "hurled at her from every side" inevitably set up confusion about the purpose and day-to-day conduct of marriage, and the same held true for her husband.[66] Nearly all agreed that marital expectations had risen dramatically. As another marriage expert phrased it, "Today we demand of our husbands or wives all the affection and companionship formerly supplied by relatives and neighbors."[67] One contributor to the journal *Marriage and Family Living* argued in 1955 that the models of marriage found in educational curricula featured such a strong "stress [on] happiness" that they "ran the risk of overselling marriage; i.e., students will expect to find things in marriage which are not actually there." Rejecting the modern focus on personal fulfillment and "togetherness," this author recommended a return to earlier definitions of marriage. "Strong marriages are the wheels of society," he argued, and in a properly run society, "the individual marries as a social responsibility and not solely as a happiness-gaining measure."[68]

As authorities' emphasis on marital happiness and companionship suggests, sex often lay at the center of this discourse. Among Kinsey's most shocking findings was his statement that "only 45.9 per cent of the total outlet of the total population is derived from marital intercourse," which helped to convince readers that nonmarital sex was seducing Americans away from (re)productive marriage.[69] Proliferating evidence that both men and women were increasingly likely to seek sexual fulfillment outside the bounds of marriage raised the possibility that marriage would be scorned altogether, and the appearance of an occasional article endorsing adult singleness exacerbated these fears. As a bachelor alarmingly summed it up in the pages of *Esquire* magazine, "A man's drive for marriage begins to slacken as the benefits he can expect from it decrease in value."[70] With domestic comforts, companionship, and sex available elsewhere, why marry?

Extracurricular sex during marriage was also presented as a cause of the marital crisis and a symptom of broader problems that plagued American marriage. After publication of the first report, experts cited Kinsey's estimate that "about half of all the married males have intercourse with women other than their wives, at some time while they are married."[71] Experts further noted that much of this adultery took place not with prostitutes or pickups but with married women who shared their partners' class and social backgrounds. This observation was strengthened by Kinsey's finding that 26 percent of the married women he surveyed confessed to at least one extramarital affair by age forty.[72] Although adultery was becoming less often a matter for the criminal courts, virtually all marriage experts saw extramarital sex as clear evidence of trouble in an individual relationship and as indicative of changing demands on all modern marriages. More broadly, the embrace of individualism and decline of social responsibility that many saw in modern life was believed to encourage extramarital involvements that weakened marital bonds. One sexologist blamed increasing infidelity on Americans' affluence and changing residential patterns. "Large cities promote infidelity because there is less chance of a scandal," he argued, and Americans' "strongly materialistic standards, the nervous strain of 'keeping up with the Joneses,' drive husbands and wives to find relaxation in night life. They can't unwind enough to enjoy quiet evenings at home, and they go a hectic pace with others in the same sphere."[73]

Implicit in the coverage of these changes was a condemnation of the American character as increasingly unable or unwilling to place group interests over selfish ones. The "other-directed" character, it seemed, was essentially selfish. Critics complained that, rather than viewing marriage as a lifelong commitment, modern Americans saw it as temporary and expendable. Identifying the increasing importance of both leisure and an ethos of sexual pleasure as potentially threatening to marriage, experts on the changing American family worried that the stresses of affluence were just as dangerous to American marriages as the privations of wartime. These critiques of modern Americans and their marriages relied upon and interwove a series of concerns: Americans were accused of selfishness and individualism, pronounced guilty of demanding personal happiness and sexual fulfillment from marriage. Americans' propensity toward adultery, and their lack of personal responsibility, evidence of which experts saw all around them, condemned the national character. In the context of such troubling changes, how was marriage to survive?

"A NEW PATTERN OF MARRIAGE": REMAKING THE MODERN MARRIAGE

Although many marriage experts saw divorce and agitation about marital unhappiness as dire signs of a decline in the viability of marriage, theirs was not the only interpretation. Other experts interpreted the same evidence more optimistically, as proof that a new ethos of marriage was emerging. They agreed that marriage was changing dramatically, but insisted that it was a change for the better. The title of one 1953 book summed up their positive assessment: *The Family: From Institution to Companionship.*[74] In replacing a model of marriage that emphasized duty with one that stressed mutual growth and fulfillment for husbands and wives, the book's authors suggested, Americans were trading up to a more difficult but infinitely more rewarding set of expectations. As one leader of the marriage-education movement pointed out, "Today we have made happiness the first demand of marriage. It is doubtful that humanity has ever sought a goal in marriage so difficult—and yet so worthy of realization."[75] Amid her pessimistic description of the "terminability" of American marriage, Margaret Mead also noted that "new ways of holding marriages together are developing."[76] Members of the most recent generation to marry were experiencing increased difficulty in forming and maintaining satisfying marriages, such an analysis suggested, but the payoff for those who did was dramatic.

Although experts who lauded the "new" marriage also saw the divorce rate as a major social problem, they insisted that it was a temporary effect of an evolving marital ideal. The new type of marriage, still in development and often under fire from traditionalists, promised postwar Americans the opportunity to lead emotionally and sexually fulfilling private lives despite the political and social anxieties that surrounded them. Armed with psychological insight and scientific knowledge, young people could form lasting marriages that contributed to the community and the nation.[77] The revitalized postwar marriage that these optimistic experts described offered ways of negotiating the dramatic social changes affecting the national character while preserving marriage for future generations.

One of the bases for this new marriage was a modified gender egalitarianism. While researching the changing American character, David Riesman noted the emergence of a "total Gestalt in which marriage itself is of a new sort: shared, communicative, emancipated, in which the husband takes an active part as more than a mere breadwinner, and the wife an active part as more than 'the little woman' of traditional culture."[78] Contemporary couples, Paul Landis agreed, based their relationships on "emotional oneness" and embraced the contemporary "goal of equality." Americans' requirements in this "new sort" of marriage included physical and emotional intimacy. Marriages had once been based on economic need, convenience, and the reproductive imperative. In the new model, men and women instead privileged emotional unity. "In this country," one postwar sociology text maintained, "husband and wife are expected to become (and often are) all things to one another—lovers, friends, companions, confidants, nurses, and all the other intimate roles that bind two persons together."[79] "Despite all the head-shaking and talk about the divorce rate," Landis wrote in 1953, "every sign points to the fact that marriage is better than it ever has been in our national history." The prevalence of divorce merely indicated that "modern couples demand more from marriage than their ancestors did."[80]

Social scientists often drew connections between the emergence of a new family structure and other contemporary social upheavals. The marriage expert Henry Bowman argued that changes in the nation's domestic life paralleled the global battle between totalitarianism and democracy. "Marriage and the family," he argued, "are passing from a form roughly paralleling dictatorship and government by force to a democratic form of organization."[81] Others concurred that Americans shaken by years of economic depression and war were self-consciously creating a new marital compact. "Our era," a journalist explained, "is seeing the emergence of a new pattern of marriage: a joining together of two people of equal status, bound by love and common interest, rather than the purchase of a sort of indentured female servant and child-bearer who is chained to her master by economic dependence."[82] This "new pattern of marriage" was defined by practitioners and observers alike as modern and egalitarian rather than old-fashioned, shaped by intense sexual and emotional bonds.

As experts' descriptions made clear, theorists of American marriage consistently looked to the past in defining the "new Gestalt." Much like the contemporary discourses of masculinity and femininity on which they drew, definitions of the "modern" marriage and family were usually framed in ambivalent relation to a Victorian model that elicited both progressive contempt and nostalgia. Nineteenth-century marriages, according to common wisdom and fifties experts on family life, had been enviably solid and stable but lacked the sexual excitement and emotional intimacy demanded by a psychologically attuned generation.[83] Marriage reformers called for a new model of heterosexual relations, marriage, and family life while gleaning what they could from the past. The "companionate marriage" of like-minded partners first lauded in the 1920s, with its emphasis on sexual compatibility, contributed to the postwar ideal.[84] The version crafted by marriage reformers was, however, largely divested of its feminism and progressive political implications by its merging with another model of family, often described as "traditional," also evoked in postwar writing about marriage and the family.

The Victorian image of a large middle-class family with an intensely private home life sheltered from the public world was also an important component of the 1950s definition of family.[85] There were, however, crucial differences between the two that experts were careful to note. The modern family was fun-loving rather than work- and duty-centered, held together by mutual affection rather than social custom, and had long ago passed many of its functions to outside institutions and services.[86] It was also far more informal, relaxed, and psychologically aware than earlier families had been and was poised at midcentury to enjoy the best that consumer culture had to offer. Marriage was assumed to require sacrifice from both partners—principally emotional ones from women and financial from men—with both agreeing that such sacrifices were merited by the rewards of a new family unit. In this model, marriage in many ways paralleled democratic government with its complementary powers and system of checks and balances. What remained intact from the earlier ideal, to be claimed and reworked by a new generation of Americans, was a focus on intimate bonds as the foundation of national identity.

The kind of marriage that experts and fiction writers described during the postwar years promised to blend the best of old and new, tempering the rigidity of Victorian roles with a new language of self-awareness and "togetherness."[87] This language addressed men and women as members of a team but also made it clear that their roles were different. For women, identity was based less upon family of origin or community than upon marriage to a man whom they could encourage and complement. Many advice books counseled that, at marriage, individual identity had to give way to a new definition of self. "All these years you have been growing up as yourself," the 1956 *Bride's Reference Book* instructed newlywed women, but now that "the time has come to be Mrs. Someone," individualism must give way to "a concrete, down-to-earth social responsibility. . . . You and your husband are a new social unit in the social fabric of your time."[88] Men were also asked to envision themselves as considerate partners, and while for women marriage may have meant no longer being "yourself," for both partners it entailed the creation of a "new social unit" based on withdrawal from the family of origin into a separate venture. By recuperating the importance of men as husbands and fathers as well as of women as wives and mothers, the new familial ideal aimed to carve out space for both sexes. The idea of couples'

"down-to-earth social responsibility" as a part of "the social fabric"
borrowed from the Victorian model, but that ideal had also been mod-
ernized, as shown by the ascendance of democracy, intimacy, and personal fulfillment as marital goals. If there was any one theme that marked
both how much American ideals of marriage clung to tradition and how
much they had changed, it was sex.

"A SENSITIVE BAROMETER":
SEXUALITY IN THE POSTWAR MARRIAGE

Postwar discourse on marriage revolved around the increasing importance of sexuality. Paul Landis cited "the fulfillment of mutual sex desire"
as a hallmark of the modern marriage, and authorities envisioned it as the
best remedy for sexual maladjustment.[89] The untutored couples, frigid
wives, and sexually aggressive yet ignorant husbands who peopled the
pages of postwar literature signified the crucial importance of marital sex.
Despite laments about the culture's focus on sexuality, it was clear to
observers that attempts to reinvigorate American marriages hinged on the
centrality of sexual behavior in the lives of "other-directed" Americans.
Many of the recent changes singled out by social scientists—egalitarian
marriage, the widespread use and acceptance of birth control, and the
entitlement of not only men but also women to sexual pleasure—had
dramatic consequences for couples' everyday practices.[90] The psychoanalyst Lena Levine, an author of several works of advice literature who
referred to the nation's changing ideas about marriage as a "'revolution of
rising expectations," noted that many of those high hopes were sexual
ones.[91] Another observer explicitly connected concerns about marriage to
changing sexual mores when he reported, "It is more and more becoming
recognized that a wife should be an equal partner in the marriage," since
women had "gained the right to decide the terms and circumstances of
sexual intercourse in marriage and to demand that they, too, be sexually
satisfied."[92] Even the conservative physician Marie Robinson, who had
diagnosed an epidemic of frigidity, agreed with this interpretation in her
1959 best-seller, *The Power of Sexual Surrender*. Because of women's
attainment of equality, their access to sexual and psychological information, and the decline of taboos, new vistas of emotional closeness and
sexual pleasure awaited modern couples. "Happiness between men and
women," she declared, "has never had such a radiant outlook as it has in
this decade."[93]

That sex and sexual information had become central to the culture was evident in the proliferation of sexual advice literature. Marriage manuals had long offered middle-class readers advice about sex alongside information on hygiene and household management, but postwar examples of the genre prioritized sex as *the* most vital indicator of a relationship's quality. "A happy bedroom," according to an advice book excerpted in the *Reader's Digest*, "takes on the attributes of a sanctuary for a married couple. Within these four walls, husband and wife reach the height and the depths [sic] of the expression of their life together."[94]

Metaphors for the place of sex in marriage continuously emphasized its importance, with one author maintaining that "the sexual relationship may be described as a sensitive barometer which reacts to every change in the climate of a marriage."[95] If attention were not paid to this barometer, squalls could build into storms that would eventually overwhelm and capsize the marital ship. Other authors preferred homelier language: "The general matrimonial structure," a leading marriage manual warned soberly, "may topple unless bound together with sound, sexual ribs."[96] Another advice author remarked that "marriage without a sex relationship is like a wall of bricks without mortar. There is nothing to hold it together, and it is easily toppled."[97] The analyst Lawrence Frank similarly argued that sex cemented marriage: if couples could "communicate sexually to each other, they are more likely to find the reassurance and support, the feeling of renewed self-confidence and trust in the other and of their need for each other, that makes possible the many tasks and obligations of their lives together." Although Frank cautioned readers that he did "not mean that sexual intercourse is the sole or complete answer to the problem of marriage," it was clear that the quality of the "sexual communication" between husband and wife played a central role in holding marriages together.[98] In its 1964 cover story on the sexual state of the nation, *Time* magazine affirmed the importance of sex when it observed that "marriages which do survive seem to be richer" partly because "Americans are becoming more sophisticated and less inhibited in bed—as just about everyone is urging them to be."[99] The minister and theology professor Reuel Howe put it most succinctly when he wrote in the *Ladies' Home Journal*, "Sex needs marriage and marriage needs sex."[100] He might have added that the nation needed marriage, and attention to the quality of marital sexuality was therefore in its best interests.

Authorities from virtually all the helping professions agreed that a mutually exciting sexual life was vital to marital success. The importance accorded sensuality marked a crucial departure from the Victorian model of marriage, a difference many Americans viewed with pride. It also offered a disturbing reminder that many of the problems besetting the postwar marriage were sexual ones. If couples' sexual problems could be addressed, it was believed, their marriages stood a much better chance of success. In 1951, spurred by concerns about the spread of divorce, the Roman Catholic Church followed the lead of groups like Family Renewal, Cana, and the Christian Family Movement in affirming the importance of fulfilling sex within marriage.[101] A few years later, an American-dominated international convention on mental health found that the "greatest single cause of unhappy marriages appears to be disappointment in expectation of how the marriage partner should play his or her sexual role."[102] Kinsey noted in his second report that, "where the sexual relationships are not equally satisfactory to both of the partners in the marriage, disagreement and angry rebellion may invade not only the marital bed, but all other aspects of the marriage." His data suggested that two-thirds of marriages "run into serious disagreement over sexual relationships," and that "in three-quarters of the divorces recorded in our case histories, sexual factors were among those that had led to the divorce."[103] Thus the crisis in American marriage was firmly rooted in an equally pervasive crisis in marital sex. At a moment when sexual pleasure was increasingly proclaimed as a right, and in which extramarital temptations beckoned, advice authors and other reformers saw it as their mission to regulate American sexual character by returning it to its proper site, the marital bed.

Authorities carefully calculated the exact relation between sexual adjustment and marital happiness. Clifford Adams, resident marriage expert at the *Ladies' Home Journal,* declared decisively that "a fourth of the wife's married happiness, and a third of her husband's, depends on the sexual adjustment they make."[104] Another counselor offered slightly different odds, proclaiming that "sixty to seventy percent of marital breakups, the records show, are indirectly due to sexual maladjustment."[105] Even a 1955 teenagers' guide to dating and marriage, which carefully downplayed the importance of sex, nevertheless presented it as a crucial and potentially marriage-threatening problem when it noted soberly that couples "agreed that it had taken longer to achieve adjustment in sex than in any other area." Only one-half reached a "satisfactory" sexual adjustment by the end of their first year of marriage, and more than 10 percent remained unhappy with the amount and quality of their marital sex after ten years or more of marriage.[106] Another sexologist contributed the staggering statistic that "four-fifths of all divorces are based on sexual disharmony."[107] Not all experts assigned a specific percentage of marital happiness to sex (or, like Adams, weighed men's interest in sex more heavily than women's), but virtually all reckoned it a crucial determinant of marital success.

Experts further observed that improved marital sex was a nearly universal expectation. When the sociologist Mirra Komarovsky explored working-class attitudes toward marital sex in the late 1950s, she found dramatic differences between contemporary couples and earlier generations. Among the couples she interviewed, "there is no mistaking their feeling that ideally wives should also experience sexual enjoyment," and, despite complaints about their husbands' performance, all the wives "agree[ed] on the ideal of sexual fulfillment."[108] As the boundaries of the middle-class expanded during the 1950s, incorporating more white ethnics of varying religions, the cultural ideals of that class were shared by a growing number of women. Clifford Adams similarly noted that the *Ladies' Home Journal*'s nationwide audience shared the same assumptions about marriage. In recent years, Adams noted, all "women's evaluation of sex and its place in marriage has undergone a profound change. Today's wife expects her marriage to be happy and well-adjusted sexually."[109]

Authorities vied to describe the potential catastrophes created by inadequate marital sex. The director of the National Desertion Bureau maintained that, when men left their wives, usually "the real diagnosis is sex maladjustment."[110] In a typically dramatic statement, Frank Caprio warned that "sexual incompatibility in marriage leads to many things, including infidelity, mental illness, divorce, and offenses that tag the culprit with the stigma, 'sex offender.' It may even lead to murder."[111] Unsatisfactory marital sex could also reach beyond the unhappy individuals it affected directly to harm future generations, since the sexual satisfaction of husbands and wives provided the proper environment for rearing healthy children.[112] "If the mother is sexually deprived," one analyst warned, she would inevitably "communicate her feelings, as well as the cultural patterns, to the male child," creating another generation of maladjusted families.[113] Although most concern was reserved for sons, daughters could also be irremediably harmed by a lack of parental sexual satisfaction: according to one physician, prostitution was often caused by a growing girl's awareness of *"manifest irregularity in the sexual life of the parents."*[114]

Married Americans were thus directed toward satisfactory sex lives to ensure not only their own happiness but also the stability of the family unit and larger community. According to one sexologist, a single couple's poor sexual adjustment could lead to spreading social upheaval: "A whole neighborhood can be infected by one unhappily married pair. Parties circulate, the atmosphere becomes not friendly but erotic at gatherings." Properly regulated marital sexuality, by contrast, offered untold civic benefits, as "a more intelligent adjustment to our sexual needs results in better parenthood, fewer divorces and sex crimes, and better citizenship for the country as a whole."[115] In the voluminous postwar literature on marriage, problems like sexual incompatibility and dissatisfaction, adultery, and divorce were represented as communicable diseases to which middle-class couples were dangerously susceptible. How were concerned couples to safeguard against such dreadful possibilities?

The answer, authorities proposed, was to cement marriage through mutually satisfying sex. Because virtually all observers of postwar marriage trends noted the increased importance of marital sex, both husbands and wives were urged to work at their "sexual partnership" within marriage and cautioned to educate themselves and their children so as to avoid tragedies of sexual ignorance.[116] Proper marital sex, authorities agreed, was every American's duty, and its theory and practice held important political implications. "The importance of sexual adjustment in marriage and the need for related scientific information," the sociologist Francis Merrill maintained, "is self-evident to the enlightened citizen of a democracy."[117] A sexologist agreed that "it is the quality of the relationship between husband and wife that determines the security of the family, the group, the country."[118] If mutually fulfilling sex was important to marriage, and marital success, in turn, was vital to the national interest, then any marriages in which one or both partners were unhappy with their sex life posed a threat to social stability.

"NOTHING DONE IN BED IS WRONG": MARITAL EXPERTS AND SEXUAL ADVICE

Virtually the entire battalion of experts who wrote on marriage promoted its maintenance through mutually fulfilling sex. The same ideology that enshrined sex as the linchpin of marital success also promised that sexual adjustment could be worked at and attained with the help of professional advice. A new imperative emerged in the work of marriage experts, in which "maturity" meant willingness to seek out expert help for any sexual problems.[119] It was a central tenet of many sexual liberals that American men and women were unprepared for the sexual side of marriage and needed remedial education. Much advice literature thus explicitly addressed those who were engaged or married and wanted to improve their sexual adjustment. Experts agreed that American couples, because of the taboos against open discussion of sexual matters, often lacked the information needed to make their marriage successful. A 1953 case study, the first entry in the *Ladies' Home Journal*'s popular "Can This Marriage Be Saved?" series, captured several common themes of the genre in its treatment of the problems caused by ignorance of sex.[120] In conversations with a marriage counselor, wife "Diana" complained of her husband's lack of interest in sex and his rough performance, while husband "Guy" described his wife as abnormally sexually demanding. The counselor's diagnosis was that Guy's behavior was "based on ignorance of the nature of sex," and that, like many modern men, he was "actually unaware that sexual satisfaction for women existed." The remedy? "Several good books on the subject enlightened him, and . . . the sexual maladjustment was solved."[121]

This narrative, in which ignorance of sex and corresponding marital distress were cured by exposure to modern advice literature, was repeated again and again in marriage experts' case studies. Frank Caprio, for example, contrasted Americans' lack of preparation for marriage to the extensive education that the state mandated for soldiers and professionals, implying that the public interest was best served by advancing the cause of sexual knowledge:

> When young soldiers are trained, the training is put into the hands of the seasoned combat veteran who knows what they will be up against. When young lawyers and doctors are trained, the training is given by experienced men in these professions.
>
> When young men and women are about to enter into marriage, they receive, with few exceptions, no training at all for its risks and responsibilities. Out of the thousands of young people about to marry, this week or next, only a handful will have enough of a sex education to enable them to deal with the sex problems that are bound to arise in the course of their married life.[122]

Like combat, marriage was a serious business that reflected a people's essential character, warded off potential dangers, and secured the nation's future.

From this perspective, the new statistical literature on American sexual behavior held the potential to make marriage more fulfilling. A writer for *Look* magazine noted approvingly that, upon perusing volumes like the first Kinsey Report, "married couples will be helped to conquer their upsetting guilt feelings and thereby attain a more satisfactory status of sexual adjustment—the road to a reduced divorce rate for our country."[123] Dr. Emily Mudd, president of the American Association of Marriage Counselors, similarly promoted Kinsey's work as promising to help the nation's marriages. Professionals, she earnestly assured readers of *Collier's* magazine, "are *using* the Kinsey findings, using them to save tottering marriages, to rebuild wrecked lives, to prevent the anguish of millions of children whose security is threatened by divorce."[124] Kinsey himself put in a bid for the usefulness of his work, noting that although some observers "have feared that a scientific approach to the problems of sex might threaten the marital institution," they were outnumbered by those "who believe that an extension of our knowledge may contribute to the establishment of better marriages.[125] Young Americans, the marriage and sex counselor Abraham Stone agreed, had been positively influenced by the effect of the reports: "Many people are talking more freely, with less fear and anxiety and with less feeling of guilt and shame about their sexual experiences. They feel freer to come for counsel, and feel less inhibited in discussing specific questions of sexual behavior."[126] Even cartoonists viewed the reports as required preparation for wedlock and a panacea for marital troubles (see figures 15 and 16).

Along with this counsel on marital sexuality came a new set of sexual imperatives. As the amount and explicitness of material on sex grew, both men and women were warned of the consequences of being sexually uneducated, inadequate, or simply uninspired. In the didactic case studies presented by marriage experts, husbands and wives who refuse to recognize sex as a marital priority are presented as uninformed, immature, and even pathologically selfish.[127] With satisfying sex seen as an increasingly important part of the normative marriage, the standards for sexual competence were constantly climbing. The psychiatrist Frank Caprio, who authored numerous studies of sexual adjustment and deviance, captured the emerging mandate in the titles of two of his works, *The Sexually Adequate Male* (1951) and *The Sexually Adequate Female* (1953).[128] A 1951 study that assessed wives' sexual responsiveness similarly divided them into two groups, branding them as either "adequate" or "inadequate" at achieving orgasm.[129] The adequacy that such experts advocated demanded that their audience consume sexual advice.

The notion of sexual adequacy, implying the existence of a body of knowledge to be mastered and sexual standards to be met, also reflected an

"ALL RIGHT, DEAR, I'LL READ THE KINSEY REPORT OVER AGAIN, AND I'LL THROW IN A GARBAGE DISPOSAL AND A CLOTHES DRIER."

"I SUGGEST YOU BOTH READ 5 PAGES OF THE KINSEY REPORT THREE TIMES A DAY."

Figures 15 and 16. The reports as a modern requirement for marriage: cartoons from Charles Preston, ed., *A Cartoon Guide to the Kinsey Report,* 45. (From the *Wall Street Journal*—permission, Cartoon Features Syndicate and Charles Preston.)

expanding understanding of what kinds of activities constituted marital sex. As social scientists pointed out, sex was shifting from its traditional function of procreation to being a new form of leisure. "No appreciable part of the coitus," Kinsey had argued, "in or outside of marriage, is consciously undertaken as a means of effecting reproduction."[130] A few experts, mostly orthodox psychoanalysts, believed that women had to welcome impregnation in order for orgasm to take place, but most postwar authorities accepted or even lauded the separation of sexual activity from procreation.[131] Although they rarely offered explicit information on birth control, the authors of sex manuals increasingly assumed that the married couples who formed their audience were conversant with modern technology and usage and sought sexual advice to increase their pleasure rather than to facilitate conception.[132] Linda Gordon notes in her study of the birth control movement that postwar advocates offered sexual advice in their clinics, reflecting authorities' belief that "the value of birth control was to promote good sex, not to offer women options other than full-time motherhood."[133] As one commentator put it, postwar literature signaled "the recognition of sex as a form of play."[134] If procreation was separate from sexual pleasure, then coitus could no longer be seen as the central sexual act.

Marriage sometimes served to authorize and legitimize sexual behaviors that then spread beyond it. Kinsey noted in 1947 that the "educated portion of the public" tended to "feel that any sort of activity which contributes to the significance of an emotional relationship between spouses is justified, and that no sort of sexual act is perverse if it so contributes to the marital relationship, even though exactly the same act between persons who were not spouses might be considered a perversion."[135] By emphasizing the importance of pleasure, experts expanded the marital sexual repertoire. The range of acceptable marital activities widened as more and more authors offered information on how to increase sexual satisfaction within marriage, recommending varied positions and techniques for intercourse, extended foreplay, and oral sex. "Now that the sex act in marriage is looked upon more and more as a part of the entire emotional relationship between man and wife," one sociological study of marriage noted, "increasing attention is given to the erotic play which precedes it." The "concrete details" and "techniques" that aided marital sex were being "elaborated in current marriage manuals," and the Kinsey studies gave these instructions "prestige and the stamp of modernity."[136] Margaret Mead attested to this eroticizing of the domestic realm when she noted that "the sort of sex-life that was once placed outside marriage, in the red-light district of the nineties, has to some extent been imported into it."[137]

Experts lent support to this process of eroticization when they maintained that any consensual sexual activity that brought pleasure to both husband and wife was acceptable and even healthy. The psychologist and sex expert Albert Ellis underlined the implications of Kinsey's findings by reminding readers that "there is no reason why orgasm must occur during coitus" and proposing that marriage counselors and other sex experts encourage women to seek sexual pleasure from other activities.[138] Marie Robinson, at the more conservative end of the spectrum, counseled readers that some practices could be unhealthy and suggested "limits to lovemaking." Specifically, Robinson felt that any activity "that does not culminate in intercourse tends to be regressive and infantile."[139] Even she, however, offered a qualified endorsement of noncoital sexuality as long as it did not displace coitus.

According to many marriage experts, virtually any sexual act was acceptable when performed within the sanctity of marriage. Advice texts urged couples to ignore taboos and refrain from worrying about whether their activities were normal. Dedication to the improvement of sex and a willingness to experiment were lauded as the signs of a truly intimate, successful marriage. "Hurried and routine sex relations," one authority warned, "are often to blame for infidelities that need never have happened."[140] As the boundaries of marital sex were redrawn, the very definition of *normal* became more fluid. Louis Berg and Robert Street's 1953 guide for married couples, which aimed "to educate the sexually incompatible, and to strengthen the foundation of the home," stated emphatically,

> In connection with normal sex, an invisible legend should hang in every bedchamber in the country: "Nothing Done in Bed Is Wrong." If every reader would implant that statement firmly in his or her mind and accept it, regardless of how far his desires may impel him, the sexual intimacy of man and woman would be vastly improved. . . . It should always be borne in mind that millions of people are doing everything the reader does or would like to do.[141]

Such an approach authorized sexual practices that would once have been outside the purview of respectable marital education. The information that authors offered on oral sex, noncoital heterosexual intercourse, and other practices which many still considered deviant was available to a wider and wider audience, a fact that could not help but change the meanings attached to all sexual acts, marital and otherwise.

Researchers who commented on the expansion of marital sex drew their observations from clinical practice. Young married Americans were increasingly exhibiting the practices of a group Kinsey approvingly dubbed the "sophisticates," a primarily upper-class group likely to make love in the nude rather than clothed and to engage in a wide variety of sexual acts.[142] As couples supposedly evolved to resemble these upper-class sophisticates, investigators confirmed that sexual pleasure was an expected part of marriage, and that its absence—for either partner—was an indication of something missing in the relationship. A male physician and a female psychologist explained, "Our society preaches that only one kind of sexual expression can be countenanced, the so-called 'normal' intercourse between husband and wife. Any other type of activity is labeled shocking, disgusting, antisocial, and perverse." Such "other" activities—a category in which they included homosexuality, masturbation, fetishism, sadism, and masochism—were far more common than many realized. Indeed, echoing Berg and Street, these authorities asserted that "everyone of us engages in all of them to some extent, consciously or unconsciously."[143]

Albert Ellis suggested the implications of this development in 1954, saying, "'Normal' sex behavior is anything and everything which we—or which the societies in which we live—declare and make it to be."[144] Ellis's critique of traditional notions of sexual normality, which was a recurring theme in his writing, sprung from his belief that any definition of sexual normalcy or deviation reflected meaningless cultural and social taboos. "Many of our clergymen and philosophers," Ellis wrote in a 1954 article, seem to know what, precisely, is 'normal' sex behavior." In actuality, he argued, "we have no absolute criterion of what is sexual 'normality'; and, in fact, 'normal' sex behavior is anything and everything which we—or which the societies in which we happen to live—declare and make it to be."[145] Addressing critics who claimed to define sexual boundaries, Ellis asked how *normal* was to be defined—by statistical prevalence, as in Kinsey's work? By the health and emotional adjustment of any group or individual, which was difficult to measure and which varied according to psychological opinion? Whatever definition was used, Ellis believed, the conclusion remained the same: "appropriate sex behavior, no matter how we conceive of it, seems to include virtually *all* kinds of sex activity."[146]

This recurrent questioning of what constituted normal worked to destabilize any easy definitions. Lucy Freeman, whose popular accounts of psychotherapy helped to familiarize audiences with Freudian terminology, reached the same conclusion, arguing, "There is really no such thing as the 'average' or 'normal' man or woman" and "no such thing as 'normal' sex behavior."[147] The sexologist Frank Caprio recognized the dilemma as well, describing a nation of men and women bewildered by the cultural and social changes around them, all beseeching the sex expert, "Where is the line between normal and the abnormal to be drawn?" Caprio's answer, which reflected the growing confusion among many authorities, was not reassuring to traditionalists. "There is no hard and fast line, no absolute norm in sex activity," he counseled readers, adding that "what is normal for one man may be shocking to another. In marital relations, these things are matters of taste and inclination."[148] Caprio's rejection of moral and medical absolutes, as well as his reliance upon an individualistic philosophy in which couples negotiated their own norms, exemplified the kind of ethos that enraged the more traditional practitioners.

Despite authors' promises of "concrete details," they rarely offered specifics, especially in comparison with the more explicit sexual advice literature that would appear in the later 1960s and the 1970s. Simple advice, such as suggesting that husbands and wives agree on how often to have sex, usually stood in for the detailed descriptions of sexual technique readers were led to expect. In fact, many authors prided themselves on *not* offering such details and condemned unnamed other guides, which presumably did, as tasteless and unscientific. Most offered some combination of basic anatomical information such as maps of male and female genitalia and definitions of terms such as *orgasm* and *frigidity*, plus a scattering of case histories. Actual advice avoided detail: Caprio, for example, typically recommended that couples kiss prior to and during coitus, suggested that contraceptives be kept accessible, and listed various sexual positions for husbands and wives to try, but his language throughout was veiled. A segment titled "Bedroom Mistakes: Faulty Technique" avoided any literal discussion of sex acts, instead warning men against demanding coitus with "tiring frequency" and advising women to avoid undertaking excessive housework when it might interfere with marital sex.[149] Navigating between titillation, scientific objectivity, and respectability, mainstream sexual guides had little in the way of explicit instruction on techniques, instead stressing the importance of fulfilling, yet vaguely defined, sexual union.

Oral sex offers a case in point. The average couple in search of sexual advice was sometimes advised to make it part of their marital repertoire and given carefully phrased guidance on how to do so. Although cunnilingus and fellatio were illegal in many states, Kinsey had established that more than half of upper-level married couples included oral-genital contact in their sex lives, and the vast majority of the authors of works containing sexual advice offered at least a qualified endorsement.[150] In typically guarded syntax, Frank Caprio reassured couples that the "oral-erotic impulse is present in every human being," and that "oral stimulations" were "regarded by many psychoanalysts as compatible with normality."[151] According to another popular marriage manual, Berg and Street's *Sex: Manners and Methods,* "oral connection" was a practice that "receives little attention and considerable neglect in literary discussions of human sexual habits." Eager to rectify this omission, the intrepid authors counseled readers that "the practice is completely normal. When millions engage in it and additional millions suppress the tendency, it can hardly be regarded otherwise."[152] Ellis similarly promoted the act when he coyly reminded readers that, "although coitus is *one* of the most satisfying of human sex experiences, it is not necessarily *the* most satisfying experience for all men and women."[153] For detailed advice, though, curious readers would have to wait.

Recommendations on how to achieve "the most satisfying sexual experience" showed concern for women's sexual pleasure. In fact, female sexual pleasure was becoming so central to modern marriage literature that authors even de-emphasized the role of the penis. Along with recommending oral sex, some experts downplayed coitus in favor of noncoital sex techniques in the interest of achieving female orgasm. The second Kinsey Report noted that "heterosexual relationships could . . . become more satisfactory if they more often utilized the sort of knowledge which most homosexual females have of female anatomy and female psychology," a finding that other experts, often reluctantly, affirmed.[154] As one team of experts admitted, "Although the penis is regarded as being the sole conveyer of pleasure for the female," nevertheless

> the disillusioning fact remains that the forefinger is a most useful asset in man's contact with the opposite sex, and that the highly vaunted male organ requires much assistance as an instrument of woman's sexual pleasure.
>
> It is time that the matter was faced. It is insistence on making the penis do something it cannot generally do that is responsible for a major proportion of sexual incompatibility. Also, it is difficult to believe that nature intended the penis to be the sole instrument of pleasure for women.

Not only were noncoital—and nonreproductive—techniques presented as biologically natural, but in some cases they were described as imperative, since the authors concluded that "to satisfy many women, a man must resort to artificial stimulation."[155] In this context, *artificial* meant digital or oral stimulation, practices that called to mind Bergler's concern, discussed earlier, that hysterical women were subverting the natural order by demanding "preparatory acts prior to insertion." The advice authors who counseled sexually troubled couples expressed the ambivalence many felt about gender roles, respectability, and sexual behavior. Although they shied away from explicit suggestions and presented sexual alternatives to their readers in language that must often have seemed frustratingly opaque, they promoted a changed vision of marital sex. Sexual experts assumed that women deserved sexual satisfaction and that men would have to adapt to women's desires.

Such recommendations rankled traditionalists, who believed that attempts to remake marriage by sexualizing it were dangerous and shortsighted. In response, they launched a conservative critique of mainstream marital advice literature. Such critics, who included clergy, social hygienists, and social scientists, along with the journalists who popularized their views, believed that reformers' and educators' attempts to incorporate sexual pleasure within marriage were likely to harm rather than rescue it. Young Americans, the sociologist Carle Zimmerman warned, were entering into marriage with "no intention of doing anything other than cohabiting sexually without observing further the implications in terms of the family."[156] The cultural critic Philip Wylie also believed that the new climate of sex consciousness endangered marriages. "American marriage," Wylie wrote, "is cracking up on an unrealistic and ridiculous philosophy" based on "an overemphasis on 'sex appeal.'"[157] By making sexual compatibility the primary quality they looked for in a mate, recent generations had ignored traditional values and would pay the price in an epidemic of unhappiness and divorce. The sociologist Pitirim Sorokin, who believed that the "American sex revolution" presaged the end of both the traditional family and the democratic political system, argued a few years later that American marriage would soon be replaced by "some sort of polygamous, or polyandrous, or anarchic, or 'communal' pseudo-marriage." Sorokin clinched his threat by reminding readers that a similar change had "quite recently occurred . . . in Soviet Russia."[158]

The importance of sex to marriage was being vastly overestimated, these worried experts maintained. A guide by the Catholic priest John O'Brien warned, "Although this topic has been played up in recent literature as the root of virtually all marital unhappiness[,] the records show that it is the major factor in but comparatively few breakups. The assumption running through this literature that so-called 'sexual incompatibility' is a cause of most marriage difficulties is a classic example of putting the cart before the horse."[159] Others agreed that the emphasis on marital sex could have a dangerous influence on susceptible readers.

By 1958 the marriage counselor Dr. David Mace was inquiring of readers of *McCall's* magazine, "Are SEX MANUALS a threat to happy marriage?"[160] The same year, the Baltimore physician and marriage counselor Hugo Boudreau mocked the jargon commonly used by liberal sex and marriage experts. The "American woman today," Boudreau observed, "is warned constantly that her marital happiness hinges upon 'proper sexual adjustment'" and "is made acutely aware that a 'vigorous and harmonious sex relationship' with her husband is vital to a successful union." Besieged by propaganda, the "American wife is beginning to feel that she must aggressively seek sexual satisfaction." Applying a different perspective to the same findings that others had hailed as liberatory and progressive, Boudreau observed with horror that women were increasingly often initiating marital sex and inciting their husbands to impossible sexual feats. Many, he predicted, would leave their families in search of the mythical sexual satisfaction promised by irresponsible "experts" and the mass media.[161] Educators who painted sex as the most important feature in marriage and endorsed the expansion of marital sex, critics complained, cheapened marriage by making it a mere legitimization of sexual excess. Many of the theorists who took this view objected to the focus on women's entitlement, but not all who called attention to the dangers of the marital sexual imperative were upholders of tradition, as evidenced by Margaret Mead's caveat. Although she generally approved of the trend toward encouraging sexual fulfillment in marriage, Mead pointed out that the new sexual imperative had a dark side when she noted that "marital sexual happiness" threatened to become "a duty like every other success-demand in America."[162]

Most of these critics saw modern marriage experts simply as deluded, but a few charged them with conspiracy to overturn the institution they ostensibly protected, with one claming, "Marriage itself has been seen by the liberators as a moralistic convention much too rigid for modern times."[163] Echoing the fictional Susan McViddy, critics insisted that the burgeoning marital sex literature lauded as the key to harmonious and sexually charged marriages instead harmed them. Some sexual education could be a good thing, many conceded, but modern manuals went too far, presenting unattainable visions of sexual bliss. By late in the decade, such warnings were increasingly common. Paul Landis cautioned that, "even though today's wives know more about sex than their mothers did, and are likely gaining more sexual satisfaction than their mothers did, they are not as happy as they should be because they are led to expect too much and are urged to strive for goals they cannot reach." Landis went on to downplay the importance of sexual fulfillment for women, arguing of the anorgasmic wife that the "only thing marring her content is her mistaken feeling that she is not measuring up to today's standard."[164] Another sex expert similarly decried the popularity of sex manuals, believing that many created "a fear that only the right 'technique' can guarantee the success of the marriage relationship."[165] A third bemoaned the modern preoccupation with equal pleasure for both husbands and wives, warning that "education has made men feel more responsible for the orgasm of their wives, the wives more critical of their husbands' potency, and mutual suspicion increases the sense of inadequacy of both."[166]

Experts like Boudreau and Landis objected less to the availability of sexual information than they did to its agenda. Contemporary Americans, they believed, were obsessed by technique but remained uninformed about the physiology and psychology of sex. "Despite modern frankness," a female minister charged, "many of those who think they know most about the subject are dangerously misinformed." The engaged and married couples whom she counseled were at once ignorant of basic anatomy and immersed in complicated data, a contradiction she blamed on the widespread availability of "modern books."[167] Sexual literature, she argued, had created unrealistic expectations, leading to the disappointment and boredom that threatened many marriages. Some took this theme further, seeing the very idea of the "sexpert" as an affront to the natural order. "The idea that the human race, or at least Western man, had to wait until the middle of the twentieth century for so-called 'sexologists' to discover the 'right' technique for the most fundamental relationship of marriage is naive if not ridiculous," O'Brien fulminated.[168]

Despite such charges, writers on marriage continued to see sex as central to a healthy marital relationship. Even those who longed to return to more traditional models of marriage acknowledged the growing importance most Americans placed on sex within marriage. In a backhanded compliment, one conservative critic of the new ethos even proposed that defenders of traditional marriage adopt the language of the sexual liberals. Howard Whitman, the author of a series of fretful articles on "America's moral crisis," offered a heartfelt defense of the institution in an angry 1957 article titled "Don't Let Them Scoff at Marriage!" Whitman fumed,

> During the past 12 years, marriage has been represented as a poor substitute for the glamour of the chase and cheesecake. The gross libel on marriage is the notion that the chase, the allure is the goal. Marriage is seen as a dull aftermath. This has been the thesis of the era of sex emancipation, the "sex revolution" as it has been called, in the dozen years since the close of World War II. It has brought us to the moral crisis of today, when marital failure is almost as popular as marital success.

Rather than demanding a simple return to "traditional" values, however, Whitman instead suggested that marriage and marital sex needed better public relations. Far from being the site of dull and routine sex, he explained, marriage was the locus of the only truly fulfilling intercourse. When couples received the proper education—not in technique, but in communication—marriage could and would become the site of "the perfect sex relationship."[169] In an ironic tribute to the power of new sexual norms, Whitman phrased his defense of marriage in the very terms used by the proponents of "sex revolution" whom he castigated as the cause of marriage's bad press. Although what he termed "the era of sex emancipation" had brought marriage to the brink of extinction, it was only by selling the "allure" of a glamorized marital sex that marriage could be revitalized and strengthened.[170] The national interest, in short, would be served by the same force that posed its primary threat: the promise of sexual pleasure.

Despite the almost universal agreement that marriage and marital sex were changing dramatically, sexual experts' recommendations and warnings encompassed profound contradictions. The fear of female sexual insatiability coexisted with stereotypes of women as essentially passive or as sexual only within the context of stable and permanent marriages. Men were castigated for their sexual crudity at the same time that aggressive sexuality was valorized. Couples were encouraged to broaden their sexual repertoires yet cautioned to retain heterosexual penetration as their central activity. Sex within marriage was ideally both a form of play and a sacred and potentially procreative trust that would strengthen traditional familial bonds. These contradictions echoed conflicting recommendations regarding marriage. At the same time that marriage experts urged its revitalization, they worried that certain changes were being taken too far, and that the kinds of sexual reforms needed to make marriage modern and attractive could not be controlled.

CONCLUSION

The contradictions embedded in American ideologies of marriage—certainty on the one hand that sexual information would help revitalize and strengthen marriage, and fear on the other that such information would accelerate its collapse—expressed fears that marriage, like the nation's sexual character, was changing irrevocably. The course that postwar experts recommended was an uneasy one, modifying traditional marriage with heightened attention to personal happiness and sexual fulfillment. Many of the much heralded innovations of the postwar marriage were far from new: marriage experts and social scientists drew on Victorian ideals and recycled pronouncements about companionate marriage from the 1920s. But 1950s models of marriage were also emphatically different from ones that had come before. As Stephanie Coontz argues, the period was "one of experimentation with the possibilities of a new kind of family," rather than "the expression of some long-standing tradition."[171] Postwar Americans insistently envisioned contemporary marriage as something new, an institution revitalized and renewed by scientific and psychological knowledge even as it was tested by anxieties about national decline, social change, transformations in gender roles, and the shock waves of the sexual revolution. With wedlock taking on such charged ideological significance, it is not surprising that experts saw American marriages as signifying the state of the "national welfare," and believed, in Caprio's words, that "the quality of the relationship between husband and wife . . . determines the security of the family, the group, the country."

Some viewed popular how-to narratives about sex as a needed component of Americans' practical education, crucial aids in the project of postwar nation building. Others instead attacked them for aiding modern Americans' self-centeredness and lack of civic interest, arguing that unhappy couples should subordinate their individual desires for sexual fulfillment to their duties to the family group and the nation. Still other critics were ambivalent about the increasing emphasis on happiness and sexual satisfaction, rather than duty and service, in marriage. Each group recognized that the meaning of marriage had changed, along with the expectations that both men and women held for it. Sex was thus both the source of a national marriage crisis and its solution. Anxieties about gender difference and the potentially disruptive effects of sexual pleasure for men and women were both elaborated and contained by an ideology of marriage that stressed its primacy in the social system and positioned it as the highest fulfillment of maturity and repository of healthy sexuality. Professionals and their audience together constructed a new vision of marriage in which both partners were entitled to sexual fulfillment.

Experts who sought to reconcile the pleasure ethos with marital and social stability recommended a careful balance between too much sexual pleasure and not enough. They often found, though, that endorsement of mutual sexual pleasure within marriage could easily shade into a call for female sexual entitlement, and the implications of the sexualization of marital roles were not always what its proponents intended. When properly channeled, sex could hold marriages together; but if it escaped its bonds it could instead destroy them. Contradictions between the many binaries that the "new" marriage was designed to manage—male and female sexual satisfaction, traditional and egalitarian gender roles, pleasure versus duty—often could not be reconciled. The kind of sexuality that marriage experts sought alternately to liberate and to tame was envisioned as potentially anarchic and disruptive, threatening to tear apart marriage and family bonds. It could also disrupt heterosexuality itself.

FIVE

"An Age of Sexual Ambiguity"

Homosexuality and National Character
in the Postwar United States

The data in the present study indicate that at least 37 per cent of the male
population has at least some homosexual experience between the beginning
of adolescence and old age. . . . This is more than one male in three of the persons that one may meet as he passes along a city street.

KINSEY, POMEROY, AND MARTIN
Sexual Behavior in the Human Male

There is nothing to be gained by shrugging off the very existence of homosexuality. It exists; we meet it only too often in everyday life. How, then,
should you, as a decent and civilized man, react to the over-friendly fellow at
the office; to your kid brother or nephew and his questionable friends; to your
own occasional shocking impulse?

JOHN McPARTLAND
"For These Are the Bedeviled"

WHEN *SEXUAL BEHAVIOR IN THE HUMAN MALE* appeared in 1948, one of its
most shocking revelations was how many American men had had sex with
other men. Kinsey found that nearly 40 percent of his male subjects had
experienced homosexual sex "to the point of orgasm," and among men who
remained unmarried until the age of thirty-five, this increased to 50 percent.[1]
The figures for American women that debuted a few years later were lower
but still unsettling: the "accumulative incidence of overt contacts to the point
of orgasm among the females reached 13%," with lesbian experience most
common among educated middle-class women. Kinsey repeatedly insisted
on a continuum with gradations between homo- and heterosexuality, in

which few Americans fell exclusively into either one category or the other. According to his figures, only 3 percent of American men and 1 percent of women had sex exclusively with members of the same gender; however, when same-sex erotic response that did not lead to orgasm was counted, as many as 50 percent of men and 28 percent of women might be termed homosexual.[2]

These numbers intensified an already heated national discussion about the extent, cause, and meaning of homosexuality in the United States. They had complex and sometimes contradictory effects: for many homosexuals, they offered reassurance of the presence of others like them, while for legal and medical experts and moral leaders they posed a series of disciplinary problems. For virtually all, they raised vital questions about the extent to which homosexuality was a part of the American sexual character. The public's fascination with narratives of gay and lesbian life grew, and commentators exploring the incidence and significance of homosexuality in the postwar United States continually evoked Kinsey's findings.

Americans had a long history of concern about homosexuality. In the early republic, same-sex sexual acts had been seen as a legal and often a moral transgression, and after the emerging science of sex "discovered" the homosexual as a species in the late nineteenth century, surveillance and discussion of homosexuals increased. By the early twentieth century, modern investigators were conducting chemical, morphological, and psychological studies to discover the roots of a preference for one's own sex. In the longer history of what Jennifer Terry calls an "American obsession," homosexuality has been framed variously as a physical or emotional disorder, a mark of primitivism or modernity, and evidence for everything from gender disintegration to social reorganization.[3]

The specter of homosexuality haunted postwar discussions of American politics and culture. In the wake of wartime social changes, its meaning seemed to be shifting as the homosexual emerged, as many phrased it, from his or her place "in the shadows" to become a visible presence.[4] Experts wanted to know how many homosexuals existed in the present-day United States and whether their numbers were increasing. Was the homosexual a specific and recognizable kind of person, differentiated from the heterosexual by his or her body, sexual behavior, gender identity, or psychology? Were male homosexuals, who received the bulk of public attention, similar to or different from lesbians?[5] Ultimately, was homosexuality a stable and recognizable category, or, as more and more worried, were hetero- and homosexual behaviors so mingled that they could not be separated? As they pondered such questions, experts often articulated the fear that modern American culture was becoming permeated with homosexuality. Was there something about the character of modern Americans that encouraged same-sex behaviors? Was homosexuality becoming what one psychiatrist referred to as a "new national disease"?[6] If so, then what elements of modern life had created this increase, and what might this mean for future generations of Americans?

As postwar Americans discussed these questions, they cast homosexuality simultaneously as dangerous, attractive, and distinctively American. Emerging as a pressing topic during the war years, homosexuality dominated Americans' imaginations in the 1950s. Homosexuality emerged as a topic in the ways that it did at this time in part because it offered the perfect site for articulating and examining widespread fears about American character.

"A PROBLEM IN SOCIETY AT LARGE": HOMOSEXUALITY AND THE WAR

Many of the phenomena that created this new cultural context of popular curiosity about homosexuality were rooted in the social and cultural changes of the war years. Among the general public, as well as within governmental, medical, and mental health circles, homosexuality became an important issue during the war. A series of developments combined to heighten public awareness of same-sex sexuality. The number of American men dismissed as physically or psychologically unfit for service prompted concern about effeminacy. Geographical mobility and the homosocial worlds of military service and wartime work fostered unprecedented opportunities for same-sex contacts.[7] Military experts and their psychiatric colleagues identified homosexuality as a growing problem in the U.S. armed forces, with one expert predicting soon after the nation's entry into the war that "the problem of the homosexual" would "become more widespread in the service as the war progresses."[8] Mounting evidence of same-sex liaisons in the services and on the home front placed homosexuality on many investigators' lists of wartime social problems.[9]

American attention to homosexuality did not end with Allied victory and demobilization. Indeed, as the war drew to a close, a number of authorities suggested that homosexuality would be an even more pressing problem in peacetime than it had been during the war. In a lecture to the staff and inmates of a New England women's reformatory, the anthropologist Margaret Mead predicted that "we are going to face [a] society that has more women than men in this generation, and female homosexuality will be a problem, not alone in the institutions but in society at large."[10] Mead's forecast rested largely on an anticipated gender imbalance after the war, but other social scientists suggested additional reasons for an imminent increase in both male homosexuality and lesbianism. The philosopher Henry Elkin suggested in 1948 that same-sex relationships would proliferate in the postwar era. Already, "numerous subtle extenuations of male homosexuality are beginning to appear," Elkin warned, and the coming battle between "perverse" and "normal" sexuality was nothing less than a "hidden conflict crucial for the future of our world."[11] When *Sexual Behavior in the Human Male* appeared, its astonishing revelation that nearly 40 percent of the nation's males engaged in sex with men fostered the growing national concern about homosexuality. In the wake of the report's widely publicized statistics, the stream of works on American homosexuality swelled to a flood.

In this unprecedented public discussion of homosexuality, three related questions recurred again and again. First, how many homosexuals were there in the United States, and how were they to be defined and counted? Second, what caused homosexuality, and why did it seem to be increasing? Last, as experts discussed homosexuality's effects, they returned again and again to questions about why it was such a feature of American life. Was homosexuality a specifically American problem? What factors in contemporary life, they asked, created and promoted homosexuality? And in turn, what influence might homosexuals have on American culture? Throughout their discussions of these and related questions, postwar authorities repeatedly expressed concern about the relation between same-sex sexuality and modern American culture, betraying a deep fear that the barriers separating heterosexuality from homosexuality would eventually dissolve.

ONE IN SIX: HOW MANY HOMOSEXUALS?

Some of Americans' most pressing questions about homosexuality during the late 1940s and 1950s centered on the number of homosexuals in the United States. Kinsey's studies, which suggested that as many as half of all men and nearly a quarter of all women could be classified as homosexual on the basis of behavior or fantasy, provided raw material for a legion of postwar commentators. The Kinsey team had cautioned readers that their own numbers were probably low, noting of their findings on homosexuality that, although "the figures are, of course, considerably higher than any which have been previously estimated[,] . . . they must be understatements, if they are anything other than the fact."[12] The numbers given were dramatic enough; with these caveats, Kinsey set off a firestorm of debate as experts from the biological and social sciences clashed over exactly how many homosexuals there were in the postwar United States.

A few critics, mostly psychoanalysts, disagreed vehemently with the report's figures. Edmund Bergler, for one, accused Kinsey of drastically inflating the number of homosexuals in his calculations and thereby alarming Americans with "the myth of a new national disease."[13] More critics, however, either accepted Kinsey's figures or agreed that, if the reports' numbers erred, it was in the direction of *under*reporting same-sex sexual activity. The psychiatrist Jule Eisenbud argued that men who defined themselves as heterosexual but had at least occasional sexual encounters with men vastly underreported their same-sex contacts because of societal taboos, a circumstance which would suggest that homosexual encounters were even more frequent than Kinsey found.[14]

Just as alarming as actual numbers was the widely expressed belief that the amount of homosexuality in the United States was increasing. When the psychoanalyst Abram Kardiner surveyed police reports, popular attitudes, and available sex studies in 1954, he concluded that "the increase in homosexuality is enormous."[15] *Time* magazine's editor, Gilbert Cant, noted a few years later that since the war "there has been a marked increase in overt homosexuality, and homosexuals are openly seeking to make converts to their abnormal pattern of life."[16] This increase was widely perceived to hold true for both men and women: in fact, since lesbians were often described as being better able than men to hide their sexual preference, homosexuality among women might well be even more widespread than among men. One sensationalist account cautioned readers after the second report that, "despite Kinsey's genius at drawing out his subjects, his statistics might be less than conclusive," and that there "is a strong possibility that among women there is an even higher percentage of homosexuality than among men."[17] "Female sexual inversion," the sexologist Frank Caprio similarly believed, was "becoming an increasingly important problem" in the United States.[18]

Writers offered staggeringly high estimates of the prevalence of homosexual inclinations or activity. Kinsey's figures had carefully distinguished between exclusive and occasional homosexuality, but such distinctions were often lost in the search for quotable numbers. One particularly alarmist document, *The Sixth Man* (1961), by the reporter Jess Stearn, maintained that one-sixth of the male population of the United States was composed of practicing or latent homosexuals. Marketed as "one of the most frightening surveys conducted since the Kinsey books," Stearn's study was greeted by an eager audience, spending twelve weeks on the *New York Times*' best-seller list.[19] A few years later, the sexual investigator Robert Masters raised the stakes when he concluded that "there are presently in the United States at least fifty million persons who are more or less susceptible to conscious sexual stimulation by members of either sex," a figure that categorized more than one in four Americans as "more or less" homosexual.[20] Such efforts to quantify the number and percentage of homosexuals were headline-grabbers, but they were also attempts to manage and contain the problem. By counting homosexuals, authorities could not only establish their mastery over homosexuality as a social problem but also attempt to cleanly separate homosexuals from heterosexuals, thus maintaining an increasingly important distinction. Even as they sought to calculate the exact number of homosexuals in the country, however, many experts revealed that their project of classification was already untenable, as the category of "the homosexual" became increasingly unstable.

"MORE DISCUSSED THAN IGNORED": HOMOSEXUALITY IN POSTWAR CULTURE

Many historians have suggested that the period during and after World War II is when sexual identity became a widely discussed and pressing issue for most Americans. Lillian Faderman argues that, during the postwar period, "knowledge of homosexuality was more widely disseminated than at any previous time in history," and Robert Corber similarly maintains that, during the 1950s, "sexual orientation became as crucial a determinate of social identity as race or gender."[21] Within the popular culture, narratives of homosexuality—information on how to identify gay men and lesbians, on whether or not they posed a security problem, on where they congregated, and on how they dressed, lived their lives, and had sex—were to be found virtually everywhere, from mass-market fiction to social science and medical journals.

Some of commentators' concerns about homosexuality sprang directly from visible changes in the size, location, and presence of the nation's homosexual communities. During and after the war years, the process of identifying a coworker, a fellow enlistee, or even oneself as homosexual took on new juridical and cultural as well as personal significance. The historian Allan Berube argues that draftees' "self-declarations began to add a political dimension to the previously sexual and social meanings of coming out."[22] George Chauncey Jr. notes that "the gay world . . . became even more extensive in the 1940s and 1950s than it had been before the war."[23] As men and women who had discovered or confirmed their homosexuality while in the service or while doing war work demobilized, many congregated in urban areas where other homosexuals lived and worked. A few formed small but influential organizations for gay men and lesbians, some with their own periodical literature. The New York–based Mattachine Society produced its own *Mattachine Review,* the lesbian organization Daughters of Bilitis published the magazine *The Ladder,* and a San Francisco Bay Area offshoot of Mattachine founded *One* magazine, a monthly dedicated to uniting homosexuals as a group and to agitating for homosexuals' civil rights.[24]

Although these periodicals had a limited circulation, they were influential and widely publicized, featuring not only coverage of homosexual life but also articles assessing publications on homosexuality and debunking popular psychological and physiological theories. One of the most prominent homophile authors, Donald Webster Cory, became nationally known and produced a stream of articles and books that educated a wide readership about the details and variety of homosexual experience and the oppression of homosexuals in American society.[25] The publication and influence of such works pointed to the dramatic shifts that were beginning to upset ideas about homosexuality and its place in national discourse. John D'Emilio argues that Cory's 1951 *The Homosexual in America* "not only provided gay men and women with a tool for reinterpreting their lives; it also implied that the conditions of life had changed sufficiently that the book's message might find a receptive audience."[26]

Whatever the reasons for their receptiveness, a mass audience for narratives of homosexuality certainly existed. Within a year of the report's release, an irritated sociologist commented, "Even a poor book on homosexuality can find a profitable market nowadays."[27] Throughout the next decade, reports on the extent and meaning of homosexuality in the United States appeared in a wide range of popular magazines and newspapers.

Many other periodicals ran stories on broader topics, such as changing gender roles, psychiatry, or sex in the United States, in which homosexuality was a major theme. Sources discussing homosexuality for a mass audience continually insisted upon the topic's vital importance: readers were urged to put aside their "apathy [and] ignorance" and pressed "to face facts" about homosexuality.[28] Ignorance and avoidance were no longer acceptable, authors warned. Instead, modern civic-mindedness demanded that Americans examine the available evidence and intelligently discuss homosexuality.

Many of these narratives were written from the outside, presenting homosexuals as an exotic or pitiable subculture that needed to be explained to or translated for a mainstream audience. Such narratives, however, were joined by works written by homosexuals themselves. A spate of works appeared after the war, ranging from serious essays by mental health experts and social scientists to real and fictional surveys of homosexual behavior, guides to gay and lesbian life, and pulp novels. These cultural productions represented a smorgasbord of information on homosexuality to appeal to any buyer. Their proliferation and continued profitability suggests that works on homosexuality appealed to heterosexual as well as homosexual readers, and further implies that positive, negative, and mixed portrayals of homosexuality were open for multiple interpretations and uses.

The wave of books on homosexuality certainly attracted attention, and disapproving reviewers and homophile activists alike commented on the topic's ubiquity. A reviewer for a literary quarterly commented that "sex deviations . . . receive somewhat exaggerated attention in recent fiction," and complained that the present-day reader "can hardly open a book without finding a spark" of what he termed "Greek fire."[29] One of the first issues of the homophile magazine *One* mocked the vogue for analyses of homosexuality in a satirical 1951 article entitled "Magazine Goldmine: Run an Article on Queers!"[30] By the next decade, Cory could point to the proliferation and popularity of works on homosexuality, including his own, and state with certainty that "today the subject of homosexuality is more discussed than ignored." Whereas "once the word homosexual could not be printed in such proper places as the columns of the *New York Times*," Cory proclaimed, nowadays "the reverse is true: It is hardly possible to read without the subject being explicitly mentioned."[31]

A glance at the *Readers' Guide to Periodical Literature* attests to both the burgeoning of information about homosexuality and the spread of a new vocabulary and frame of reference for its discussion. During and briefly after the war years, articles dealing with homosexuality were filed under "Sex Perversion." "Homosexuality" first appeared as a subject heading in 1947 but merely carried the notation "See Sex Perversion." The guide shifted its classificatory system rapidly in response to increasing interest in and information on the topic, soon listing relevant articles only under "Homosexuality" and adding "Lesbian" as a subclassification in 1959.[32]

The effects of this explosion of attention and rapid mass diffusion of information about same-sex sexuality have usually been theorized as wholly negative for homosexuals and for the public status of homosexuality. Lillian Faderman, for example, follows her contention that in the 1950s *homosexuality* became a household word with the argument that the unprecedented coverage of the topic worked primarily to pathologize homosexuality, fixing its status as "sick or subversive." Throughout the 1950s, Faderman concludes, "the demarcation that separated 'homosexual' from 'heterosexual' was now more clear than ever."[33] In a 1996 study of twentieth-century lesbians, the historian Trisha Franzen has similarly maintained that postwar lesbians who searched for information on sexuality found only "uniformly negative images of twisted and pathetic lives."[34] Jonathan Ned Katz agrees, maintaining that the postwar era "was a period in which the predominance of the hetero norm went almost unchallenged, an era of heterosexual hegemony."[35] What many of these and other historians of sexuality in the postwar period have concentrated on is the ways in which available popular knowledge pathologized gay men and lesbians, both by building on long-standing notions of their physical, psychological, and moral deviance and by inscribing them within newer discourses that framed them as threats to national security and sexual character.

I read the postwar proliferation of popular and expert attention to homosexuality and its place in American culture somewhat differently. Rather than becoming clearer to observers during this period, the line between hetero- and homosexuality seemed dangerously blurred and often threatened to collapse altogether. This is not to suggest that homosexuality was described favorably. Experts repeatedly presented same-sex sexuality as a locus of secrecy and shame and a source of public danger, and psychiatric and government rhetoric authorized campaigns against homosexuality in the streets and the workplace that had a real and highly negative influence on gay Americans. In the widely cited words of the psychoanalyst Edmund Bergler, homosexual men and women were inherently neurotic, untrustworthy, and "sick inwardly," unhappy because they "want to be disappointed."[36] A physician summed up the medical view of homosexuals as "a revolting group of individuals," "pathetic freaks of nature."[37] The American Psychiatric Association categorized homosexuality as a "psychopathic personality disorder" in 1952, and when a committee of the Group for the Advancement of Psychiatry assessed the suitability of homosexuals for government employment three years later, they agreed that adult homosexuality was inevitably "a symptom of a severe emotional disturbance."[38] Homosexuality, *Coronet* magazine agreed, often led to mental anguish, "social isolation," and suicide.[39]

Although such commentary characterized homosexuals as predatory, dangerous, evil, or at best ill, the effects of this outpouring of analysis were not always clear-cut. The rhetoric of danger and deviance, pervasive though it was, was only one side of a multifaceted and often contradictory discourse about homosexuality. Much of both medical and popular information about homosexuality was indeed characterized by warnings about abnormality and advice on how to recognize and expose homosexuals, but the range and overall tone of available information was often more complex and ambivalent than a focus solely on negative representations would suggest. Mainstream sources also featured discussions of homosexuality that debunked negative stereotypes: when the columnist Max Lerner penned an eleven-part series on the topic in 1950, which was published in the *New York Post,* he continually expressed empathy with homosexuals and called for reason rather than bigotry. Sources with a less positive spin often mixed their messages, albeit begrudgingly: *Newsweek* magazine, for example, featured an article that both warned of the presence of "at least 500,000 men and women inverts in New York City alone" and acknowledged that "most of them [homosexuals] control their social conduct within the same bounds as do people of normal sexual inclinations."[40] Likewise, the same journalist who castigated homosexuality as "revolting . . . [and] socially dangerous behavior," admitted a few paragraphs later that homosexual criminality and misconduct were "not nearly so widespread as is popularly supposed."[41]

Hendrik Ruitenbeek's 1963 collection of essays, *The Problem of Homosexuality in Modern Society,* offers an illustration of the complexity with which the topic was often presented. The book's cover, which depicted two figures painted in murky colors, mingled negative iconography—shadows and an obscured face—with signs of acceptance and toleration, such as the calm gaze of the seated figure and the supportive hands on his shoulders (see figure 17). The book's contents similarly blended attacks on

Figure 17. The ambiguous position of the homosexual:
cover, Hendrik M. Ruitenbeek, ed., *The Problem of
Homosexuality in Modern Society.*

homosexuality with more measured assessments of its meaning and calls
for normalization and acceptance. Even vitriolic denunciations of same-
sex sexuality could perform important cultural work by asserting the social
significance of homosexuality and placing it on the national agenda.
Through their insistence upon the difficulty of detecting homosexuals,
exposure of how many apparently heterosexual men and women engaged

in same-sex sexual behaviors, and anxious attention to why such acts attracted so many, postwar experts did not merely condemn homosexuality but also broadened public discussion of it. And they—sometimes deliberately, sometimes unintentionally—destabilized traditional sexual norms by questioning whether homosexuality had any fixed meaning.

"WHAT, PRECISELY, DO WE MEAN WHEN WE USE THE TERM HOMOSEXUAL?"

As a number of authorities noted, the wildly varying estimates produced by observers begged questions about how they defined and diagnosed homosexuality. Kinsey's, Masters's, and Stearn's differing counts of homosexuals, for example, pointed to the difficulties of making such assessments: by what criteria was one out of every three, four, or six men in the United States homosexual? In pursuing definitions of homosexuality, investigators asked several questions: Was homosexuality located in the body or in the mind? Did it take specific sexual acts to brand a person homosexual, or were that person's emotions or desires enough to classify him or her as such? Could one's sexual identity or propensities be measured? Was "the homosexual" a particular kind of person, or, as many increasingly believed, were same-sex behaviors the result of an innate biological or psychological capacity shared by all modern Americans? In short, what exactly constituted homosexuality?[42]

Postwar definitions of homosexuality both borrowed from earlier projects and sharply moved away from them. During the nineteenth and early twentieth centuries, everyday sexual classification accepted some same-sex activities as falling within the realm of normal. This understanding was based both on assumptions about situational behaviors and on an active/passive model of sexual relations in which, for example, a man who fellated another might be viewed as homosexual while his partner was not. By the postwar era, this no longer held true: in such situations, partners were increasingly often understood as equal participants in a shared act, and the "occasional" and habitual homosexual as sharing some essential identity.[43] Studies of sexual behavior during the 1920s and 1930s had repeatedly searched for roots of homosexuality in the body, exploring anatomy and hormones with detours to the psyche for psychological tests and family histories. As postwar investigators struggled to define homosexuality, they borrowed from all these earlier models. To some observers, a single adult same-sex sexual encounter, or merely the desire for one, rendered a person homosexual. According to dominant psychoanalytic thought, youthful same-sex behavior could be a phase or experiment, but any later same-sex preferences, whether acts or mere urges, signified neurosis. To others, it took repeated incidents of same-sex sexual behavior for a man or woman to merit the homosexual label.

Definitions of both hetero- and homosexuality were becoming increasingly contested, and the first report only muddied the waters further. "One of the troubles about the discussion of homosexuals in the government service," Max Lerner pointed out acerbically in 1950, "is that the term is used so loosely you could drive several tanks through it."[44] Attempting to create clear diagnostic categories, some experts distinguished between random homosexual acts and the more serious phenomenon of homosexuality as a clinical entity. "Homosexual acts per se do not constitute homosexuality," the psychiatrist Samuel Hadden advised colleagues in the pages of the *Pennsylvania Medical Journal* in 1957, adding that even recurring homosexual behavior could be "regarded as a normal phase in the course of psychosexual development." It took more than a few orgasms to determine sexual orientation, he insisted, and "only careful evaluation of many factors can determine whether an individual is homosexual."[45]

A few studies even suggested that homosexuality was as normal or abnormal as heterosexuality, and that it should be accepted as a benign sexual preference akin to finding brunettes more attractive than blondes. Evelyn Hooker, a Los Angeles psychologist who studied homosexual men's emotional adjustment and level of functioning, pointed out that arguments about homosexuals' emotional instability were often based on studies of men who were institutionalized or sought psychiatric treatment, and not on assessments of the stability of those who functioned well within the broader society. After comparing a group of homosexual men—volunteers from the Mattachine Society—to a heterosexual control group, Hooker concluded that the two groups did not demonstrate dramatic psychological differences. Clinically speaking, Hooker maintained, homosexuality "does not exist. Its forms are as varied as are those of heterosexuality." Following Kinsey, she concluded that same-sex erotic behavior was "a deviation in sexual pattern that is within the normal range, psychologically."[46] Hooker's studies of male homosexuals began appearing in psychology journals in the mid-1950s and, as a result of word of mouth and homophile literature, were avidly discussed in West Coast homosexual circles.

Both sexual liberals and conservatives confessed to confusion over how to define and recognize homosexuality. When two Army psychiatrists surveyed experts' opinions, they found that "an occasional homosexual act does not constitute sexual inversion any more than an occasional drink of whiskey constitutes chronic alcoholism."[47] The phenomenon of bisexuals further confused definitions: in one of its periodic worried updates on the topic, *Time* magazine reported with some amazement that "homosexuality is not an all-or-nothing quality."[48] Excessive interest in heterosexual sex could easily cross over into homosexuality: "The cloak of Don Juan conceals a latent homosexual," one homophile author warned.[49] To a public that correlated homosexuality with same-sex acts, such distinctions were undoubtedly confusing.

If same-sex sexual behavior alone was not enough to define someone as homosexual, then could diagnoses be based on gendered characteristics? Popular stereotypes of mannish lesbians and effeminate homosexual men persisted, but experts warned that they were misleading and worked to undercut the linking of homosexuality with gender-inappropriate behavior. George Corner, of the National Research Council's Committee for Research in Problems of Sex, argued that the "popular picture of the effeminate pervert must be replaced by the realization that homosexual behavior is something in which a rather large proportion of boys and men are liable to engage under conducive circumstances, whatever their physical build."[50] "Not all homosexuals," another sex expert observed, "are of the 'sissy' type," adding that "during the war the writer saw a number of fighter pilots who were homosexuals and could be dangerous if provoked."[51] Such authors' insistence that morphology and appearance were not correlated with homosexuality ran counter to persistent popular stereotypes, causing a great deal of confusion. The police who patrolled Times Square in the 1940s and 1950s repeatedly "complained that the boys in what they deemed 'Queens County' were 'not easy to identify,' devoid of tell-tale marks of effeminacy."[52] A psychiatrist similarly cautioned readers against assuming that homosexuals displayed traits of the opposite sex, noting that the "major percentage of homosexuals are indistinguishable from others of their sex," and that he had known homosexual "marine sergeants, professional football players, world champion boxers, steeplechase riders" and others "whose appearance and public behavior might well be the envy of almost any man."[53]

Gendered cues, such sources warned, could mislead. The ability to wear high heels or apply makeup was no guarantee against lesbianism, and men with homosexual desires could engage in a convincing masquerade of heterosexuality. Indeed, as some of the very behaviors that had once indicated heterosexuality (such as promiscuity) became recast as clues to homosexuality, the categories seemed to blur. In Hooker's study, several members of an initial control group of heterosexuals proved to be participating in the study under false pretenses. Although each one of them had been recommended by community leaders as a "thorough-going heterosexual," more than 10 percent had to be eliminated from the study because further questioning revealed that, "though married and functioning in the community[,] they had had extensive homosexual experience."[54] Hooker thus argued in another paper that her research "raises as many questions about heterosexuality as it does about homosexuality." The term *heterosexual,* she held, was just as limited and unsatisfactory a diagnostic label as *homosexual,* because neither reflected consideration of an individual's sexual behaviors and psychic processes or of the context in which his or her sexual choices were made.[55]

Some authorities navigated these complex considerations by suggesting that there were multiple types of homosexuals, which could be sorted by the strength of their response to members of the same sex. Addressing a conference of law enforcement professionals, the sex researcher Alfred Gross asked rhetorically, "What, precisely, do we mean when we use the term homosexual?" The "rough definition of the homosexual as a man who receives sexual gratification from his own sex" was problematic, he explained, because it lumped the "schoolboy experimenting with the boy next door" in with the chronic "exhibitionist." "There are," Gross concluded somewhat enigmatically, "homosexuals and homosexuals."[56] Others offered more specific taxonomies of homosexuality: the reporter Max Lerner quoted an unnamed "eminent psychiatrist" as describing three types: the "exploratory" homosexual, who dabbled briefly in same-sex sexual behavior before abandoning it; the "facultative homosexual," who "may have a faculty for homosexual relations" but often lives "a heterosexual life and even a married life, as well," and, last, the clearer case of the *"obligatory or compulsive homosexual,"* who was magnetically and inevitably drawn to same-sex relations. Only the latter could be reliably identified even by the expert.[57]

As authorities proposed multiple and often conflicting definitions of homosexuality, a dizzying variety of possible models and nosologies emerged. Bergler described the familiar class of homosexuals and lesbians who "cover up their homosexuality with a camouflage of heterosexuality," but also proposed a new diagnostic category of "spurious homosexuality," a syndrome affecting heterosexuals who pretended to be homosexual out of neurosis or to seem modern and interesting.[58] Further muddying the waters, a sociologist alerted the public to the existence of "pseudo homosexuals," essentially heterosexual individuals who experimented with same-sex activity on occasion.[59] The New York physician Dr. George Silver proposed that "there may be several kinds of homosexuality, one of which may be a basic character trait; another, part of normal personal or social development and so temporary; still another, a permanent form derived from social and/or personal factors."[60]

Homophiles often embraced this blurring of boundaries, asserting that homosexuality was "not a separate entity, but a question of degree." Following Kinsey, one argued in the early 1950s that "over the population as a whole there is an imperceptible gradation from wholly homosexual to wholly heterosexual. A man may be completely homosexual or completely heterosexual, but the great majority of men come somewhere between these two extremes."[61] Another homophile writer, J. D. Mercer, agreed that the most important things Kinsey's book did was disclose "the widespread incidence of homosexual behavior among American males" and reveal "to what extent it is *intermingled* with heterosexual relations."[62] Sexologists agreed that it was increasingly impossible to determine or categorize any individual's sexuality. As ways to diagnose sexual subjectivity multiplied, the categories themselves became a mockery. Charles Berg and Clifford Allen maintained that "it might be true to say that a 'diagnosis' based on characteristics no deeper than the *unconscious* mind (even without morphology and genetics) would have to declare everybody bisexual *and* more or less of an intersex."[63]

This crisis in psychoanalytic and medical categories was reflected in popular culture. In *The Hypocritical American,* an impassioned appeal to Americans to rethink national taboos about sex, the novelist and critic James Lincoln Collier drew on Kinsey to argue that, "clearly, there is a distinction between homosexuality and homosexuals. Not all men and women who occasionally have homosexual sex can be called homosexuals."[64] As authorities wrangled over definitions, the criteria of what defined a homosexual seemed increasingly meaningless. One wartime study of enlisted men, for example, defined the term with the observation that "by 'homosexuality' we refer only to cases of frank inversion; we do not mean the occasional, casual, passive homosexual experience," while a later study defined homosexuality as the existence of "prominent homosexual impulses."[65] Little wonder that, according to *Sexology* magazine, homosexuality "more than any other sexological subject, has remained a very confused issue in the average reader's mind."[66]

Another factor that served to complicate simple definitions was the concept of latency, which spread from psychoanalytic thought throughout postwar popular culture. Freud had viewed the years between five and ten as a "latency period" in which children repress polymorphous sexual urges. As psychiatric attention to sexuality intensified, the concept was simplified to mean any same-sex potential or interest, however minor and buried. According to a psychiatrist and a sex researcher writing in the *Journal of Social Hygiene*, latent homosexuals "at a conscious level, have no interest in homosexual relations and even react with disgust to such an idea," but "have strong homosexual drives at an unconscious level," which "come out in some disguised fashion."[67] The "disguised fashion" of those drives could be curious indeed. "Strangely enough," one team of advice authors noted, "heterosexuality can itself be a defense against latent homosexual tendencies."[68] The concept was pervasive and powerful: the cultural critic Nora Sayre recalls of male friends in the 1950s that "the idea of 'latent' homosexuality was a tremendous threat for them—some worried that they might wake up one morning and discover themselves to be gay."[69] In the postwar coming-of-age classic *The Catcher in the Rye,* a would-be sophisticate waxes eloquent on the subject, warning the protagonist, Holden Caulfield, that "half the married guys in the world were flits and didn't even know it[;] . . . you could practically turn into one overnight, if you had all the traits and all."[70] Latency could be an almost infinitely flexible concept, encoding layers of deceptive behaviors and cravings. *Newsweek* magazine even described a lesbian featured in a psychoanalytic case study as having "strong, if latent, normal desire."[71]

Latency presented troubling problems not least because authorities who credited the concept believed that latent homosexuality affected a great many Americans. The editors of *Sexology* magazine maintained in 1951 that their estimate of 4 million homosexuals in the United States was "only the estimated number of 'overt' homosexuals. If those having latent and partial homosexual traits are included[,] the total figure would undoubtedly be several times 4,000,000."[72] The social hygienist Edward Glover emphasized how easily latent homosexuality could be hidden when he noted that the "'unconscious homosexual' may show no signs of conscious homosexual interest," concealing secret inclinations so thoroughly that "the only manifest signs present in adult life" are minor "peculiarities of character and social reaction."[73] The latent homosexual, as John D'Emilio and Robert Corber have noted, parallels another, equally distressing bogey, the concealed Communist; both harbor a secret essence that threatens social stability.[74]

The unsuspecting figure of the latent homosexual resembles Raymond Shaw, the brainwashed victim in the cold war classic film *The Manchurian Candidate* (1962). Outwardly a war hero, Shaw is brainwashed by American and Chinese Communists to assassinate a presidential candidate, hastening a Communist takeover of the United States. The horror of Shaw's position lies in his lack of self-knowledge; under orders from his masters, he even murders his beloved bride. The only way he can destroy his hidden self is by suicide.[75] Latency suggested a similar danger, as desires could be invisible not only to observers but also to homosexuals themselves. The concept of latency not only inspired the psychoanalyst Irving Bieber's hopeful suggestion that "every homosexual is a latent heterosexual" but also authorized the philosopher-analyst Ernest van den Haag's assumption that "every heterosexual can be described as a latent homosexual—one who does not use his homosexual potential—and every homosexual as a latent heterosexual."[76] Latency pointed to a troubling slippage between sexual categories: potentially, every American was always already homosexual.

Concern about the permeability of any boundary between heterosexuality and homosexuality suffused postwar writing on sexuality. In his 1964 *The Grapevine,* a report on "the secret world of the lesbian," Jess Stearn noted that his extensive sojourn among Sapphists had convinced him that "the boundaries of female homosexuality were so vague that many women slipped into lesbianism without realizing they were lesbians."[77] This phrase, which publishers found striking enough to reproduce on the book's jacket, drew on a conflicting set of meanings that structured popular literature on homosexuality. In this view, the space separating hetero- from homosexuality was both a "boundary" to be policed and a mutable space of sexual potential. Women could "slip" into lesbianism without realizing it, but the category of "the lesbian" still existed and was transparent to the outside observer. Regardless of the self-definition of a woman who might "slip" out of heterosexuality and into lesbianism "without realizing" it, her lesbianism is still definable as such by experts. This tension between a vision of sexuality that separated homosexuals from heterosexuals and one that insisted on their similarities preoccupied many of the social scientists and others who wrote about homosexuality's growing influence in American culture. Their search for an elusive line that would definitively mark the separation between heterosexuality and homosexuality under-wrote a variety of theories of sexuality and culture.

As postwar experts failed to reach consensus on defining homosexuality, a few proposed rejecting the category altogether. "Fifty years ago," the psychiatrist Hendrik Ruitenbeek explained, "there was no question about what a 'homosexual' was. . . . Since then, the issue has been complicated" by Kinsey's discovery of the ubiquity of same-sex sexual behavior and the emergence of conflicting diagnostic categories and psychoanalytic theories.[78] The psychoanalyst Clara Thompson agreed that the category no longer had any clear definition. "The term 'homosexual,'" she complained shortly after the war, "has come to be a kind of wastebasket in which are dumped all forms of relationship with one's own sex. The word may be applied to activities, attitudes, feelings, thoughts, or repression of any of these."[79] Given this confusing proliferation of analytical and popular meanings, Thompson felt that the term *homosexual,* and perhaps even the concept, held little clinical value. More and more often, experts asked whether it was possible to define or categorize any sexuality. How were heterosexuals, homosexuals, and anyone in between—as individuals and as group members—to be defined and categorized? The answer was disturbingly unclear, and an underlying concern emerged that there might be no clear separation between the two.[80]

THE SEARCH FOR CAUSES OF HOMOSEXUALITY

As experts sought to account for the apparent rise in homosexuality in the United States, they offered a host of theories about where this upsurge in same-sex sexual behavior had come from, why it appeared when it did, and what its future effects might be. A few scientists argued that homosexuality was genetically determined.[81] The Kinsey team had avoided any extensive exploration of these issues, arguing simply that homosexuality was "an expression of capacities that are basic in the human animal."[82] Other commentators, however, instead saw homosexuality as triggered by some combination of familial, environmental, and social circumstances. The physician George Silver saw a "natural complexity about homosexuality, since it may be buried in the *individual's* psyche or physiology or chemistry, enforced from without by the *family* psychological setting, or arise from the *social* organization."[83] As such, it could potentially affect anyone, even emerging late in life after lying dormant for years.

The news media paid close attention to reports of homosexuality in other countries; a typical article on same-sex love in England noted gleefully that "the latest report on homosexuality at Oxford would hardly deepen the roar of the proud British lion."[84] However, reports on homosexuality abroad usually served to highlight the phenomenon as primarily an American problem, accentuating worries about the deleterious effect of American sexuality on the nation's status. The novelist Saul Bellow even argued that "America's chief export to Europe had become its homosexuals."[85] The anxious association of domestic homosexuality and declining national prestige emerged clearly in Edmund Bergler's charge that Kinsey's figures on homosexuality could "be politically and propagandistically used against the United States abroad, stigmatizing the nation as a whole in a whisper campaign."[86] Authorities questioned why rates of homosexuality seemed to be higher in the United States than in other countries. Was the national increase in same-sex behavior a physiological or sociological phenomenon? Could it be connected to environmental or social factors? As authorities explored these questions, many of the theories that they offered connected sexual behavior to cultural change, continuing the ideological linkage of American sexuality and the changing national character.

Some believed that the apparent upsurge in American homosexuality was rooted in recent history. The depression, one author maintained, "creating as it did a huge army of unemployed youth, provided ideal conditions for the culture and development of the virus of inversion."[87] Most commentators who saw historical developments as important to the nation's rising tide of homosexuality, however, looked to more recent phenomena, including World War II and the postwar economic boom. The war was widely seen as having encouraged homosexuality among GIs in Europe or Asia, since men stationed there lacked access to appropriate female partners and turned to situational homosexuality.[88] More troubling, the stresses of combat and the homosocial atmosphere of camp life could conspire to render some formerly "normal" men homosexual for life.[89] The psychiatrist Abram Kardiner, for one, speculated that former soldiers "tend to drift towards males because they have lived through battles in which male cooperation contrasts violently with images of the demanding, uncooperative woman. Many of these men between the ages of nineteen and twenty-four whose lives were dislocated by the war and who have trouble readjusting to civilian life turn to homosexuality regardless of their previous interest in women."[90]

When they returned home at the end of the war, Kardiner and others believed, this new population of homosexually inclined men initiated others into their ranks. "The backwash of World War II," an unnamed policeman told reporter Jess Stearn, "swept the flotsam and jetsam of the deviate world into the huge city," where "they could do as they pleased."[91] Other experts agreed that in many locales homosexuality was "washed up by the war," so that after 1945 the problem "had a new dimension."[92] "Postwar periods," the chief of social medicine at a major New York hospital noted, "particularly seem to stimulate homosexuality."[93] The war functioned as a causative agent in other analyses as well: according to psychoanalytically inclined experts, home-front conditions had encouraged women to flaunt their economic and sexual freedom, emasculating husbands and lovers and creating homosexual children.[94] Despite their often vituperative tone, such theories furthered a cultural rather than biologistic view of homosexuality by stressing the malleable nature of sexual behavior.

Although war made a tempting target, for many of the experts who worried about homosexuality it provided insufficient explanatory power. Distressingly, causes had to be located closer to home. Like other varieties of deviant or excessive sexuality, homosexuality was seen as an effect of modern life, triggered by changes in everyday conditions. Rapid economic and technological changes, it seemed, went hand in hand with homosexuality, making it inevitable in modern American life. The stress of "urban life," one writer believed, "frequently drives sensitive, introverted men and women to seek refuge in sexual aberrations," while ambitious young men sought same-sex contacts to escape "the fast-paced 20th century economic struggle."[95] Another authority blamed alleged increases in homosexual behavior on the "pressures of environment: high-tension city living, replacement of human contact by impersonal mechanization, and the haunting insecurities of the atomic era."[96]

A few homophiles built on such arguments to defend the social utility of homosexuality. In the advanced industrial society of the postwar United States, they argued, tasks had become increasingly differentiated. The alleged increase in the number and visibility of homosexuals, therefore, was the result of a natural process of sexual specialization that reflected this increasing specialization of labor. In the modern world, the homophile activist Jim Kepner reasoned in a 1957 article in *One* magazine, society had "learned the advantages of division of labor, and each job, including reproduction, is left to specialists." Countering conservative rhetoric, such as Marynia Farnham's assertion that "homosexual members are dead cells" in modern society, Kepner applied a libertarian free-market analysis to homosexuality. Rather than a "dead cell," the homosexual was an example of human specialization. "We don't expect every man to be farmer, carpenter, and lawyer all at once," Kepner argued; hence, "why expect everyone to have children?"[97] Kepner's theories on the social utility of homosexuality went further than those of most homophiles—he argued that homosexuals were perfectly adapted to jobs that required extensive travel or exposure to dangerous mutagens, and that a growing homosexual population was ideally fitted to adapt to modern industrial development—but his belief that the dictates of modern life encouraged homosexuality echoed the themes found in other theories.[98]

Chief among the social changes authorities discussed were those affecting gender roles, and homosexuality was commonly attributed to a national decline in traditional masculinity and femininity.[99] Robert Odenwald's *The Disappearing Sexes* warned that, as gender roles became less differentiated, the nation was "moving towards a one-sex society" dominated by homosexuals.[100] Another psychologist suggested that women's presence in the workplace accelerated American men's retreat into homosexuality by "making the female a competitor" and "stepping up the requirements of masculinity."[101] Was homosexuality the inevitable outcome of America's changing gender roles?

Unfortunately for the tradition-minded, family life was just as often described as the cause of homosexuality. As Kardiner explained, maternal overinvolvement and distant fathers were "probably one of the main factors in the increase in male homosexuality.[102] And too little mothering was as bad as too much. The move of middle-class women into the workplace, many argued, created homosexual sons and daughters by leaving children and adolescents bereft of maternal guidance at a critical developmental juncture. Fatherhood could also foster homosexuality: the difficulty of providing for a family could tempt men to shrink from the responsibilities of heterosexuality and marriage and seek comfort in the arms of other men. "Homosexuality," reasoned one authority, provided American men with "an opportunity to relax from the high demands of masculinity."[103] The analyst Robert Lindner, whose best-selling books offered cautionary case studies of a nation under stress, maintained that homosexuality offered American men one of the few available ways to rebel against prescribed social roles.[104] Just as during the war years some army examiners had feared that heterosexual men would feign homosexual tendencies in order to escape military induction, so postwar experts worried that homosexuality offered benefits that would tempt previously heterosexual men.[105]

The same social changes that rendered men susceptible to the attractions of homosexuality could also turn American women into lesbians. What Frank Caprio termed women's "overdesire for emancipation" could lead to same-sex practices, and women's participation in paid labor, as well as shifts in their fashions, smoking habits, and participation in sports, signaled increasing lesbianism among American women. "It is not surprising, Caprio opined, that "in the face of all the changes that are taking place that many lonesome as well as pleasure-seeking women prefer to replace heterosexuality with an exploitation of sexuality among themselves."[106] For many, the choice of a same-sex relationship by a woman implied a childish avoidance of mature heterosexuality and family life.

Finally, a number of authorities charged Kinsey and his popularizers with encouraging homosexuality—with, in effect, creating the phenomena on which they reported. As one physician phrased it, Kinsey's "endorsement of tolerance raises questions of social policy." Matter-of-fact discussion of homosexuality could, "like a removal of quarantine, multiply the infection"; and, as a result of sexological surveys, "those who never would have known what the strange stirrings were, would now be informed, and succumb. Others who might have exercised restraint, might now loose [sic] it."[107] According to the philosopher Henry Elkin, Kinsey's first report "defends the man with homosexual impulses who wishes to consider himself normal."[108] Others concurred in the fear that work like Kinsey's served at best as an apologia for, and at worst as incitement to, same-sex sexual behaviors. To such commentators, it seemed that the widespread availability of information on homosexuality served to advance, rather than discourage, its spread.

FROM "NATIONAL DISEASE" TO "NEW TASTE":
NATIONAL CHARACTER AND HOMOSEXUALITY

This torrent of commentary raises unavoidable questions: Why was homosexuality—as opposed to, for example, venereal disease, alcohol, or birth control, each of which had been at the center of earlier moral panics—singled out as such an extreme threat to the public? Why did worries about it focus on the United States, and why at this moment? As others have argued, homosexuals' new visibility during and after war served as a catalyst for increased attention, as did the conservative (even paranoid) political climate of the postwar years. So did the shift from physical to psychological and psychoanalytic nosology, and the appearance of statistics such as Kinsey's, suggesting that homosexuality was more common than many had believed.

The primary reason homosexuality emerged as such a crucial topic in the postwar United States, however, is that it provided an ideal site for articulating widespread fears and hopes about American character. In postwar discourse, homosexuality often served as a signifier for sexual abandon, mirroring broader concerns about American character after World War II. A reviewer for *The Nation* made this clear when he argued that homosexuality was dangerous not because of any direct harm it caused but because the "ease of homosexual fulfillment" could lure those of "passive, dependent character." Such indolence stood in sharp contrast to the "aggression, self-sufficiency, and responsibility which are necessary to establish a heterosexual way of life."[109] Many contemporaries, worried about the effects of affluence, saw "self-sufficiency" and "responsibility" as qualities in which modern-day Americans were sadly lacking. Homophile authors underlined this point in their writing, commonly noting that heterosexuals displayed their share of instability and degenerate sexuality. As an author tartly pointed out in *One* magazine, "Picture[s] of happy heterosexual life" were "more common in story books than in real life."[110] The cluster of fears discussed in previous chapters—that modern Americans were becoming lazy and sensual, incapable of sustaining the nation—coalesced around the figure of the homosexual.

Although theories about the cause of homosexuality varied widely, they shared one distressing similarity: nearly all implicated the nation itself in the development of homosexuality. American institutions ranging from the military to the nuclear family were accused of fostering same-sex attractions and behaviors, suggesting that factors central to modern American culture and everyday life, rather than aberrant subcultures, promoted homosexuality. Drawing on cross-cultural anthropological work, the psychiatrist Robert Laidlaw commented of the United States that "our very cultural mores tend in some degree to promote the homosexual pattern." Laidlaw favored "a freer, more permissive attitude towards sexual behavior," but his larger point was echoed by others who did not share his laissez-faire philosophy.[111]

The idea that something essential in Americans and their culture was to blame for the increase in homosexuality resurfaced again and again; indeed, to a number of experts, the figure of the homosexual exemplified the central dilemmas confronting modern American society. Arthur Schlesinger Jr. had called attention to the relationship between homosexuality and modern life in "The Crisis of American Masculinity," stating that "this is an age of sexual ambiguity" and suggesting that it was "no accident that homosexuality, that incarnation of sexual ambiguity, should be enjoying a cultural boom new in our history."[112] At the end of the war, the journalist John McPartland linked same-sex sexual activity to an emerging type that anticipated the worst features of the character David Riesman would soon describe as "other-directed." According to McPartland, "The homosexual is the prototype of an individual-centered culture. Sterile, sensual, urban and tragic, the homosexual has always appeared to keen over a dying society."[113] The death and anomie associated here with the modern homosexual resonated with national concerns in the wake of a world war and the unleashing of the atomic bomb. In a culture focused on rebuilding a normative society and celebrating fecundity, what could be more threatening than sterility? Homosexuals could be seen at once as an advance guard representing new values and as the newest representatives of an ancient character type. The homosexual—here envisioned persistently as male, as alone, and as both troubled and dangerous—thus presaged the emergence of a new kind of American sexual character.

Mainstream and homophile writers agreed that the homosexual mirrored the dilemmas common to all Americans of the postwar era. "The social significance of homosexuality," Abram Kardiner stated, "reaches deep into the social distresses of our time. It is both a symptom of distress and a safety valve."[114] J. D. Mercer, the pseudonymous author of a voluminous 1959 study of homosexuals' roles in society, believed that the "ambiguous status of the homosexual" reflected the existential "disbalance" and "mass chaos" that were "glaring tragedies of the modern age."[115] Robert Lindner similarly argued that the situation of the homosexual in the present-day United States "presents the major contentions of our era in the clearest possible terms," representing "the basic issue of man versus society, of individualism versus conformity."[116] The homosexual was the paradigmatic rebel. Mirroring national social changes, the modern homosexual was not merely responding to deviant individual desires, but instead literally enacting through his own body and psyche the growing pains of all of postwar society. Homosexuality was seen by sympathetic as well as hostile commentators as synchronous with generational pessimism, despair over the atomic bomb, and a general sense that the contemporary United States was a "dying society."

Scholars in the humanities similarly viewed homosexuality as being imbued with larger cultural meanings. In "Come Back to the Raft Ag'in, Huck Honey!," a controversial essay first published in the *Partisan Review* in 1948, the literary critic Leslie Fiedler argued that homosexuality—and, in particular, the interracial male couple, exemplified by Mark Twain's Huck and Jim—was a central trope of the national literary imagination. Male authors, Fiedler maintained, often shared a fantasy of a homosocial world without marriage or family responsibilities. The figure of the homosexual, he noted, had become a "stock literary theme" at a time when "the exploration of responsibility and failure has become again a primary concern of our literature." American authors returned again and again to homosexual situations and characters, Fiedler speculated, because they were fascinated by "homosexual passion" and invested in "a national myth of masculine love."[117] Readers, likewise, were simultaneously drawn to and repelled by same-sex desire.

Similarly, some postwar whites looked to African American culture in search of an escape from the constrictions of their own lives.[118] The imaginative correlation of homosexuality and racial difference worked on another level as well: homophile authors repeatedly analogized the two, as when Donald Webster Cory drew on Gunnar Myrdal's *An American Dilemma* to suggest that the oppression of homosexuals paralleled that of Negroes and of Jews. "The homosexual minority," Cory observed, "displays remarkable parallels in its position in modern culture to the minorities of ethnic, racial and religious origin."[119] Luther Allen, in the pages of the *Mattachine Review,* similarly argued that, just as "the white man has held the Negro down . . . [and then] has called him shiftless, . . . the heterosexual world likewise often blames the homosexual for defects which that world itself has created."[120] Like civil rights leaders who appealed to international opinion during the cold war, homophiles used the language of democracy to claim freedom and respect. Cory drew on these principles often, arguing in one speech that "peoples of the free world are watching America, hopeful that out of this land will come new vistas of progress, yet skeptical of the meaning of American democracy and culture in terms of human values."[121] Such rhetoric served as a less than subtle reminder that the eyes of the world—especially of those nations whose good opinion and allegiance the United States wished to court—were upon it. The nation's treatment of its minorities, including homosexuals, would support or condemn its democratic claims.

Authorities who analyzed Americans' opinions on homosexuality argued that an elaborate system of fears regarding same-sex love pervaded the national culture and structured social relations. A number of authors suggested that what one critic called "that oppressive contempt which America, in fear of its own shadow side, turns on the homosexual" was excessive and overdetermined.[122] The sociologist Edgar Friedenberg, noting the fear of homosexuality common among Americans, commented that "the horror seems overdone," and the British anthropologist Geoffrey Gorer agreed.[123] "Among the generality of Americans," he observed, affection between men "is seen as an immediate and personal threat." This threat loomed large, such commentators agreed, because it emanated not from without, but from within. Unlike in other countries and cultures, Gorer maintained, homosexuality was seen as a dangerous, often unconscious, ever-present potential to be guarded against. "In America, as opposed to Western Europe, the homosexual is a threat, not to the young and immature, but above all to the mature male; *nobody is sure that he might not succumb.*" As a result of this intense concern, "all relationships between American males are colored by this panic fear of their own potential homosexuality."[124] The novelist James Baldwin similarly viewed homosexuality as the "shadow side" of Americanism, arguing in a 1949 essay that "our obsession with [the homosexual] corresponds with the debasement of the relation between the sexes," with homosexual men sharing the "ambiguous and terrible" position assigned to women and to emotion in postwar culture.[125]

As Gorer's remarks suggest, "potential homosexuality" was ripe for psychoanalyzing, and a number of commentators proposed that Americans' violent repudiation of homosexuality hid a secret attraction. According to J. D. Mercer, many "very manly men" harbored aberrant desires beneath their denunciations of same-sex sexual activity.[126] The editors of *One* magazine routinely interpreted angry letters as evidence of the authors' own repressed homosexuality, but this thesis had other adherents as well.[127] The psychiatrist William Menninger noted that "those who denounce adult homosexual individuals with feelings of great hostility may very possibly be overreacting to their own unconscious wishes in that direction." The British social scientist Gordon Westwood, whose 1953 *Society and the Homosexual* compared British and American sexual attitudes, agreed that "prejudice regarding homosexuality can be traced to a common cause, namely the tendency of the average man to castigate in others the impulses that lie hidden in his own unconscious mind."[128]

Experts and "manly men" saw their antihomosexual motives held up for examination—one book reviewer who otherwise agreed with Edmund Bergler's *Homosexuality: Disease or Way of Life?* naively wondered "what intimate psychodynamic need Bergler satisfies by his all-out attack on homosexuality."[129]

In the work of homophile writers and their allies, panicked heterosexuals were assailed for their fears and repression. "Our biggest national problem concerning sex," one woman wrote in an early issue of *One,* "belongs exclusively to the majority that calls itself normal." Heterosexual Americans, she argued, saw sex everywhere, placing it at the center of all human behavior, while most homosexuals took a far more balanced view. This "terrible monomania" had created "a sex-starved nation" of heterosexuals who attributed their own desires to homosexuals.[130] Albert Ellis even argued in one article that "the exclusive heterosexual," or any individual who is "utterly afraid of trying all non-heterosexual outlets and is compulsively tied to heterosexual ones," was by definition "indubitably neurotic or perverted."[131] J. D. Mercer argued that it was the heterosexual who threatened American morals since he "demands a partner . . . from the ranks of the young and innocent."[132] By rewriting a script of sexual danger in which excess, corruption, and threat emanated from *hetero*sexuals, Mercer and others drew on seemingly oppositional discourses in order to advocate a critical reading of the ways in which the normal and abnormal were opposed.

Again and again, authors who explained homosexuality to the general public stressed its attractions. Homosexuals, they informed their readers, had a dangerous allure to which Americans responded in record numbers. A Senate committee investigating the effects of homosexuality on government had declared that "one homosexual can pollute a Government office," a finding that stressed both the danger and the powerful pull of same-sex sexual practices.[133] Another author reported in distress that "the 'gay boys' have . . . a glamour and attractiveness" that captivated previously heterosexual young men. "Consequently, the ranks of homosexuals are swelling."[134] A psychoanalyst writing in *The Nation* cautioned that tolerant media coverage of homosexuality would undoubtedly lead more and more putative heterosexuals to turn to same-sex behaviors.[135]

Lesbianism held an equally seductive force. Kinsey had suggested in the second report that heterosexual relationships could be improved by a close study of lesbian techniques, a comment that one unhappy reviewer greeted with the observation that the "criticism here implied of heterosexual relationships on the average in our society is, to say the least, devastating to the male ego."[136] And according to "Dr. Goldman," the fictitious author of a "authoritative medical-sociological-psychological study" of single women, many of those who experimented casually with lesbian sex found themselves powerless to return to heterosexuality. Recklessly mixing his metaphors, "Goldman" warned women who believed "that they can shed the homosexual coat for the heterosexual as soon as the opportunity presents itself" that they were instead "opening a Pandora's box of troubles." Rather than retaining her essential heterosexuality, the unwary woman "may learn to rely so heavily on the erotic pleasures she experiences in such a relationship that she literally 'spoils herself' for a man."[137] This fictitious theorist drew on the same rhetoric of homosexual compulsion presented by real authorities: the penal reformer Katharine Sullivan argued in the mid-1950s that "the number of confirmed female homosexuals has increased to a marked degree" because, despite the "degrading sorrow" of such a life, even a "normal girl can become addicted to homosexuality very quickly."[138] The logic that underwrote such warnings was clear. If homosexuality was so addictive, then every American was vulnerable, always already a potential homosexual.

Not only were homosexuals themselves literally seducing Americans, experts informed their readers, but their culture was doing so metaphorically. By the mid-1950s many of the cultural codes that signified homosexuality had become widely disseminated and were readily understood by an increasing number of consumers. Popular stage and film productions, including *The Immoralist, Tea and Sympathy, Strangers on a Train,* and *Some Like It Hot,* featured overtly gay themes and characters, and even more often, popular entertainment alluded to homosexuality without naming it openly.[139] A physician speculated that average Americans who read about homosexuality "might let themselves be more easily seduced by an attractive world of artists, poets, dancers, designers."[140] The influence of homosexuality was being seen in all aspects of modern American life, where it was "diffused," as one critic put it, "among all classes of the population."[141]

A 1953 series in the newsmagazine *American Mercury, Homosexuality in American Culture,* was typical in its depiction of homosexuality as an increasingly important influence in Americans' daily lives. The *Mercury* charged that a homosexual conspiracy was changing contemporary moral standards, and promised to expose "the sinister influences, the peculiar values, of the effeminate, super-sensitive, 'new taste' that is seeping through the arts in America."[142] Cultural critics who inveighed against the power of homosexuality painted a lurid portrait in which the hetero-sexuality of "innocent outsiders" could be threatened by pastimes such as reading the works of sexual advice authors and journalists or watching a play or film with a homosexual theme. The *New York Times* drama critic Howard Taubman, for instance, spoke out repeatedly against "the increasing incidence and influence of homosexuality" in the arts. According to Taubman, the "infiltration of homosexual attitudes occurs in the theater at many levels," ranging from costuming to plot content. Most troubling, however, were the "furtive, leering insinuations that have contaminated some of our arts."[143] More and more plays contained clearly homosexual characters and themes, and even those with innocuous content starred "specimens of homosexual content" whose appearance on stage was "difficult, often disguised," and likely to confuse the "literal-minded and unsophisticated" theatergoer. Moved by their plight, the critic offered naive arts patrons a guide to recognizing and avoiding homosexual themes.[144]

Critics stressed the power of such covert influences in terms that again drew parallels between homosexuality and Communism. Left-wing politics and homosexuality were sometimes connected directly, as when suspected homosexuality led to dismissal from government positions, or when Arthur Schlesinger Jr. speculated that the Communist party attracted American adherents by offering perverts the "sexual fulfillment they cannot obtain in existing society."[145] More broadly, subversion and homosexuality were analogized as parallel behaviors. "While often hidden," one popular work on male homosexuality reported grimly, "the impact of the homosexual is consistently at work, influencing American thought and gaining greater acceptance for homosexuality."[146] In the theater, critics viewed homosexual themes in a production, the presence of homosexual actors or producers, and jokes about homosexuality as equally dangerous to the vulnerable consumer. The psychologist Robert Odenwald warned that "the casting of an unsuspected homosexual as a hero in dramatic presentations may have a greater impact than anyone can imagine."[147] An outraged critic charged that "homosexuals in charge of cultural outlets . . . transfer their own emotional instability to other people." This "instability," he continued, "turns their taste, all too often directly connected with their sexual preferences, into an arbiter of what the audience can see and what it cannot."[148]

This vision of homosexuals as cultural vampires engaged in leeching the vitality from American culture and shaping it to reflect their own agenda vividly captured the fears common to many observers. Depictions of homosexuals often displayed an ambivalent admiration for their artistic talent, but the danger they posed was seen as expanding along with their cultural space. Homosexuality now reached beyond the worlds of fashion and the theater, the magazine warned. Instead of remaining a ghetto, however brightly lit, homosexuality had become "a universe . . . through which many innocent outsiders wander," and its values had "permeated the thinking and manner of culturally conscious non-homosexuals."[149]

Increasingly, homosexuality was seen not merely as the province of an aberrant minority but as a set of practices and an identity that held powerful attractions. Critics often charged that popular sources made homosexuality appear alluring and attractive, a seductive lifestyle offering sensuality and excitement. Homophile authors were also uncomfortable with the sensational tones in which homosexuality was sometimes described to the public. "The paperback stereotype," the activist Donald Webster Cory noted with disapproval, did not depict the complexity of lesbian life but instead portrayed it as "exciting and glamorous[,] . . . a series of cocktail parties, smart-dressed exotic beauties, and wealthy male escorts fighting to oust wealthy female escorts."[150]

Although fiction and theatrical productions came in for heavy criticism, nonfiction literature sympathetic to homosexuality was also vehemently denounced. Publications by politically motivated homosexuals, one psychiatrist wrote in disapproval, have "done much to remove the sense of shame the deviant once felt. Now deviation is flaunted openly."[151] Bergler similarly charged modern homosexuals with disseminating "a kind of romantic aura" through their "homosexual propaganda-machine."[152] Another reviewer, who in like fashion condemned the "obscene propaganda drive" of American homosexuals, charged that the works of Donald Webster Cory "could be far more seductive of the near-innocent man than any mere Kinsey statistics."[153] This vision of a sexual attraction so potent that it could lure heterosexuals from the path of righteousness suggests the strength of authorities' fear that Americans were not innocent and in need of protection so much as they were sexually curious and potentially licentious. Many of the authors who railed against homosexuality and warned of its extraordinary allure suspected that their audience might actively seek out homosexual experience. The obsessive fear that same-sex erotic bonds would overpower one's self-control and even one's duties as a citizen attests to the allure and power that homosexuality held in the popular mind. Ironically, although their intent was often to further pathologize homosexuality, many of the authors who wrote about it also spread knowledge about how available and attractive an option it was for modern, sexually informed Americans.

CONCLUSION

In the postwar years, homosexuality was described variously as a serious topic about which Americans needed to educate themselves; a recent social phenomenon caused by changes in American life; evidence of dramatic flaws in the national character; a threat to the United States' political stability, family life, and future; a glamorous and appealing lifestyle; a common behavior for which all Americans shared a capacity; and an ineradicable essence. Confusingly, experts could offer neither a clear count of the number of homosexuals in the country nor an authoritative definition of what a homosexual was, and no single theory emerged to account for the cause or apparent increase of homosexuality. Efforts to draw a clear boundary between hetero- and homosexuality were confounded by the proliferation of conflicting models: was homosexuality caused by the blurring of boundaries between masculinity and femininity, the breakdown of sexual taboos, or some other factors? Even classificatory schemes confused observers—since homosexuals could be classified as "overt" or "latent," "exploratory" or "obligatory," "pseudo," "unconscious," or "spurious," many of those who consumed the burgeoning literature on homosexuality must have given up on reaching any clear understanding of the topic.

Readers of the Kinsey Reports and the host of materials that interpreted and surrounded them were exposed to an unprecedented amount of information about homosexuality, but its meanings remained elusive. Even while a conservative psychoanalyst like Edmund Bergler attacked Kinsey's figures, preached the dangers of homosexuality, and decried popular interest in it, his own outline of no less than seven types of homosexuals contributed to a more complex portrait of homosexuality. Although scientific and popular literature about homosexuality featured denunciations of its moral and emotional costs, the messages readers encountered were far from monolithic. For example, in "For These Are the Bedeviled," the 1950 article from *Esquire* magazine quoted at the beginning of this chapter, homosexuality is presented as a factor in everyday life, a familiar social reality to be met with calm analysis and open discussion. The author, John McPartland, who wrote widely on questions of sexuality and social values for popular magazines, at one point even invites the reader to consider himself as potentially homosexual. Encouraging him to "face the possibility," McPartland sketches a scenario in which

> you suddenly find that you yourself are thinking brief, surprising, unwanted thoughts. You may be just an adolescent, or you may be a fat old codger with a trunkful of memories of women you've known. At such a moment, if you can talk to yourself honestly, you may think, with a flash of revulsion, "Is there something wrong with me? Maybe I'm not completely normal." . . . a great many men have to face a situation of this sort at some time in their lives. Some experts even insist that the subject of homosexuality is unpleasant and repulsive to most of us chiefly *because* we've had these disturbing periods of uncertainty about ourselves.[154]

"For These Are the Bedeviled" demonstrates how competing notions of homosexuality circulated in the postwar United States. Homosexuality is associated with "a flash of revulsion," and homosexuals are described as "bedeviled" by a problematic desire. At the same time, however, they are also presented as victims of social oppression whose plight calls for liberal education and tolerance. Last, homosexual desire is viewed as a potential inherent in "a great many men," including the urbane reader of *Esquire*.

As the rhetoric of "For These Are the Bedeviled" suggests, the effects of this new attention to homosexuality were mixed. Many authorities certainly believed that diffusion of information on same-sex behaviors led to their increase: as early as 1945, military experts noted that the collapse of consensus on what constituted homosexuality had resulted in a greater tolerance for sexual variation.[155] In her study of the Women's Army Corps, which was the site of heated debates about homosexuality during the war, the historian Leisa Meyer argues that, for some women, "this 'new' awareness generated questions about their own sexuality or led to a 'tolerant' attitude toward sexual diversity. For others it gave them a language of heterosexual privilege with which to expand their own authority."[156] A similar dynamic characterized national discourses on homosexuality in the postwar years. Experts' proposals that homosexuality was on the rise, that homosexual culture possessed a dangerous attraction, and that anyone could be a latent homosexual without even knowing it, all made homosexuality appear to be an inevitable part of the future. Similarly, many of the theories accounting for rising homosexuality held frightening implications.

If economic depression, war, prosperity, or changing family patterns could create homosexual tendencies where none had previously existed, then perhaps other social forces could too.

In an ironic twist, many of the factors repeatedly implicated in the increase of homosexuality were the very same features of modern American life of which social scientists were proudest—leisure, affluence, an efficient war machine that had triumphed in a world war, increasing specialization in work, intimate family bonds—in short, modern American life itself. Boundaries between hetero- and homosexuality were policed so rigorously precisely because of the nagging fear that they were breaking down altogether. Homosexuality was thus seen as dangerous not only in and of itself but also because, for many Americans, it stood as a signifier for broader social transformations. A nation enthralled by homosexuality featured a populace utterly sexualized, degendered, and cast adrift from their families, with too much leisure and too little ambition.

Whether sympathetic or condemnatory, coverage of homosexuality reconfigured debates about all kinds of sexuality in America. As I argue throughout this book, postwar Americans, especially members of the white middle class, embraced and celebrated the idea of an essential American character. As authorities increasingly incorporated personal life and sexual behavior into this cultural ideal, they were forced to recognize that American sexual character carried with it a propensity toward same-sex sexual behavior. This belief drove the reaction against homosexuality evident within government and much of the medical and psychiatric professions. Homosexuality stood, for many, as an extreme and condensed set of the same values associated with heterosexual license and unrestrained consumption. The volubility and range of Americans' discussions of homosexuality, as well as the wildly varying causes and effects that they assigned to it, testify to how fraught the topic was. Sexual identity, whether heterosexual or homosexual, had become a crucial component of modern American character.

"All America Is One Big Orgone Box"
American Sexual Character Revisited

SHORTLY BEFORE THE THIRD REPORT from the Kinsey Institute appeared in 1958, the president of Vassar College resignedly predicted that, given Americans' insatiable curiosity about sex, the book—a survey called *Pregnancy, Birth, and Abortion*—"can be expected to evoke the same sensational treatment" accorded the earlier Kinsey Reports.[1] Unlike *Sexual Behavior in the Human Male* and *Sexual Behavior in the Human Female*, however, *Pregnancy, Birth, and Abortion* aroused little attention. Contemporaries suggested that the book's topic was too clinical to command mass interest, or that the public had forgotten Kinsey in the two years since his death. More to blame, however, were shifts in the sexual climate of the United States in the decade since Kinsey's first survey was published.

Between World War II and the mid-1960s, the place of sex in American culture changed. Observers at the time, and historians since, documented intensified attention to sexual issues in civic culture as sexuality became viewed both as central to personal identity and as knowable—that is, as accessible to measurement and description. The Kinsey Reports and the debates they prompted played a crucial role in this process in the postwar United States. According to the Kinsey biographer James Jones, the reports "precipitated the most intense and high-level dialogue on human sexuality in the nation's history." Before Kinsey, Jones argues, "Americans had debated a variety of sex-related issues, including prostitution, venereal disease, birth control, sex education, and Freud's theories. But the cultural debate that greeted *Sexual Behavior in the Human Male* was far more important. . . . However awkward, prurient, or naughty they might feel, Americans suddenly had permission to talk about sex. Kinsey gave them that right, and he did so in the name of science."[2] The very lack of controversy occasioned by Kinsey's third volume thus signaled a profound change in the cultural climate. By the time it was published, interested readers could choose from a flood of sexual studies, and the topic had become accepted as one of public importance. The era that Kinsey had helped to usher in was firmly established, and many of the values his work represented, especially a belief in the importance of producing and disseminating information about sex and furthering the open discussion of sexual behaviors and attitudes in America, had apparently triumphed.

During the decade and a half after the war, Americans were introduced to a new sexual vocabulary and inundated with information about sex. Homosexuality emerged into the public sphere and was discussed to an unprecedented extent. A range of popular sexual experts appeared, as Americans struggled to decide who was entitled to speak about sex. As a host of social and cultural problems were attributed to or seen as caused by changing sexual behaviors, the search for an ideal or at least a usable sexuality preoccupied experts across the nation. Attention to one's sex life became, in the eyes of experts and reformers, a tenet of American freedom. But since few could agree on what constituted a proper sex life, little clear consensus emerged; instead, as this book documents, authorities battled over such topics as the sexualization of public discourse, the import of men and women's changing behaviors, the proper place of sex in marriage, and the meaning of homosexuality.

The injection of sexual themes and topics into public discourse could not be reversed. Sex became a central theme in civic debates, and even conservative commentators who were interested in the maintenance of traditional family norms, and who wished to downplay the importance of sexuality, adopted the emerging discourse of pleasure and entitlement. Postwar Americans used the language of sexuality to discuss the problems of modern life, relating concerns about political subversion, changing family structures, consumption, and gender roles to the state of American sexuality. The 1950s were a pivotal moment in the transformation of the United States into a society that viewed sexual beliefs and behaviors as privileged keys to personality and character. As authorities discussed social problems, including the nation's image abroad, declining masculinity, failing marriages, women's roles, the rise of a national consumer economy, and the apparent increase in homosexuality, among other issues, they repeatedly proposed that solutions lay in a different type or amount of, or a new approach to, sex.

These debates were about power as well as about sex, but the story of these developments is not as simple as one of winners and losers. Some participants in the expanding postwar discourse of sex, such as sexologists and other social science professionals, gained new cultural authority and forged careers through writing and talking publicly about sex. For most Americans, however, the postwar centrality of sexuality had more ambiguous results. Gay men and lesbians gained increased visibility and access to an increasingly important language of sexual civil rights, fostering the development of modern gay rights movements.[3] By opening up the public discussion of homosexuality, however, Kinsey's statistics also provided ammunition for witch hunts directed against gay men and lesbians and authorized increasing surveillance of homosexuality. The heterosexuals examined in the reports and addressed in advice literature found themselves affected in similarly complex ways by postwar changes in the discourse of sex: they were simultaneously "liberated" to express their desires and encouraged to confine these desires and behaviors to a heterosexual, monogamous, and preferably married model. For both sexes, the standards of proper sexual knowledge and performance were raised, and as sexual knowledge and "adequacy" were expected of modern American men and women, it became difficult to reject or ignore what Foucault referred to as "all this garrulous attention which has us in a stew over sexuality."[4] The reports, along with the reviews, rejoinders, revisions, and appropriations that followed them, worked to further a process in which many social problems were viewed as at least in part sexual. As sex assumed center stage, it was no longer possible to see it as merely a private or individual matter.

SEXUAL REVOLUTIONS

In the early 1950s, the sociologist Pitirim Sorokin had used the trope *revolution* to describe what he saw as a dramatic change in the nation's sexual practices and ethos, and warned that if Americans did not move to reverse current trends, the nation would fall into irreversible cultural decline. The term was a popular one, and by the early 1960s, sexual revolution was widely perceived as a fait accompli.[5] In early 1964, belatedly recognizing that the nation had already undergone what it termed "a second sexual revolution," *Time* magazine offered a vivid image that reflected the magnitude of recent sexual and social changes. In his cover article on this "revolution of mores and morals," *Time*'s editor, Henry Anatole Grunwald, likened the contemporary United States to an Orgone Box, a 1940s invention of psychoanalyst-philosopher-sexologist Wilhelm Reich. Reich believed that his Orgone Box, a structure resembling an icebox, conferred special powers, including concentrated libido and enhanced orgasm, on anyone willing to spend time inside it. As Grunwald explained his comparison,

> The narrow box, simply constructed of wood and lined with sheet metal, offered cures for almost all the ills of civilization and the body; it was also widely believed to act as a powerful sex stimulant for the person sitting inside it. Hundreds of people hopefully bought it before the United States government declared the device a fraud and jailed its inventor. And yet, in a special sense, Dr. Reich may have been a prophet. For now it sometimes seems that all America is one big Orgone Box.[6]

Grunwald's vision of a sexually obsessed nation—in which isolated individuals crouched in separate compartments hoping vainly for sexual transcendence, submitting to the ministrations of fraudulent "experts," and needing rescue by the state—captured several key themes of postwar discourse about American sexuality and social change. Sex, or at least certain kinds of sex, was indeed proposed as the cure for many "ills of civilization" in the postwar United States. In the same way that many of Americans' political and economic dilemmas were interpreted through the analytic lens of national sexual character, individual problems—including failing marriages, domestic disharmony, imperiled masculinity, and gender confusion—were defined as sexual crises that could be addressed through the regulation or liberation of sexual behavior.

As the 1950s gave way to the 1960s, even many liberal critics argued that the sexual revolution had gone too far. The open discussion of sexual behavior was an important step in the breakdown of antiquated taboos, such critics believed, but the oversexualization of American culture had removed the secrecy that lent sexual activity its allure. Once divested of its much deplored burden of Puritan guilt, sex was boring. The philosopher and literary critic Robert Elliot Fitch complained that, as a result of the ever increasing explicitness of authors and the explorations by biological and social scientists, the mystique that had once surrounded sexual pleasure was rapidly disappearing. When taboos ruled the national imagination, "sex used to be hot stuff, but now," Fitch complained, "it smokes like a piece of dry ice[;] . . . by the time the modern intelligence is through with it, what sex gives us is not a burn but a frostbite. It isn't wicked any more and it isn't any fun. Its [sic] just biologic."[7] The psychologist Rollo May agreed, writing that, since the postwar expansion of public discourse about sex,

> we therapists rarely get in our consulting-offices any more patients who exhibit repression of sex. In fact we find just the opposite: a great deal of talk about sex, a great deal of sexual activity, practically no one complaining of any cultural prohibitions over his going to bed as often or with as many partners as he wishes. But our patients do complain of a lack of feeling and passion; so much sex and so little meaning or even fun in it.[8]

Claims that overexposure had stripped sex of its mystery and meaning betrayed a deep uneasiness with many aspects of contemporary sexual culture. Mental health professionals identified an epidemic of new forms of sexual anxiety as another unwanted effect of the new sexual norms. Echoing an observation made first by traditionalists, a number of liberal psychological and medical experts felt that new expectations and demands—that one be constantly sexually desirable and desirous, that one master techniques of lovemaking, and that one be au courant with the latest scientific research and studies—had replaced earlier prohibitions on the public discussion of sex. These new norms, they reported with surprise, were as harmful to Americans as had been the climate of repression they allegedly replaced.

Simple psychological problems engendered by sexual denial and guilt were disappearing, but the new cultural prescriptions around sexuality were creating new types of sexual and social malaise. May assessed the changing state of awareness of sexuality in the United States in terms reminiscent of Riesman's warnings about the other-directed man, noting that "sexual knowledge is available at any bookstore, contraception is available outside Boston, [and] external social anxiety is lessened. But internalized anxiety and guilt have increased, and in some ways these are more morbid, harder to handle, and impose a heavier burden than external anxiety and guilt." Sexual performance and prowess had become expected. "Whereas the Victorian person didn't want anyone to know that he or she had sexual feelings," May argued, "now we are ashamed if we do not."[9] The critic Alfred Kazin agreed, observing, "More and more, the sexual freedom of our time seems to be a way of mentally getting even, of confused protest" rather than "the pagan enjoyment of instinct."[10] The crusade to offer accurate and help-ful counsel about sex had apparently created demanding new standards against which Americans felt compelled to measure themselves. Intense verbosity had replaced repressive silence, but for average men and women the effects were equally injurious.

Betty Friedan offered a similar critique in 1963 in *The Feminine Mystique*, where she noted that "in the past decade there has been an enormous increase in the American preoccupation with sex." Adding a rare feminist perspective to public discussions of the effects of the sexual revolution, Friedan saw what she termed "the sexual sell" as a key element in middle-class women's oppression. Rather than liberating women into a new realm of freedom and enjoyment, the increasing emphasis on sex distracted Americans from real problems and opportunities. She complained,

> Instead of fulfilling the promise of infinite orgiastic bliss, sex in the
> America of the feminine mystique is becoming a strangely joyless
> national compulsion, if not a contemptuous mockery. The sex-glutted
> novels become increasingly explicit and increasingly dull; the sex kick of
> the women's magazines has a sickly sadness; the endless flow of manuals
> describing new sex techniques hint at an endless lack of excitement. . . .
> The frustrated sexual hunger of American women has increased, and
> their conflicts over femininity have intensified, as they have reverted
> from independent activity to search for their sole fulfillment through
> their sexual role in the home.[11]

In the next decade, many theorists of the second wave of feminism would echo Friedan's analysis as they examined how female sexuality had been ignored or manipulated. Even as many launched a renewed quest for female sexual empowerment and pleasure, their manifestoes often harshly criticized the ideology of sexual liberation.

Not only did the sexual revolution produce disappointing sex and new varieties of neurosis, critics complained, it also promoted an increased commodification of sexuality. In *The Sane Society*, his 1955 critique of middle-class American mores, the psychoanalyst Erich Fromm argued that, in contemporary sexual discourse, "making love" did not liberate human potential but instead expressed "the pleasure of unrestricted con-sumption, push-button power, and laziness."[12] That same year, the Marxist philosopher Herbert Marcuse wrote approvingly in *Eros and Civilization* that, "compared with the Puritan and Victorian periods, sexual freedom has undoubtedly increased," but he also warned readers that "sexual relations themselves have become much more closely assimilated with social relations; sexual liberty is harmonized with profitable conformity."[13] By 1961, when he added a new preface to the book, Marcuse had become pessimistic about the liberatory potential of eroticism. As sexuality "obtains a definite sales value or becomes a token of prestige and of playing according to the rules of the game," he observed with gloom, "it is itself transformed into an instrument of social cohesion."[14] In this view, "authentic" sexuality was nearly impossible to attain within the confines of consumer culture, and sex seemed less and less likely to generate positive transformations in American lives and values.

Even as Fromm, Marcuse, and other commentators despaired of the progressive and redemptive possibilities of sex, a series of new sexual revolutions were being proclaimed, reflecting the changing behaviors and agendas of youth movements and the counterculture, feminism, and gay liberation, among others. With each new incarnation of sexual change, observers proposed new models for personal and national identity, gender relations, and politics and also reworked a number of themes and questions raised earlier by Kinsey and his contemporaries.

As at earlier moments, sex surveys provided both evidence of and inspiration for the sexual revolutions of the 1960s and 1970s. Although Kinsey's loss of funding signaled a lull in behavioral sex research, smaller-scale and more specific projects flourished in subsequent decades, as did advice literature promising better sex. No subsequent survey would be as large or as wide ranging as Kinsey's, but privately funded projects continued to appear, and several caught the public's attention and prompted widespread debate. The most important surveys to appear in the two decades after Kinsey's, conducted by William Masters and Virginia Johnson in the 1960s and Shere Hite in the 1970s, elicited very different pictures of American sexual behavior.

Human Sexual Response, Masters and Johnson's 1966 best-seller, was based on clinical observations of seven hundred men and women who were measured, probed, and observed while engaging in a range of sexual behaviors. The study offered a physiological take on many of Kinsey's findings. Like their predecessor, Masters, a gynecologist, and Johnson, a psychologist, viewed sex as a set of biological behaviors best understood through mapping and measuring, and they placed orgasm at the heart of their project. Public reactions to their work centered on their findings regarding women's capacity for multiple orgasm. Their data suggested that heterosexual intercourse, as many 1950s experts had feared, was not the ideal route to sexual pleasure for many women. Their methodology and presentation of data in *Human Sexual Response* (along with its follow-up, *Human Sexual Inadequacy*) also echoed familiar assumptions about the role of sexology in improving American heterosexuality and marriage, as their therapy practice accepted only married couples.[15]

A decade later, the researcher Shere Hite released a study based on her collection of the sexual experiences and reflections of close to three thousand women.[16] Unlike Kinsey, Masters, and Johnson, Hite lacked academic and institutional backing. *The Hite Report*'s methodology, in which data was gathered through a mass mailing to one hundred thousand women, reflected a feminist faith in experience and distrust of "experts," as did the author's questionnaire asking open-ended questions. Hite believed that personal narrative, rather than observation, standardized questions, or measurements of physiology, was the best tool for eliciting truths about sex. The survey, along with a follow-up study of men, was criticized for its methodology but attracted media attention for its grim picture of heterosexuality. The novelist Erica Jong, herself an active participant in contemporary discussions of feminism and sexuality, underlined women's pervasive discontent when she summarized Hite's major findings in her review of the study. "Most of the respondents to Hite's questionnaires," Jong reported, "thought that the sexual revolution was a myth, that it had left them free to say yes (but not to say no), that the double standard was alive and well, [and] that the quantity of sex had gone up, not the quality." Despite these caveats, Jong expressed optimism about feminism and sex in the title of her review: "If Men Read It, Sex Will Improve."[17]

A decade apart, and in different ways, *Human Sexual Response* and *The Hite Report* reaffirmed some of Kinsey's central ideas and testified to Americans' simultaneous enduring hopes for sex and pessimism about realizing them. The findings and reception of these two surveys, and of many smaller ones undertaken after Kinsey, demonstrated the nation's continuing anxiety about what kinds of sex Americans engaged in. They also reflect some of the social and sexual changes of the 1960s and 1970s, including the effect—small in 1966, but growing rapidly by 1976—of feminism. These studies and their feminist commentators claimed that, when it came to sex, American ideologies—whether the watered-down advice literature of the previous generation or the sexist "revolutionary" assumptions of men with whom they organized, battled, and slept—ignored female pleasure and imposed false and rigid norms of female sexuality.

Sexuality was a central issue for second-wave feminism, and as women's liberation spread across the country, analyses of female sexuality and recommendations for an appropriate and healthy sex life proliferated.[18] Some women's liberation groups and leaders vowed to reform and improve heterosexuality; some advocated temporary or permanent celibacy; and some saw lesbianism as the model not only for healthy egalitarian relationships but also for the most fulfilling sex. Second-wave feminists examined sexual behavior with an eye to exploring violence against women and theorizing new understandings of female sexual pleasure. Many lauded Masters and Johnson's clinical researches, embracing their discoveries that orgasms were clitoral rather than vaginal and that women's sexual pleasure was largely divorced from the penetrative intercourse enshrined as real sex. Criticizing "sexual liberation" as a form of exploitation, they charged men alternately with sexual ignorance and with incompetence—accusations very similar to those heard in 1950s marital advice literature—and also applied a new term, *sexism.*

As feminists debated the meaning of sexual liberation, some of their observations and complaints struck a familiar note. In an ironic twist, many second-wave criticisms of American sexuality had been voiced nearly twenty years before not only by postwar homophiles and sexual radicals but also by opponents of the Kinsey Reports who objected to much of the agenda of sexual liberalism. Susan McViddy's decision that vacuuming a chandelier was the path to contentment would have prompted ridicule from consciousness-raising groups of the early 1970s, but her critique of cultural expectations about female sexuality in many ways resonated with their own. Despite the wide disjuncture between their beliefs, both socially conservative commentators in the 1950s and feminists of the 1970s objected to how male experts had theorized women's desires and behaviors. Similarly, some of the same issues that postwar authorities discussed—how cultural expectations about gender shaped sex, whether sex surveys could accurately measure behaviors, and whether public discussion of sexual practices served to promote them—would continue to provoke, reflect, and shape American culture a half century later.

THE SEX SURVEY IN THE 1990S

In the 1990s, controversies over another nationwide sex survey suggested again both how familiar a cultural staple the genre had become and how unsettling its premises remained. In 1987, the researchers Edward Laumann, Robert Michael, and John Gagnon, working through the National Opinion Research Center at the University of Chicago, responded to a call for research on sex by the U.S. Department of Health and Human Services' National Institutes of Health and received federal funding for a projected survey of the sexual behavior of twenty thousand Americans. This survey, intended largely to gather information on HIV transmission in order to combat the AIDS epidemic, became the subject of intense debate in Congress and in the national media. Once again, a sex survey was in the spotlight. Senators discussed the purpose and likely effect of such studies, and, following a protest led by Republican congressmen Jesse Helms of North Carolina and William Dannemeyer of California, the George H. W. Bush administration withdrew funding in 1991. Funding for a significantly reduced project was subsequently obtained from several private foundations, and the researchers released their study, entitled the *National Health and Social Life Survey,* in 1994.[19]

Scientific expectations of this survey were high, surpassed only by its political stakes. The project was heralded as the first comprehensive and reputable scientific study since *Sexual Behavior in the Human Male* and *Sexual Behavior in the Human Female* nearly a half century before. The scaled-down study that eventually appeared, based on interviews with 3,432 people, repeatedly contrasted Kinsey's methodology and findings to its own, emphasizing the debt its authors felt to their predecessor. As in the Kinsey studies, investigators interviewed adult subjects about their sexual histories, querying their behavior from childhood to the present. But if the 1990s survey's political fortunes mirrored those of Kinsey's study, its findings differed dramatically: the 1990s survey found lower rates of partnered heterosexual sex, extramarital sex, and homosexuality than Kinsey's team had. Laumann, Michael, and Gagnon also took a fundamentally different view of sexual behavior than Kinsey had, seeing most identities and acts as shaped by culture, rather than by human biological capacity.[20] The Chicago team's books attended to ethnic and racial categories, which Kinsey's had not, and also considered factors in sexual life not addressed in Kinsey's published works, including alcohol and drug use, sexual coercion and abuse, and the epidemiology of sexually transmitted diseases.

This study depicts an American sexual landscape narrower and less variegated than Kinsey had found. Heterosexual penile-vaginal intercourse, which respondents saw as "the act that defines an event as sexual" (157), is more central in Americans' sexual histories than in the earlier study. The data on homosexuality appears even more removed from Kinsey's findings, as the 1990s authors found far lower rates of same-sex sexual behavior in the United States than Kinsey had in the 1930s and '40s.[21] Attuned to the ways in which Kinsey's data was mobilized decades earlier, the authors warn against attempts to read their findings as either "good news" or "bad news," and they disassociate themselves from the cultural and political uses often attached to sexual information (544). Their warning was prescient, but futile: despite the authors' repeated caution that their survey likely underreported many types of activity, especially homosexuality, it was widely hailed as establishing a new and drastically lower benchmark for rates of same-sex and other stigmatized sexual behaviors (70, 254).

Class was another area of difference. Kinsey's studies, which appeared in the context of social upheavals after the war, an expansion of the middle class, and a celebration of common Americanism, had emphasized contact between groups as well as within them, and in many ways attempted to translate the sexual mores of different groups across lines of class, age, and subculture. The study by Laumann, Michael, and Gagnon instead stresses the balkanized nature of sexual behavior in the United States, noting that sexual networks usually replicate existing social arrangements, and that most Americans therefore not only work and socialize with but also interact sexually with people demographically very much like themselves. Continuities between the two studies did emerge: female orgasm, the authors believe, "is now considered both a right (for women) and a responsibility (for men)," a model many sexual experts advocated in the 1950s (114). Similarly, the study asserts that, while oral sex has become more common, it is still a "contested" behavior for many Americans (157). Overall, however, many of the Chicago study's findings support the conclusions and agenda of the conservative politicians who moved to block its federal funding. The news media were quick to note that the 1990s survey, in contrast to Kinsey's, offered a portrait of American sexual practices that repudiated the apparent triumph of a major "sexual revolution."

This survey and the controversies it prompted indicate ways in which American attitudes toward sexual information continue to mirror postwar ideas, as well as how much they have changed. In the heated and heavily politicized discussion of the 1994 survey, several themes that had dominated postwar debate about Kinsey's surveys recurred. First, during these later discussions, possible respondents to the Chicago survey were almost universally divided by the commentators into two groups, variously categorized as honest versus dissimulating, modest versus immodest, and ultimately, sexually respectable versus perverse. Senator Jesse Helms, who led congressional opposition to federal funding for the original survey, charged that the "only people who are willing to respond to these purportedly scientific studies are those who have a desire to share the graphic details of their sexual intimacies, real or imagined—people who obviously favor lewd or perverse sexual behavior."[22] The study's design itself supported an epidemiological version of this split between "good" and "bad" sexuality: the letter soliciting potential respondents identified one of its goals as "better understand[ing] the nature and extent of harmful and of healthy sexual behavior in our country," terms that vividly recall postwar debates about sexual and social change.[23]

Another theme familiar from postwar discussions of the Kinsey Reports was the attribution of great cultural power to the sex survey, with many Americans crediting it with the ability to influence individuals' sexual behavior and beliefs. In a 2000 examination of the sex survey as an example of modern knowledge production, Mary Poovey argues that such surveys offer a "cultural fantasy about how much and what kind of sex is properly American," and that responses to them affirm the belief that "to produce knowledge about something—no matter what the form that knowledge takes—is to promote it."[24] The Senate Republican Policy Commission maintained that the organizers of the projected survey would "use . . . American taxpayers' money" to "show that promiscuous, perverted, sexual practices are normal and, therefore, socially acceptable."[25] Robert Knight, a representative of the conservative Family Research Council who testified against the authorization of surveys of sexual behavior, argued in more specific terms that any such research would inevitably promote promiscuity and homosexuality. According to Knight, questions about sexual behavior were "calculated to increase curiosity about deviant behavior" and would inevitably lead to increased sexual experimentation, since "through sheer repetition of reference, harmful activities can lose their power to inspire natural resistance."[26] As in the 1940s and 1950s, concerns about same-sex sexual behavior lay at the heart of this fear, and homosexuality was specifically singled out as a set of behaviors that presented a dangerous allure against which American youth must be guarded.

Last, the study's political travails and the uses to which its findings were put suggest that sex surveys continue to provoke concern and even alarm. In 1999, in the midst of national attention to a presidential sex scandal that hinged on defining *sex,* the staid *Journal of the American Medical Association* published an article by researchers affiliated with the Kinsey Institute that examined new survey data on exactly what behaviors college-age Americans counted as constituting sex. The study suggested that many Americans, like their chief executive, did not define oral sex as "sex" proper.

After protest from commentators who saw the article's appearance as inappropriate and politically motivated, the journal's editor was fired and the journal apologized for carrying the piece.[27] More recently, a planned 2002 survey of sexual behavior that was to be undertaken by a psychologist at Mercer University, a Baptist-affiliated institution in Macon, Georgia, was halted by administrators after drawing unfavorable comments from university backers.[28] Such controversies suggest that many Americans continue to see sexual knowledge as potentially dangerous, and that information based on actual behaviors, such as survey data, carries particular power. Information about sex—whether accurate or not—is viewed as capable of influencing both individuals, who will model what they read about, and any culture that engages in such risky inquiries.

AMERICAN SEXUAL CHARACTER IN THE NEW MILLENNIUM

Changes in American sexual behavior, politics, and popular culture in the years since publication of the reports bear out many of the best hopes and the worst fears of postwar commentators. Gay and lesbian civil rights are increasingly recognized in both the public and private spheres, in the shape of antidiscrimination legislation and cultural acceptance. Discussions of minority sexual behaviors such as sadomasochism and fetishism are far more common. By 2000, the national divorce rate hovered at levels far higher than those that had so alarmed Americans after World War II, while both homosexual and heterosexual cohabitation outside of wedlock had also risen dramatically. The nation's popular culture, traditionalists and liberals agree, has been saturated with increasingly explicit sexual imagery.

Despite—or perhaps because of—these changes, Kinsey's project and its alleged effects on American culture are still in the news. A new film about Kinsey is slated for release. The end of the twentieth century brought a renewed flurry of attention to the reports, as did the fiftieth anniversary of the books' appearance. For many, the reports and their author stand as positive emblems of sexual liberalism. The political magazine *Counterpunch* was one of several sources to cite the reports among the twentieth century's most influential works, and the authors of the 1994 Chicago survey credit Kinsey for setting in motion the journey that transformed the United States "from a society in which sexual matters were covert and unmentionable to one in which sexuality is overt and ever-present."[29] It is difficult, they argue, "even for those of us who were alive in those days before 1948, when Kinsey's first book on sexual practices was published, to recall how empty was the erotic landscape in American society."[30]

For other groups, however, Kinsey's alleged responsibility for the nation's changing sexual patterns elicits blame rather than praise. The Intercollegiate Studies Institute, a conservative educational organization, named *Sexual Behavior in the Human Male* third on its list of the fifty worst books of the century (in company with volumes by Alger Hiss, Malcolm X, and Eldridge Cleaver), describing it as a "pervert's attempt to demonstrate that perversion is 'statistically' normal."[31] In many socially and religiously conservative organizations, allegations about Kinsey's methods of data collection, motives, and private behavior still abound, and calls for a congressional investigation into his methodology recently mounted, nearly a half century after his death.[32] According to a 1997 news release by the conservative evangelical group Concerned Women for America, "Kinsey's goal was to change the way Americans view sex." His "false 'science'" and "tainted philosophy," the group argues, have been so successful that they "can still be found impacting our society almost fifty years later," necessitating their call for volunteers "to take down Kinsey!"[33]

Kinsey's work, such critics believe, laid the groundwork for homosexual rights, feminism, and sexual education in the public schools.[34] The reports often take center stage in theories about the spread of sexual liberalism, with Kinsey serving as a degenerate prophet. Kinsey's most vehement critic, the media specialist Judith Reisman, argues that his studies "revolutionized this nation": the values and beliefs she terms the "Kinsey pathology" served to "breed a nation swarming with impotent, dependent, violent sex and drug addicts, afraid of love and commitment and increasing [sic] brutal to each other and to children people [sic]."[35] Whether hailed as a liberator or castigated for single-handedly ruining the morals of generations, Kinsey, and the surveys that bear his name, are often seen as having fundamentally altered American life. Two rather recent biographies capture this duality: one lauds Kinsey as a "social reformer, liberator, [and] pioneer scientist" who was a "much maligned, courageous, difficult and great man," while the other takes a harsh view, describing him as a victim of "sexual dysfunction" whose "private demons . . . also bedeviled the nation."[36]

In the new millennium, American marriage and threats to it are still front-page news. Works on the benefits and future of marriage crowd bestseller lists, offering analyses from a dizzying range of vantage points. Attacks on America's "divorce culture" and its effects proliferate, as do calls to remake marriage, often by endorsing a return to "traditional" patterns of earlier wedlock, to deferral of women's careers for childbearing, and to male authority within the home. Other critics point instead to the continuing burdens that marriage places on women, and call for changes in gendered assumptions about careers, children, and domesticity.[37] Unlike the citizens of some other Western democracies, Americans have not rejected marriage, which—whether undertaken for the first, second, or third time—remains at the center of the real and imagined lives of the majority. Politicians as well as pundits continue to link civic good to matrimony: in 2001, several state governors vowed to "promote and honor marriage" through programs that endorse Bible-based "covenant marriages" and limit divorce options, while others considered what economic measures would best encourage wedlock. President George W. Bush advocated federal incentives encouraging women to view marriage as their best route out of poverty, and his 2002 welfare reform program earmarked $300 million for programs to promote marriage among single mothers receiving public assistance.[38]

Other contemporary jeremiads regarding American sexual and cultural mores also strike familiar themes. Patrick Buchanan, a 2000 presidential candidate, greeted the new century with a book, *The Death of the West: How Dying Populations and Immigrant Invasions Imperil Our Country and Civilization,* in which he argued that middle-class Americans were dooming the nation by embracing secularization and using contraceptives. Many of Buchanan's laments and proposed programs echo those of postwar authorities, most notably his plan to promote wedlock by taxing the unmarried and his argument that American decadence threatens the national culture, which can only be redeemed by embracing traditional morality.[39] Some links between postwar and contemporary discourses on sexuality, marriage, and politics are even more direct: David Popenoe, one of the leading spokesmen for the conservative evangelical campaign Focus on the Family, is the son and spiritual heir of the postwar marriage counselor and eugenics expert Paul Popenoe. Echoing an earlier generation's dire predictions, David Popenoe argues that current trends point to "the gradual elimination of marriage in favor of casual liaisons," a scenario in which "children will be harmed, adults will probably be no happier, and the social order could collapse."[40]

As both Bush's and Buchanan's programs suggest, the concept of "character" continues to play a prominent role in political and popular discourse. Presidential and other campaigns in the late twentieth century repeatedly revolved around the issue of candidates' character, a term often understood as equating moral fitness with the ability to govern. In the late 1990s, as a sexual intrigue between then President William Clinton and a female

White House employee exploded into the headlines and culminated in a congressional vote on articles of impeachment, the phrase "the character issue" came into vogue as a shorthand term linking public fitness with sexual probity. The incident and its aftermath also renewed national conversations about American sexual behavior, with pundits simultaneously criticizing the president's recklessness, estimating the extent of oral sex and adultery (the prime sexual charges against the chief executive), and questioning what relevance private sexual behavior might have for a politician's public performance. Alan Keyes, a conservative talk-show host and candidate for the Republican presidential nomination in 1996, was one of many observers who diagnosed a contemporary "crisis of character" in the United States, in his case seeing proper character as synonymous with a firm stance against abortion and gay rights.[41]

For many Americans, ideas about the proper place of sex have been articulated most clearly through campaigns for sexual education for children and youth. School-based curricula teaching the basics of physiology and sexual behavior were widespread by the 1980s, and took on new urgency with the spread of HIV and AIDS. Opposition to sexual education programs also grew along with the AIDS crisis, however, and the 1990s saw a growing movement for abstinence-based education, a pedagogical approach encouraging youth to avoid sex before marriage. Such programs, which often have religious and moral overtones, have been aided by federal programs and endorsed by many politicians.[42] Despite controversy, abstinence-based education has proven popular with many parents and school districts, and a 1999 study found that nearly one-quarter of sexual-education programs in the United States exclude any mention of contraceptives and teach that total sexual abstinence is the only method of disease and pregnancy prevention.[43] Underlining the popular and political connection between moral character and the promotion of sexual abstinence, a number of faith-based groups such as Focus on the Family currently promote school-based "character education," a program of moral and philosophical pedagogy to which conservative teachings about sexuality—including the rejection of homosexuality and affirmation of premarital chastity—are central. As in related debates over sex surveys, the political agendas behind battles over sexual education reflect two widely held beliefs: that public discussion of sexual behaviors will translate directly into an increase in those behaviors, and that silence about such behaviors as premarital sex, contraceptive use, and homosexuality will limit their incidence.

What is at stake in these very different uses of Kinsey's work and assessments of how it affected American sexual mores? The rhetoric of both Kinsey's critics and his supporters suggests that many of the controversies raised by *Sexual Behavior in the Human Male* and *Sexual Behavior in the Human Female* remain relevant to contemporary American culture. The boundaries of American sexual character may have changed, but the concept remains a powerful one, as sexual behavior and ideology continue to be key to changing representations of citizenship and of the good society. Much as antimiscegenation laws in the nineteenth and twentieth centuries attempted to shape citizenship, and social purity movements in the Progressive Era helped middle-class women and men define themselves in relation to new immigrants and people of color, discussions of sexual behavior and ideology in the 1950s offered Americans one way in which to articulate and interpret the social changes they saw happening around them, and they continue to serve similar functions.

Postwar authorities warned Americans that unless traditional restraints were resurrected marriage would vanish, homosexuality would become endemic, and sexual anarchy would bring about the nation's moral and political collapse. These scenarios never came to pass, but the new narratives of sexual possibility and constraint produced by postwar theorists not only bespoke very real anxieties but also reflected equally real changes under way in the nation's economy and culture. Many of the contemporary developments that helped to drive such visions—including the changing importance of leisure, rising expectations of personal relationships, and the increasing centrality of consumer capitalism—would significantly reshape individual and collective national identity during the next half century. A number of the shifts that commentators lamented are still on the public mind, as some of the most important themes in postwar sexual discourse—the civil rights of sexual minorities, the mutability and collapse of sexual categories, the effect of private sexual behavior on public life, and the search for happiness in a consumer culture—remain pressing today.

Several processes that accelerated during the 1950s continue into the present. Americans still eagerly consume authoritative sexual advice, as measured by best-seller lists, newspaper and Internet counsel, chat rooms, and water cooler conversations. In a nod to the industry of sexual advice that has expanded since Kinsey, Laumann, Michael, and Gagnon opted to publish their data in two volumes, a detailed one for social scientists and health professionals, and a second, aimed at a popular audience eager to consume sexual data.

The specifics of exactly which sexual behaviors and identities most Americans deem acceptable continue to shift. At least some of the adult heterosexual behaviors widely condemned in Kinsey's era have been integrated into a developmental narrative in which premarital petting and different forms of intercourse lead eventually to social and sexual maturity, a model suggested by Kinsey's conclusions. It is now primarily children and teens, rather than adults, who are considered to be at moral and physical risk from inappropriate sex. Largely due to queer activism, homosexuality has also become at least partially normalized in the eyes of many Americans. By the turn of the twenty-first century, in the midst of debates about homosexuality in the military, gay adoptions, and civil unions, acceptance seemed to grow of at least some gay individuals and unions, particularly long-term monogamous couples. Other acts, relationships, and identities, however, remain outside the charmed circle of normalcy, emerging into public consciousness in moments of scandal or panic.[44] Discussions of the place of gay men and lesbians in the national sexual and civic landscape have been haunted by the HIV pandemic, which prompted many Americans to resurrect older notions of national character and to invoke nationalistic models of sexual practice and ideology to "explain" HIV and AIDS in terms that were often racist and xenophobic. The exact mechanisms by which national identity and sexuality are intertwined may have changed, but the two remain intimately linked and mutually supportive: in the 1980s and 1990s, as Cindy Patton reminds us, "the AIDS epidemic became a vehicle through which to renegotiate the meaning of being a good American."[45]

Postwar discussions and uses of sexuality were crucial in creating an era in which modernists cannot escape from the idea of sexual identity, the view that sexual behavior is intimately connected to and constitutive of the self and even the soul. One trend illustrating the apparent centrality of sexual activity to most Americans' definition of the good life is that in many cases it is now the lack of sexual interest and activity, rather than their presence, that calls for medical intervention. Following the wildly successful 1998 introduction of Viagra, a drug targeting male erectile dysfunction, pharmacological approaches to problems of sexual desire or performance were hailed as a new Holy Grail. The former Republican presidential candidate Bob Dole touted Viagra's benefits in a national advertising campaign, and it became a staple in comedy routines, even as the drug's sales pulled in unprecedented revenues and researchers scrambled to find equivalent treatments for female sexual dysfunction. Sexual pleasure, the discourse around Viagra insisted, was an American entitlement: as the drug's manufacturer Pfizer phrases it in their promotional materials, by creating "improved erections" the drug helps men to "reclaim an important part of their lives."[46] These ideas were explored by 1950s experts who linked sexual identity and desire to the modern self and, alternately—and sometimes simultaneously—celebrated increasing openness about sex, deplored the modern focus on sexual behavior, and queried the kinds of social changes that Kinsey's work seemed to promote.

The idea that true human happiness lies in or through sex has a long history in American social thought, with individuals and groups seeking liberation or transcendence variously through polygamy, communal marriage, celibacy, and various forms of sexual freedom. Popular belief in an authentic and empowering sexuality—whatever those terms might mean— endures, and authoritative discourses about sexuality, whether statistical, medical, psychological, or political, still hold tremendous cultural power.[47] Kinsey's work furthered an ever increasing cultural volubility about sex, making the nation into a metaphorical Orgone Box. Many of the questions Americans ask about sex—What kinds of sexual behavior are pleasurable? Which are likely to produce a good society? What behaviors are harmful? And who decides?—remain both contested and compelling.

NOTES

INTRODUCTION

1. Kinsey, Pomeroy, and Martin, *Sexual Behavior in the Human Male;* Kinsey et al., *Sexual Behavior in the Human Female.* The bomb metaphor was a common one: for example, see "Bombs, H and K," 57; and Milburn, "Sex, Sex, Sex, and the World Crisis," 230. Elaine Tyler May discusses the metaphorical connection between atomic power and sexuality in *Homeward Bound,* 92–113.

2. Albert Deutsch compared Kinsey to scientific martyrs in his "Kinsey, the Man and His Project," 2. The characterization of one or both of the reports as Soviet propaganda is an implicit theme in many reviews and articles; for an explicit statement of this, see John Chapple, editorial.

3. For the postwar authors whose work I examine here, the term *American*—as in *American culture, American studies,* or *American sexual behavior*—denoted the United States only and did not include Latin America or Canada.

4. Eley and Suny, eds., *Becoming National,* 4.

5. Anderson, *Imagined Communities,* 15.

6. Eley and Suny argue that the postwar era saw a resurgence of nationalism; see *Becoming National,* 3. Examples of studies focusing on national identity in the postwar era include Corber, *In the Name of National Security;* Henriksen, *Dr. Strangelove's America;* and Sharp, *Condensing the Cold War.*

7. Significantly, sexuality and gender have emerged as vital and often overlooked components of discourses of nationalism, leading Eley and Suny to call for attention to "the relationship between the politics of sexuality and the

discourse of belonging to the nation" (introduction to *Becoming National: A Reader* [New York: Oxford University Press, 1996], 27). See also Berlant, *The Queen of America Goes to Washington City;* and McClintock, "No Longer in a Future Heaven," 260–84.

8. Kinsey et al., *Sexual Behavior in the Human Female*, 469.

9. Kinsey, Pomeroy, and Martin, *Sexual Behavior in the Human Male*, 199.

10. Foucault, *The History of Sexuality*, 2:3; 1:6, 11.

11. *Readers' Guide to Periodical Literature* (Minneapolis: H. W. Wilson), vol. 12 (1937–39), vol. 20 (1953–55), vol. 22 (1957–59).

12. Riesman, with Glazer and Denney, *The Lonely Crowd*.

13. Dubinsky, *Improper Advances*, 3, 144. See also Mosse, *Nationalism and Sexuality*.

14. See chapter 1.

15. Rumming, "Dr. Kinsey and the Human Female," 8.

16. Reich, *The Mass Psychology of Fascism*, xxvi. The Federal Food and Drug Administration banned Reich's devices.

17. An important earlier document that drew parallel connections, though one rarely mentioned by postwar American authorities, was Otto Weininger's 1898 jeremiad, *Sex and Character;* see Sengoopta, *Otto Weininger*.

18. Sorokin, *The American Sex Revolution*, 5.

19. On postwar liberalism, see Pells, *The Liberal Mind in a Conservative Age;* and Feldstein, *Motherhood in Black and White*. Morris Ernst, who wrote widely on sex issues, offers an ideal example of the complexities of cold war liberalism: a liberal anti-Communist lawyer, he both served as cocounsel for the American Civil Liberties Union and worked closely with J. Edgar Hoover to feed information to the Federal Bureau of Investigation. See Schrecker, *Many Are the Crimes*, 21.

20. Archer, "The Backwash of Dr. Kinsey," 6–11; Riesman, with Glazer and Denney, *The Lonely Crowd*, 145–48.

21. See May, *Homeward Bound;* Corber, *In the Name of National Security;* and Cuordileone, "Politics in an Age of Anxiety," 515–45.

22. Ellis, "Ten Indiscreet Proposals," 10.

23. These movements have been studied intensively. In an extensive literature on the social purity movements and prostitution, see Bristow, *Making Men Moral;* Pivar, *Purity Crusade;* Gilfoyle, *City of Eros;* and Hobson, *Uneasy Virtue*. On the marriage reform movement of the 1920s, see Simmons, "Marriage in the Modern Manner"; and White, *The First Sexual Revolution*.

24. Duggan, *Sapphic Slashers*, 5.

25. The concept of "moral panic," on which I draw implicitly throughout this book, is discussed by Simon Watney in *Policing Desire*, 38–57.

26. Ellis, *The American Sexual Tragedy*. This topic so intrigued the *Digest* that it featured a two-part article: "Must We Change Our Sex Standards?

A Symposium," 1–6, and "Must We Change Our Sex Standards? A Reader's Symposium," 129–32.

27. Brecher and Brecher, "The New Kinsey Report Has a Moral," 28–31, 78–80; "Do Americans Commercialize Sex? A Symposium," 68–69; Johnstone, "Check Your Sex I.Q.," 15–17.

28. Meyerowitz, "Sex Change and the Popular Press," 160.

29. Geddes, ed., *An Analysis of the Kinsey Reports on Sexual Behavior in the Human Male and Female*.

30. Mayer, "Gender Ironies of Nationalism," 1, 2.

31. In modern Europe, George Mosse writes, especially in periods of war and of international reorganization, nationalism "helped control sexuality, yet it also provided the means through which changing sexual attitudes could be absorbed and tamed into respectability." As nationalism "assumed a sexual dimension of its own," stereotypes of masculinity, femininity, marriage, and deviance all reflected national ideals. *Nationalism and Sexuality*, 10.

32. See Costigliola, "The Nuclear Family," 163–83; and Cuordileone, "Politics in an Age of Anxiety."

33. See "Are Yanks Lousy Lovers?," 10; Minot, "Sex in Puerto Rico," 55–60; Rosenthal, "Sex Habits of European Women vs. American Women," 52–59; Sandomirsky, "Sex in the Soviet Union," 199–209; "Teen-Agers and Sex in Australia," 113.

34. Foucault, *The History of Sexuality*, 1:11. Earlier examples of the process of putting sex into public discourse abound: for relevant examples, see Bristow's analysis of the World War I Commission on Training Camp Activities in *Making Men Moral* and Jennifer Terry's discussion of campaigns around homosexuality in *An American Obsession*.

35. The phrase "right use of sex," which formed part of the American Social Hygiene Association's "Platform for Social Hygiene," often appeared in bold on the back cover of its publications.

36. Strathern, "Enterprising Kinship," 3.

37. In a controversial 1997 biography of Kinsey, the historian James H. Jones argues that Kinsey's public pose as a dispassionate scientist masked an obsessive zeal for social engineering, and that his research findings—especially those pertaining to homosexuality—were shaped by a private sexual agenda. My approach to Kinsey's data is very different: although I occasionally comment on the internal logic of Kinsey's studies and on his public utterances about his work, I focus primarily on the effects of his studies and on the ways in which they took up or responded to contemporary ideas about sexuality. Jones, *Alfred C. Kinsey*.

38. For an indication of the volume and variety of published responses to the two reports, see the selected bibliography given in Himelhoch and Fava, eds., *Sexual Behavior in American Society*, 417–35.

39. Sexual problems of and threats to youth are a theme in postwar literature on American sexuality, but for most of the authors I consider, the theme remains a submerged one. I discuss this issue in more detail in chapters 1 and 5.

40. Cuordileone, "Politics in an Age of Anxiety," 526.

CHAPTER ONE. "SEXUAL ORDER IN OUR NATION"

1. Luce, *The American Century*, 1, 3.

2. A 1997 study refers to the postwar United States as a "culture of anxiety," based on the pervasiveness and strength of worries about social and individual collapse. See Henriksen, *Dr. Strangelove's America*, 116.

3. Merrill, *Social Problems on the Home Front*, 30.

4. See Michel, "American Women and the Discourse of the Democratic Family in WWII," 154–67; and Westbrook, "I Want a Girl, Just Like the Girl That Married Harry James," 587–614.

5. Tenenbaum, "The Fate of Wartime Marriages," 531.

6. "Women: They Think of the Moment," 18.

7. Patrick, "Are Morals Out of Date?," 23.

8. Ibid., 63, 68, 70.

9. Groves, foreword to *Sex Problems of the Returned Veteran*, v.

10. Burgess, "The Sociologic Theory of Sexual Behavior," 27.

11. For a discussion of World War I–era responses to sexual disorder, see Bristow, *Making Men Moral;* and Brandt, *No Magic Bullet.*

12. "To Tell or Not to Tell Is the Worry of Home-Bound GIs," 3. An illicit war romance and the child that resulted were plot points in Sloan Wilson's popular novel and film *The Man in the Gray Flannel Suit.*

13. For a discussion of heterosexual mores and ideologies during World War II, see Costello, *Virtue under Fire.* Allan Berube discusses the wartime experiences of gay men and lesbians in *Coming Out under Fire.*

14. Despite the prominence of the family in postwar culture, children and youth were, perhaps surprisingly, not at the center of these debates. Adults were considered as independent sexual actors, while youth figured in discussions of the nation's changing sexual patterns most often as victims of increasingly lax morals or indicators of social change.

15. Mead, "Preface to the Mentor Edition," vii.

16. According to the study, approximately 88 percent of men petted before marriage; between 67 percent and 98 percent (depending on class and educational background) engaged in premarital sex; 50 percent violated their marriage vows; and nearly as many were sexually active during their adult life with both male and female partners. Kinsey, Pomeroy, and Martin, *Sexual Behavior in the Human Male*, 245, 552, 569, 585.

Although both reports were compiled and authored by a team of coresearchers, they were viewed as the work of one man, as the popular name "Kinsey Reports" indicates. Throughout this study, I follow contemporary usage and refer to Kinsey as the reports' main author, alluding to "his" statistics or findings.

17. According to *Sexual Behavior in the Human Male,* "nearly 50% of the females in our sample had had coitus before they were married" (p. 286); approximately 16 percent "had engaged in extra-marital petting although they had never allowed extra-marital coitus" (p. 427); and 26 percent of married women had had extramarital coitus by age forty (p. 416).

18. Lyndon Johnson, "Address before Jefferson-Jackson Dinner, Raleigh, NC," 18 March 1957, p. 3885; quoted in Goodwin, *Lyndon Johnson and the American Dream,* 157.

19. The best overall assessment of responses to Kinsey's work is Morantz, "The Scientist as Sex Crusader," 563–89; see also discussions in Gathorne-Hardy, *Sex: The Measure of All Things;* and Jones, *Alfred C. Kinsey.*

20. "Town Hall," 9.

21. Cited in Whitfield, *The Culture of the Cold War,* 185; "Kinsey, Again," 561.

22. *Catholic News,* 10 July 1954; quoted in Irvine, *Disorders of Desire,* 64.

23. Deutsch, "Kinsey, the Man and His Project," 1.

24. Benjamin, "The Kinsey Report," 400. Another reviewer similarly held that Kinsey would be the "man from which an era would take its name." Parry, "Kinsey Revisited," 196; quoted in Jones, *Alfred C. Kinsey,* 567.

25. Lee, introduction to *I Accuse Kinsey!,* viii; Niebuhr, "Kinsey and the Moral Problem of Man's Sexual Life," 63–70.

26. See Myers-Shirk, "To Be Fully Human," 112–36.

27. J. Edgar Hoover, cited in *Reader's Digest:* "Must We Change Our Sex Standards? A Symposium," 6. The ironies of this statement are manifest, given Hoover's own closeted life as a gay man who apparently cross-dressed.

28. Mari Jo Buhle sketches the popularization of psychoanalysis in *Feminism and Its Discontents,* especially chap. 4: "Ladies in the Dark," 165–205. Eli Zaretsky describes the field as "rigid, ossified, and text-bound" and says it serves as "an agent of rationalization, a virtual emblem of the organization-man conformity and other-directedness the age so dreaded." "Charisma or Rationalization?," 379. See also Hale, *The Rise and Crisis of Psychoanalysis in the United States.*

29. For an example, see Hobbs and Kephart, "Professor Kinsey," 614–20.

30. Daniels, *I Accuse Kinsey!,* 5.

31. Duvall, "Christ, Kinsey, and Mickey Spillane," 22.

32. Podell and Perkins, "A Guttman Scale for Sexual Experience—A Methodological Note," 420–22.

33. Kinsey, Pomeroy, and Martin, *Sexual Behavior in the Human Male,* 656.

34. For these estimates, see Stearn, *The Sixth Man.*

35. Cited in Whitman, "America's Moral Crisis," 172.

36. Berkman, "The Cult of Super-Sex," 52, 149.

37. Zimmerman, "A Sociologist Looks at the Report," 95.

38. Ogburn and Nimkoff, *Technology and the Changing Family,* 52, 54.

39. Pilpel and Zavin, "Sex and the Criminal Law," 238.

40. See Freedman, "Uncontrolled Desires," 83–106; and Chauncey, "The Postwar Sex Crime Panic," 160–78.

41. Kinsey, Pomeroy, and Martin, *Sexual Behavior in the Human Male,* 603. Authorities noted that prostitution was declining: in a typical midcentury assessment of the state of prostitution, an official of the American Social Hygiene Association reported that even in "the worst cities" it "takes [a] diligent search to find a prostitute." Kinsie, "Prostitution—Then and Now," 247.

42. Frank, "How Much Do We Know about Men?," 55.

43. Schauffler, "Today It Could Be *Your* Daughter," 43. For an interpretation of the influence of race upon perceptions of unwed pregnancy, see Solinger, *Wake Up Little Susie.*

44. Henry, *All the Sexes,* rear dustcover copy. Confusingly, following a title broaching a multiplicity of sexes, the book's subtitle was *A Study of Masculinity and Femininity.* For a discussion of Henry's work, see Terry, *An American Obsession.*

45. Odenwald, *The Disappearing Sexes,* 4.

46. "Speaking of S-e-x," 56–57.

47. Viereck, "The Erotic Note in Recent American Fiction," 166.

48. Whitman, "Don't Let Them Scoff at Marriage!," 101.

49. Redman, "Sex and Literary Art," 412.

50. Towne, "Homosexuality in American Culture," 4–5. Towne seems to have anticipated the blockbuster novel *Peyton Place,* which opened with the infamous lines "Indian summer is like a woman. Ripe, hotly passionate, but fickle, she comes and goes as she pleases." Metalious, *Peyton Place,* 1.

51. Gaithings Committee report, cited in Davis, *Two-Bit Culture,* 220.

52. Sargeant, "The Cult of the Love Goddess in America," 82.

53. This campaign is discussed in Coleman, "Maidenform(ed)," 3–22.

54. Packard, *The Hidden Persuaders,* 85, 88.

55. The gradual breakdown of the code and adoption of a system of ratings according to age is detailed in Leff and Simmons, *The Dame in the Kimono;* and in Walsh, *Sin and Censorship.*

56. Cited in Leff and Simmons, *The Dame in the Kimono,* 136; cited in Savran, *Communists, Cowboys, and Queers,* 121.

57. Crosby, "Movies Are Too Dirty," 8, 11. The plot of *Suddenly, Last Summer* (dir. Joseph Manckiewicz, 1959) also dealt with homosexual prostitution and incest.

58. DeGrazia, *Girls Lean Back Everywhere,* 323.

59. The film in question was a French adaptation of D. H. Lawrence's *Lady Chatterley's Lover,* undergoing its own widely publicized and important court battle in London at that time; see deGrazia, *Girls Lean Back Everywhere,* 339.

60. Homophile organizations were also formulating a version of rights discourse at this time. See D'Emilio, *Sexual Politics, Sexual Communities* and my discussion in chapter 5.

61. Sorokin, *The American Sex Revolution,* 5. For reviews, see Cort, "Sex Scares the Professor," 255–56; and Malcolm, "A Comedy of Eros," 19.

62. Duvall, "Sex Fictions and Facts," 50.

63. Mumford, *In the Name of Sanity,* 30.

64. Gerould, *Sexual Practices of American Women,* 129, 133.

65. DeMenasce, "Sexual Morals and Sexualized Morality," 167–68.

66. Gordon, Gordon, and Gumpert, *The Split-Level Trap,* 18–19.

67. Bailey and Farber, *The First Strange Place,* 215. Bailey and Farber argue that the postwar era reflects the attempts of Americans to come to terms with the sexual, racial, political, and gender differences—both between the United States and other nations and among diverse Americans—that became evident during the war years.

68. Sandeen, *Picturing an Exhibition,* 39.

69. Commager, *The American Mind,* 2.

70. Commager, "Portrait of the American," 3.

71. Prominent examples include Benedict, *The Chrysanthemum and the Sword;* Schaffner, *Fatherland;* and Adorno et al., *The Authoritarian Personality.* Ellen Herman discusses the importance of character studies to wartime psychology in chap. 2 of *The Romance of American Psychology,* 17–47.

72. Potter, *People of Plenty,* 14.

73. Mart, "Tough Guys and American Cold War Policy," 359. Other diplomatic historians have suggested that this rhetoric was a worldwide one (India, for example, as Andrew Rotter argues, reformulated the dominant image to cast the United States as a sexual aggressor threatening a female nation-state), but gendered rhetoric seems to have been particularly heated in the United States ("Gender Relations, Foreign Relations," 53; see also Costigliola, "The Nuclear Family").

74. At times, nations and their interests were even cast in sexual terms. In her 2000 analysis of cold war ideology and American identity, Joanne P. Sharp notes that "the relationship between the superpowers was itself written as a sexual one." *Condensing the Cold War,* 103.

75. See Mead, "The Study of National Character," 70–85.

76. Gorer, *The American People,* 22. Gorer was a protégé of Margaret Mead's.

77. Mead, *And Keep Your Powder Dry,* 21.

78. See Wilkinson, *The Pursuit of American Character.*

79. Wise, "'Paradigm Dramas' in American Studies," 307.

80. These references are taken from Trilling, "Our Country and Our Culture"; Commager, *The American Mind.* See also Commager, *America in Perspective;* Reisman, "Psychological Types and National Character"; Savelle, *Seeds of Liberty.* For an annotated collection, see Wilkinson, ed., *American Social Character.* The U.S. population grew from about 140 million in 1945 to 180.6 million in 1960; see Bremner and Reichard, eds., *Reshaping America,* ix.

81. Perry, *Characteristically American,* 4–5.

82. See Susman, "'Personality' and the Making of Twentieth-Century Culture," 271–86.

83. Donald, "How English Is It?," 32.

84. Postwar ideologies of American character fit Pierre Bourdieu's model of social and cultural capital; see his "The Forms of Capital," 241–58.

85. "The Family," 36.

86. This formulation is influenced by Priscilla Wald's discussion of literary nation building in *Constituting Americans.*

87. Hixson, *Parting the Curtain,* 118.

88. Riesman, *The Lonely Crowd;* and Whyte, *The Organization Man.*

89. "What Is the American Character?," 22.

90. Myerson, "The Great Unlearning," 533.

91. Ellis, *The American Sexual Tragedy,* 11.

92. "A Scientist Looks at America's Sexual Behavior," 34.

93. Frank, *The Conduct of Sex,* 112.

94. Riesman, *The Lonely Crowd,* 142–47.

95. I am indebted to Regina Morantz-Sanchez for suggesting that many of the changes postwar critics feared were grounded in actual social changes of the time, and for urging me to stress the role of consumer capitalism.

96. Potter, *People of Plenty.*

97. Scanlon, introduction to *The Gender and Consumer Culture Reader,* 2.

98. Cohen, "From Town Center to Shopping Center," 260 and passim.

99. Herberg, *Protestant-Catholic-Jew.*

100. Bell, *The Cultural Contradictions of Capitalism,* 432–33. The title essay was originally published in 1970.

101. The centerpiece of a wide scholarship on consumption and American identity is Lasch, *Culture of Narcissism,* an influential blend of historical, economic, and Freudian criticism first published in 1979. Lasch accused Americans and their culture of being self-centered and morally impoverished and lamented both the depredations of consumer capitalism and what Lasch saw as a decline in the strength of community and the family unit. Significantly, Lasch continued a theme found in earlier criticism when he noted of the modern narcissist that "his emancipation from ancient taboos brings him no sexual peace" (23).

102. Astley, "Fidelity and Infidelity," 80.

103. Whitman, *Let's Tell the Truth about Sex,* 224.

104. Schauffler, "Today It Could Be *Your* Daughter," 43.

105. War brides from Allied or occupied nations who married American soldiers and, usually, migrated to the United States with them after the war received a great deal of attention, much of it negative, in the American press. For examples, see Padovar, "Why Americans Like German Women," 354–57; Pannitt, "Those English Girls," 5; and "German Girls," 38. For a later assessment of the GIs' rush to marry foreign brides that framed it as a cautionary tale for American women, see South, "The Secret of Love," 23, 112–13.

106. Dudziak, "Josephine Baker, Racial Protest, and the Cold War," 544.

107. McPartland, *Sex in Our Changing World,* 3.

108. Visson, *As Others See Us,* 162.

109. Hirsch, *Sexual Misbehavior of the Upper-Cultured,* 51.

110. Sandomirsky, "Sex in the Soviet Union," 199.

111. Christian, "Sex Cultism in America," 66; David Loth, *The Erotic in Literature,* 15.

112. Gorer, "The Erotic Myth of America," 590, 591.

113. On America's efforts to improve its image abroad, see Pells, *Not Like Us;* Pells's reference to "cultural diplomacy" is on p. 87. Mary Dudziak also discusses postwar efforts to export useful images of the United States in *Cold War Civil Rights;* and Walter Hixson addresses efforts focusing on the Soviet Union in *Parting the Curtain.*

114. Heineman, "The Hour of the Woman," 382.

115. "National Council of Catholic Women Meets," B20.

116. Bergler, "The Myth of a New National Disease," 87.

117. Sandomirsky, "Sex in the Soviet Union," 199.

118. Sorokin, *The American Sex Revolution,* 104.

119. Stone, "The Kinsey Studies and Marriage Counseling," 173.

120. Folsom, "Sociological Implications of the Report," 87.

121. Sorokin, *The American Sex Revolution,* 153.

122. Caprio, *The Power of Sex,* 5–6.

123. Rusk, "Concerning Man's Basic Drive," 24.

124. Cited in D'Emilio and Freedman, *Intimate Matters,* 282.

125. Whitman, "America's Moral Crisis," 219. For a discussion of the diagnostic category of "sex addiction," see Irvine, "Reinventing Perversion," 429–50. Unlike the 1990s models Irvine examines, the trope of addiction to certain sexual images or behaviors appears in postwar discussions of America's changing culture of consumption as a national, not an individual, affliction.

126. Zimmerman, "A Sociologist Looks at the Report," 104.

127. Averill, "Sexuality in Crisis," 1196.

128. Berlant, *The Queen of America Goes to Washington City,* 1.

129. Dubinsky, *Improper Advances,* 35.

1. Honigmann, "An Anthropological Approach to Sex," 7.
2. Ernst, "The Kinsey Report and Its Contributions to Related Fields," 282.
3. Philip Wylie had earlier blamed much marital disarray on American men's "missing *sense of maleness* which has driven so many wives to bleak despair, so many others to divorce." "What's Wrong with American Marriages?," 38, emphasis in original.
4. Schlesinger, "The Crisis of American Masculinity," 64.
5. Bristow, *Making Men Moral*, 23.
6. Fortuna, "The Magnificent American Male," 54–55, 148–49.
7. A similar dynamic emerged following the Vietnam War; see Jeffords, *The Re-Masculinization of America*.
8. Elkin, "Aggressive and Erotic Tendencies in Army Life," 408–13.
9. Kitching, *Sex Problems of the Returned Veteran*, 56.
10. Futterman, "Changing Sex Patterns and the War," 29.
11. Whitman, "Wolf! Wolf!," 14.
12. Menninger, *Psychiatry in a Troubled World*, 363–64. Menninger notes that 4.2 million claims for disability compensation had been filed by veterans by the end of 1947, attesting to the tremendous physical and emotional damage wrought by the war. For similar predictions, see Cherne, "The Future of the Middle Class," 75–78.
13. Robins et al., "Hysteria in Men," 677–85.
14. Hoover, "Mankind at Its Worst," 55. Hoover's title played on *Esquire's* claim to represent "Man at His Best."
15. See Wylie, *Generation of Vipers;* and Strecker, *Their Mothers' Sons*. Wylie coined the term "Momism" in *Generation of Vipers*. Antifeminist theorists like Edward Strecker and Edmund Bergler also relied on the term, and in wartime and postwar literature on masculinity and the changing American character it became a trope for female incompetence, greed, and control over men.
16. Popularized by H. M. Overstreet's best-selling *The Mature Mind, maturity* was an important term in postwar psychological thought, where it came to mean the ability to handle crucial developmental tasks including marriage, parenthood, and breadwinning. For an example of contemporary usage, see Drury, "Are You Mature?," 38–40.
17. Solinger, *Wake Up Little Susie*, 91.
18. Stern, "The Miserable Male," 42, 53.
19. Ibid., 542.
20. Connell, *Masculinities*, 23.
21. Mead, *Male and Female*, 236.
22. Pollock, "How Masculine Are You?," 49, 55.
23. Hunt, "The Decline and Fall of the American Father," 23, 24.
24. Montagu, *The Natural Superiority of Women*, 174.

25. Marmor, "Psychological Trends in American Family Relationships," 146.

26. Frank, "How Much Do We Know about Men?," 52.

27. Mead, "American Man in a Woman's World," 11, 22.

28. Hunt, "What Keeps a Husband Faithful?," 39–41; Russell Lynes, "Husbands," 85–87; Hacker, "The New Burdens of Masculinity," 227–33; Lawrenson, "What Has Become of the Old-Fashioned Man?," 42–43, 114–15; Landis and Landis, "The U.S. Male," 22–23, 48.

29. Willig, "Lament for Male Sanctuary," 19.

30. "The Playboy Panel: The Womanization of America," 43. Ogersby, *Playboys in Paradise.*

31. Drake, "Why Men Leave Home," 26.

32. Hunt, *Her Infinite Variety,* 133.

33. Hinkle, "Spinsters and Bachelors," 159. Research in endocrinology, which had assumed an increasingly large place in the human sciences since the 1920s, sometimes filtered down to the popular culture and was used to question the biological basis of gender.

34. Landis and Landis, "The U.S. Male," 22.

35. See Meyerowitz, "Sex Change and the Popular Press."

36. Lal, "Science and Sex Conversion," 39.

37. Schlesinger, "The Crisis of American Masculinity," 65.

38. Parsons, "The Social Structure of the Family," 271.

39. Riesman and Glazer, *The Lonely Crowd;* and Whyte, *The Organization Man.*

40. Marcuse, *Eros and Civilization,* 89.

41. Hacker, "The New Burdens of Masculinity," 232.

42. Jurca, *White Diaspora,* 137–38. Wilson, *The Man in the Gray Flannel Suit.* Addressing these narratives of suburban discontent, Jurca argues that imagining oneself as oppressed became a crucial element of middle-class identity for white men. For other examples of this genre, see Keats, *The Crack in the Picture Window;* Elliott, *Parktilden Village;* and Yates, *Revolutionary Road.*

43. Gordon, Gordon, and Gumpert, *The Split-Level Trap,* 12, 34. The authors argued that it was middle-aged wives, not commuting husbands and fathers, who were most victimized by the suburban lifestyle they described.

44. Lyndon, "Uncertain Hero," 107.

45. Mailer, in "The Playboy Panel: 'The Womanization of America,'" 142.

46. Gorer, *The American People,* 49.

47. Ogburn and Nimkoff, eds., *Technology and the Changing Family,* 5, table 1.

48. Lyndon, "Uncertain Hero," 41.

49. Wassersug, "Why Men Envy Women," 12; Bowman, "Are Husbands Slaves to Women?," 111–14. Another observer went so far as to dub the middle-class American husband—in contrast to his more assertive European counter-part—"an oppressed minority . . . a volunteer for slavery." Amaury de Rien-

court, quoted in Pope, "Is It True What They Say about American Husbands?," 85.

50. Hunt, "Decline and Fall of the American Father," 20.

51. Ibid., 22.

52. See Marsh, *Suburban Lives*.

53. Averill, "Sexuality in Crisis," 1198. For a similar argument, see Fontaine, "Are We Staking Our Future on a Crop of Sissies?," 154–56.

54. Bettelheim, "Growing Up Female," 122.

55. Averill, "Sexuality in Crisis," 1198. Psychoanalytic case studies frequently cited inadequate fathers as a primary cause of adult homosexuality in both men and women; for a typical example, see Wittels, *The Sex Habits of American Women*, 133.

56. Marmor, "Psychological Trends in American Family Relationships," 146.

57. Jarrell, "A Sad Heart at the Supermarket," 99.

58. Barth, "What's Wrong with American Men?," 24. See also Baldridge, "Why I Love Italian Men," 58–60.

59. Barrett, "New Innocents Abroad," 286.

60. Experts consistently described mass culture as feminine; see, for example, essays in Rosenberg and White, eds., *Mass Culture*. See also Huyssen, "Mass Culture as Woman," 188–208.

61. Arthur Schlesinger Jr., cited in May, *Homeward Bound*, 98. Schlesinger's 1958 article repeated this plea, hoping for a "virile political life" that "will be definite and hard-hitting." "The Crisis of American Masculinity," 66.

62. Cuordileone, "Politics in an Age of Anxiety," 518.

63. Popular and legal commentary on the Rosenbergs' alleged gender transgression is discussed in Carmichael, *Framing History*, 95–107.

64. Leonard, "The American Male," 97.

65. Moskin, "The American Male," 76.

66. Thompson, "The New Mr. Caspar Milquetoasts," 11, 121.

67. Magnus Hirschfeld, with preface and additional chapters by Edward Podolsky, *The Sexual History of the World War* (New York: Cadillac Publishing, 1946), 287, 300–3, emphasis in original. Podolsky's sympathies were not only with men: he outlined six different types of frigidity that the stresses of war caused women, 304–5.

68. Fry, "A Report on Sex Life," 547.

69. Kinsey, Pomeroy, and Martin, *Sexual Behavior in the Human Male*, 197. Further references in this chapter are given in the text.

70. This process has been described as "sexual embourgeoisment"; see Weinberg and Williams, "Sexual Embourgeoisment? Social Class and Sexual Activity: 1938–1970," 33–48.

71. Harper, "Legal Considerations in Relation to the Report," 47.

72. Kardiner, *Sex and Morality,* 66, emphasis added.

73. Kirkendall, "Toward a Clarification of the Concept of Male Sex Drive," 367.

74. Montagu, *The Natural Superiority of Women,* 45.

75. Mead, *Male and Female,* 218.

76. DeMenasce, "Sexual Morals and Sexualized Morality," 168.

77. Clark, "The American Male," 31; "The Impotent Male," 48.

78. Clark, "The American Male," 32. See also Lawrenson, "New York," 35.

79. Pampanini, "American Men Bore Me . . . ," 59.

80. Caprio, *The Power of Sex,* 1, capitalization in original.

81. Caprio, *The Sexually Adequate Male,* 2, 4.

82. Brown, "What American Men Want to Know about Sex," 125.

83. Johnstone, "Check Your Sex I.Q.," 15, emphasis in original.

84. Caprio, *Variations in Sexual Behavior,* 307–8.

85. Riesman, "Permissiveness and Sex Roles," 214.

86. Alan Nadel makes this argument about *Playboy* in *Containment Culture,* 129–36. For other analyses of *Playboy* and its role in consolidating postwar male consumerism, see Bailey, *Front Porch to Back Seat,* 102–7; Ogersby, *Playboys in Paradise;* and Ehrenreich, *The Hearts of Men.*

87. Peterson, *The Century of Sex,* 229.

88. Lunbeck, *The Psychiatric Persuasion,* 235–36.

89. Rubin, *Glands, Sex, and Personality,* 163. Such descriptions often hinted at repressed or latent homosexuality, which I discuss in chapter 5.

90. Caprio, *The Sexually Adequate Male,* 4.

91. Cooper, "Education for Responsible Husbandhood," 97.

92. Caprio, *The Sexually Adequate Male,* 80.

93. Ibid., 17.

94. Moskin, "The American Male," 78.

95. Hilliard, "The Act of Love," 42. See also Hilliard, *A Woman Doctor Looks at Love and Life,* cited in James, "The American Wife," 36.

96. Landis and Landis, "The U.S. Male," 23.

97. Clark, "The American Male," 31–32, emphasis in original.

98. Bergler and Kroger, *Kinsey's Myth of Female Sexuality,* 112; emphasis in original.

99. Odenwald, *The Disappearing Sexes,* 38–39; "The Impotent Male," 48.

100. Popenoe, *Sexual Inadequacy of the Male,* 35.

101. Ellis, *The American Sexual Tragedy,* 71.

102. Gorer, "Justification by Numbers," 285.

103. Burgess, "The Sociologic Theory of Psychosexual Behavior," 15.

104. Frazier, "The Entrenchment of the American Witch," 100.

CHAPTER THREE. "MUCH THE SAME DESIRES AS MEN"

1. "For Women Only . . . What Every Woman Should Know about Kinsey," 78.

2. Farnham and Lundberg, *Modern Woman*, 275. Similar works from the period include Strecker and Lathbury, *Their Mothers' Daughters;* and Strecker, *Their Mothers' Sons.* For contemporary critiques of these authors' ideas, see Herschberger, *Adam's Rib;* and Montagu, *The Natural Superiority of Women.*

3. Robinson, *The Power of Sexual Surrender,* 77. Robinson saw her work as offering a psychoanalytic corrective to Kinsey's views.

4. Meyer, *Creating G.I. Jane,* 33.

5. McPartland, *Sex in Our Changing World,* 9.

6. Wittels, *The Sex Habits of American Women,* 45.

7. Kardiner, *Sex and Morality,* 76–77.

8. Robinson, *The Power of Sexual Surrender,* 7, 67.

9. Cited in May, *Barren in the Promised Land,* 174. Definitions of *frigidity* varied, but many experts used the term to mean the inability to reach orgasm through heterosexual intercourse.

10. Popenoe, "Can This Marriage Be Saved?," 49. Popenoe's eugenics and his crusade to sexually reinvigorate middle-class marriage are discussed in Kline, *Building a Better Race;* and Ladd-Taylor, "Eugenics, Sterilization, and Modern Marriage in the USA," 298–327.

11. Bender, "How Much Women Change—and How Little," 128; Widdemer, "Cad's Paradise," 55.

12. Merrill, *Social Problems on the Home Front,* 102.

13. Sharp, "Men Are the Sucker Sex," 33.

14. For examples of postwar concern about women's changing roles, see Hacker, "Women as a Minority Group," 60–69; Kluckhohn, "American Women and American Values," 179–99; and White, "The Changing Context of Women's Education," 291–95.

15. Scheinfeld, "What's Wrong with Sex Studies," 16.

16. Meyerowitz, "Beyond the Feminine Mystique," 234, 241.

17. Weise, "Live the Life of McCall's," 27, emphasis in original.

18. Mayer, "Gender Ironies of Nationalism," 7.

19. Joanne Meyerowitz discusses women's private and public roles in "Beyond the Feminine Mystique." Melani McAlister has traced the representation of women in postwar film as "spunky" foils for a degraded and oppressed femininity set elsewhere or in the past; see *Epic Encounters,* chap. 1.

20. See May, *Homeward Bound,* 16–19; and Kozol, *Life's America,* 7–9.

21. *Sexual Behavior in the Human Female* was originally scheduled for publication in 1951; after several postponements, it finally appeared in late 1953. See the editor's note in Brecher and Brecher, "The New Kinsey Report Has a Moral," 29.

22. For examples of articles appearing before the second report that predicted its conclusions, see Block, "What Are Women Telling Dr. Kinsey?," 25–30; Block, "What Women Are Telling Dr. Kinsey," 40–45; Cooley, "What Kinsey Is Discovering about Women," 36–40; Deutsch, "Have Women Talked Frankly to Dr. Kinsey?," 24–25, 58–59; Deutsch, "What Dr. Kinsey Is Up To Now, Part I," 81–82, 84–86, and "What Dr. Kinsey Is Up To Now, Part II," 85–86, 88, 90; Ernst, "What Kinsey Will Tell," 36–37, 86–90; and Grant, "The Kinsey Report on Women," 17.

23. "Ask Press to Play Down the Kinsey Report," 693.

24. "Dr. Kinsey's Sex Study of Women," 1.

25. Examples of authors recounting their Kinsey interview experiences include "What I Told Dr. Kinsey about My Sex Life," 44–46; Caro, "The Kinsey Interview Experience (as Seen by a Psychiatric Social Worker)," 189–201; Scott, "I Was Interviewed by Dr. Kinsey," 26–29; "The Sexual Behavior of an American Woman as Revealed by Her to Dr. Alfred C. Kinsey," 24–25, 58–61; and Skinner, "Trial by Kinsey," 29–31.

26. *Newsweek* poll cited in Brinkman, "Dr. Alfred C. Kinsey and the Press," 115.

27. Strecker, "The Silver Cord," 138.

28. "From the Editors," 11.

29. Banning, "What Women Won't Tell Dr. Kinsey," 110.

30. "Dr. Kinsey's Sex Study of Women," 1.

31. Bergquist, "Check Your Sex Life against the New Kinsey Report," 22.

32. Mudd, "Implications for Marriage and Sexual Adjustment," 137.

33. Havemann, "The Kinsey Report on Women," 53; Norris, "Incredible!," 59; Hurst, "Nourishing," 52.

34. Cochran et al., *Statistical Problems of the Kinsey Report*, 1.

35. "Review of *Sexual Behavior in the Human Female*," 120.

36. Hobbs and Kephart, "Professor Kinsey," 615.

37. Kinsey et al., *Sexual Behavior in the Human Female*, 4. Further references in this chapter appear in the text.

38. Grant, "The Kinsey Report on Women," 17–18.

39. Banning, "What Women Won't Tell Dr. Kinsey," 45.

40. Bergquist, "Check Your Sex Life against the New Kinsey Report," 17, emphasis added.

41. "Sex vs. America," 20.

42. Wylie, "Virginity and Pre-Marital Sex Relations," 27.

43. Batdorff, "American Women vs. the Kinsey Report," 121–24.

44. *Indianapolis Star*, 15 August 1953, cited in Jones, *Alfred C. Kinsey*, 699. Some coverage attempted to place Kinsey within a familial framework; see Nanette Kutner, "Yes, There Is a Mrs. Kinsey," 17, 92–94.

45. Zolotow, "Love Is Not a Statistic," 8.

46. Norris, "Incredible!," 59–60.

47. Banning, "What Women Won't Tell Dr. Kinsey," 109.

48. Hobbs and Kephart, "Professor Kinsey," 614.

49. Banning, "What Women Won't Tell Dr. Kinsey," 109.

50. Landis, "The Women Kinsey Studied," 110, 112.

51. Bergler and Kroger, *Kinsey's Myth of Female Sexuality,* 2, 110, emphasis in original.

52. Scheinfeld, "Kinsey's Study of Female Sex Behavior," 5.

53. Cartoon, *Milwaukee Sentinel* and *Los Angeles Examiner,* 1953, "Women" binder, Kinsey Institute for Research in Sex, Gender, and Reproduction, 9.

54. Vincent, "So You Want to Stay Single?," 59.

55. "Our 'Unsavory Character' Resents Speed Ratings Applied to Women," 12.

56. James, "The American Wife," 20.

57. Reik, *Of Love and Lust,* 431.

58. Mead, introduction to *Women,* 16.

59. Sherwin, "Female Sex Crimes," 183.

60. Ellis, "Female Sexual Response and Marital Relations," 154.

61. McPartland, *Sex in Our Changing World,* 87.

62. Odenwald, *The Disappearing Sexes,* 62–63.

63. "More Harm Than Good," 6. The figure of "Mrs. Jones," the archetypal woman next door who sets community norms, is also invoked as the subject of the report in Archer, "Keeping Up with Mrs. Jones' Sex Life," 33–36.

64. Landis, "What Is 'Normal' Married Love?," 127. See also Landis, "Don't Expect Too Much of Sex in Marriage," 25–27.

65. Poling, "The Dangers in the Marriage Manuals," 41–45.

66. Gordon, Gordon, and Gumpert, *The Split-Level Trap,* 73–75.

67. Hobbs and Kephart, "Professor Kinsey," 619–20. Hobbs, a conservative sociologist, was a vehement critic of Kinsey's work. Three months after this review was published, his testimony before an investigative committee was instrumental in Kinsey's loss of Rockefeller Foundation funding. See Jones, *Alfred C. Kinsey,* 334–35.

68. Wylie, *Generation of Vipers,* 186.

69. Postwar discussions of the proper demeanor and attitude of the corporate wife offer one example of this trend; see Whyte, *The Organization Man,* 158–59, 258–59, 363; Palmer, "What Kind of Wife Has He?," 7–39; and the film *Woman's World* (dir. Jean Negulesco, 1954), in which a group of men competing for a management position are interviewed along with their wives, and the women's appearance and demeanor decide the matter.

70. Muret, "Marriage as a Career," 30–31.

71. Robinson, *The Power of Sexual Surrender,* 49–50.

72. Franzblau, *The Road to Sexual Maturity,* 143.

73. Ibid., 147.

74. Robinson, *The Power of Sexual Surrender,* 27.

75. Thigpen and Cleckley, *The Three Faces of Eve,* rear-cover review. Further page references are given in the text.

76. *Decatur (Ala.) Daily,* 31 August 1953; and the *Ottawa (Ill.) Republican-Times,* 4 September 1953, "Women" binder 12, Kinsey Institute for Research in Sex, Gender, and Reproduction, ellipses in original. The reference is to Rudyard Kipling's "The Ladies," which, after noting pointedly that "the things you will learn from the Yellow an' Brown / They'll 'elp you a lot with the White!," concludes with the lines "For the Colonel's Lady an' Judy O'Grady / Are sisters under their skins!"

77. Preston, ed., *A Cartoon Guide to the Kinsey Report,* 33, 125, 112–13. A similar scene, in which an angry informant strikes a surveyor, appears in Wenzel, ed., *The Flimsey Report,* 10.

78. Folsom, "Sociological Implications of the Report," 78.

79. Berg and Street, *Sex,* 24.

80. Results are from the Kelly Longitudinal Study, discussed in May, *Homeward Bound,* chap. 5.

81. Seen for sale on the eBay auction Website, www.ebay.com, accessed on September 15, 2000.

82. Caprio, *The Sexually Adequate Male,* 54; emphases in original.

83. Whitbread and Cadden, "Susan McViddy Finds Out What She's Missing," 40. Further page references are given in the text.

84. For more on Kinsey's taxonomy, see Gould, *The Flamingo's Smile,* 159.

85. Morrison, *Playing in the Dark,* 51–52.

86. On the importance of race in postwar constructions of American womanhood, see Dudziak, "Josephine Baker, Racial Protest, and the Cold War"; Feldstein, "I Wanted the Whole World to See"; and Kunzel, "White Neurosis, Black Pathology," 263–303, 304–34.

87. Maslin, "A Tragically Fallen Star Smolders in Memory," C15.

88. Bergquist, "Check Your Sex Life against the New Kinsey Report," 17.

89. The sociologist Janice Irvine argues in her analysis of the reports that Kinsey "colluded in the racial exclusion so pervasive in sex research." As I note in the chapter, I suspect that, although his wish for statistical validity played a part in this decision, his exclusion of African Americans may also have been prompted by a shrewd assessment of American postwar racial ideologies: that findings pertaining to white women would be less likely to be dismissed. See Irvine, *Disorders of Desire,* 43.

90. "What I Told Dr. Kinsey about My Sex Life," 45.

91. McKensie, "Pursuit of Democracy," 6. I am grateful to Ruth Feldstein for providing this citation.

92. "Why Negro Women Are Not in the Kinsey Report," 109.

93. "Some Say Kinsey Should Use Colored Interviewers," 111.

94. Dr. Rose Hum Lee, cited in "Sociologist Says Minorities Get 'Tired of Being Studied,'" 112.

95. Menzies and Bernard-Luc, *The Fig Leaf.*

96. Train, *Miss Kinsey's Report,* 158.

97. Smythe, *The Sex Probers.*

98. The film version of *The Chapman Report* was released in 1962, directed by George Cukor and starring Shelley Winters, Jane Fonda, Claire Bloom, and Efrem Zimbalist Jr. At least one film depicted a sex survey of men: in *Boys' Night Out* (dir. Michael Gordon, 1962), a graduate student in sociology (Kim Novak) poses as a prostitute to live in an apartment maintained by four male friends, one of whom (James Garner) is single. The film revolves around Novak's manipulation of the men, each of whom expects sex from her but instead confesses his marital and sexual history, which she records for her research. A love affair develops between the characters played by Novak and Garner, and following confrontations between Novak, her subjects, and their wives, she abandons her studies and pursues love instead.

99. Wallace, *The Chapman Report,* 6. Further page references are given in the text. The film version incorporates significant changes in the plot; my discussion here is based on the novel.

100. Pont, "Review of *The Chapman Report,*" 26.

101. Ibid.

102. Rumming, "Dr. Kinsey and the Human Female," 8.

103. Kidd, "Sexual Behavior in the American Advertiser," 41.

104. Poovey, *Uneven Developments,* 12.

105. The terms *overt* and *covert* appear throughout both volumes. Introducing a section of the report on premarital coitus, Kinsey wrote, "Because of this public condemnation of pre-marital coitus, one might believe that such contacts would be rare among American females and males. But this is only the overt culture, the things that people openly profess to be and do. Our previous report (1948) on the male has indicated how far publicly expressed attitudes may depart from the realities of behavior—the covert culture." Kinsey et al., *Sexual Behavior in the Human Female,* 285.

106. Nancy Cott has argued that Victorian beliefs in female sexual passivity and lack of desire were sometimes strategically deployed by nineteenth-century women who wished to avoid unwanted sexual demands and the risks of pregnancy. See "Passionlessness," 162–88.

CHAPTER FOUR. "I'M A MUCH BETTER CITIZEN
THAN IF I WERE SINGLE"

1. Montaigne, *The Origins and Nature of Marriage,* 87.

2. Ditzion, *Marriage, Morals, and Sex in America,* 398.

3. The American Association of Marriage Counselors was founded in 1944 partly in response to worries about the mass failure of wartime marriages. See Carson, "Afraid of Love," 95. Beth Bailey discusses the academic marriage-education movement, which reached its peak in influence and popularity during the 1950s, in *Front Porch to Back Seat*, 119–40.

4. Social scientists repeatedly observed that postwar Americans were beginning to prepare carefully for marriage. One sociologist found that "the older view that marriage really required no preparation is being challenged by the younger generations who believe in giving their courtships much forethought and attention." Koller, "Some Changes in Courtship Behavior in Three Generations of Ohio Women," 370. Another article contrasted modern marriages to those of the past with the observation "Young people themselves . . . are beginning to demand a better deal." Carson, "Afraid of Love," 95. Marriage and sex educators often justified their work on the grounds that the public demanded sexual information.

5. The intense pronatalism of the postwar years is discussed in Marsh and Ronner, *The Empty Cradle;* and May, *Barren in the Promised Land.* For a contemporary opinion on the importance of children to a healthy marriage, see Naismith, "The Problem of Infertility," 27–30.

6. Whitman, "Sex and Early Marriage," 40.

7. Dr. J. G. Auerbach, cited in Whitman, "Sex and Early Marriage," 40–41. The equation between sexual self-denial and emotional or mental illness was often featured in cultural productions, where it competed with the traditional narrative of sexual ruin: for example, in the film *Splendor in the Grass* (dir. Elia Kazin, 1961), the heroine, played by Natalie Wood, suffers from a mental and emotional breakdown clearly coded as the result of her sexual refusal of the hero, played by Warren Beatty. Such narratives suggested that, in at least some cases, premarital chastity might not be worth its emotional cost.

8. Truxal, Merrill, *The Family in American Culture,* 134; May, *Barren,* 134.

9. "Isaac," quoted in Whitman, "Sex and Early Marriage," 148.

10. Nancy Cott argues that "the institution of marriage is and has been a public institution and a building block of social policy," and emphasizes that "presumptions about and provisions for the obligations and benefits of marriage have always been built into many legal and governmental structures in the United States[,] . . . enforcing privileges along with obligations." See "Giving Character to Our Whole Civil Polity," 107.

11. Caprio, *The Power of Sex,* 93–94, 11.

12. Merrill, *Social Problems on the Home Front,* 103.

13. *The Best Years of Our Lives* (dir. William Wyler, 1946).

14. The success or failure of wartime marriages took on international political dimensions as well—in 1945, as thousands of British war brides awaited transport to the United States, the British embassy in Washington warned that

"these women will prove an increasingly important factor in Anglo-American relations." Cited in Reynolds, *Rich Relations,* 417.

15. Berg and Street, *Sex,* 14.

16. Menninger, *Psychiatry in a Troubled World,* 393.

17. Tenenbaum, "The Fate of Wartime Marriages," 530.

18. "The Family," 36.

19. Truxal and Merrill, *The Family in American Culture,* 676, emphasis in original.

20. For example, see Churchill, "Your Chances of Getting Married," 38. Literature on the responsibilities of American women to returning war veterans is discussed in Gerber, "Heroes and Misfits," 545–74; Hartmann, "Prescriptions for Penelope," 223–39; and Michel, "Danger on the Home Front," 447–66. In the extensive primary literature, see especially Kitching, *Sex Problems of the Returned Veteran.*

21. Dr. Coleman R. Griffith, quoted in Katz, *Home Fires,* 8.

22. Culman, "You Married Him, Now Stick with Him," 17.

23. Desmond, "The Plight of the Unmarried," 528.

24. Whitman, "Let's Help Them Marry Young," 1.

25. Ibid., 1.

26. Before World War II, unofficial separations far outnumbered legal ones; see Hartog, *Man and Wife in America.*

27. U.S. Bureau of the Census, *Statistical Abstract of the United States,* tables no. 78: "Marriage and Divorce Rates"; and no. 79: "Median Age at First Marriage," 70. Governmental estimates of marriages projected to end in divorce rose from a little under one in four in 1945 to over four in ten by 1965. See May, *Homeward Bound,* table 5: "Percentage of Marriages Projected to End in Divorce," 8. Divorce was becoming more easily obtained, as decrees from different states began to be recognized nationally and the legal process became simpler and less expensive for many. Weatherford, *American Women's History,* s.v. "divorce," 107–8.

28. Kline, *Building a Better Race,* 124–25.

29. Paul Landis, quoted in Coontz, *The Way We Never Were,* 33.

30. Zaretsky, "Charisma or Rationalization?," 381.

31. "Phobias Keep Some Single," 370.

32. Gibson, "How Neurotic Are You?," 64.

33. Farnham and Lundberg, *Modern Woman,* 356–59.

34. In 1955, the American Law Institute issued a declaration "deem[ing] it inappropriate for the Government to attempt to control behavior that has no substantial significance except as to the morality of the actor." Langum, *Crossing over the Line,* 219–20.

35. Duvall, *Before You Marry,* 185.

36. Franzblau, *The Road to Sexual Maturity*, 207. In these scenarios the non-racially-marked partner is assumed to be physically impaired or emotionally or mentally disturbed.

37. Riesman, "The Saving Remnant," 140.

38. Polatin and Philtine, "Who Shouldn't Marry?," 163.

39. Levey, "Imagining the Family in Postwar Popular Culture," 125.

40. Whitman, *Let's Tell the Truth about Sex*, 21.

41. Caprio, *The Power of Sex*, 11.

42. McPartland, "Footnote on Sex," 213.

43. Bossard, "Divorce," 97.

44. Mead, "What Is Happening to the American Family?," 323.

45. Putnam, "Divorce Is No Solution," 62.

46. Ibid., 60.

47. Berg and Street, *Sex*, 227.

48. Sbarbaro, *Marriage Is on Trial*, xii, 111, 112–13.

49. Montagu, *The Natural Superiority of Women*, 153–70; Farnham and Lundberg, *Modern Woman*, 359–71.

50. "No Permits for Promiscuity," 1124.

51. Bossard and Boll, *Why Marriages Go Wrong*, 12.

52. Bossard, "Divorce," 97.

53. Whitman, "America's Moral Crisis," 220. See also Whitman, "Divorce Granted!," 11–16. Whitman's figures may have overestimated the actual incidence of American divorce vis-à-vis that of other countries: for comparative statistics, see Phillips, *Putting Asunder*, 560, fig. 13.3.

54. The divorce rate in 1940 had been 8.8; after rising during the war years and peaking at a high of 17.9 per thousand in 1946, it remained between 8.9 and 10.3 throughout the 1950s. U.S. Bureau of the Census, *Statistical Abstract of the United States*, 70. To complicate estimates, the rising divorce rate reflected the decrease of the once common practice of informally dissolving marriages by desertion rather than by legal decree. Also, rates were not uniformly reported, causing confusion over exactly how many divorces occurred. See Riley, *Divorce*, 157–80.

55. Whitman, "America's Moral Crisis," 221.

56. This new coupling is authorized by the film's portrayal of wife #1 (Virginia Mayo) as a gold-digging victory girl who eventually leaves her unemployed veteran husband (Dana Andrews) for a wealthier man.

57. Bossard and Boll, *Why Marriages Go Wrong*, 13.

58. Averill, "Sexuality in Crisis," 1198.

59. Appel, "Problems with Which People Want Help in Sex and Marriage," 4.

60. Gordon, Gordon, and Gumpert, *The Split-Level Trap*, 110; Landis, "The Changing Family," 28.

61. Duvall, *Before You Marry*, 242.

62. Caprio, *Marital Infidelity*, 76.

63. Sociological literature on the suburbs often noted that arriving residents, especially the mothers of young children, were isolated. The mobility of modern Americans is discussed in Riesman and Glazer, *The Lonely Crowd;* and Landis, "The Changing Family."

64. Adams, "Making Marriage Work" (January 1953): 28; (July 1953): 28; (January 1956): 26.

65. Stone, "The Kinsey Studies and Marriage Counseling," 165.

66. Boudreau, as told to Lester David, "Myths That Imperil Married Love," 172.

67. Landis, "Marriage Has Improved," 14.

68. Kephart, review of *Women in the Modern World,* by Mirra Komarovsky, 76.

69. Kinsey, Pomeroy, and Martin, *Sexual Behavior in the Human Male,* 544.

70. Eimerl, "Why Bachelors Stay Single," 81. See also Ogersby, *Playboys in Paradise.*

71. Kinsey, Pomeroy, and Martin, *Sexual Behavior in the Human Male,* 585.

72. Kinsey speculated about the female partners in *Sexual Behavior in the Human Male* (588); the figures on female extramarital intercourse are given in *Sexual Behavior in the Human Female* (416).

73. Caprio, *Marital Infidelity,* 14–15.

74. Burgess and Locke, *The Family.*

75. Landis, "Marriage Has Improved," 13.

76. Mead, "The Contemporary American Family," 9.

77. The benefits of expert advice are outlined in Gretta Palmer, "Marriage Control," 51–54; and in Carson, "Afraid of Love."

78. Riesman, "Permissiveness and Sex Roles," 213.

79. Landis, "Marriage Has Improved," 14; Truxal and Merrill, *The Family in American Culture,* 509.

80. Landis, "Marriage Has Improved," 14.

81. Bowman, *Marriage for Moderns,* 215. This contrast between two types of family organization, often referred to as "traditional" or "patriarchal" versus "domestic," was a common one: for one example, see the descriptions and suggested exercises for high school students in Landis and Landis, *Personal Adjustment, Marriage, and Family Living,* 238–45.

82. Hunt, "What Keeps a Husband Faithful?," 41. This particular brand of retrospective feminism was common among marriage educators—placing sexism and the repression of female sexuality firmly in the past helped to frame their own recommendations as modern and progressive.

83. The continual re-creation of Victorian family and sexual models is a recurring theme in American conceptualizations of sexuality; see Degler, "What Ought to Be and What Was," 1469–77; Foucault, *The History of Sexuality,*

vol. 1; and Simmons, "Modern Sexuality and the Myth of Victorian Repression," 157–77.

84. For a discussion of the "companionate marriage" ideal, see Simmons, "Marriage in the Modern Manner"; Trimberger, "Feminism, Men, and Modern Love," 131–52; and White, *The First Sexual Revolution.*

85. Other aspects of postwar ideology drew on older ideas about national identity and domestic life—consider the 1950s resurgence of "colonial" domestic style based on an idealized image of the national past as safely free of racial difference, international conflict, and anxiety. Significantly, a recurrent theme in postwar social science is the argument that early Americans were psychologically simpler and healthier, with no time for neuroses.

86. Many of these differences, of course, mirrored Riesman's description of the differences between the "inner-directed" Americans of the past and their contemporary "other-directed" descendants.

87. The term *togetherness,* coined by *McCall's* magazine in 1954 to describe the new family-centered lifestyle of modern America, passed instantly into everyday language. Weise, "Live the Life of McCall's," 27.

88. *The Bride's Reference Book* (New York: *Bride's Magazine,* 1956), cited in Harvey, *The Fifties,* 68.

89. Landis, "Marriage Has Improved," 14.

90. Each of these developments was singled out by authorities; see Ogburn and Nimkoff, *Technology and the Changing Family,* 5, table 1.

91. Levine and Loth, *The Emotional Sex,* 83.

92. Montaigne, *The Origins and Nature of Marriage,* 80.

93. Robinson, *The Power of Sexual Surrender,* 9.

94. Hilliard, "Too Tired to Love?," 69.

95. Morrison, "A Descriptive Study of Responses to the Sex Attitude Inquiry," 1. Sex is also described as the "barometer" to marital success in Truxal and Merrill, *The Family in American Culture,* 523.

96. Berg and Street, *Sex,* 214.

97. Caprio, *The Power of Sex,* 162.

98. Frank, *The Conduct of Sex,* 67.

99. Grunwald, "The Second Sexual Revolution," 12.

100. Howe, "Sex and Religion," 82.

101. Pope Pius XII acknowledged that the rhythm method could be a part of Catholic marriages. See Shannon, *The Lively Debate,* 16, 28. My thanks to Joanne Melish for drawing this issue to my attention.

102. The group was the International Committee on Mental Health. See Whitman, "Don't Let Them Scoff at Marriage!," 100.

103. Kinsey et al., *Sexual Behavior in the Human Female,* 12.

104. Adams, "Making Marriage Work: 'We Agree on Almost Everything Except Sex,'" 32.

105. Carson, "Afraid of Love," 17.

106. Landis and Landis, *Personal Adjustment, Marriage, and Family Living,* 200.

107. Caprio, *Variations in Sexual Behavior,* 307.

108. Komarovsky, *Blue-Collar Marriage,* 83.

109. Adams, "Making Marriage Work: What Factors Favor Good Sexual Adjustment and a Happy Marriage?," 28.

110. Heggie, "Runaway Husbands," 149.

111. Caprio, *Variations in Sexual Behavior,* 307. Caprio's sympathy for those judged "sex offenders" is evident, a stance that mirrors Kinsey's.

112. Although the 1950s family ideal included children, and postwar authorities produced a flood of information on parenting, the authors I discuss in this chapter rarely commented on the presence of children except in passing, such as when noting that parental sex required a space removed from the sounds of children. Literature for and on women sometimes discussed their conflicts at being torn between the roles of wife/lover and mother and generally advised that the two functions be kept separate. But beyond a few concrete suggestions, such as occasionally serving children their dinner early or engaging a babysitter to ensure that adults had time for communication and romance, offspring are strikingly absent from postwar discussions of marital sexuality. They appeared symbolically as a generation at risk from improper parental relationships, but the sexual bond between husband and wife is primary.

113. Frank, *The Conduct of Sex,* 130.

114. Glover, "The Abnormality of Prostitution," 263; emphasis in original.

115. Caprio, *The Power of Sex,* 5–6, 207. Although "swinging" did not yet receive widespread attention in the news media, coverage of the suburban middle class sometimes alluded to licentious partying and mate swapping.

116. Fittipoldi, "Sexual Partnership in Marriage," 183.

117. Merrill, "The Kinsey Report," 328.

118. Caprio, *The Power of Sex,* 11.

119. See, for example, Stone, "The Kinsey Studies and Marriage Counseling," 165.

120. Originally introduced as a six-month feature, "Can This Marriage Be Saved?" was brought back the following year and soon became a regular monthly feature, one that can still be found in the *Journal.*

121. Popenoe, "Can This Marriage Be Saved?," 41.

122. Caprio, *The Power of Sex,* 89–90.

123. Clemenko, "Toward a Saner Sex Life," 106.

124. Mudd, with Davidson, "How Dr. Kinsey's Report on Women May Help Your Marriage," 113, emphasis in original.

125. Kinsey et al., *Sexual Behavior in the Human Female,* 13.

126. Stone, "The Kinsey Studies and Marriage Counseling," 165.

127. For example, see Adams, "Making Marriage Work: 'I Hate Being Pregnant and I Hate Sex,'" 28.

128. Talcott Parsons had commented on the importance of "adequacy" to Americans' self-image in a 1947 essay, noting that Americans tended to "be hypersensitive to any suggestion of inferiority or incapacity to achieve goals." "Patterns of Aggression in the Western World," 310.

129. Terman, "Correlates of Orgasm Adequacy in a Group of 556 Wives," 115–72.

130. Kinsey et al., *Sexual Behavior in the Human Female*, 313.

131. This viewpoint is discussed in May, *Barren in the Promised Land*, 173–78.

132. Many sexual advice authors assumed that their readers used contraceptives, such as barrier methods, to space pregnancies. Few went into any detail regarding birth control methods, with the exception of "safe days" (see, for example, the chapter "Theory of the Safe Days" in Berg and Street, *Sex*, 193–200), but passing references to contraceptive use were common. A 1943 public opinion poll found that nearly 85 percent of women surveyed believed that contraceptive information should be readily available to all married women, with 60 percent extending that freedom to unmarried women as well. See Roper, "Birth Control, the *Fortune* Survey," 247–48.

133. Gordon, *Woman's Body, Woman's Right*, 366. See also Chesler, *Woman of Valor*, especially the chapter "From Birth Control to Family Planning," 371–95.

134. Foote, "Sex as Play," 240.

135. Kinsey, Pomeroy, and Martin, *Sexual Behavior in the Human Male*, 572.

136. Bossard and Boll, *Why Marriages Go Wrong*, 195.

137. Mead, *Male and Female*, 218.

138. Ellis, "Female Sexual Response and Marital Relations," 154.

139. Robinson, *The Power of Sexual Surrender*, 188.

140. Caprio, *Marital Infidelity*, 253.

141. Berg and Street, *Sex*, 10, 209.

142. Kinsey, Pomeroy, and Martin, *Sexual Behavior in the Human Male*, 574.

143. Levy, and Munroe, "Sexual Satisfaction," 143–44.

144. Ellis, "What Is Normal Sex Behavior?," 41.

145. Ibid.

146. Ibid., 49, emphasis in original.

147. Freeman, "Sex and Emotional Health," 62.

148. Caprio, *The Power of Sex*, 173.

149. Caprio, *The Sexually Adequate Female*, 108, 140–41.

150. Marriage was, of course, no legal safeguard. The attorney Robert Veit Sherwin, a critic of U.S. sex laws, pointed out in a law guide for lay readers that

even "a husband and wife" could be "guilty of committing Sodomy when they engage in the act of Cunnilingus or Fellatio," since "regardless of statistics or of modern day opinions, all of the practices mentioned are as illegal for married people as they are for unmarried people." *Sex and the Statutory Law (in All Forty-Eight States),* 37–38.

151. Caprio, *Variations in Sexual Behavior,* 267.

152. Berg and Street, *Sex,* 159.

153. Ellis, *The American Sexual Tragedy,* 89, emphasis in original.

154. Kinsey et al., *Sexual Behavior in the Human Female,* 468.

155. Berg and Street, *Sex,* 115–16.

156. Zimmerman, *Family and Civilization,* 764.

157. Wylie, "What's Wrong with American Marriages?," 37.

158. Sorokin, *The American Sex Revolution,* 14.

159. O'Brien, *Happy Marriage,* 222.

160. Mace, "Are SEX MANUALS a Threat to Happy Marriage?," 23, capitalization in original.

161. Boudreau, "Myths That Imperil Married Love," 172–73, 175.

162. Mead, *Male and Female,* 218, 219.

163. Whitman, "America's Moral Crisis," 220.

164. Landis, "What Is 'Normal' Married Love?," 129, 131.

165. Mace, "What the Sex Manuals Don't Tell You," 59.

166. Kardiner, *Sex and Morality,* 235.

167. Johnstone, "What Those I Counsel Don't Know about Sex," 12, 14.

168. O'Brien, *Happy Marriage,* 222.

169. Whitman, "Don't Let Them Scoff at Marriage!," 58, 103.

170. The more liberal Frank Caprio also maintained that sexual pleasure within marriage was more fulfilling for its participants: "As far as sexual happiness goes," he noted, "the affair never produces the good sex adjustment that is part of a happy marriage." *The Power of Sex,* 73.

171. Coontz, *The Way We Really Are,* 36.

CHAPTER FIVE. "AN AGE OF SEXUAL AMBIGUITY"

1. Kinsey, Pomeroy, and Martin, *Sexual Behavior in the Human Male,* 650, emphasis in original.

2. Kinsey et al., *Sexual Behavior in the Human Female,* 475. Between the publication of the first and second reports, a number of authorities had proposed that lesbianism would be found to be even more widespread than male homosexuality (475, n. 19).

3. Terry, *An American Obsession.* See also Minton, *Departing from Deviance.*

4. Both fiction and nonfiction works used such tropes; see, for example, Aldrich, *We Walk Alone;* and Mercer, *They Walk in Shadow.*

5. In postwar discourse, *homosexual* sometimes referred only to men, but at other times incorporated lesbians. In this chapter my focus is on how commentators viewed homosexuals as a group, but I try to note differences in the representation of lesbians and of gay men.

6. Bergler, "The Myth of a New National Disease."

7. World War II has been widely viewed as a watershed for gay and lesbian self-awareness, visibility, and cultural identity. See, for example, D'Emilio, *Sexual Politics, Sexual Communities;* D'Emilio and Freedman, *Intimate Matters;* Meyer, *Creating G.I. Jane;* Timmons, *The Trouble with Harry Hay;* and Berube, *Coming Out under Fire.*

8. Letter from the navy surgeon general's office to the psychiatrist and military advisor Winifred Overholser, August 1942; quoted in Berube, *Coming Out under Fire,* 44.

9. Real and anticipated sexual problems predominate in many analyses of the social effects of war on the United States. For a typical sociological account, in which homosexuality is a veiled but powerful concern, see Merrill, *Social Problems on the Home Front.*

10. Mead's 1944 address at the Massachusetts Reformatory for Women, quoted in Freedman, *Maternal Justice,* 263.

11. Elkin, "The Sexual Crisis of Our Time," 11.

12. Kinsey, Pomeroy, and Martin, *Sexual Behavior in the Human Male,* 625.

13. Bergler, "The Myth of a New National Disease," 66. Although he thought Kinsey had overestimated the number of male homosexuals, Bergler believed that the second report *under*reported the extent of female homosexuality.

14. Eisenbud, "A Psychiatrist Looks at the Report," 20–27.

15. Kardiner, "The Flight from Masculinity," 18.

16. Cant, "The Malady of Sexual Inversion," 25.

17. Steiner, *Sex Behavior of the Lesbian, with Case Histories,* 12.

18. Caprio, *The Sexually Adequate Female,* 145.

19. Stearn, *The Sixth Man,* front cover.

20. Masters, *Forbidden Sexual Behavior and Morality,* 173.

21. Faderman, *Odd Girls and Twilight Lovers,* 160; Corber, *In the Name of National Security,* 9.

22. Berube, *Coming Out under Fire,* 7.

23. Chauncey, *Gay New York,* 9.

24. *One* was probably the most influential of these journals. For a discussion of the rise of the gay and lesbian press, see Streitmatter, *Unspeakable.*

25. "Donald Webster Cory" was a pseudonym for Edward Sagarin, a sociologist and member of the New York Mattachine Society who later turned against the homophile movement. I refer to him in this book by his chosen pseudonym of the time. See D'Emilio, *Sexual Politics, Sexual Communities,* 167–68; and Minton, *Departing from Deviance,* 246–52.

26. D'Emilio, *Sexual Politics, Sexual Communities,* 33.

27. Zimmerman, "A Sociologist Looks at the Report," 95.

28. Major, "New Moral Menace to Our Youth," 101. My use of the male pronoun here is deliberate: commentary on sexuality took male homosexuals as its principal subject more than it did lesbians, and most considerations of homosexuality were gendered. For more on this topic, see Adams, "Making the World Safe for the Missionary Position," 255–74; Black, "Perverting the Diagnosis," 201–16; Kennedy and Davis, *Boots of Leather, Slippers of Gold;* Meyer, *Creating G.I. Jane;* Penn, "The Meanings of Lesbianism in Postwar America," 196–224; and Terry, *An American Obsession.*

29. Viereck, "The Erotic Note in Recent American Fiction," 168.

30. Winters and Freeman, "Magazine Goldmine," 2–12.

31. Cory, *The Lesbian in America,* 21.

32. *Readers' Guide to Periodical Literature,* vol. 17 (1947–49); vol. 20 (1953–55); vol. 22 (1957–59); and vol. 23 (1959–61).

33. Faderman, *Odd Girls and Twilight Lovers,* 140, 160.

34. Franzen, *Spinsters and Lesbians,* 135.

35. Katz, "The Invention of Heterosexuality," 20.

36. Bergler, "The Myth of a New National Disease," 77, and Bergler, "Differential Diagnosis between Spurious Homosexuality and Perversion Homosexuality," 405.

37. Hadden, "Attitudes toward and Approaches to the Problem of Homosexuality," 1195. Hadden later published widely on his "cures" of homosexuals; see "Treatment of Male Homosexuals in Groups," 13–22, and "A Way Out for Homosexuals," 107–20.

38. Bayer, *Homosexuality and American Psychiatry,* 39; Committee on Cooperation with Governmental (Federal) Agencies of the Group for the Advancement of Psychiatry, *Report on Homosexuality with Particular Emphasis on This Problem in Governmental Agencies,* report no. 30 (January 1955), 2, cited in Hooker, "Adjustment of the Male Overt Homosexual," 18.

39. Berkman, "The Third Sex," 129.

40. "A Delicate Problem," 99, 101.

41. Berkman, "The Third Sex," 129.

42. On conflicts over defining homosexuality, see Terry, *An American Obsession;* Kenen, "Who Counts When You're Counting Homosexuals?"; and Carlston, "A Finer Differentiation," 177–96, 197–218.

43. George Chauncey examines this earlier understanding of male same-sex sexual activity in "Christian Brotherhood or Sexual Perversion?," 294–317.

44. Lerner, "Scandal in the State Dept: II—The Scientists Speak," 5.

45. Hadden, "Attitudes toward and Approaches to the Problem of Homosexuality," 1195.

46. Hooker, "The Adjustment of the Male Overt Homosexual," 31. See also Hooker, "Inverts Are Not a Distinct Personality Type," 20–22, and "A Preliminary Analysis of Group Behavior of Homosexuals," 217–25.

47. Greenspan and Campbell, "The Homosexual as a Personality Type," 686.

48. "What Is a Homosexual?," 44.

49. Mercer, *They Walk in Shadow,* 179.

50. Corner, "The Origin, Methods, and Findings of the Report—*Sexual Behavior in the Human Male,*" 16–17.

51. Berg and Allen, *The Problem of Homosexuality,* 55.

52. Cited in Senelick, "Private Parts in Public Places," 340.

53. Hadden, "Attitudes toward and Approaches to the Problem of Homosexuality," 1198.

54. Hooker, "The Adjustment of the Male Overt Homosexual," 20.

55. Hooker, "Male Homosexuality in the Rorschach," 52.

56. Gross, "The Troublesome Homosexual," 14.

57. Lerner, "Scandal in the State Dept.: II—The Scientists Speak," 23, emphasis in original.

58. Bergler, "Lesbianism," 328, and "Differential Diagnosis between Spurious Homosexuality and Perversion Homosexuality," 405, 408.

59. Burgess, "The Sociologic Theory of Psychosexual Behavior," 20. A theory of pseudo homosexuality is also proposed in Westwood, *Society and the Homosexual.*

60. Silver, "The Homosexual," 452.

61. Westwood, *Society and the Homosexual,* 23.

62. Mercer, *They Walk in Shadow,* 202, emphasis in original.

63. Berg and Allen, *The Problem of Homosexuality,* 141, emphases in original.

64. Collier, *The Hypocritical American,* 111–12.

65. Hohman and Schaffner, "Sex Lives of Unmarried Men," 507; Mendelsohn and Ross, "An Analysis of 133 Homosexuals Seen at a University Health Service," 246.

66. "Can Homosexuality Be Cured?," 146.

67. Bowman and Engle, "The Problem of Homosexuality," 3.

68. Berg and Allen, *The Problem of Homosexuality,* 149.

69. Sayre, *Previous Convictions,* 152.

70. Salinger, *The Catcher in the Rye,* 143. Holden later reacts with disgust to what he interprets as a pass from his former teacher Mr. Antolini, suddenly viewing the man as a "pervert" (192).

71. "These Tragic Women," 62.

72. Editor's comment in Cory, "Can Homosexuality Be Cured?," 155.

73. Glover, "The Abnormality of Prostitution," 261.

74. See D'Emilio, "The Homosexual Menace," 226–40; and Corber, *Homosexuality in Cold War America,* and *In the Name of National Security.*

75. *The Manchurian Candidate* (dir. John Frankenheimer, 1962).

76. Bieber, *Homosexuality,* 220; van den Haag, "Notes on Homosexuality and Its Cultural Setting," 291.

77. Stearn, *The Grapevine,* 4–5.

78. Kardiner, "The Flight from Masculinity," 19.

79. Thompson, "Changing Concepts of Homosexuality in Psychoanalysis," 40.

80. Jonathan Ned Katz categorizes Kinsey as one of a group of sexual liberals whose work "actually helped to secure the dominance of the heterosexual ideal" and "reaffirmed the idea of a sexuality divided between the hetero and homo." (*The Invention of Heterosexuality,* 96–97). As I argue here, its effects were far more varied.

81. See, for example, Kallman, "Comparative Twin Studies on the Genetic Aspects of Male Homosexuality," 283–98.

82. Kinsey, Pomeroy, and Martin, *Sexual Behavior in the Human Male,* 866.

83. Silver, "The Homosexual," 451, emphases in original.

84. "Lavender and Old Blues," 82.

85. Saul Bellow, quoted in Barrett, "New Innocents Abroad," 294.

86. Bergler, "The Myth of a New National Disease," 87.

87. Anomaly, *The Invert and His Social Adjustment,* 208. This volume was first published in 1928; the author, Robert Henry Thouless, a psychologist, took his pseudonym from the writings of Edward Carpenter and Havelock Ellis. The publication of a revised edition in 1948—retaining the pseudonym, but with an introduction penned by Thouless under his own name—suggests the increasing market for and interest in accounts of homosexuality.

88. Both military rules and cultural assumptions declared local—often nonwhite—women off-limits to white military personnel; see Meyer, *Creating G.I. Jane;* and Westbrook, "I Want a Girl, Just Like the Girl That Married Harry James." For a parallel analysis of World War I, see Bristow, *Making Men Moral.*

89. For a typical postwar analysis of how wartime experiences contributed to homosexuality, see Berg and Allen, *The Problem of Homosexuality,* 49.

90. Kardiner, "The Flight from Masculinity," 30.

91. Stearn, *The Sixth Man,* 113.

92. Ibid., 11.

93. Silver, "The Homosexual," 451.

94. The best-known examples of such polemics were Strecker, *Their Mothers' Sons;* and Wylie, *Generation of Vipers.*

95. Major, "New Moral Menace to Our Youth," 106–7.

96. Berkman, "The Third Sex," 132. For a similar argument linking homosexuality to hectic modern life, see Ruitenbeek, "Men Alone," 81.

97. Jim Kepner, "It Just Isn't Natural," 9. Farnham's "dead cell" argument appears in her "The Unmentionable Minority" (116).

98. For a variant of this view, see Luther Allen's argument that "homosexuality as an alternative form of love . . . is a sort of sexual and social safety valve rather than a menace." "Homosexuality, Morality, and Religion," 25.

99. There is a voluminous literature on twentieth-century theories that relate homosexuality to gender ideology. For a few examples, see Minton, *Departing from Deviance,* and Terry, *An American Obsession.*

100. Odenwald, *The Disappearing Sexes,* 4.

101. Kardiner, *Sex and Morality,* 18, 21, 32. For a similar argument, see Ruitenbeek, "Men Alone," 85.

102. Kardiner, *Sex and Morality,* 147.

103. Ibid., 33.

104. Lindner, "Homosexuality and the Contemporary Scene," 40.

105. Berube, *Coming Out under Fire,* 20.

106. Caprio, *The Sexually Adequate Female,* 146.

107. Silver, "The Homosexual," 451.

108. Elkin, "The Sexual Crisis of Our Time," 11.

109. Sapirstein, "The 'Happy' Homosexual," 552.

110. Kepner, "It Just Isn't Natural," 12.

111. Laidlaw, "A Clinical Approach to Homosexuality," 41.

112. Schlesinger, "The Crisis of American Masculinity," 64.

113. McPartland, *Sex in Our Changing World,* 269.

114. Kardiner, "The Flight From Masculinity," 37.

115. Mercer, *They Walk in Shadow,* 7.

116. Lindner, *Must You Conform?,* 75.

117. "Come Back to the Raft Ag'in, Huck Honey!," reprinted in Leslie Fiedler, *An End to Innocence,* 142–60.

118. Normal Mailer's *The White Negro,* which celebrated both homosexuality and blackness as identities that could be appropriated to free American men from conformity, offers another case in point. A number of historians have discussed the postwar contours of white fascination with African American culture, especially among teens: see Breines, *Young, White, and Miserable.*

119. Cory, "Homosexual Attitudes and Heterosexual Prejudices," 420.

120. Allen, "Homosexuality: Is It a Handicap?," 9–10. For another example of homophiles drawing on the emergent Civil Rights movement to position homosexuality as parallel to blackness; see "I Pass," 14–15.

121. Cory, "Changing Attitudes towards Homosexuals," 427–28.

122. Barrett, "New Innocents Abroad," 287.

123. Friedenberg, *The Vanishing Adolescent,* 183.

124. Gorer, *The American People,* 125–29, emphasis added.

125. Baldwin, "Preservation of Innocence," 16.

126. Mercer, *They Walk in Shadow,* 179.

127. For one example, see the letter to the editor from "Mr. E." of Rome, New York, and the accompanying comment, in *One* 4, no. 1 (January 1956): 28.

128. Menninger, *Psychiatry in a Troubled World,* 223; Westwood, *Society and the Homosexual,* 16.

129. Cant, "The Malady of Sexual Inversion," 25.

130. Walker, "The Terrible Monomania," 2–3. A similar satire, calling for the "mandatory registration of known heterosexuals," appeared earlier that year: see Lambert, "The Griffum Atrocity," 20–21.

131. Ellis, "Are Homosexuals Necessarily Neurotic?," 11. This article was reprinted verbatim in Mercer, *They Walk in Shadow,* 92–99.

132. Mercer, *They Walk in Shadow,* 498. This passage rewrites one paragraph of Ralph Major's polemic "New Moral Menace to Our Youth."

133. *The Employment of Homosexuals and Other Sex Perverts in Government,* 20.

134. Leslie, *Casebook,* 15.

135. Sapirstein, "Hindering the Search for Morality," 252–53.

136. Simpson, "Nonsense about Women," 49–56.

137. Preston, *Sex Habits of Single Women,* 8, 79.

138. Kathleen Sullivan, *Girls on Parole* (Boston: Houghton Mifflin, 1956), cited in Freedman, *Maternal Justice,* 331–32.

139. On theater, see Curtin, *"We Can Always Call Them Bulgarians";* Chauncey, *Gay New York,* 9. George Chauncey later describes this approach to material on homosexuality as "using connotative codes rather than denotative codes" (357). It is important to note that this increased awareness of homosexuality brought with it increased risks—of harassment, assault, job loss, and so on—for many suspected homosexuals.

140. Silver, "The Homosexual," 451.

141. Towne, "Homosexuality in American Culture: The New Taste in Literature," 6.

142. Advertisement for the Homosexuality in American Culture series, *American Mercury* (August 1951): 2.

143. Taubman, "Not What It Seems," 1x–2x.

144. Taubman, "Modern Primer," 1x–2x.

145. Schlesinger, *The Vital Center,* 50.

146. Stearn, *The Sixth Man,* 17.

147. Odenwald, *The Disappearing Sexes,* 149.

148. Towne, "Homosexuality in American Culture: The New Taste in Literature," 8.

149. Ibid., 3, 7.

150. Cory, *The Lesbian in America,* 116.

151. Odenwald, *The Disappearing Sexes,* 142.

152. Bergler, "Lesbianism," 328.

153. Cant, "The Malady of Sexual Inversion," 25–26.

154. McPartland, "For These Are the Bedeviled," 51, emphasis and ellipsis in original.

155. Greenspan and Campbell, "The Homosexual as a Personality Type," 686.

156. Meyer, *Creating G.I. Jane,* 163.

EPILOGUE. "ALL AMERICA IS ONE BIG ORGONE BOX"

1. Blanding, "Educators Educated," 12.

2. Jones, *Alfred C. Kinsey,* 574.

3. John D'Emilio notes in *Sexual Politics, Sexual Communities* that many leaders of the homophile groups of the 1950s, who participated in and drew on postwar work on sexual orientation, were the forefathers of gay liberation.

4. Foucault, *The History of Sexuality,* 1:36.

5. For another use of the term, see Boroff, "Sex," 96. Beth Bailey historicizes the concept in "Sexual Revolution(s)," 235–62.

6. Grunwald, "The Second Sexual Revolution," 1.

7. Fitch, *The Decline and Fall of Sex,* 95. For an earlier lament of the evil effects of too much sexual information, see Allen, "I'm Sick of Sex," 15–17.

8. May, "The New Puritanism," 162, emphasis in original.

9. Ibid., 161.

10. Kazin, "The Freudian Revolution Analyzed," 40.

11. Friedan, *The Feminine Mystique,* 261–62. Although her focus was on female heterosexuality, Friedan shared in cold war concerns about homosexuality, which she described as "spreading like a murky smog over the American scene" (274).

12. Fromm, *The Sane Society,* 178.

13. Marcuse, *Eros and Civilization,* 86.

14. Ibid., ix–x.

15. Masters and Johnson, *Human Sexual Response.*

16. Hite, *The Hite Report.*

17. Jong, "If Men Read It, Sex Will Improve," B-22.

18. On second-wave feminists' analyses of sex, see Gerhard, *Desiring Revolution.*

19. The study's history is detailed in Coughlin, "The Sex Lives of Americans," A8; Pollitt, "Subject to Debate," 484; and Elmer-Dewitt, "Now for the Truth about Sex," 63–69.

20. Laumann, Gagnon, Michael, and Michaels, *The Social Organization of Sexuality,* especially 104–5 and 133. Further references to this text are given parenthetically.

21. The highest rate of same-sex practices that the Chicago survey elicited was under 5 percent for women and 9 percent for men; other approaches (for example, asking about sex since puberty rather than over the life course, or asking face-to-face rather than soliciting written and sealed answers) garnered lower numbers of same-sex partners, approximately 4.1 percent for women and 4.9 percent for men (294–96). Laumann and his colleagues attribute this difference partly to Kinsey's lack of probability sampling and his focus on fantasy as well as practice (289).

22. H.R. 2507, Helms Amendment 1757. "N.I.H. Reauthorization Act," 102d Cong., 2d sess., 2 April 1992, p. S-4758, vote no. 65.

23. Michael, Gagnon, Laumann, and Kolata, *Sex in America,* 55.

24. Poovey, "Sex in America," 92, 105.

25. H.R. 2507, Simon Amendment 1756. "N.I.H. Reauthorization Act," 102d Cong., 2d sess., 2 April 1992, p. S-4758, vote no. 64.

26. Testimony of Robert H. Knight, director of Cultural Studies, Family Research Council, regarding HR 1271, before the Committee on Governmental Affairs of the United States Senate, November 9, 1995. Www.frc.org/frc/podium/pd95k3pa.html, accessed in February 1998.

27. Sanders and Reinisch, "Would You Say You 'Had Sex' If . . . ?," 275–77; Kolata, "Editor of A.M.A. Journal Is Dismissed over Sex Paper," A10.

28. Wilson, "An Ill-Fated Sex Survey," A10.

29. This list of the twentieth century's most influential works is archived at http://counterpunch.org/top100nf.html, accessed on 4 February 1998.

30. Michael et al., *Sex in America,* 12.

31. Www.isi.org/publications/ir/50worst.html, accessed on 2 February 1998.

32. James Jones's 1997 biography *Alfred C. Kinsey: A Public/Private Life,* which depicts Kinsey as a dedicated propagandist for sexual liberalism and homosexuality, prompted new assessments of the influence and legacy of his work. Reviews include Duberman, "Kinsey's Urethra," 40–43; Thomas Laqueur, "Sexual Behavior in the Social Scientist: Was Alfred Kinsey a Pioneer or a Pervert?," *Slate* (4 November 1997), http://slate.msn.com/?id = 3021, accessed in November 1997.

Allegations about Kinsey's use of data from adult men who had sex with children have surfaced in a series of documents by conservative authors, including Reisman and Eichel, *Kinsey, Sex, and Fraud;* and a film documentary, *The Children of Table 34,* directed by Robert H. Knight, director of cultural studies for the Family Research Council.

33. Concerned Women for America, "Press Conference Held Oct. 2, 1977." For the text of this and other critiques of Kinsey by this group, see www.cwfa .org/newsflash/news-kinsey1097.html, accessed in December 1997. For Indiana University's response to these and other allegations, see Indiana University, "Controversy over Alfred Kinsey's Research," October 1998, www.indiana.edu/ ~kinsey/controversy.html#CContents, accessed in December 1997.

34. Restoring America to Constitutional Principles, a California organization whose issues include campaigning against the Internal Revenue Service and urging supporters to purchase gold, argued in a 2001 article entitled "Alfred Kinsey and the Carnage Left Behind" that educators and scientists who back Kinsey's work are "either totally stupid or a bunch of queers and perverts on the hunt for new victims." Www.devvy.com/reisman_20001110.html, accessed on 12 January 2002.

35. Judith Reisman, "The Deadbeat Dad of the Sexual Revolution: Kinsey, Crimes and Lies," June 24, 1998, Washington, D.C.; archived at www .academia.org/conservativeuniversity/lecturehall/reisman1.htm, accessed on 15 January 2002. See also www.drjudithreisman.org, accessed on 15 January 2002.

36. Gathorne-Hardy, *Sex: The Measure of All Things*, 454; Jones, *Alfred C. Kinsey*, 772.

37. Whitehead, *The Divorce Culture;* Waite and Gallagher, *The Case for Marriage;* and Hewlett, *Creating a Life*. In an extensive literature, other books that received wide media attention include Paul, *The Starter Marriage and the Future of Matrimony;* Heatherington and Kelly, *For Better or for Worse;* and Wallerstein et al., *The Unexpected Legacy of Divorce*.

38. Goldstein, "Tying Marriage Vows to Welfare Reform," A01.

39. Buchanan, *The Death of the West*.

40. Popenoe and Elshtain, *Promises to Keep*, 248, quoted in www.family.org/ cforum/research/papers/a0002274.html, accessed on 15 January 2002. Popenoe's ideological links to his father are discussed perceptively in Kline, *Building a Better Race*, 161–63.

41. Keyes and Grant, *Our Character, Our Future;* see also Keyes's updated Website, www.issues2002.org/Archive/Our_Character_Alan_Keyes.htm, accessed on 4 January 2003.

42. According to the Sexuality Information and Education Council of the United States (SIECUS), abstinence-only curricula exploded in popularity in the 1990s, spurred by the 1996 creation of a federal program allocating $50 million per year for such programs. SIECUS, "Toward a Sexually Healthy America," 7.

43. Darroch, Landry, and Singh, "Changing Emphases in Sexuality Education in U.S. Public Secondary Schools," 204–11.

44. Gayle Rubin has argued that sexual behaviors and identities are commonly deemed acceptable or unacceptable based on their closeness to the privileged model of monogamous heterosexual marriage, in which sexual activity is partnered and conventionally "vanilla." Therefore, homosexuals are most likely to be accepted when they meet at least some of these criteria. See her "Thinking Sex," 3–44.

45. Patton, *Fatal Advice,* 7.

46. Quotations are from Pfizer's Website, www.viagra.com, accessed in March 2003. Viagra's success also underlines the resurgence of popular and scholarly belief in biological theories of sexual identity and behavior.

47. The 1990s also saw sex surveys, which had long been a tool of American social conservatives, undertaken by conservative groups for very different ends. The sociologist Paul Cameron, whose work has been repeatedly criticized by experts in the field, draws on social-scientific discourse, particularly the authority of numbers, to attack sexual behaviors he sees as dangerous and immoral. As Cameron argues on his Website, "Rather than fearing that American public officials will persecute them, gay activists have realized that the social and political climate has swung in their favor. And what better way to cement their status as an official minority than to become a government statistic!" See www.family researchinst.org/FRR_01_12.html, accessed on 3 January 2002.

SELECTED BIBLIOGRAPHY

MANUSCRIPT COLLECTIONS

Kinsey Institute for Research in Sex, Gender, and Reproduction, Indiana University, Bloomington, Indiana.

BOOKS, ARTICLES, FILMS, AND WEBSITES

Adams, Clifford. "Making Marriage Work: Are You Enhancing Your Appeal?" *Ladies' Home Journal* (January 1953): 28.

———. "Making Marriage Work: Ask Yourself: Am I a Successful Working Wife?" *Ladies' Home Journal* (January 1956): 26.

———. "Making Marriage Work: 'I Hate Being Pregnant and I Hate Sex.'" *Ladies' Home Journal* (July 1958): 28.

———. "Making Marriage Work: We Agree on Almost Everything Except Sex." *Ladies' Home Journal* (October 1958): 32.

———. "Making Marriage Work: What Factors Favor Good Sexual Adjustment and a Happy Marriage?" *Ladies' Home Journal* (July 1953): 28.

———. "Making Marriage Work: What Factors Favor Good Sexual Adjustment and a Happy Marriage?" *Ladies' Home Journal* (August 1958): 28.

Adams, Kate. "Making the World Safe for the Missionary Position: Images of the Lesbian in Post–World War II America." In *Lesbian Texts and Contexts: Radical Revisions,* ed. Joanne Glasgow and Karla Jay, 255–74. New York: New York University Press, 1990.

Adorno, T. W., et al. *The Authoritarian Personality.* New York: W. W. Norton, 1950.

Aldrich, Ann. *We Walk Alone.* New York: Fawcett, 1955.

Allen, Clifford. "The Problem of Homosexuality." *International Journal of Sexology* (1951): 31–32.

Allen, Luther. "Homosexuality: Is It a Handicap?" *Mattachine Review* (July–August 1955): 6–10.

———. "Homosexuality, Morality, and Religion." *Mattachine Review* (February 1956): 25–29.

Allen, Robert T. "I'm Sick of Sex." *Reader's Digest* (April 1950): 15–17.

Anderson, Benedict. *Imagined Communities: Reflections on the Origin and Spread of Nationalism.* New York: Verso, 1991.

Anomaly. *The Invert and His Social Adjustment.* With an introduction by R. H. Thouless. London: Balliere, Tindall, and Cox, 1948.

Appel, Kenneth E. "Problems with Which People Want Help in Sex and Marriage." In *Man and Wife: A Source Book of Family Attitudes, Sexual Behavior, and Marriage Counseling,* ed. Emily H. Mudd and Aron Krich, 3–13. New York: W. W. Norton, 1957.

Archer, Jules. "The Backwash of Dr. Kinsey: Report on Sexual Behavior of Women Is Dangerous Sex Advice." *Life Today* (December 1953–January 1954): 6–11.

———. "Keeping Up with Mrs. Jones' Sex Life." *Life Today* (August–September 1951): 33–36.

"Are Yanks Lousy Lovers?" *Reader's Digest* (December 1945): 10.

"Ask Press to Play Down Kinsey Report." *Christian Century* (7 June 1950): 693.

Astley, M. Royden. "Fidelity and Infidelity." In *Man and Wife: A Source Book on Family Attitudes, Sexual Behavior, and Marriage Counseling,* ed. Emily Mudd and Aron Krich, 80–96. New York: W. W. Norton, 1957.

Averill, Lloyd. "Sexuality in Crisis." *Christian Century* (2 October 1963): 1196–99.

Bailey, Beth. *From Front Porch to Back Seat: Courtship in Twentieth-Century America.* Baltimore: Johns Hopkins University Press, 1988.

———. "Sexual Revolution(s)." In *The Sixties: From Memory to History,* ed. David Farber, 235–62. Chapel Hill: University of North Carolina Press, 1994.

Bailey, Beth, and David Farber. *The First Strange Place: The Alchemy of Race and Sex in World War II Hawaii.* New York: Free Press, 1992.

Baldridge, Letitia. "Why I Love Italian Men." *Reader's Digest* (July 1957): 58–60.

Baldwin, James. "Preservation of Innocence." *Zone* (summer 1949): 14–22.

Banning, Margaret Culkin. "What Women Won't Tell Dr. Kinsey." *Cosmopolitan* (September 1951): 44–45, 108–10.

Barrett, William. "New Innocents Abroad." In *The Scene before You: A New Approach to American Culture,* ed. Chandler Brossard, 268–84. New York: Rinehart, 1955.

Barth, Ramona. "What's Wrong with American Men?" *Reader's Digest* (November 1949): 23–25.

Batdorff, Virginia Roller. "American Women vs. the Kinsey Report." *American Mercury* (August 1953): 121–24.

Bayer, Ronald. *Homosexuality and American Psychiatry: The Politics of Diagnosis.* Princeton, N.J.: Princeton University Press, 1987.

Bell, Daniel. *The Cultural Contradictions of Capitalism.* New York: Basic Books, 1976.

Bender, James F. "How Much Women Change—and How Little." *Reader's Digest* (July 1947): 127–28.

Benedict, Ruth. *The Chrysanthemum and the Sword: Patterns of Japanese Culture.* Boston: Houghton Mifflin, 1946.

Benjamin, Harry. "The Kinsey Report: Book Review and Roundup of Opinion." *American Journal of Psychotherapy* (July 1948): 398–416.

Berg, Charles, and Clifford Allen. *The Problem of Homosexuality.* New York: Citadel Press, 1958.

Berg, Louis, and Robert Street. *Sex: Manners and Methods.* New York: McBride Company, 1953.

Bergler, Edmund. "Differential Diagnosis between Spurious Homosexuality and Perversion Homosexuality." *Psychiatric Quarterly* (July 1947): 399–409.

———. "Lesbianism: Fact and Fiction." In *Sex, Society, and the Individual,* ed. A. P. Pillay and Albert Ellis. Bombay: *International Journal of Sexology,* 1953. First published in *International Journal of Sexology* (1947): 328–36.

———. "The Myth of a New National Disease: Homosexuality and the Kinsey Report." *Psychiatric Quarterly* (January 1948): 66–88.

Bergler, Edmund, and William Kroger. *Kinsey's Myth of Female Sexuality: The Medical Facts.* New York: International University Press, 1953.

Bergquist, Laura. "Check Your Sex Life against the New Kinsey Report." *Pageant* (October 1953): 16–25.

Berkman, Ted. "The Cult of Super-Sex." *Coronet* (June 1955): 149–53.

———. "The Third Sex: Guilt or Sickness?" *Coronet* (November 1955): 129–33.

Berlant, Lauren. *The Queen of America Goes to Washington City: Essays on Sex and Citizenship.* Raleigh, N.C.: Duke University Press, 1997.

Berube, Allan. *Coming Out under Fire: The History of Gay Men and Lesbians in WWII.* New York: Free Press, 1990.

The Best Years of Our Lives. Dir. William Wyler. Samuel Goldwyn Company, 1946.

Bettelheim, Bruno. "Growing Up Female." *Harper's* (October 1962): 120–28.

Bieber, Irving. *Homosexuality: A Psychoanalytic Study of Male Homosexuals.* New York: Basic Books, 1962.

Black, Allida. "Perverting the Diagnosis: The Lesbian and the Scientific Basis of Stigma." *Historical Reflections* (summer 1994): 201–16.

Blanding, Sarah Gibson. "Educators Educated." *Saturday Review* (31 May 1958): 12.

Block, Maxine. "What Are Women Telling Dr. Kinsey?" *Your Life* (25 July 1949): 25–30.

———. "What Women Are Telling Dr. Kinsey." *Marriage Magazine* (September 1952): 40–45.

"Bombs, H and K." *Newsweek* (31 August 1953): 57.

Boroff, David. "Sex: The Quiet Revolution: Among the Fallen Idols, Virginity, Chastity, and Repression." *Esquire* (July 1961): 96–99.

Bossard, James H. S. "Divorce: Some Selected Repercussions." In *Man and Wife: A Source Book of Family Attitudes, Sexual Behavior, and Marriage Counseling,* ed. Emily Hartshorne Mudd and Aron Krich, 97–111. New York: W. W. Norton, 1957.

Bossard, James H. S., and Eleanor Stoker Boll. *Why Marriages Go Wrong: Hazards to Marriage and How to Overcome Them.* New York: Ronald Press Company, 1958.

Boudreau, Hugo, as told to Lester David. "Myths That Imperil Married Love." *Coronet* (December 1948): 172–76.

Bourdieu, Pierre. "The Forms of Capital." In *Handbook of Theory and Research for the Sociology of Education,* ed. John Richardson, 241–58. New York: Greenwood Press, 1986.

Bowman, Claude C. "Are Husbands Slaves to Women?" *Coronet* (April 1950): 111–14.

Bowman, Henry A. *Marriage for Moderns.* New York: McGraw-Hill, 1948.

Bowman, Karl, and Bernice Engle. "The Problem of Homosexuality." *Journal of Social Hygiene* (January 1953): 2–16.

Boys' Night Out. Dir. Michael Gordon. Warner Brothers, 1962.

Brandt, Allan. *No Magic Bullet: A Social History of Venereal Disease in the United States since 1880.* New York: Oxford University Press, 1987.

Brecher, Edward, and Ruth Brecher. "The New Kinsey Report Has a Moral: We Must Face the Facts about Sex." *Redbook* (September 1953): 28–31, 78–80.

Breines, Wini. *Young, White, and Miserable: Growing Up Female in the Fifties.* Boston: Beacon, 1992.

Bremner, Robert H., and Gary W. Reichard, eds. *Reshaping America: Society and Institutions, 1945–1960.* Columbus: Ohio State University Press, 1982.

Brinkman, Paul Delbert. "Dr. Alfred C. Kinsey and the Press: A Historical Case Study of the Relationship of the Mass Media to a Pioneering Behavioral Scientist." Ph.D. diss., Indiana University, 1971.

Bristow, Nancy K. *Making Men Moral: Social Engineering during the Great War.* New York: New York University Press, 1996.

Brown, Fred. "What American Men Want to Know about Sex." *Journal of Social Psychology* (1948): 119–25.

Buchanan, Patrick. *The Death of the West: How Dying Populations and Immigrant Invasions Imperil Our Country and Civilization.* New York: St. Martin's Press, 2001.

Buhle, Mari Jo. *Feminism and Its Discontents: A Century of Struggle with Psychoanalysis.* Cambridge: Harvard University Press, 1998.

Burgess, Ernest W. "The Sociologic Theory of Psychosexual Behavior." In *Sexual Behavior in American Society: An Appraisal of the Two Kinsey Reports,* ed. Jerome Himelhoch and Sylvia Fleis Fava, 12–28. New York: W. W. Norton, 1955.

Burgess, Ernest W., and Harvey J. Locke. *The Family: From Institution to Companionship.* New York: American Book Company, 1953.

"Can Homosexuality Be Cured?" *Sexology* (October 1951): 146.

Cant, Gilbert. "The Malady of Sexual Inversion." *New Leader* (7 January 1957): 25–26.

Caprio, Frank. *Marital Infidelity.* New York: Citadel Press, 1953.

———. *The Power of Sex.* New York: Citadel Press, 1952.

———. *The Sexually Adequate Female.* New York: Citadel Press, 1953.

———. *The Sexually Adequate Male.* New York: Citadel Press, 1951.

———. *Variations in Sexual Behavior: A Psychodynamic Study of Deviations in Various Expressions of Sexual Behavior.* New York: Citadel Press, 1955.

Carlston, Erin. "'A Finer Differentiation': Female Homosexuality and the American Medical Community, 1926–1940." In *Sciences and Homosexualities,* ed. Vernon Rosario, 197–218. New York: Routledge, 1997.

Carmichael, Virginia. *Framing History: The Rosenberg Story and the Cold War.* Minneapolis: University of Minnesota Press, 1993.

Caro, Jo. "The Kinsey Interview Experience (as Seen by a Psychiatric Social Worker)." In *The Sex Life of the American Woman and the Kinsey Report,* Albert Ellis, 189–201. New York: Grunwald, 1954.

Carson, Ruth. "Afraid of Love: Fears and Inhibitions Wreck Marriages." *Collier's* (14 September 1946): 17, 95.

The Chapman Report. Dir. George Cukor. Warner Brothers, 1962.

Chapple, John. Editorial. *Ashland Press,* 16 March 1949.

Chauncey, George Jr. "Christian Brotherhood or Sexual Perversion? Homosexual Identities and the Construction of Sexual Boundaries in the World War I Era." In *Hidden from History: Reclaiming the Gay and Lesbian Past,* Martin Duberman et al., 294–317. New York: New American Library, 1989.

———. *Gay New York: Gender, Urban Culture, and the Making of the Gay Male World, 1890–1940.* New York: Basic Books, 1994.

———. "The Postwar Sex Crime Panic." In *True Stories from the American Past,* ed. William Graebner, 160–78. New York: McGraw-Hill, 1993.

Cherne, Leo M. "The Future of the Middle Class." *Atlantic Monthly* (June 1944): 75–78.

Chesler, Ellen. *Woman of Valor: Margaret Sanger and the Birth Control Movement in America.* New York: Simon and Schuster, 1992.

The Children of Table 34. Dir. Robert H. Knight. Family Research Council, 1994. Film documentary.

Christian, Frederick. "Sex Cultism in America." *Cosmopolitan* (April 1958): 66–67.

Churchill, Judith. "Your Chances of Getting Married." *Good Housekeeping* (October 1946): 38–39, 313–19.

Clark, Amory. "The American Male: His Sex Habits." *Cosmopolitan* (May 1957): 30–32.

Clemenko, Harold B. "Toward a Saner Sex Life." *Look* (9 December 1947): 106–7.

Cochran, William G., Frederick Mosteller, and John Tukey. *Statistical Problems of the Kinsey Report.* Washington, D.C.: ASA, 1954.

Cohen, Lizabeth. "From Town Center to Shopping Center: The Reconfiguration of Community Marketplaces in Postwar America." In *The Gender and Consumer Culture Reader,* ed. Jennifer Scanlon, 245–66. New York: New York University Press, 2000.

Coleman, Barbara. "Maidenform(ed): Images of American Women in the 1950s." *Genders* (1995): 3–22.

Collier, James Lincoln. *The Hypocritical American: An Essay on Sex Attitudes in America.* New York: Bobbs-Merrill, 1964.

Commager, Henry Steele. *America in Perspective: The United States through Foreign Eyes.* New York: Random House, 1947.

———. *The American Mind: An Interpretation of American Thought and Character since the 1880s.* New Haven, Conn.: Yale University Press, 1950.

———. "Portrait of the American." In *Years of the Modern: An American Appraisal,* ed. John W. Chase, 3–34. New York: Longmans, Green, 1949.

Connell, R. W. *Masculinities.* Berkeley: University of California Press, 1995.

Cooley, Donald G. "What Kinsey Is Discovering about Women." *Your Marriage* (spring 1950): 36–40.

Coontz, Stephanie. *The Way We Never Were: American Families and the Nostalgia Trap.* New York: Basic Books, 1992.

———. *The Way We Really Are: Coming to Terms with America's Changing Families.* New York: Basic Books, 1997.

Cooper, William M. "Education for Responsible Husbandhood." *Marriage and Family Living* (summer 1949): 96–97, 104.

Corber, Robert. *Homosexuality in Cold War America: Resistance and the Crisis of Masculinity.* Durham, N.C.: Duke University Press, 1997.

———. *In the Name of National Security: Hitchcock, Homophobia, and the Political Construction of Gender in Postwar America.* Durham, N.C.: Duke University Press, 1993.

Corner, George. "The Origin, Methods, and Findings of the Report—*Sexual Behavior in the Human Male.*" In *Problems of Sexual Behavior,* ed. American Social Hygiene Association, 1–19. New York: ASHA, 1948.

Cort, David. "Sex Scares the Professor." *The Nation* (23 March 1957): 255–56.

Cory, Donald Webster. "Can Homosexuality Be Cured?" *Sexology* 18 (October 1951): 146–56.

———. "Changing Attitudes toward Homosexuals." Address delivered to the International Committee for Sex Equality at the University of Frankfort, September 1952. Reprinted in *One* (February 1953): 2–11; and in *Homosexuality: A Cross-Cultural Approach,* ed. Donald Webster Cory, 427–40. New York: Julian Press, 1956.

———. "Homosexual Attitudes and Heterosexual Prejudices." *International Journal of Sexology* (February 1952); reprinted in Donald Webster Cory, ed., *Homosexuality: A Cross-Cultural Approach,* 420–26. New York: Julian Press, 1956.

———. *The Homosexual in America: A Subjective Approach.* New York: Greenberg, 1951.

———. *The Lesbian in America.* New York: Citadel Press, 1964.

Costello, John. *Virtue under Fire: How World War II Changed Our Social and Sexual Attitudes.* Boston: Little, Brown, 1985.

Costigliola, Frank. "The Nuclear Family: Tropes of Gender and Pathology in the Western Alliance." *Diplomatic History* (spring 1997): 163–83.

———. "'Unceasing Pressure for Penetration': Gender, Pathology, and Emotion in George Kennan's Formation of the Cold War." *Journal of American History* (March 1997): 1309–39.

Cott, Nancy. "Giving Character to Our Whole Civil Polity: Marriage and the Public Order in the Late Nineteenth Century." In *U.S. History as Women's History: New Feminist Essays,* ed. Linda Kerber et al., 107–21. Chapel Hill: University of North Carolina Press, 1995.

———. "Passionlessness: An Interpretation of Victorian Sexual Ideology, 1790–1850." In *A Heritage of Her Own,* ed. Cott and Elizabeth Pleck, 162–88. New York: Simon and Schuster, 1979.

Coughlin, Ellen. "The Sex Lives of Americans." *Chronicle of Higher Education* (12 October 1994): A8.

Crosby, John. "Movies Are Too Dirty." *Saturday Evening Post* (10 November 1962): 8, 11.

Cuber, John, and Robert Harper. *Problems of American Society: Values in Conflict.* 2d rev. ed. New York: Henry Holt, 1951.

Culman, Irene Stokes. "You Married Him, Now Stick with Him." *Good Housekeeping* (May 1945): 17.

Cuordileone, K. A. "'Politics in an Age of Anxiety': Cold War Political Culture and the Crisis in American Masculinity, 1949–1960." *Journal of American History* (September 2000): 515–45.

Curtin, Kaier. *"We Can Always Call Them Bulgarians": The Emergence of Lesbians and Gay Men on the American Stage.* Boston: Alyson Publications, 1987.

Daniels, E. J. *I Accuse Kinsey!* Orlando: Christ for the World, 1954.

Darroch, Jacqueline E., David J. Landry, and Susheela Singh. "Changing Emphases in Sexuality Education in U.S. Public Secondary Schools, 1988–1999." *Family Planning Perspectives* (September–October 2000): 204–11.

Davis, Katherine Bement. *Factors in the Sex Life of 2,200 Women.* New York: Harper, 1929.

Davis, Kenneth C. *Two-Bit Culture: The Paperbacking of America.* Boston: Houghton Mifflin, 1984.

Davis, Maxine. *The Sexual Responsibility of Women.* New York: Permabooks, 1957.

Degler, Carl. "What Ought to Be and What Was: Women's Sexuality in the Nineteenth Century." *American Historical Review* (1974): 1469–77.

deGrazia, Edward. *Girls Lean Back Everywhere: The Law of Obscenity and the Assault on Genius.* New York: Vintage Books, 1992.

"A Delicate Problem." *Newsweek* (14 June 1954): 99–101.

DeMenasce, Jean C. "Sexual Morals and Sexualized Morality." *Commonweal* (24 November 1950): 167–69.

D'Emilio, John. "The Homosexual Menace: The Politics of Sexuality in Cold War America." In *Passion and Power: Sexuality in History,* ed. Kathy Peiss and Christina Simmons, 226–40. Philadelphia: Temple University Press, 1989.

————. *Sexual Politics, Sexual Communities: The Making of a Homosexual Minority, 1940–70.* Chicago: University of Chicago Press, 1983.

D'Emilio, John, and Estelle Freedman. *Intimate Matters: A History of Sexuality in America.* New York: Harper and Row, 1988.

Desmond, Thomas C. "The Plight of the Unmarried." *American Mercury* (May 1948): 527–34.

Deutsch, Albert. "Have Women Talked Frankly to Dr. Kinsey?" *Redbook* (July 1952): 24–25, 58–59.

————. "The Kinsey Report and Popular Culture." In *Sexual Behavior in American Society: An Appraisal of the Two Kinsey Reports,* ed. Jerome Himelhoch and Sylvia Fleis Fava, 383–85. New York: W. W. Norton, 1955.

———. "Kinsey, the Man and His Project." *Sex Habits of American Men: A Symposium on the Kinsey Report,* ed. Albert Deutsch. New York: Prentice-Hall, 1948.

———. "What Dr. Kinsey Is Up to Now, Part I." *Look* (8 May 1951): 81–82, 84–86.

———. "What Dr. Kinsey Is Up to Now, Part II." *Look* (22 May 1951): 85–86, 88, 90.

Ditzion, Sidney. *Marriage, Morals, and Sex in America: A History of Ideas.* New York: W. W. Norton, 1953.

"Do Americans Commercialize Sex? A Symposium." *Ladies' Home Journal* (October 1956): 68–69.

Donald, James. "How English Is It? Popular Literature and National Culture." *New Formations* (winter 1988): 31–48.

Drake, St. Clair. "Why Men Leave Home." *Negro Digest* (April 1950): 24–26.

"Dr. Kinsey's Sex Study of Women." *Your Life* (September 1953): 1–4.

Drury, Michael. "Are You Mature?" *Reader's Digest* (April 1958): 3840.

Duberman, Martin. "Kinsey's Urethra." *The Nation* (3 November 1997): 40–43.

Dubinsky, Karen. *Improper Advances: Rape and Heterosexual Conflict in Ontario, 1880–1929.* Chicago: University of Chicago Press, 1993.

Dudziak, Mary L. *Cold War Civil Rights: Race and the Image of American Democracy.* Princeton, N.J.: Princeton University Press, 2000.

———. "Josephine Baker, Racial Protest, and the Cold War." *Journal of American History* (September 1994): 543–70.

Duggan, Lisa. *Sapphic Slashers: Sex, Violence, and American Modernity.* Chapel Hill, N.C.: Duke University Press, 2001.

Duvall, Sylvanus. *Before You Marry.* New York: Association Press, 1959.

———. "Christ, Kinsey, and Mickey Spillane." *Pastoral Psychology* (October 1956): 22–25.

———. "Sex Fictions and Facts." *Look* (12 April 1960): 47–52.

Ehrenreich, Barbara. *The Hearts of Men: American Dreams and the Flight from Commitment.* New York: Anchor Books, 1983.

Eimerl, Sarel. "Why Bachelors Stay Single." *Esquire* (1958): 81–82.

Eisenbud, Jule. "A Psychiatrist Looks at the Report." In *Problems of Sexual Behavior,* ed. American Social Hygiene Association, 20–27. New York: ASHA, 1948.

Eley, Geoff, and Ronald Grigor Suny, eds. *Becoming National: A Reader.* New York: Oxford University Press, 1996.

Elkin, Henry. "Aggressive and Erotic Tendencies in Army Life." *American Journal of Sociology* (March 1956): 408–13.

———. "The Sexual Crisis of Our Time." *Christianity and Society* (autumn 1948): 8–13.

Elliott, George P. *Parktilden Village.* Boston: Beacon Press, 1958.

Ellis, Albert. *The American Sexual Tragedy.* Boston: Twayne, 1954.

———. "Are Homosexuals Necessarily Neurotic?" *One* (April 1955): 8–12.

———. "Female Sexual Response and Marital Relations." *Social Problems* (April 1954): 152–55.

———. "Ten Indiscreet Proposals." *Pageant* (November 1958): 6–15.

———. "What Is Normal Sex Behavior?" *Complex* (1954): 41–51.

Elmer-Dewitt, Philip. "Now for the Truth about Sex." *Time* (17 October 1994): 63–69.

The Employment of Homosexuals and Other Sex Perverts in Government. Washington: Government Printing Office, 1950.

Ernst, Morris. "The Kinsey Report and Its Contributions to Related Fields: The Kinsey Report and the Law." *Scientific Monthly* (May 1950): 279–94; reprinted in *Sexual Behavior in American Society: An Appraisal of the Two Kinsey Reports,* ed. Jerome Himelhoch and Sylvia Fleis Fava, 244–50. New York: W. W. Norton, 1955.

———. "What Kinsey Will Tell." *Redbook* (May 1950): 36–37, 86–90.

Faderman, Lillian. *Odd Girls and Twilight Lovers: Lesbianism in Twentieth-Century America.* New York: Columbia University Press, 1991.

"The Family." *Life* (24 March 1947): 36.

Farnham, Marynia. "The Unmentionable Minority." *Cosmopolitan* (May 1949): 116–18.

Farnham, Marynia, and Ferdinand Lundberg. *Modern Woman: The Lost Sex.* New York: Harper, 1947.

Feldstein, Ruth. "'I Wanted the Whole World to See': Race, Gender, and Constructions of Motherhood in the Death of Emmett Till." In *Not June Cleaver: Women and Gender in Postwar America, 1945–1960* ed. Joanne Meyerowitz, 263–303. Philadelphia: Temple University Press, 1994.

———. *Motherhood in Black and White: Race and Sex in American Liberalism, 1930–1965.* Ithaca: Cornell University Press, 2000.

Fiedler, Leslie. *An End to Innocence: Essays on Culture and Politics.* Boston: Beacon Press, 1955.

Fitch, Robert Elliot. *The Decline and Fall of Sex; with Some Curious Digressions on the Subject of True Love.* New York: Harcourt, Brace, 1957.

Fittipoldi, William. "Sexual Partnership in Marriage." In *Man and Wife: A Source Book of Family Attitudes, Sexual Behavior, and Marriage Counseling,* ed. Emily Mudd and Aron Krich, 180–93. New York: W. W. Norton, 1957.

Folsom, Joseph K. "Sociological Implications of the Report." In *Sex Habits of American Men,* ed. Albert Deutsch, 74–87. New York: Prentice-Hall, 1948.

Fontaine, Andre. "Are We Staking Our Future on a Crop of Sissies?" *Better Homes and Gardens* (December 1950): 154–56.

Foote, Nelson. "Sex as Play." In *Sexual Behavior in American Society: An Appraisal of the Two Kinsey Reports,* ed. Jerome Himelhoch and Sylvia Fleis Fava, 237–43. New York: W. W. Norton, 1955.

Fortuna, Gene. "The Magnificent American Male." *Esquire* (July 1945): 54, 147–49.

"For Women Only . . . What Every Woman Should Know about Kinsey." *Look* (8 September 1953): 78.

Foucault, Michel. *The History of Sexuality.* Vol. 1: *An Introduction.* Trans. Robert Hurley. New York: Vintage Books, 1980.

———. *The History of Sexuality.* Vol. 2: *The Use of Pleasure.* Trans. Robert Hurley. New York: Vintage Books, 1982.

Frank, Lawrence K. *The Conduct of Sex: Biology and Ethics of Sex and Parenthood in Modern Life.* New York: Black Cat Books, 1961.

———. "How Much Do We Know about Men?" *Look* (17 May 1955): 52–57.

Franzblau, Abraham. *The Road to Sexual Maturity.* New York: Simon and Schuster, 1954.

Franzen, Trisha. *Spinsters and Lesbians: Independent Womanhood in the United States.* New York: New York University Press, 1996.

Frazier, George. "The Entrenchment of the American Witch." *Esquire* (February 1962): 100–103, 138.

Freedman, Estelle. *Maternal Justice: Miriam Van Waters and the Female Reform Tradition.* Chicago: University of Chicago Press, 1996.

———. "Uncontrolled Desires: The Response to the Sexual Psychopath, 1920–60." *Journal of American History* (1987): 83–106.

Freeman, Lucy. "Sex and Emotional Health." In *The Sex Life of the American Woman and the Kinsey Report,* ed. Albert Ellis, 58–72. New York: Greenwood, 1954.

Friedan, Betty. *The Feminine Mystique.* New York: W. W. Norton, 1963.

Friedenberg, Edgar Z. *The Vanishing Adolescent.* New York: Dell, 1959.

Fromm, Erich. *The Sane Society.* Greenwich, Conn.: Fawcett Books, 1955.

"From the Editors." *Life Today* (December 1953–January 1954): 11.

Fry, Clements C. "A Report on Sex Life." *Yale Review* (spring 1948): 547–49.

Futterman, Captain Samuel. "Changing Sex Patterns and the War." *Marriage and Family Living* (May 1946): 29–30.

Gathorne-Hardy, Jonathan. *Sex: The Measure of All Things: A Life of Alfred C. Kinsey.* Bloomington: Indiana University Press, 2000.

Geddes, Donald Porter, ed. *An Analysis of the Kinsey Reports on Sexual Behavior in the Human Male and Female.* New York: New American Library, 1954.

Gerber, David. "Heroes and Misfits: The Troubled Social Reintegration of Disabled Veterans in *The Best Years of Our Lives.*" *American Quarterly* (December 1994): 545–74.

Gerhard, Jane. *Desiring Revolution: Second-Wave Feminism and the Rewriting of American Sexual Thought, 1920 to 1982.* New York: Columbia University Press, 2001.

"German Girls." *Life* (23 July 1945): 38.

Gerould, Christopher. *Sexual Practices of American Women: A Report on Female Behavior.* New York: Lion Books, 1953.

Gibson, John. "How Neurotic Are You?" *Ladies' Home Journal* (March 1958): 64.

Gilfoyle, Timothy J. *City of Eros: New York City, Prostitution, and the Commercialization of Sex, 1790–1920.* New York: W.W. Norton, 1994.

Glover, Edward. "The Abnormality of Prostitution." In *Women: The Variety and Meaning of Their Sexual Experience* ed. A.M. Krich, 247–73. New York: Dell, 1953.

Goldstein, Amy. "Tying Marriage Vows to Welfare Reform: White House Push for State Strategies to Promote Family Ignites Dispute." *Washington Post,* 1 April 2002, A01.

Goodwin, Doris Kearns. *Lyndon Johnson and the American Dream.* New York: St. Martin's Press, 1991.

Gordon, Linda. *Woman's Body, Woman's Right: Birth Control in America.* New York: Penguin, 1977.

Gordon, Richard, Katherine Gordon, and Max Gumpert. *The Split-Level Trap.* New York: Random House, 1960.

Gorer, Geoffrey. *The American People: A Study in National Character.* New York: W.W. Norton, 1947.

———. "The Erotic Myth of America." *Partisan Review* (July–August 1950): 590–94.

———. "Justification by Numbers: A Commentary on the Kinsey Report." *American Scholar* (summer 1948): 280–86.

Gould, Stephen Jay. *The Flamingo's Smile: Reflections in Natural History.* New York: W.W. Norton, 1985.

Grant, Edward G. "The Kinsey Report on Women." *Magazine Digest* (January 1951): 17–19.

Greenspan, Herbert, and John Campbell. "The Homosexual as a Personality Type." *American Journal of Psychiatry* (March 1945): 682–89.

Gross, Albert. "The Troublesome Homosexual." *Focus* (January 1953): 13–16.

Groves, Ernest. Foreword to *Sex Problems of the Returned Veteran,* by Howard Kitching. New York: Emerson Books, 1946.

Grunwald, Henry Anatole. "The Second Sexual Revolution." *Time* (24 January 1964): 54–59.

Hacker, Helen Mayer. "The New Burdens of Masculinity." *Marriage and Family Living* (August 1957): 227–33.

———. "Women as a Minority Group." *Social Forces* (1951): 60–69.

Hadden, Samuel B. "Attitudes toward and Approaches to the Problem of Homosexuality." *Pennsylvania Medical Journal* (1957): 1195–98.

———. "Treatment of Male Homosexuals in Groups." *International Journal of Group Psychotherapy* (January 1966): 13–22.

———. "A Way Out for Homosexuals." *Harper's* (March 1967): 107–20.

Hale, Nathan G. *The Rise and Crisis of Psychoanalysis in the United States: Freud and the Americans, 1917–1985.* New York: Oxford University Press, 1995.

Harper, Fowler V. "Legal Considerations in Relation to the Report." In the *Problems of Sexual Behavior, ed.* American Social Hygiene Association, 47–57. New York: ASHA, 1948.

Hart, James D., ed. *The Oxford Companion to American Literature.* 5th ed. New York: Oxford University Press, 1983.

Hartmann, Susan M. *The Home Front and Beyond: American Women in the 1940s.* Boston: Twayne, 1982.

———. "Prescriptions for Penelope: Literature on Women's Obligations to Returning World War II Veterans." *Women's Studies* (1978): 223–39.

Hartog, Hendrik. *Man and Wife in America: A History.* Cambridge: Harvard University Press, 2000.

Harvey, Brett. *The Fifties: A Women's Oral History.* New York: HarperCollins, 1993.

Havemann, Ernest. "The Kinsey Report on Women: Long-Awaited Study Shows They Are Not Very Interested In Sex." *Life* (24 August 1953): 41–44, 48, 53–56.

Heatherington, E. Mavis, and John Kelly. *For Better or for Worse: Divorce Reconsidered.* New York: W.W. Norton, 2002.

Heggie, Barbara. "Runaway Husbands." *Good Housekeeping* (October 1950): 58, 146–50.

Heineman, Elizabeth. "The Hour of the Woman: Memories of Germany's 'Crisis Years' and West German National Identity." *American Historical Review* (April 1996): 354–95.

Henriksen, Margot. *Dr. Strangelove's America: Society and Culture in the Atomic Age.* Berkeley: University of California Press, 1997.

Henry, George. *All the Sexes: A Study of Masculinity and Femininity.* New York: Rinehart, 1955.

Herberg, Will. *Protestant-Catholic-Jew: An Essay in American Religious Sociology.* Chicago: University of Chicago Press, 1955.

Herman, Ellen. *The Romance of American Psychology: Political Culture in the Age of Experts.* Berkeley: University of California Press, 1996.

Herschberger, Ruth. *Adam's Rib.* 1948; reprint, New York: Harper and Row, 1970.

Hewlett, Sylvia Ann. *Creating a Life: Professional Women and the Quest for Children.* New York: Talk Miramax Books, 2002.

Hilliard, Marion. "The Act of Love: Woman's Greatest Challenge." *Reader's Digest* (June 1957): 43–46.

———. "Too Tired to Love?" *Reader's Digest* (April 1960): 69–72.

Himelhoch, Jerome, and Sylvia Fleis Fava, eds. *Sexual Behavior in American Society: An Appraisal of the First Two Kinsey Reports.* New York: W. W. Norton, 1955.

Hinkle, Beatrice. "Spinsters and Bachelors." In *Why Are You Single?*, ed. Hilda Holland. 159–72. New York: Farrar, Straus, 1949.

Hirsch, Arthur Henry. *Sexual Misbehavior of the Upper-Cultured: A Mid-Century Statistical Analysis of Behavior Outside Marriage in the United States since 1930 (Limited to White Persons).* New York: Vantage Press, 1955.

Hite, Shere. *The Hite Report: A Nationwide Study on Female Sexuality.* New York: Macmillan, 1976.

Hixson, Walter L. *Parting the Curtain: Propaganda, Culture, and the Cold War, 1945–61.* New York: Macmillan, 1997.

Hobbs, A. H., and W. M. Kephart. "Professor Kinsey: His Facts and His Fantasy." *American Journal of Psychiatry* (February 1954): 614–20.

Hobson, Barbara Meil. *Uneasy Virtue: The Politics of Prostitution and the American Reform Tradition.* Chicago: University of Chicago Press, 1987.

Hohman, Leslie B., and Bertram Schaffner. "Sex Lives of Unmarried Men." *American Journal of Sociology* (May 1947): 501–7.

Holland, Hilda, ed. *Why Are You Still Single?* New York: Farrar, Straus, 1949.

Honigmann, John J. "An Anthropological Approach to Sex." *Social Problems* (July 1954): 7–16.

Hooker, Evelyn. "The Adjustment of the Male Overt Homosexual." *Journal of Projective Techniques* (March 1957): 18–31.

———. "Inverts Are Not a Distinct Personality Type." *Mattachine Review* (January–February 1955): 20–22.

———. "Male Homosexuality in the Rorschach." *Journal of Projective Techniques* (1958): 33–54.

———. "A Preliminary Analysis of Group Behavior of Homosexuals." *Journal of Psychology* (August 1956): 217–25.

Hoover, J. Edgar. "Mankind at Its Worst." *Esquire* (April 1951): 55, 145–47.

Howe, Reuel. "Sex and Religion: The Pastor Speaks of Sex and Love." *Ladies' Home Journal* (July 1958): 52, 82–83.

Hunt, Morton. "The Decline and Fall of the American Father." *Cosmopolitan* (April 1955): 20–25.

———. *Her Infinite Variety: The American Woman as Lover, Mate, and Rival.* New York: Harper and Row, 1962.

———. "What Keeps a Husband Faithful?" *Reader's Digest* (June 1958): 39–41.

Hurst, Fannie. "Nourishing." *Life* (24 August 1953): 59, 62, 65.

Huyssen, Andreas. "Mass Culture as Woman: Modernism's Other." In *Studies in Entertainment: Critical Approaches to Mass Culture,* ed. Tania Modleski, 188–208. Bloomington: Indiana University Press, 1986.

"The Impotent Male." *Newsweek* (10 April 1950): 48.

Institute for Sex Research. *Pregnancy, Birth, and Abortion.* New York: Harper, 1958.

"I Pass." *One* (1956): 14–15.

Irvine, Janice. *Disorders of Desire: Sex and Gender in Modern American Sexology,* Philadelphia: Temple University Press, 1990.

———. "Reinventing Perversion: Sex Addiction and Cultural Anxieties." *Journal of the History of Sexuality* (April 1995): 429–50.

Jacobs, Norman, ed. *Culture for the Millions: Mass Media In Modern Society.* Boston: Beacon Press, 1959.

Jacobson, Paul H. *American Marriage and Divorce.* New York: Rinehart, 1959.

James, T. F. "The American Wife: A Symposium." *Cosmopolitan* (January 1958): 20–37.

Jarrell, Randall. "A Sad Heart at the Supermarket." In *Culture for the Millions? Mass Media in Modern Society,* ed. Norman Jacobs, 97–111. Boston: Beacon Press, 1959.

Jeansonne, Glen. *Women of the Far Right: The Mothers' Movement and World War II.* Chicago: University of Chicago Press, 1996.

Jeffords, Susan. *The Re-Masculinization of America: Gender and the Vietnam War.* Indiana University Press, 1989.

Johnstone, Margaret Blair. "Check Your Sex I.Q." *Collier's* (14 March 1953): 15–17.

———. "What Those I Counsel Don't Know about Sex." *Reader's Digest* (January 1953): 12–14.

Jones, James H. *Alfred C. Kinsey: A Public/Private Life.* New York: W. W. Norton, 1997.

Jong, Erica. "If Men Read It, Sex Will Improve." *New York Times,* 3 October 1976, B-22.

Jurca, Catherine. *White Diaspora: The Suburb and the Twentieth-Century American Novel.* Princeton, N.J.: Princeton University Press, 2001.

Kallman, F. J. "Comparative Twin Studies on the Genetic Aspects of Male Homosexuality." *Journal of Nervous and Mental Diseases* (1952): 283–98.

Kardiner, Abram. "The Flight from Masculinity." In *The Problem of Homosexuality in Modern Society,* ed. Hendrik M. Ruitenbeek, 17–39. New York: Dutton, 1963.

———. *Sex and Morality.* New York: Bobbs-Merrill, 1958.

Katz, Donald. *Home Fires: An Intimate Portrait of One Middle-Class Family in Postwar America.* New York: HarperCollins Publishers, 1992.

Katz, Jonathan Ned. "The Invention of Heterosexuality." *Socialist Review* (1990): 7–33.

————. *The Invention of Heterosexuality.* New York: Dutton, 1995.

Kazin, Alfred. "The Freudian Revolution Analyzed." *New York Times Magazine* (6 May 1956): 22.

Keats, John. *The Crack in the Picture Window.* Boston: Houghton Mifflin, 1956.

Kelly, G. Lombard. *Sex Manual.* Augusta, Ga.: Southern Medical Supply Company, 1953.

Kenen, Stephanie. "Who Counts When You're Counting Homosexuals? Hormones and Homosexuality in Mid-Twentieth-Century America." In *Sciences and Homosexualities,* ed. Vernon Rosario, 177–96. New York: Routledge, 1997.

Kennedy, Elizabeth, and Madeline Davis. *Boots of Leather, Slippers of Gold: The History of a Lesbian Community.* New York: Routledge, 1992.

Kephart, William. Review of *Women in the Modern World,* by Mirra Komarovsky. *Journal of Marriage and Family Living* (February 1955): 75–76.

Kepner, Jim. "It Just Isn't Natural." *One* (October–November 1957): 8–11.

Keyes, Alan, with George Grant. *Our Character, Our Future.* New York: Zondervan, 1996.

Kidd, Elizabeth J. "Sexual Behavior in the American Advertiser: Why the New Kinsey Study Is Significant." *Printers' Ink* (11 September 1953): 41–43.

"Kinsey, Again." *Catholic Mind* (September 1949): 560–62.

Kinsey, Alfred C., Wardell Pomeroy, and Clyde Martin. *Sexual Behavior in the Human Male.* Philadelphia: W. B. Saunders, 1948.

Kinsey, Alfred C., Wardell Pomeroy, Clyde Martin, and Paul Gebhard. *Sexual Behavior in the Human Female.* Philadelphia: W. B. Saunders, 1953.

Kinsie, Paul M. "Prostitution—Then and Now." *Journal of Social Hygiene* (June 1953): 241–48.

Kirkendall, Lester A. "Toward a Clarification of the Concept of Male Sex Drive." *Marriage and Family Living* (November 1958): 367–72.

Kitching, Howard. *Sex Problems of the Returned Veteran.* New York: Emerson Books, 1946.

Kline, Wendy. *Building a Better Race: Gender, Sexuality, and Eugenics from the Turn of the Century to the Baby Boom.* Berkeley: University of California Press, 2001.

Kluckhohn, Florence. "American Women and American Values." In *Facing the Future's Risks,* ed. L. Bryson, 179–99. New York: Harper, 1953.

Kolata, Gina. "Editor of A.M.A. Journal Is Dismissed over Sex Paper." *New York Times,* 16 January 1999, A10.

Koller, Marvin. "Some Changes in Courtship Behavior in Three Generations of Ohio Women." *American Sociological Review* (1951): 366–70.

Komarovsky, Mirra. *Blue-Collar Marriage.* New York: Vintage Books, 1962.

Kozol, Wendy. Life's *America: Family and Nation in Postwar Photo-Journalism.* Philadelphia: Temple University Press, 1994.

Kunzel, Regina. "White Neurosis, Black Pathology: Constructing Out-of-Wedlock Pregnancy in the Wartime and Postwar United States." In *Not June Cleaver: Women and Gender in Postwar America, 1945–1960,* ed. Joanne Meyerowitz, 304–34. Philadelphia: Temple University Press, 1994.

Kutner, Nanette. "Yes, There Is a Mrs. Kinsey." *McCall's* (July 1948): 17, 92–94.

Ladd-Taylor, Molly. "Eugenics, Sterilization, and Modern Marriage in the USA: The Strange Career of Paul Popenoe." *Gender and History* (August 2001): 298–327.

Laidlaw, Robert W. "A Clinical Approach to Homosexuality." *Marriage and Family Living* (February 1952): 39–46.

Lal, Gobind Behari. "Science and Sex Conversion." *American Mercury* (February 1953): 39–44.

Lambert, William. "The Griffum Atrocity." *One* (February 1953): 20–21.

Landis, Judson T. "The Women Kinsey Studied." In *Sexual Behavior in American Society: An Appraisal of the First Two Kinsey Reports,* ed. Jerome Himelhoch and Sylvia Fleis Fava, 108–12. New York: W. W. Norton, 1955.

Landis, Judson T., and Mary G. Landis. *Personal Adjustment, Marriage, and Family Living.* New York: Prentice-Hall, 1955.

———. "The U.S. Male: Is He First-Class?" *Collier's* (19 July 1952): 22–23, 48.

Landis, Paul. "The Changing Family." *In Readings in Marriage and the Family,* ed. Judson T. Landis and Mary G. Landis, 28–41. New York: Prentice-Hall, 1952.

———. "Don't Expect Too Much of Sex in Marriage." *Reader's Digest* (December 1954): 25–27.

———. "Marriage Has Improved." *Reader's Digest* (June 1953): 13–15.

———. "What Is 'Normal' Married Love?" *Coronet* (October 1957): 126–30.

Langum, David. *Crossing over the Line: Legislating Morality and the Mann Act.* Chicago: University of Chicago Press, 1994.

Lasch, Christopher. *Culture of Narcissism: American Life in an Age of Diminishing Expectations.* New York: W. W. Norton, 1991.

Laumann, Edward O., John H. Gagnon, Robert T. Michael, and Stuart Michaels. *The Social Organization of Sexuality: Sexual Practices in the United States.* Chicago: University of Chicago Press, 1994.

"Lavender and Old Blues." *Newsweek* (20 July 1959): 82.

Lawrenson, Helen. "New York: Crack-Up City." *Esquire* (July 1953): 35, 112–13.

———. "What Has Become of the Old-Fashioned Man?" *Esquire* (February 1951): 42–43, 114–15.

Lee, Robert D. Introduction to *I Accuse Kinsey!*, ed. E. J. Daniels. Orlando, Fla.: Christ for the World, 1954.

Leff, Leonard, and Jerold Simmons. *The Dame in the Kimono: Hollywood, Censorship, and the Production Code from the 1920s to the 1960s.* New York: Grove Weidenfeld, 1990.

Leonard, George B. "The American Male: Why Is He Afraid to be Different?" *Look* (18 February 1958): 95–102.

Lerner, Max. "THE WASHINGTON SEX STORY: No. I—Panic on the Potomac." *New York Post,* 10 July 1950: 4, 24.

———. "Scandal in the State Dept.: II—The Scientists Speak." *New York Post,* 11 July 1950: 5, 23.

———. "Scandal in the State Dept.: III—How Many Homosexuals?" *New York Post,* 12 July 1950: 5, 34.

———. "Scandal in the State Dept.: VII—Sen. Wherry's Crusade." *New York Post,* 17 July 1950: 2, 20.

———. "Scandal in the State Dept.: VIII—Blick of the Vice Squad." *New York Post,* 18 July 1950: 2, 26.

———. "Scandal in the State Dept.: XII—What Can We Do about It?" *New York Post,* 22 July 1950: 2, 64.

Leslie, Robert. *Casebook: Homophile.* New York: Dalhousie Press, 1966.

Levey, Jane. "Imagining the Family in Postwar Popular Culture: The Case of *The Egg and I* and *Cheaper by the Dozen.*" *Journal of Women's History* (autumn 2001): 125–50.

Levine, Lena, and David Loth. *The Emotional Sex: Why Women Are the Way They Are Today.* New York: William Morrow, 1964.

Levy, John., M. D., and Ruth Munroe, Ph.D. "Sexual Satisfaction." In *Why You Do What You Do,* ed. Robert N. Linscott and Jess Stein, 139–48. New York: Random House, 1956.

Lindner, Robert. "Homosexuality and the Contemporary Scene." In *The Problem of Homosexuality in Modern Society,* ed. Hendrik M. Ruitenbeek, 52–79. New York: Dutton, 1963.

———. *Must You Conform?* New York: Rinehart, 1956.

Loth, David. *The Erotic In Literature.* New York: MacFadden-Bartell, 1961.

Lowe, Donald M. *The Body in Late Capitalist USA.* Durham, N.C.: Duke University Press, 1995.

Luce, Henry R. *The American Century.* New York: Furman and Rinehart, 1941.

Lunbeck, Elizabeth. *The Psychiatric Persuasion: Knowledge, Gender, and Power in Modern America.* Princeton, N.J.: Princeton University Press, 1994.

Lyndon, Louis. "Uncertain Hero: The Paradox of the American Male." *Woman's Home Companion* (November 1956): 41–43, 76.

Lynes, Russell. "Husbands: The New Servant Class." *Reader's Digest* (March 1955): 85–87.

Mace, David R. "Are SEX MANUALS a Threat to a Happy Marriage?" *McCall's* (January 1958): 23, 53.

——. "What the Sex Manuals Don't Tell You." *Reader's Digest* (January 1958): 59–61.

Mailer, Norman. *The White Negro.* San Francisco: City Light Books, 1957.

Major, Ralph H. "New Moral Menace to Our Youth." *Coronet* (September 1950): 101–8.

Malcolm, Donald. "A Comedy of Eros." *New Republic* (18 March 1957): 19.

The Manchurian Candidate. Dir. John Frankenheimer. United Artists, 1962.

Marcuse, Herbert. *Eros and Civilization: A Philosophical Inquiry into Freud.* New York: Vintage, 1955.

Marmor, Judd. "Psychological Trends in American Family Relationships." *Marriage and Family Living* (fall 1951): 145–47.

Marsh, Margaret. *Suburban Lives.* New Brunswick, N.J.: Rutgers University Press, 1990.

Marsh, Margaret, and Wanda Ronner. *The Empty Cradle: Infertility in America from Colonial Times to the Present.* Baltimore, Md.: Johns Hopkins University Press, 1996.

Mart, Michelle "Tough Guys and American Cold War Policy: Images of Israel, 1948–1960." *Diplomatic History* (1995): 357–80.

Maslin, Janet. "A Tragically Fallen Star Smolders in Memory: Hollywood's Tryst with Dorothy Dandridge Inspires Real Love at Last." *New York Times,* 19 June 1997, C15.

Masters, R.E.L. *Forbidden Sexual Behavior and Morality.* New York: Julian Press, 1962.

Masters, William, and Virginia Johnson. *Human Sexual Inadequacy.* Boston: Little, Brown, 1970.

——. *Human Sexual Response.* Boston: Little, Brown, 1966.

May, Elaine Tyler. *Barren in the Promised Land: Childless Americans and the Pursuit of Happiness.* New York: Basic Books, 1995.

——. *Great Expectations: Marriage and Divorce in Post-Victorian America.* Chicago: University of Chicago Press, 1980.

——. *Homeward Bound: American Families in the Cold War Era.* New York: Pantheon Books, 1988.

May, Rollo. "The New Puritanism." In *Sex in America,* ed. Henry Anatole Grunwald, 161–64. New York: Bantam, 1964.

Mayer, Tamar. "Gender Ironies of Nationalism: Setting the Stage." In *Gender Ironies of Nationalism: Sexing the Nation,* ed. Tamar Mayer, 1–24. New York: Routledge, 1999.

McAlister, Melani. *Epic Encounters: Culture, Media, and U.S. Interests in the Middle East, 1945–2000.* Berkeley: University of California Press, 2001.

McClintock, Anne. "'No Longer in a Future Heaven': Nationalism, Gender, and Race." In *Becoming National: A Reader,* ed. Geoff Eley and Ronald Grigor Suny, 260–84. New York: Oxford University Press, 1996.

McKensie, Marjorie. "Pursuit of Democracy: Negro Woman Still Has Her Privacy in the Wake of Kinsey." *Pittsburgh Courier,* 5 September 1953. 6.

McPartland, John. "Footnote on Sex." *Harper's* (February 1946): 212–14.

———. "For These Are the Bedeviled." *Esquire* (July 1950): 51, 137–42.

———. *Sex in Our Changing World.* New York: Rinehart, 1947.

Mead, Margaret. "American Man in a Woman's World." *New York Times Magazine* (10 February 1957): 11, 20–23.

———. *And Keep Your Powder Dry.* New York: William Morrow, 1942.

———. "The Contemporary American Family." In *Readings in Marriage and the Family,* ed. Judson T. Landis and Mary G. Landis, 1–9. New York: Prentice-Hall, 1952.

———. Introduction to *Women: The Variety and Meaning of Their Sexual Experience,* ed. A. M. Krich, 9–24. New York: Dell, 1953.

———. *Male and Female: A Study of the Sexes in a Changing World.* New York: Mentor, 1955.

———. "Preface to the Mentor Edition." *Male and Female: A Study of the Sexes in a Changing World.* 1949. Reprint, New York: Morrow and Company, 1955.

———. "The Study of National Character." In *The Policy Sciences: Recent Developments in Scope and Method,* ed. David Lerner, 70–85. Stanford, Calif.: Stanford University Press, 1951.

———. "What Is Happening to the American Family?" *Journal of Social Casework* (November 1947): 323–30.

Mendelsohn, Fred, and Matthew Ross. "An Analysis of 133 Homosexuals Seen at a University Health Service." *Diseases of the Nervous System* (1959): 246–50.

Menninger, William. *Psychiatry in a Troubled World.* New York: Macmillan, 1948.

Menzies, Victor, and Jean Bernard-Luc. *The Fig Leaf.* London: Peter Owen, 1954.

Mercer, J. D. *They Walk in Shadow.* New York: Comet Press Books, 1959.

Merrill, Francis E. "The Kinsey Report: Manifest and Latent Implications." In *Sexual Behavior in American Society: An Appraisal of the Two Kinsey Reports,* ed. Jerome Himelhoch and Sylvia Fleis Fava, 326–31. New York: W. W. Norton, 1955.

———. *Social Problems on the Home Front: A Study of War-Time Influences.* New York: Harper and Brothers, 1948.

Metalious, Grace. *Peyton Place.* New York: Dell, 1956.

Meyer, Leisa D. *Creating G.I. Jane: Sexuality and Power in the Women's Army Corps during World War II.* New York: Columbia University Press, 1996.

Meyerowitz, Joanne. "Beyond the Feminine Mystique: A Reassessment of Postwar Mass Culture, 1946–1958." In *Not June Cleaver: Women and Gender in Postwar America, 1945–1960,* ed. Meyerowitz, 229–62. Philadelphia: Temple University Press, 1994.

———. "Sex Change and the Popular Press: Historical Notes on Transsexuality in the United States, 1930–1955." *GLQ* 4 (1998): 159–87.

Michael, Robert T., John H. Gagnon, Edward O. Laumann, and Gina Kolata. *Sex in America: A Definitive Survey.* New York: Little, Brown, 1994.

Michel, Sonya. "American Women and the Discourse of the Democratic Family in WWII." In *Behind the Lines: Gender and the Two World Wars,* ed. Margaret Higgonet et al., 154–67. New Haven, Conn.: Yale University Press, 1988.

———. "Danger on the Home Front: Motherhood, Sexuality, and Disabled Veterans in American Postwar Films." In *American Sexual Politics,* ed. John Fout and Maura Tantillo, 447–66. Chicago: University of Chicago Press, 1994.

Milburn, George. "Sex, Sex, Sex, and the World Crisis: Reflections on Kinsey." *The Nation* (19 September 1953): 230–31.

Minot, Peter. "Sex in Puerto Rico." *American Mercury* (September 1951): 55–60.

Minton, Henry. *Departing from Deviance: A History of Homosexual Rights and Emancipatory Science in America.* Chicago: University of Chicago Press, 2002.

Montagu, Ashley. *The Natural Superiority of Women.* New York: Macmillan, 1952.

Montaigne, Lewis. *The Origins and Nature of Marriage.* New York: Citadel Press, 1953.

Morantz, Regina Markell. "The Scientist as Sex Crusader: Alfred Kinsey and American Culture." *American Quarterly* (winter 1979): 563–89.

"More Harm Than Good." *Life Today* (December 1953–January 1954): 6.

Morrison, Lucile Phillips. "A Descriptive Study of Responses to the Sex Attitude Inquiry." Master's thesis, Pepperdine College, Los Angeles, 1957.

Morrison, Toni. *Playing in the Dark: Whiteness and the Literary Imagination.* Cambridge: Harvard University Press, 1992.

Moskin, John. "The American Male: Why Do Women Dominate Him?" *Look* (4 February 1958): 76–80.

Mosse, George. *The Image of Man: The Creation of Modern Masculinity.* New York: Oxford University Press, 1996.

———. *Nationalism and Sexuality: Respectability and Abnormal Sexuality in Modern Europe.* New York: Howard Fertig, 1985.

Mudd, Emily. "Implications for Marriage and Sexual Adjustment." In *An Analysis of the Kinsey Reports on Sexual Behavior in the Human Male and Female,* ed. Donald Porter Geddes, 130–37. New York: Mentor Books, 1954.

Mudd, Emily Hartshorne, with Bill Davidson. "How Dr. Kinsey's Report on Women May Help Your Marriage." *Collier's* (18 September 1953): 112–17.

Mumford, Lewis. *In the Name of Sanity.* New York: Harcourt, Brace, 1954.

Murdoch, George P. *Social Structure.* New York: Macmillan, 1949.

Muret, Charlotte. "Marriage as a Career." In *Women Today: Their Conflicts, Their Frustrations, and Their Fulfillments,* ed. Elizabeth Bragdon, 26–41. New York: Bobbs-Merrill, 1953.

"Must We Change Our Sex Standards? A Readers' Symposium." *Reader's Digest* (September 1948): 129–32.

"Must We Change Our Sex Standards? A Symposium." *Reader's Digest* (June 1948): 1–6.

Myerson, Abraham. "The Great Unlearning." *American Mercury* (November 1950): 533–57.

Myers-Shirk, Susan. "'To Be Fully Human': Protestant Psychotherapeutic Culture and the Subversion of the Domestic Ideal, 1945–1965." *Journal of Women's History* (spring 2000): 112–36.

Nadel, Alan. *Containment Culture: American Narratives, Postmodernism, and the Atomic Age.* Durham, N.C.: Duke University Press, 1995.

Naismith, Grace. "The Problem of Infertility." *Reader's Digest* (June 1954): 27–30.

"National Council of Catholic Women Meets." *New York Times,* 15 September 1948, sec. 2: 20.

Niebuhr, Reinhold. "Kinsey and the Moral Problem of Man's Sexual Life." In *An Analysis of the Kinsey Reports,* ed. Donald Porter Geddes, 62–70. New York: Mentor Books, 1954.

"No Permits for Promiscuity." *Christian Century* (7 October 1953): 1124.

Norris, Kathleen. "Incredible!" *Life* (24 August 1953): 59–60.

O'Brien, John A. *Happy Marriage.* New York: Popular Library, 1956.

Odenwald, Robert P. *The Disappearing Sexes.* New York: Random House, 1965.

Ogburn, W. F., and M. F. Nimkoff, eds. *Technology and the Changing Family.* Cambridge: Riverside Press, 1955.

Ogersby, Bill. *Playboys in Paradise: Masculinity, Youth, and Leisure-Style in Modern America.* New York: Berg, 2001.

"Our 'Unsavory Character' Resents Speed Ratings Applied to Women." *Saturday Evening Post* (3 October 1953): 12.

Overstreet, H. M. *The Mature Mind.* New York: W. W. Norton, 1953.

Packard, Vance. *The Hidden Persuaders.* New York: Pocket Books, 1957.

Padovar, Saul. "Why Americans Like German Women." *American Mercury* (September 1946): 354–57.

Palmer, Gretta. "Marriage Control: A New Answer to Divorce." *Reader's Digest* (August 1947): 51–54.

———. "What Kind of Wife Has He?" *Reader's Digest* (March 1948): 37–39.

Pampanini, Silvana. "American Men Bore Me . . ." *Esquire* (June 1953): 108–9, 124.

Pannitt, Merrill. "Those English Girls." *Ladies' Home Journal* (September 1945): 5.

Parry, Hugh J. "Kinsey Revisited." *International Journal of Opinion and Attitude Research* (summer 1948): 196–97.

Parsons, Talcott. "Patterns of Aggression in the Western World." In *Essays in Sociological Theory*, ed. Parsons, 310–28. New York: Free Press, 1954.

———. "The Social Structure of the Family." In *The Family: Its Function and Destiny*, ed. Ruth Anshen, 271–88. New York: Harper and Bros., 1959.

Patrick, G. T. W. "Are Morals Out of Date?" *Ladies' Home Journal* (October 1944): 23, 62–63, 65–70.

Patton, Cindy. *Fatal Advice: How Safe-Sex Education Went Wrong.* Durham, N.C.: Duke University Press, 1996.

Paul, Pamela. *The Starter Marriage and the Future of Matrimony.* New York: Villard Books, 2002.

Pells, Richard. *The Liberal Mind in a Conservative Age: American Intellectuals in the 1940s and 1950s.* New York: Harper and Row, 1985.

———. *Not Like Us: How Europeans Have Loved, Hated, and Transformed American Culture since World War II.* New York: Basic Books, 1997.

Penn, Donna. "The Meanings of Lesbianism in Postwar America." In *Gender and American History since 1890*, ed. Barbara Melosh, 106–26. New York: Routledge, 1993.

Perry, Ralph Barton. *Characteristically American.* New York: Alfred A. Knopf, 1949.

Peterson, James. *The Century of Sex: Playboy's History of the Sexual Revolution, 1900–1999.* New York: Grove Press, 1999.

Phillips, Roderick. *Putting Asunder: A History of Divorce in Western Society.* New York: Cambridge University Press, 1988.

"Phobias Keep Some Single." *Science News-Letter* (15 December 1956): 370.

Pilpel, Harriet F., and Theodora Zavin. "Sex and the Criminal Law." *Marriage and Family Living* (August 1953): 238–44.

Pivar, David J. *Purity Crusade: Sexual Morality and Social Control, 1868–1900.* Westport, Conn.: Greenwood Press, 1973.

"The Playboy Panel: 'The Womanization of America.'" *Playboy* (June 1962): 43–50, 133–34, 139–44.

Podell, Lawrence, and John C. Perkins. "A Guttman Scale for Sexual Experience— a Methodological Note." *Journal of Abnormal and Social Psychology* (1957): 420–22.

Podolsky, Edward. "Sexual Neurosis in Soldiers." In *The Sexual History of the World War,* by Magnus Hirschfeld, chap. 26. Preface and additional chapters by Edward Podolsky. New York: Cadillac Publishing, 1949.

Polatin, Phillip, and Ellen C. Philtine. "Who Shouldn't Marry?" In *Why You Do What You Do,* ed. Robert N. Linscott and Jess Stein, 163–74. New York: Random House, 1956.

Poling, James. "The Dangers in the Marriage Manuals." *Coronet* (September 1960): 41–45.

Pollitt, Katha. "Subject to Debate." *The Nation* (31 October 1994): 484.

Pollock, Jack Harrison. "How Masculine Are You?" *Nation's Business* (June 1950): 49–55.

Pont, Manard. "Review of *The Chapman Report.*" *San Francisco Chronicle,* 5 June 1960, 26.

Poovey, Mary. "Sex in America." In *Intimacy,* ed. Lauren Berlant, 86–112. Chicago: University of Chicago Press, 2000.

———. *Uneven Developments: The Ideological Work of Gender in Mid-Victorian Britain.* Chicago: Chicago University Press, 1989.

Pope, Elizabeth. "Is It True What They Say about American Husbands?" *Reader's Digest* (November 1958): 85–86.

Popenoe, David, with Jean Bethke Elshtain. *Promises to Keep: Decline and Renewal of Marriage in America.* New York: Bowman and Littlefield, 1996.

Popenoe, Paul. "Can This Marriage Be Saved?" *Ladies' Home Journal* (January 1953): 41–43, 129–31.

———. *Sexual Inadequacy of the Male: A Manual for Counselors.* Los Angeles: American Institute of Family Relations, 1946.

Potter, David. *People of Plenty: Economic Abundance and the American Character.* Chicago: University of Chicago Press, 1954.

Preston, Charles, ed. *A Cartoon Guide to the Kinsey Report.* New York: Avon Publications, 1954.

Preston, Lillian. *Sex Habits of Single Women.* Boston: Beacon Press, 1964.

Putnam, Nina Wilcox. "Divorce Is No Solution." *Reader's Digest* (September 1948): 60–62.

Redman, Ben Ray. "Sex and Literary Art." *American Mercury* (October 1946): 412–17.

Reich, Wilhelm. *The Mass Psychology of Fascism.* New York: Farrar, Straus and Giroux, 1969.

Reik, Theodor. *Of Love and Lust: On the Psychoanalysis of Romantic and Sexual Emotions.* New York: Farrar, Straus and Cudahy, 1957.

Reisman, Judith, and Edward W. Eichel. *Kinsey, Sex, and Fraud: The Indoctrination of a People.* Lafayette, La.: Lochinvar-Huntington House, 1990.

"Review of *Sexual Behavior in the Human Female.*" *New Yorker* (19 September 1953): 120.

Reynolds, David. *Rich Relations: The American Occupation of Britain, 1942–45.* New York: Random House, 1995.

Riesman, David. "Permissiveness and Sex Roles." *Marriage and Family Living* (August 1959): 211–17; reprinted as "The New College Atmosphere" in *Sex in America: What Are the Facts about Today's Sexual Revolution?*, ed. Henry Anatole Grunwald, 29–38. New York: Bantam, 1964.

———. "Psychological Types and National Character: An Informal Commentary." *American Quarterly* (winter 1953): 325–43.

———. "The Saving Remnant: A Study of Character." In *Years of the Modern: An American Appraisal*, ed. John W. Chase, 115–49. New York: Longmans, 1949.

Riesman, David, with Nathan Glazer and Reuel Denney. *The Lonely Crowd: A Study of the Changing American Character.* New Haven, Conn.: Yale University Press, 1950.

Riley, Glenda. *Divorce: An American Tradition.* New York: Oxford University Press, 1991.

Roberts, Mary Louise. *Civilization without Sexes: Reconstructing Gender in Postwar France, 1917–1927.* Chicago: University of Chicago Press, 1994.

Robins, Eli, et al. "'Hysteria' in Men." *New England Journal of Medicine* (1 May 1952): 677–85.

Robinson, Marie N. *The Power of Sexual Surrender.* Garden City, N.Y.: Doubleday and Company, 1959.

Roper, Elmo. "Birth Control, the *Fortune* Survey." In *Readings in Marriage and the Family*, ed. Judson T. Landis and Mary G. Landis, 247–48. New York: Prentice-Hall, 1952.

Rosenberg, Bernard, and David Manning White, eds. *Mass Culture: The Popular Arts in America.* New York: Free Press, 1957.

Rosenthal, Herbert C. "Sex Habits of European Women vs. American Women." *Pageant* (March 1951): 52–59.

Rotter, Andrew J. "Gender Relations, Foreign Relations: The United States and South Asia, 1947–1964." *Journal of American History* (September 1994): 518–42.

Rubin, Gayle. "Thinking Sex: Notes for a Radical Theory of the Politics of Sexuality." In *The Lesbian and Gay Studies Reader*, ed. Henry Abelove, Michele Aina Barale, David Halperin, et al., 3–44. New York: Routledge, 1992.

Rubin, Herman H. *Glands, Sex, and Personality.* New York: Wilfred Funk, 1952.

Ruitenbeek, Hendrik M. "Men Alone: The Male Homosexual and the Disintegrated Family." In *The Problem of Homosexuality in Modern Society*, ed. Hendrik M. Ruitenbeek, 80–93. New York: Dutton, 1963.

Rumming, Eleanor. "Dr. Kinsey and the Human Female." *Saturday Night* (15 August 1953): 8–11.

Rusk, Howard A. "Concerning Man's Basic Drive." *New York Times Review of Books* (4 January 1948): 2–4.

Salinger, J.D. *The Catcher in the Rye.* New York: Little, Brown, 1951.

Sandeen, Eric. *Picturing an Exhibition: The Family of Man and 1950s America.* Albuquerque: University of New Mexico Press, 1995.

Sanders, Stephanie, and June Reinisch. "Would You Say You 'Had Sex' If . . . ?" *Journal of the American Medical Association* (1999): 275–77.

Sandomirsky, Vera. "Sex in the Soviet Union." *Russian Review* (July 1951): 199–209.

Sapirstein, Milton. "The 'Happy' Homosexual," review of *The Homosexual in America,* by Donald Webster Cory. *The Nation* (22 December 1951): 551–52.

———. "Hindering the Search for Morality." *The Nation* (15 March 1952): 252–53.

Sargeant, Winthrop. "The Cult of the Love Goddess in America." *Life* (10 November 1947): 81–84.

Savelle, Max. *Seeds of Liberty: The Genesis of the American Mind.* New York: Knopf, 1948.

Savran, David. *Communists, Cowboys, and Queers: The Politics of Masculinity in the Work of Arthur Miller and Tennessee Williams.* Minneapolis: University of Minnesota Press, 1992.

Sayre, Nora. *Previous Convictions: A Journey through the 1950s.* New Brunswick, N.J.: Rutgers University Press, 1995.

Sbarbaro, John A. *Marriage Is on Trial.* New York: Macmillan, 1947.

Scanlon, Jennifer. Introduction to *The Gender and Consumer Culture Reader,* ed. Jennifer Scanlon. New York: New York University Press, 2000.

Schaffner, Bertram. *Fatherland: A Study of Authoritarianism in the German Family.* New York: Columbia University Press, 1949.

Schauffler, Dr. Goodrich C. "Today It Could Be *Your* Daughter." *Ladies' Home Journal* (January 1958): 43, 112–13.

Scheinfeld, Amram. "Kinsey's Study of Female Sex Behavior." *Reader's Digest* (October 1953): 5–8.

———. "What's Wrong with Sex Studies." *Cosmopolitan* (August 1953): 15–19.

Schlesinger, Arthur Jr. "The Crisis of American Masculinity." *Esquire* (November 1958): 64–66.

———. *The Vital Center: The Politics of Freedom.* Boston: Houghton Mifflin, 1949.

Schrecker, Ellen. *Many Are the Crimes: McCarthyism in America.* New York: Little, Brown, 1998.

"A Scientist Looks at America's Sexual Behavior." *Science Illustrated* (2 December 1947): 34–37, 99.

Scott, Sarah Nell. "I Was Interviewed by Dr. Kinsey." *Your Life* (27 July 1950): 26–29.

Senelick, Laurence. "Private Parts in Public Places." In *Inventing Times Square: Commerce and Culture at the Crossroads of the World,* ed. William R. Taylor, 329–55. New York: Russell Sage, 1991.

Sengoopta, Chandak. *Otto Weininger: Sex, Science, and Self in Imperial Vienna.* Chicago: University of Chicago Press, 2000.

"The Sexual Behavior of an American Woman as Revealed by Her to Dr. Alfred C. Kinsey." *Today's Woman* (18 July 1948): 24–25, 58–61.

Sexuality Information and Education Council of the United States (SIECUS). "Toward a Sexually Healthy America." New York: SIECUS, 2001.

"Sex vs. America." *Newsweek* (7 September 1953): 20.

Shannon, William H. *The Lively Debate: Responses to* Humanae Vitae. New York: Sheed and Ward, 1970.

Sharp, Cameron. "Men Are the Sucker Sex." *Nation's Business* (October 1952): 32–33, 86–89.

Sharp, Joanne P. *Condensing the Cold War:* Reader's Digest *and National Identity.* Minneapolis: University of Minnesota Press, 2000.

Sherwin, Robert Veit. "Female Sex Crimes." In *The Sex Life of the American Woman and the Kinsey Report,* ed. Albert Ellis, 175–87. New York: Greenwood, 1954.

———. *Sex and the Statutory Law (in All Forty-Eight States).* New York: Oceana Publications, 1949.

Silver, George A. "The Homosexual: Challenge to Science." *The Nation* (25 May 1957): 451–54.

Simmons, Christina. "'Marriage in the Modern Manner': Sexual Radicalism and Reform in America, 1914–1941." Ph.D. diss., Brown University, 1982.

———. "Modern Sexuality and the Myth of Victorian Repression." In *Passion and Power: Sexuality in History,* ed. Kathy Peiss and Christina Simmons, 157–77. Philadelphia: Temple University Press, 1989.

Simpson, George. "Nonsense about Women." *Humanist* (March–April 1954): 49–56; reprinted in *Sexual Behavior in American Society: An Appraisal of the Two Kinsey Reports,* ed. Jerome Himelhoch and Sylvia Fleis Fava, 59–67. New York: W. W. Norton, 1955.

Skinner, Cornelia Otis. "Trial by Kinsey." *New Yorker* (27 May 1950): 29–31.

Smythe, Joseph Hilton. *The Sex Probers.* Boston: Beacon Press, 1961.

"Sociologist Says Minorities Get 'Tired of Being Studied.'" *Ebony* (October 1953): 111–13.

Solinger, Rickie. *Wake Up Little Susie: Single Pregnancy and Race before Roe v. Wade.* New York: Routledge, 1992.

"Some Say Kinsey Should Use Colored Interviewers." *Ebony* (October 1953): 111.

Sorokin, Pitirim A. *The American Sex Revolution.* Boston: Porter Sargent, 1956.

South, Betty. "The Secret of Love: Have American Girls Forgotten?" *Esquire* (February 1951): 23, 112–13.

"Speaking of S-e-x." *Newsweek* (21 February 1949): 56–57.

Splendor in the Grass. Dir. Elia Kazin. Warner Brothers, 1961.

Stearn, Jess. *The Grapevine.* Garden City, N.J.: Doubleday, 1964.

———. *The Sixth Man.* New York: MacFadden, 1961.

Steiner, Lucius. *Sex Behavior of the Lesbian, with Case Histories.* Hollywood, Calif.: Genell, 1964.

Stern, Edith. "The Miserable Male." *American Mercury* (November 1948): 537–42.

Stone, Abraham. "The Kinsey Studies and Marriage Counseling." In *Sexual Behavior in American Society: An Appraisal of the Two Kinsey Reports,* ed. Jerome Himelhoch and Sylvia Fleis Fava, 164–74. New York: W. W. Norton, 1955.

Strathern, Marilyn. "Enterprising Kinship: Consumer Choice and the New Reproductive Technologies." *Cambridge Anthropology* (1990): 3–24.

Strecker, Edward. "The Silver Cord." In *Women Today: Their Conflicts, Their Frustrations, and Their Fulfillments,* ed. Elizabeth Bragdon, 138. New York: Bobbs-Merrill, 1953.

———. *Their Mothers' Sons: The Psychiatrist Examines an American Problem.* Philadelphia: J. B. Lippincott, 1946.

Strecker, Edward A., and Vincent Lathbury. *Their Mothers' Daughters.* Philadelphia: J. B. Lippincott, 1956.

Streitmatter, Rodger. *Unspeakable: The Rise of the Gay and Lesbian Press in America.* Boston: Faber and Faber, 1995.

Suddenly, Last Summer. Dir. Joseph Manckiewicz. Columbia Pictures, 1959.

Susman, Warren. "'Personality' and the Making of Twentieth-Century Culture." In *Culture as History: The Transformation of American Society in the Twentieth Century,* ed. Warren Susman, 271–86. New York: Pantheon, 1984.

Taubman, Howard. "Modern Primer: Helpful Hints to Tell Appearances vs. Truth." *New York Times,* 28 April 1963, 1x–2x.

———. "Not What It Seems: Homosexual Motif Gets Heterosexual Guise." *New York Times,* 5 November 1961, 1x.

"Teen-Agers and Sex in Australia." *Ladies' Home Journal* (January 1958): 113.

Tenenbaum, Samuel. "The Fate of Wartime Marriages." *American Mercury* (November 1945): 530–36.

Terman, Lewis. "Correlates of Orgasm Adequacy in a Group of 556 Wives." *Journal of Psychology* (1951): 115–72.

Terry, Jennifer. *An American Obsession: Science, Medicine, and the Place of Homosexuality in Modern Society.* Chicago: University of Chicago Press, 1999.

———. "Theorizing Deviant Historiography." *differences* (1991): 55–74.

"These Tragic Women." *Newsweek* (15 June 1959): 62–63.

Thigpen, Corbett, and Hervey Cleckley. *The Three Faces of Eve.* New York: Popular Library, 1957.

Thompson, Clara. "Changing Concepts of Homosexuality in Psychoanalysis." In *The Problem of Homosexuality in Modern Society,* ed. Hendrik M. Ruitenbeek, 40–51. New York: Dutton, 1963.

Thompson, Dorothy. "The New Mr. Caspar Milquetoasts." *Ladies' Home Journal* (August 1958): 11–12, 121.

Timmons, Stuart. *The Trouble with Harry Hay: Founder of the Modern Gay Movement.* Boston: Alyson Publications, 1990.

"To Tell or Not to Tell Is the Worry of Home-Bound GIs." *Stars and Stripes* (28 June 1946): 3.

Towne, Alfred. "Homosexuality in American Culture: The New Taste in Humor." *American Mercury* (September 1951): 22–27.

———. "Homosexuality in American Culture: The New Taste in Literature." *American Mercury* (August 1951): 3–9.

"Town Hall." *Good Housekeeping* (July 1948): 8–9.

Train, Ray. *Miss Kinsey's Report.* Cleveland, Ohio: Chevron, 1967.

Trilling, Diana. "Men, Women, and Sex." *Partisan Review* (April 1950): 366–69.

Trilling, Lionel. "Our Country and Our Culture." *Partisan Review* (August 1952).

Trimberger, Ellen Kay. "Feminism, Men, and Modern Love: Greenwich Village, 1900–1925." In *Powers of Desire: The Politics of Sexuality,* ed. Ann Snitow et al., 131–52. New York: Monthly Review Press, 1983.

Truxal, Andrew G., and Francis Merrill. *The Family in American Culture.* New York: Prentice-Hall, 1947.

U.S. Bureau of the Census. *Statistical Abstract of the United States: 1960.* 81st ed. Washington, D.C., 1960.

van den Haag, Ernest. "Notes on Homosexuality and Its Cultural Setting." In *The Problem of Homosexuality in Modern Society,* ed. Hendrik M. Ruitenbeek, 291–302. New York: E. P. Dutton, 1963.

Viereck, George Sylvester. "The Erotic Note in Recent American Fiction." *American Aphrodite* (1954): 166–75.

Vincent, Heywood. "So You Want to Stay Single?" *Cosmopolitan* (August 1954): 58–61.

Visson, Andrè. *As Others See Us.* New York: Doubleday, 1948.

Waite, Linda J., and Maggie Gallagher. *The Case for Marriage: Why Married People Are Happier, Healthier, and Better Off Financially.* New York: Doubleday, 2001.

Wald, Priscilla. *Constituting Americans: Cultural Anxiety and Narrative Form.* Chapel Hill: Duke University Press, 1995.

Walker, Dorothy. "The Terrible Monomania." *One* (November 1953): 2–3.

Walkowitz, Judith. *City of Dreadful Delight: Narratives of Sexual Danger in Late-Victorian London.* Chicago: University of Chicago Press, 1992.

Wallace, Irving. *The Chapman Report.* New York: Signet, 1960.

Wallerstein, Judith S., et al. *The Unexpected Legacy of Divorce: A Twenty-Five-Year Landmark Study.* New York: Hyperion, 2001.

Walsh, Frank. *Sin and Censorship: The Catholic Church and the Motion Picture Industry.* New Haven, Conn.: Yale University Press, 1996.

Wassersug, J.D. "Why Men Envy Women." *Science Digest* (July 1950): 12–16.

Watney, Simon. *Policing Desire: Pornography, AIDS, and the Media.* Minneapolis: University of Minnesota Press, 1987.

Weatherford, Doris, ed. *American Women's History: An A to Z of People, Organizations, Issues, and Events.* New York: Prentice Hall, 1994.

Weinberg, Martin, and Colin Williams. "Sexual Embourgeoisment? Social Class and Sexual Activity: 1938–70." *American Sociological Review* (February 1980): 33–48.

Weise, Otis L. "Live the Life of *McCall's.*" *McCall's* (May 1954): 27.

Wenzel, Bill, ed. *The Flimsey Report; or, Sex Is Here to Stay.* New York: Farrell Publishing Company, 1953.

Westbrook, Robert B. "'I Want a Girl, Just Like the Girl That Married Harry James': American Women and the Problem of Political Obligation in World War II." *American Quarterly* (December 1990): 587–614.

Westwood, Gordon. *Society and the Homosexual.* New York: E. P. Dutton, 1953.

"What Is a Homosexual?" *Time* (16 June 1958): 44.

"What Is the American Character?" *Time* (27 September 1954): 22–25.

"What I Told Dr. Kinsey about My Sex Life." *Ebony* (4 December 1948): 44–46.

While the City Sleeps. Dir. Fritz Lang. RKO Radio Pictures, 1956.

Whitbread, Jane, and Vivian Cadden. "Susan McViddy Finds Out What She's Missing." *Good Housekeeping* (February 1950): 40, 185–86.

White, Kevin. *The First Sexual Revolution: The Emergence of Male Heterosexuality in Modern America.* New York: New York University Press, 1993.

White, Lynn Jr. "The Changing Context of Women's Education." *Marriage and Family Living* (November 1955): 291–95.

Whitehead, Barbara Defoe. *The Divorce Culture: Rethinking Our Commitments to Marriage and Family.* New York: Vintage, 1998.

Whitfield, Stephen J. *The Culture of the Cold War.* Baltimore: Johns Hopkins University Press, 1990.

Whitman, Howard. "America's Moral Crisis: Sex as It Was Meant to Be." *Better Homes and Gardens* (August 1957): 58, 98, 100–103.

———. "America's Moral Crisis: The Slavery of Sex Freedom." *Better Homes and Gardens* (June 1957): 59, 172, 218–21.

———. "Divorce Granted!" *Reader's Digest* (October 1954): 11–16.

———. "Don't Let Them Scoff at Marriage!" *Better Homes and Gardens* (August 1957): 100–102.

———. "Let's Help Them Marry Young." *Reader's Digest* (October 1947): 1–4.

———. *Let's Tell the Truth about Sex.* New York: Pellegrini and Cudahy, 1948.

———. "Sex and Early Marriage." *Better Homes and Gardens* (August 1947): 40–41, 146–49.

———. "Wolf! Wolf!" *Woman's Home Companion* (July 1948): 12–14.

"Why Negro Women Are Not in the Kinsey Report." *Ebony* (8 October 1953): 109–15.

Whyte, William H. *The Organization Man.* New York: Simon and Schuster, 1956.

Widdemer, Margaret. "Cad's Paradise." *Good Housekeeping* (October 1950): 55, 238–42.

Wilkinson, Rupert. *The Pursuit of American Character.* New York: Harper and Row, 1988.

———, ed. *American Social Character: Modern Interpretations from the '40s to the Present.* New York: HarperCollins, 1992.

Willig, John. "Lament for Male Sanctuary." *New York Times Magazine* (10 March 1957): 19, 72, 78.

Wilson, Robin. "An Ill-Fated Sex Survey." *Chronicle of Higher Education* (2 August 2002): A10.

Wilson, Sloan. *The Man in the Gray Flannel Suit.* New York: Simon and Schuster, 1955.

Winters, Jeff, and David Freeman. "Magazine Goldmine: 'Run an Article on Queers!'" *One* (June 1953): 2–12.

Wise, Gene. "'Paradigm Dramas' in American Studies: A Cultural and Intellectual History of the Movement." *American Quarterly* (1979): 293–337.

Wittels, Fritz. *The Sex Habits of American Women.* New York: Eton Books, 1951.

Woman's World. Dir. Jean Negulesco. Twentieth Century Fox, 1954.

"Women: They Think of the Moment." *Time* (26 February 1945): 18–19.

Wylie, Philip. *Generation of Vipers.* New York: Rinehart, 1945.

———. "Virginity and Pre-Marital Sex Relations." In *Sex Life of the American Woman and the Kinsey Report,* ed. Albert Ellis, 25–41. New York: Greenberg, 1954.

———. "What's Wrong with American Marriages?" *Reader's Digest* (August 1946): 337–39.

Yates, Richard. *Revolutionary Road.* New York: Vintage, 1961.

Zaretsky, Eli. "Charisma or Rationalization? Domesticity and Psychoanalysis in the United States in the 1950s." In *Intimacy,* ed. Lauren Berlant, 378–404. Chicago: University of Chicago Press, 2000.

Zimmerman, Carle C. *Family and Civilization.* New York: Harper and Brothers, 1947.

———. "A Sociologist Looks at the Report." In *Problems of Sexual Behavior,* ed. American Social Hygiene Association, 82–105. New York: ASHA, 1948.

Zolotow, Maurice. "Love Is Not a Statistic." *Reader's Digest* (April 1954): 8–9.

INDEX

Page numbers in italics indicate illustrations.

Hefner, Hugh, 78
Helms, Jesse, 208, 209–10
Henry, George, 30
Herberg, Will, 42
The Hidden Persuaders (Packard), 31
High Noon (film), 68
Hite, Shere, 205, 206
The Hite Report (Hite), 206
Hobbs, A.H., 102, 106–7
homophile movement, 171, 188
The Homosexual in America (Cory), 171
homosexuality: and American character, 166–67, 187–93; and appearance, 178–79; causes of, 183–87, 230n55; and Communism, 194; and the Depression, 184; and government, 192; incidence of, in United States, 28, 168–70, 181; Kinsey statistics on, 165; latent, 181–82; as a minority identity, 190, 249n118; in other countries, 184; place of, in postwar United States, 170–78; political organizations, 171; and popular culture, 170–76, *175*, 193–94; postwar theories of, 166–67, 176–83; in pulp novels, 172; surveys of, 176, 208; types of, 179–81; World War II and, 167, 171, 184–85. *See also* lesbianism
Homosexuality: Disease or Way of Life? (Bergler), 192
Hooker, Evelyn, 177, 179
Hoover, J. Edgar, 27, 58–59
Howe, Reuel, 147
Howl (Ginsberg), 33
Human Sexual Inadequacy (Masters and Johnson), 206
Human Sexual Response (Masters and Johnson), 205–6
Hunt, Morton, 62, 66–68, 70
Hurst, Fannie, 95–96
The Hypocritical American (Collier), 180

The Immoralist (Goetz), 193
impotence, 76
Indianapolis Star, 98
Institute for Psychological Research, 48
Intercollegiate Studies Institute, 212

Jarrell, Randall, 68
Johnson, Lyndon, 25
Johnson, Virginia, 205–7
Johnstone, Margaret Blair, 77
Jones, James, 199–200, 221n37, 252n32
Jong, Erica, 206
Jorgensen, Christine, 30, 63
Journal of the American Medical Association, 210
Journal of Social Hygiene, 181

Kardiner, Abram, 169, 184–85, 186, 189
Katz, Jonathan Ned, 173
Kazin, Alfred, 203–4
Kephart, W.H., 102, 106–7
Kepner, Jim, 185–86
Keyes, Alan, 214
Khrushchev, Nikita, 92
Kidd, Elizabeth, 125
Kinsey, Alfred, 1–2, 5; biographies of, 199–200, 212, 221n37, 252n32; photograph of, with female subject, *93;* photograph of, with team, *22*
Kinsey Reports, 5–6, 13–14; class in, 25, 155; extramarital sex in, 141–42; homosexuality in, 165, 168–69; impact of, 1–2, 200–1; methodology of, *23*, 24, 72; race in, 24, 235n89; silences in, 14. See also *Sexual Behavior in the Human Female; Sexual Behavior in the Human Male*
Kirkendall, Lester, 75
kitchen debate (Nixon and Khrushchev), 92
Kline, Wendy, 133
Knight, Robert, 210
Komarovsky, Mirra, 149
Kroeger, William S., 27

The Ladder, 171
Ladies' Home Journal, 19, 90, 111, 127, 140, 147, 148, 149, 151
La Dolce Vita (film), 32
Laidlaw, Robert, 188
Landis, Judson, 81, 102
Landis, Mary, 81
Landis, Paul, 105–6, 139, 143–44, 146, 160–61

Laumann, Edward, 207–9, 215
legal system, 32–33
Lerner, Max, 174, 177, 179
lesbianism, 245n5; attractions of, 192–93; causes of, 187; estimates of prevalence of, 168–69; images of, in fiction, 195; political organizations, 171; theories of, 182; in Women's Army Corps, 197. *See also* female sexuality; homosexuality
Levine, Lena, 146
Life, 39, 95–96, 132
Life Today, 105
Lindner, Robert, 186, 189
Lolita (Nabokov), 33
Look, 62, 69, 81, 151
Luce, Henry, 17
Lunbeck, Elizabeth, 79
Lundberg, Ferdinand, 88, 137

Mace, David, 159
Mailer, Norman, 65, 249n118
"Making Marriage Work" (Adams), 140
male heterosexuality: and homosexuality, 83; and inadequacy, 77–83; normative, 75–76, 78–79
The Manchurian Candidate (film), 182
The Man in the Gray Flannel Suit (Wilson), 65
Marcuse, Herbert, 64, 204–5
The Mark (film), 32
marriage, 128–30, 132–41; and citizenship, 130–31; civic benefits of, 150–51; and class, 138–40; companionate, 144; contemporary threats to, 212–13; early, 132–33; and female sexuality, 107–9, 158; interracial, 134; rates of, 133, 238n27; sex in, 146–62; and sexual advice, 150–62; and the state, 134; unhappiness in, 138–40; Victorian, 144–46, 240n83; and World War II, 131–32. *See also* divorce
Marriage and Family Living, 141
marriage manuals, 140
Marsh, Margaret, 67
Mart, Michelle, 38
Martin, Clyde, 22

masculinity: American versus other nations', 76–77; and the family, 65–67; and male heterosexuality, 70–71; normative, 83–84; postwar crisis of, 54–57, 59–63; and race, 62; and women's changing roles, 67; in the workplace, 63–65; and World War II, 57–59
Masters, Robert, 170
Masters, William, 205–7
Mattachine Review, 171, 190
Mattachine Society, 171, 177
May, Elaine Tyler, 130
May, Rollo, 203
Mayer, Tamar, 91–92
McCall's, 91, 159
McKensie, Marjorie, 115
McPartland, John, 44, 89, 105, 165, 189, 196–97
Mead, Margaret, 20–21; on dating, 38; on divorce, 136; on lesbianism, 168; on marital sex, 154, 160; on marriage, 143; on masculinity, 60–62, 76; on national identity, 52; on women's sexual expectations, 104–5
Menninger, William, 132, 191
Menzies, Victor, 118
Mercer, J.D., 180, 189, 191, 192
Merrill, Francis, 18, 150
Metalious, Grace, 31, 224n50
Meyer, Leisa, 89, 197
Meyerowitz, Joanne, 10, 91
Michael, Robert, 207–9, 215
Miller, Henry, 31
Miss Kinsey's Report (Train), 119; cover of, *119*
Modern Woman: The Lost Sex (Farnham and Lundberg), 88
"Momism" (concept), 107, 228n15
Montagu, Ashley, 61, 75–76, 137
Morrison, Toni, 115
Mudd, Emily, 95, 152
Mumford, Lewis, 35
Muret, Charlotte, 108
Myrdal, Gunnar, 190

Nabokov, Vladimir, 33
The Nation, 188, 192

Sbarbaro, John, 136–37
Scanlon, Jennifer, 42
Schauffler, Goodrich, 30
Scheinfeld, Amram, 91
Schlesinger, Arthur Jr., 54–55, 61, 63, 68, 189, 194
Science Illustrated, 41
Senate Republican Policy Commission, 210
sex: education, 214; as liberatory, 8; marital, 146–62; sex experts, 11, 14, 107, 200–1; and state interests, 34–35
Sex: Manners and Methods (Berg and Street), 157
Sexology, 180, 181
The Sex Probers (Smythe), 118–20; cover of, *119*
sexual adequacy, 152–53
Sexual Behavior in the Human Female (Kinsey et al.), 22, 77, 86–87, 92–107; and "average" American woman, 97–99; cartoon treatments of, 46–47, 100–1, 103, 112–13, 153; Kinsey interviewing subject for, *93;* race in, 114–18, 235n89; subjects of, 93, 101–3
Sexual Behavior in the Human Male (Kinsey et al.), 21, 54, 70; class differences in; 71–73; coded interview sheet, *72;* findings of, 71–74; homosexuality in, 168–69; illegal behavior in, 74–75; impotence in, 76; race in, 74–75; sources of outlet chart from, *23*
The Sexually Adequate Female (Caprio), 152
The Sexually Adequate Male (Caprio), 152
Sexual Practices of American Women (Gerould), 35
Sex Variants (Henry), 30
Shane (film), 68
Silver, George, 180, 183
singles, 133–35
The Sixth Man (Stearn), 170
Smythe, Joseph Hilton, 118–20, *119*
Society and the Homosexual (Westwood), 191
soldiers, 18–19, 57–58, 131, 180. *See also* World War II
Solinger, Rickie, 59
Some Like It Hot (film), 193

Sorokin, Pitirim, 33–34, 41, 47–49, 52, 159, 201
Splendor in the Grass (film), 237n7
The Split-Level Trap (Gordon and Gordon), 36–37, 65, 105
Sputnik, 40
Stearn, Jess, 170, 182, 185
Stern, Edith, 60
Stewart, Potter, 33
Stone, Abraham, 48, 76, 81, 140, 152
Strangers on a Train (film), 193
Strathern, Marilyn, 12
Street, Robert, 155, 157
Streker, Edward, 94
suburbs, 36
Suddenly, Last Summer (film), 32, 224n57
Sullivan, Katharine, 193
"Susan McViddy Finds Out What She's Missing" (Whitbread and Cadden), 111–14
Susman, Warren, 39

Taubman, Howard, 194
Tea and Sympathy (film), 193
Terry, Jennifer, 166
Thompson, Clara, 183
Thompson, Dorothy, 69–70
The Three Faces of Eve (Cleckley and Thigpen), 109–10
Time, 32, 40, 169, 178, 202
"togetherness" (concept), 91, 145, 241n87
Towne, Alfred, 31
Train, Ray, 119, *119*
Trilling, Diana, 17
Tropic of Cancer (Miller), 31

United States of America, image abroad of, 44–48
USSR, 40, 44, 46, 91, 159

Van den Haag, Ernest, 182
Viagra, 216–17
Victim (film), 32
victory girls, 89, 131
Viereck, George, 31
Virgin Spring (film), 32
Visson, Andre, 44
The Vital Center (Schlesinger), 68

Text:	Adobe Garamond
Display:	11.25/13.5 AGaramond
Compositor:	International Typesetting & Composition
Printer and Binder:	Thomson-Shore, Inc.